A European Elizabethan

A European Elizabethan

The Life of Robert Beale, Esquire

DAVID SCOTT GEHRING

OXFORD
UNIVERSITY PRESS

Great Clarendon Street, Oxford, OX2 6DP,
United Kingdom

Oxford University Press is a department of the University of Oxford.
It furthers the University's objective of excellence in research, scholarship,
and education by publishing worldwide. Oxford is a registered trade mark of
Oxford University Press in the UK and in certain other countries

© David Scott Gehring 2024

The moral rights of the author have been asserted

Published in the United States of America by Oxford University Press
198 Madison Avenue, New York, NY 10016, United States of America

British Library Cataloguing in Publication Data
Data available

Library of Congress Control Number: 2023950713

ISBN 9780198902911

DOI: 10.1093/9780198902942.001.0001

Printed and bound by
CPI Group (UK) Ltd, Croydon, CR0 4YY

Acknowledgements

A lot of people and institutions have made this book possible. Without their help, Robert Beale would remain obscured by the passage of time. With their help, I hope to have shone a light on this complex character and his perspective of the sixteenth century. In the most practical of ways, I have received assistance from staff at archives across Europe and the United States who have gone above and beyond to make material accessible to me both physically and electronically. Of special note are the staff in the Manuscripts Reading Room of the British Library, the Bodleian Library, Aberdeen University Library, and Brigham Young University. Staff at smaller archives have also provided key documents with patience and kindness at Balliol College, Oxford; Magdalen College, Cambridge; and at county record offices in Coventry, Kent, Norfolk, and Staffordshire. The staff in the upper reading room of the Institute of Historical Research are to be thanked for reminding me how to operate a microfilm reader. I am particularly grateful to those who permitted me to use and quote from material in their private archives, namely His Grace the Duke of Rutland, the Marquess of Bath, the Marquess of Salisbury, and Lord De L'Isle. To Anne Monro-Davies I am grateful for the glimpse into aspects of Milbourne House, one of Beale's homes; for the photos sent via email I am indebted to Sue Evans. For the custom map of Europe, Michael Athanson deserves all the credit; it's a shame we couldn't work in a pirate joke. During the depths of the pandemic of 2020–2, progress on this book was enabled by digital photography and electronic file transfer from many of these people. Long may they continue to help others similarly.

Audiences at seminars and conferences in the USA, Canada, United Kingdom, and Germany have helped me to think about this book in challenging but fruitful ways. The book is better on account of their questions. On a more individual level, friends and colleagues have offered constructive criticism and encouragement at various stages; others have simply lent an ear while I thought something through. At the University of Nottingham, my time has been enriched by a community of friends, especially Dave Appleby, Dean Blackburn, Harry Cocks, Onni Gust, Dan Hucker, and Liudmyla Sharipova. Farther afield and over several years I've received helpful advice and friendly conversation from Simon Adams, Stephen Alford, Tim Crowley, Cesare Cuttica, Sue Doran, Stefanie Freyer, Matt and Roberta Markovina, Noah Millstone, Dmitra Pavlina Nikita, Eric and Elisabeth Platt, Nick Popper, Alec Ryrie, Elizabeth Williamson, and Neil Younger. The efforts of the team at Oxford University Press have been appreciated, as have been the very helpful comments from those who read the proposal and full manuscript. Miranda Bethell, as copy editor, is to be recognized for her keen eye, humanity regarding idiom, and sense of humour. The University of Nottingham has funded much of my work on this book, especially by way of archival trips and reproduction, conferences, library acquisitions, and research leave. To the taxpayers who continue to fund education in this country and elsewhere, thank you. Students, both undergraduate and (post)graduate, are to be recognized for their enthusiasm and energy that can be contagious, even if they haven't done all the reading. In July 2023, Dekai Liu read the manuscript in full twice while on exchange from the University of Nottingham Ningbo, and I am grateful for his suggestions both general and specific.

In 2017 a companion of many years left us. He had been rather good at reminding me about the importance of putting aside academic concerns and taking time to sit in the sun or go for a run—if only to think things through. Arthur's legacy has lived on in two most unlikely characters. I have learned much from Eleanora Blanche and Fitzroy Humphrey since 2018, not the least of which is how to hold students' attention while teaching seminars remotely via video conference. With me for the whole of my time with Beale, from my first archival trip to Germany in 2008 to retrace Beale's steps in 1577, to my very last pages of writing in 2023, has been my best friend. She has weathered more stories than anyone else, read the manuscript in full, and done it all with only occasional visible lapses in attention. If that isn't stamina, I'm not sure what is. Thank you, Dr Friend.

Contents

List of Figures

Abbreviations

AGR	David Scott Gehring, *Anglo-German Relations and the Protestant Cause: Elizabethan Foreign Policy and Pan-Protestantism* (London, 2013).
AUL	Aberdeen University Library
BL	British Library
Bodleian	The Bodleian Library, Oxford
BYU	Brigham Young University
Collinson	Patrick Collinson, *The Elizabethan Puritan Movement* (London, 1967).
CP	Cecil Papers, Hatfield House
CSPF	*Calendar of State Papers, Foreign Series, Elizabeth*
CUL	Cambridge University Library
DB	*Deutsche Biographie*, online at www.deutsche-biographie.de
HoP:HoC	*History of Parliament: House of Commons*, online at www.historyofparliamentonline.org
LMA	London Metropolitan Archives
Longleat	Longleat House
LPL	Lambeth Palace Library
ODNB	*Oxford Dictionary of National Biography*, online at www.oxforddnb.com
STC	A. W. Pollard and G. R. Redgrave, *A Short-title Catalogue of Books Printed in England, Scotland, & Ireland and of English Books Printed Abroad 1475–1640*, 2nd edn rev., W. A. Jackson, F. S. Ferguson, and K. F. Pantzer (London, 1976–91), online at http://estc.bl.uk
Taviner	Mark Taviner, 'Robert Beale and the Elizabethan Polity', unpublished PhD thesis, University of St Andrews, 2000.
TCD	Trinity College Dublin
TNA	The National Archives, Kew, London
USTC	*Universal Short Title Catalogue*, online at http://ustc.ac.uk/index.php
VD16	*Verzeichnis der im deutschen Sprachbereich erschienenen Drucke des 16. Jahrhunderts*, online at www.gateway-bayern.de

Conventions

The year is taken to begin on 1 January rather than 25 March, and all dates are, unless otherwise stated, according to the 'old style' (i.e. Julian calendar) used in England and elsewhere in Protestant Europe during the sixteenth century. Spelling in quotations has preserved the original spelling in the documents, but, to assist the reader, abbreviations have been silently expanded, additional punctuation has been supplied in square brackets, and the thorn 'y' has been replaced with 'th' (as in 'the'). It may help the reader to know that £50 in 1572, the yearly salary for a clerk of the Privy Council, is roughly equal to £15,000 in 2023 (according to TNA's online tool at https://www.nationalarchives.gov.uk/currency-converter/ and adjusting for inflation since 2017). For the sake of comparison, a building craftsman at this time earned a little over nine pence per day as a wage, which amounted to roughly £12 per year (according to https://www.measuring-worth.com/datasets/ukearncpi/earnstudyx.pdf). Final letters as sent have been preferred over copies and are designated as '(orig.)' in the footnotes; where '(orig.)' is not noted, the letter is a later copy or earlier draft; copies have sometimes been noted to illuminate issues of dating or dissemination. Similarly, preference has been given to the manuscripts themselves over printed abstracts and transcriptions in calendars or other editions. Where such documents have been consulted, references in footnotes do not include the relevant entries in the *Calendar*(s) *of State Papers*, *Historical Manuscripts Commission* reports, or other series in print or on *British History Online*. Knights are not denoted 'Sir' for the sake of keeping things simple, and nobles are sometimes referred to as, for example, 'Leicester', 'Burghley', or 'Bedford'. Non-anglophone proper names and places have been spelled according to their original languages and as locals used them—unless doing so would confuse the reader regarding commonly known people and places like, for example, William of Orange, King Philip of Spain, the Palatinate, and Germany. References to biographical dictionaries are supplied where possible, and citations to online databases are current to summer 2023.

Genealogy

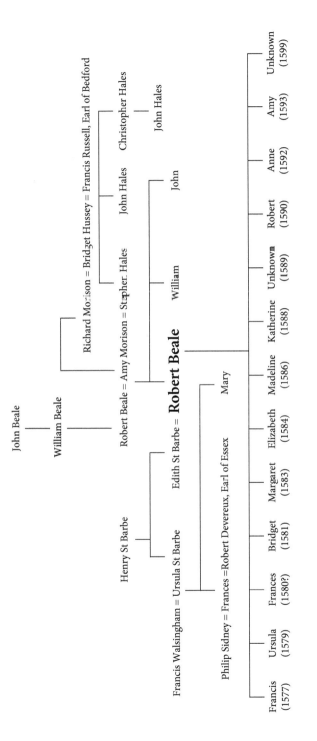

Map of Europe

Western Europe, c.1600
with locations of interest to Robert Beale

——— Holy Roman Empire

0   500 mi

1

Europe in England

To reduce a life to a book seems unfair, but to leave it in obscurity is worse still. As an exercise in both compression and compassion, writing a fair and meaningful account of another's life is no mean feat or insignificant task. The challenge becomes the greater when the subject lived a long life during an age far removed from the present and was active on several levels in multiple circles inside and outside government. The undertaking is even more considerable still when the relevant source material is either comparatively scarce or, less frequently, unexpectedly abundant. In the case of Robert Beale, an Elizabethan and government administrator of the second tier and for whom these issues apply, the difficulties are further compounded by the fact that, alongside source material in the usual locations, he was a voracious collector of books and manuscripts, and he retained whatever he could in his personal library and archive. Most unusually, that archive has survived nearly intact from the year of his death, 1601, to the present.[1] The enormity of his collection and the additional relevant papers is of such a scale that, rather than continue to illuminate Beale's life and character evermore, it tends to cloud the historian's view and cast doubt on the feasibility of such a project. An account of Beale's life would require sifting and winnowing through hundreds of volumes, many thousands of pages, in archives across the United Kingdom and across the seas. There are plenty of clear and present reasons why Beale has been left in relative obscurity and why, as Patrick Collinson remarked, 'no-one has dared to write a biography of Beale'.[2]

This book is an attempt to get past the paperwork of an industrious administrator to get a sense of their personal life and thinking, but to do so is not to cast

---

[1] The collection was used sporadically by scholars before its thorough cataloguing in 1994, but the introductory matter and indexing to the catalogue dramatically increased its accessibility and use: *The British Library Catalogue of Additions to the Manuscripts: The Yelverton Manuscripts [...]*, 2 vols (London, 1994). Stray items and volumes are found in other collections at the BL and elsewhere.

[2] The abundance and encumbrance of personal papers was not, of course, unique to Beale. The same applies to Francis Walsingham. See Chapter 6, n. 2. Patrick Collinson, 'Servants and Citizens: Robert Beale and other Elizabethans', *Historical Research*, 79:206 (2006), 501. Collinson was no stranger to writing biographies, having written *Archbishop Grindal, 1519–1583: The Struggle for a Reformed Church* (London, 1979), and over two dozen entries by 2004 for the *ODNB*, including that for Queen Elizabeth I, which was published separately by Oxford University Press in 2007; published posthumously was his *Richard Bancroft and Elizabethan Anti-Puritanism* (Cambridge, 2013). Biography as a historical methodology has had its detractors, but its advocates and practitioners have, it seems, won the argument. See, e.g. Diarmaid MacCulloch's difference of opinion from that of his doctoral advisor, Geoffrey Elton, in MacCulloch's *Thomas Cromwell: A Life* (London, 2018), 3–4.

that paperwork aside. Paper was very much part of who Beale was; his library and archive represent, as it were, a palimpsest of his life. He worked for nearly forty years at the centre of the Elizabethan regime—as clerk of the Privy Council and at multiple points as Member of Parliament—so any effort to understand his life and experiences must necessarily consider that activity and the paper it generated. When commenting on the excellent but necessarily restricted work by Mark Taviner on Beale and the limitations of the voluminous sources, Collinson remarked that 'we know so little about [Beale] on a personal level' and that details regarding a toothache in 1576 and gifts for his wife, Edith, in 1587 were exceptional.[3] As will be seen, the historical record actually tells much more. We can see, for example, his insecurities, professional and otherwise, his care and concern for his wife and many children, his health struggles with bladder stones and gout, his property holdings in London and elsewhere, his financial concerns throughout his life, and his correspondence networks with friends and associates near and far.

A Bitter, Insecure Man

The whole Beale analysed here brings together some parts of the man described by others. The earliest historian of Elizabethan England, William Camden, described Beale as a 'vehement man and austerely bitter' most likely due to Beale's firm religious convictions in sympathy with some Puritans. Another of an even more anti-Puritan bent, Peter Heylyn, followed suit in describing Beale's 'impetuosity and edge' directed against the archbishop of Canterbury, John Whitgift: 'This Beal was in himself a most eager Puritan, trained up by [Francis] Walsingham to draw dryfoot after [i.e. track] Priests and Jesuits, his extream hatred to those men, being looked on as the only good quality which he could pretend to [...] being over-blinded by zeal and passion, he was never able to distinguish rightly between truth and falshood'. Thomas Fuller, writing about the same time and much in the same vein as Heylyn, and quoting Camden, admitted Beale's abilities in serving his queen but concluded '[w]ell knew queen Elizabeth what tools to use on knotty timber'.[4] These characterizations proved tenacious in the twentieth century. In what was probably Joan Henderson's most important biographical entry for The History of Parliament, Beale's 'twin interests of religion

---

[3] Collinson, 'Servants and Citizens', 501, with n. 52 referring to Taviner as 'the most authoritative account of any aspect of Robert Beale's career'.

[4] William Camden, Annales Rervm Anglicarvm, et Hibernicarvm, Regnante Elizabetha (London, 1615) (STC 4496), 338, 'hominem vehementem & austere acerbum'; cf. the English translation as 'a man very austere and sharpe' (London, 1625) (STC 4497), Bk 3, 33, and later, 'a man vehement and austerely sowre' (3rd edn, London, 1635) (STC 4501), 249. Peter Heylyn, Aërius Redivivus, or, The History of the Presbyterians [...] (London, 1672), 264. Thomas Fuller, The Church-History of Britain (London, 1655), 149. Camden's conservative Protestantism can be seen in the Annales, but see also ODNB for a discussion of his earlier years at Oxford.

and law' dominated his life inside and outside of the House of Commons, and his confrontations with Whitgift and ecclesiastical jurisdiction eventually brought his downfall. Elements of Henderson's understanding and treatment of Beale can be seen in John Neale's analysis of Beale's activity in multiple parliaments; Henderson's caution in avoiding a description of Beale as a Puritan was, however, not to be found in Neale, who saw Beale as a subversive Puritan. Collinson remarked late in life that Beale was, for Henderson, 'the study of a lifetime' and her 'longstanding friend', but one might reasonably say the same for him.[5] From Collinson's doctoral thesis in 1957 forward, Beale commanded attention. Understandably given the focus of his work, and as with Henderson's view, Collinson gave pride of place to the religious and legal dimensions of Beale. Here one finds an Elizabethan Puritan of principle who sympathized with and was a mouthpiece for those opposing Whitgift, and who tried to work in the Commons for reformation of abuses in the Church. As a parliamentarian, Beale was, for Collinson, a prime example of the Elizabethan 'men of business' to be called upon for efficient and thorough research and administrative tasks 'as part of the dynamic machinery of government, as decision makers and policy formers, not as passive tools or instruments'.[6] Additional doctoral theses have continued to flesh out scholarly understandings of Beale in his role as clerk of the Privy Council and collector of books and manuscripts for that very purpose, but the most substantial work by far has been that of Taviner.[7]

One of the principal strengths of Taviner's work is its attempt to see Beale in the round and consider his collecting and archiving practices as integrated with his activities as clerk, secretary, and ambassador. By addressing fine-grained issues of watermarks and palaeography, and benefiting from the British Library's catalogue of the collection, Taviner was able to analyse issues of provenance and dating of acquisition. With encouragement from Collinson to pursue Beale, Taviner consulted as much modern scholarship and primary material as he could in print and manuscript, and while at points he recognized the wider,

---

[5] *HoP:HoC*. J. E. Neale, *Elizabeth I and her Parliaments*, 2 vols (London, 1953; 1957). Collinson, 'Servants and Citizens', 491, 500, with commentary on Henderson and Neale at 488–9.

[6] Patrick Collinson, 'The Puritan Classical Movement in the Reign of Elizabeth I', PhD thesis, University of London, 1957; the index to the thesis (essentially Vol. 3, later prepared by Collinson's mother in 1960) demonstrates Collinson's engagement with Beale in the fact that Beale has more entries than Archbishop Edmund Grindal and that other 'man of business', Thomas Norton, and ranks among the top ten Elizabethans by way of entries; the thesis was later revised and published as *The Elizabethan Puritan Movement* (London, 1967). Patrick Collinson, 'Puritans, Men of Business and Elizabethan Parliaments', *Parliamentary History*, 7 (1988), 197. NB Collinson's declaration that 'I would not claim Robert Beale as a friend' was primarily because he knew little about Beale on a personal level. 'Servants and Citizens', 501.

[7] Patricia Ann Brewerton, 'Paper Trails: Re-Reading Robert Beale as Clerk to the Elizabethan Privy Council', PhD thesis, Birkbeck College, University of London, 1998. Jacqueline D. Vaughan, 'Secretaries, Statesmen and Spies: The Clerks of the Tudor Privy Council, c.1540–c.1603', PhD thesis, University of St Andrews, 2007. Taviner. Although Gary Bell's entry on Beale in the *ODNB* refers to the published works of Henderson, Collinson, and others, these theses have not been used.

international context and Beale's connections overseas, his primary focus remained the domestic sphere of Elizabethan governance, and some errors persisted. Beale's importance has also been discussed briefly by various others for particular purposes apart from religion. Scholars have long used and cited Beale's manuscript treatise on the office of the principal secretary, first printed in 1925 as an appendix to Conyers Read's biography of Francis Walsingham, Beale's brother-in-law. Beale's arguments in the 1580s and 1590s for parliamentary supremacy and his use of history have drawn attention, as have his archival practices as emblematic of broader trends in the development of the state. Also noted but not sufficiently recognized is the fact that Beale did not fit into any one 'faction' at the Elizabethan court, if such factions even existed between William Cecil and Robert Dudley, earl of Leicester; rather, like several others, no clear line of allegiance seemed to apply for Beale.[8] Probably one of the elements of Beale's life most frequently cited by scholars has been his notion, put forward in his treatise on the office of the principal secretary, to separate documents public (i.e. state) and private (i.e. personal). Leaving aside for the moment whether Beale fully and consistently demarcated between the two in his own collections (he did not), his experience as an ambassador, clerk, and specialist in foreign affairs alerted him to the necessity of easy and efficient record retrieval in what would eventually become known as the state paper office. In England, he was not alone in developing his own archive, but his most immediate inspiration was not English. In fact, Beale appears to have taken his initial cues from Johann Sturm, whose Gymnasium at Strasbourg Beale attended in the 1550s, and whose methods of organizing and retrieving information set the pattern for many others. Also, although Beale was never a part of the enterprises of ecclesiastical history led by Matthias Flacius Illyricus at Magdeburg, he knew from an early age the importance of collecting material and documenting the past for present purposes. In the English context, Matthew Parker, archbishop of Canterbury, led a similarly major project in collecting materials of ecclesiastical history, while Cecil and Walsingham retained as much of their own materials as they could for the purposes of the state. Beale's thinking in this respect was representative of broader trends during Elizabeth's reign, when the collection, copying, circulation, and retention of paper far exceeded the practices of previous reigns and set the tone

---

[8] Conyers Read, *Mr Secretary Walsingham and the Policy of Queen Elizabeth*, 3 vols (Oxford, 1925), 1.423–3. Alexandra Gajda, 'The Elizabethan Church and the Antiquity of Parliament', in Paul Cavill and Alexandra Gajda (eds), *Writing the History of Parliament in Tudor and Early Stuart England* (Manchester, 2018), 77–105, esp. 94–6; cf. Ian Archer's chapter, 'Elizabethan Chroniclers and Parliament', 133–52. Arnold Hunt, 'The Early Modern Secretary and the Early Modern Archive', in Liesbeth Corens, Kate Peters, and Alexandra Walsham (eds), *Archives and Information in the Early Modern World* (Oxford, 2018), 105–30, esp. 118–28. Nicholas Popper, 'From Abbey to Archive: Managing Texts and Records in Early Modern England', *Archival Science*, 10 (2010), 249–66, esp. 256–8; Nicholas Popper, 'An Information State for Elizabethan England', *The Journal of Modern History*, 90 (2018), 503–35, esp. 516–18. Simon Adams, 'Favourites and Factions at the Elizabethan Court', repr. in Simon Adams, *Leicester and the Court: Essays on Elizabethan Politics* (Manchester, 2002), 59.

for the century ahead. The difference with Beale, though, was a matter of station.[9] He never became as mighty as Walsingham or Cecil, but his role and significance have been summarized:

> Beale was a powerful character, a plainly spoken man of passionate Protestantism and high intelligence, an experienced bureaucrat and a master of government business. Over his long career, Beale collected the kinds of papers he and his colleagues needed to use every day, organized by themes and topics. Though rebound in the seventeenth century, Beale's volumes [...] allow us to understand an Elizabethan archive, to touch it and feel it: the stiff pale animal hide spines and covers, the leather ties to keep the books closed, the indexes for speedy reference, and Beale's explanatory notes in what [...] is one of the vilest hands of sixteenth-century England—uncompromising and bluntly effective like, indeed, the man himself.[10]

As will be seen, the comparison between Beale's hand and character is entirely appropriate.

The development and survival of Beale's massive archive of manuscripts have been the primary areas of study for scholars because his library of printed books, although very considerable at the time, has not come down alongside his papers, which were eventually deposited in the British Museum in the twentieth century. His books, along with those collected subsequently by the Yelverton family in the seventeenth and eighteenth centuries, were sold at public auction in London in 1784, but a manuscript catalogue of the library as it existed in 1694 can offer clues.[11] To ascertain which books in the Yelverton library were his is a matter of

[9] On Sturm and Flacius, see Chapter 2. In addition to the works by Hunt and Popper cited above, see the fullest account taking developments into the 17th century, Nicholas Popper, *The Specter of the Archive: Political Practice and the Information State in Early Modern Britain* (Chicago, IL, 2024); I am grateful to the author for providing me with relevant chapters in advance of publication. As Popper notes, Beale's working relationship with William Cecil, Lord Burghley, in the 1590s included Beale's frequent visits to the Tower to consult records on Burghley's behalf. Use with caution because of overstatement, F. Jeffrey Platt, 'The Elizabethan "Foreign Office"', *The Historian*, 56 (1994), 725–40. The 'Office of Her Majesty's Papers and Records for Business of State and Council' was officially chartered in 1575, but most Elizabethan counsellors retained their papers, public or private, within their families and friends. Popper, 'From Abbey to Archive', 255–6. For related discussions, see Alan Stewart, 'Familiar Letters and State Papers: The Afterlives of Early Modern Correspondence', in James Daybell and Andrew Gordon (eds), *Cultures of Correspondence in Early Modern Britain* (Philadelphia, PA, 2016), 237–52; Angela Andreani, *The Elizabethan Secretariat and the Signet Office: The Production of State Papers, 1590–1596* (London, 2017); Noah Millstone, *Manuscript Circulation and the Invention of Politics in Early Stuart England* (Cambridge, 2016).

[10] Stephen Alford, *The Watchers: A Secret History of the Reign of Elizabeth I* (London, 2012), 19.

[11] William Camden, *Britannia, or, a Chorographical Description of the Flourishing Kingdoms of England, Scotland, and Ireland[...]*, trans. Richard Gough (London, 1789), 2.178, which also noted that 'the MSS only wait for a purchaser'. Catalogue of the Yelverton library, 1694, BL, Hargrave MS 107. At his death, Beale seems not to have left any of his books to his old grammar school in Coventry established by John Hales. Given his close connections to Coventry and its people throughout his life, the lack of even a small bequest is slightly surprising. CUL, MSS Add. 4467-8. When in dire financial straits in the 1590s, Beale might have needed to start selling his books. See Chapter 8.

conjecture in some ways, but one can reasonably suspect that he owned a book listed in the catalogue if elsewhere he referred to it and obviously used it for his written compositions. Similarly, when we can document that he received books from others, and those books are found in the catalogue compiled nearly a century after his death, the credibility of the catalogue improves. Beale's vast and deep learning in theology, history, law, medicine, and other subjects can be accounted for if one takes a liberal but cautious view of the catalogue and from the likelihood that Beale owned many of the titles printed before the late 1590s, when his financial situation probably prevented him from adding much to his library.

The slipperiness of the library catalogue is reflected both in the fact that no likeness of Beale has survived (if ever drawn) and across his papers. A search in the nineteenth century for a print or portrait of Beale found nothing, and descriptions of Beale's appearance are scant.[12] Regarding his papers, much of what he kept was for his own purposes in serving his queen and for later reference. As a working reference archive of political and religious affairs domestic and foreign, his papers shed little light on Beale as a person; such was not their purpose. By considering his working life as found in his archive in light of other sources—such as his letters to others, parish registers, and patent rolls—gaps can be filled, shadows illuminated, and errors corrected; and yet, despite the historian's best efforts, some sources simply no longer survive, however obliquely we know of them.[13] The following pages provide the fullest account at present by using the widest base of the known relevant sources in their original forms where feasible, but it is nevertheless recognized that any description and analysis of a life over four centuries past cannot be complete, cannot be perfect, and can only be partial because Beale was reluctant to commit too much to paper; he knew the danger of doing so. The depiction, as it were, of Beale here shows how an adolescent from a middling but comfortable family in London was sent abroad in flight from Catholic persecution during the 1550s, travelled considerably on his own in the

---

[12] In *The Gentlemen's Magazine* (May 1825), 386, an inquirer regarding Beale was informed by the editor that a certain 'C.S.B. can confidently assure [the inquirer] that there is no print (portrait) of Robert Beale extant; nor has he learned that there is any painting of him'; that Beale 'rendered himself conspicuous in his day', according to the editor, is dubious at least regarding any attempt to have himself depicted. See the observation in 1600 that Beale was heavy and paunch-bellied: John Herbert to Robert Cecil, 15 May 1600, CP, 79/49 (orig.); see Chapter 8.

[13] Basic factual errors persist regarding, e.g. Beale's location at key moments, date of death, and number of children. In an otherwise reasonable if brief entry in the *ODNB* for Beale, the reader is informed that Beale was in Paris during the St Bartholomew's Day Massacre in 1572 (he was almost certainly in London), and that he died on 27 May 1601 (he died two days earlier). In an otherwise excellent book, Alexandra Walsham repeats the error that Beale had one child, his daughter who married Henry Yelverton. There were many others, including Francis Beale, a future MP. Alexandra Walsham, *Generations: Age, Ancestry, and Memory in the English Reformations* (Oxford, 2023), 496, citing Stewart, 'Familiar Letters', 251, which simply refers to the BL's catalogue for the Yelverton collection. An example of correspondence with Beale of which only a trace remains is that of the Puritan Thomas Wilcox, who apparently corresponded with both Beale and his wife, Edith, about 1578. Collinson, 'Puritan Classical Movement', 60, 819, citing Dr Williams' Library, MS Morrice, Vol. 2, 'A Chronological Account of Eminent Persons', 517(4).

Holy Roman Empire and France during the 1560s, and found official government employment in London in the 1570s. With the assistance of patrons in high places, Cecil above all, and through his own industry and connections, Beale rose to the height of his power in the 1580s, even serving as a temporary principal secretary on occasion. A man of firm legal principles and religious scruples, he was known to challenge Archbishop Whitgift and his proceedings on several occasions, even doing so in Whitgift's own home and on the floor of the House of Commons. In the 1590s and with an older generation giving way to a new, Beale found the limits of his power when he was ejected from Parliament, placed under house arrest, and no longer within Elizabeth's good graces. Nevertheless, by 1600 Beale again had enough of Elizabeth's confidence for him to considered for the role of principal secretary in his own right.

For all his rise from being an informal servant and informal intelligencer abroad to a clerk of the Privy Council and secretary of the Council of the North with properties in London, Surrey, and Warwickshire, and for all his bluster before a primate and conviction in his writings, Beale was deeply insecure. He came not from a noble or particularly wealthy background, and he was dependent upon the protection of his social superiors. His entrée onto the political scene in the early 1560s was in proving the legitimacy of a potentially rival Protestant claim to the royal succession, and his role in that drama was not forgotten by Elizabeth or others. A major element of his motivation to build a library and archive was to make himself useful to the regime, but the fact that he never earned a university degree restricted how high up the social and political ladder he could climb, and he resented that others with such degrees but with less knowledge and expertise found advancement and security that eluded him. Although he had frequently grumbled about his costs in serving the queen in the 1570s and 1580s, after his fall in 1593 his financial security was so imperilled that he became seriously concerned about the welfare of his wife and children were he to die suddenly in an accident. His concern for his family was sincere and consistent. Edith was pregnant over a dozen times, giving birth to eleven named children between 1577 and 1593, with six surviving in 1600. Robert and Edith appear by all accounts to have been in a loving relationship, and his preference for enjoying the married life was known to others.[14] In a series of desperate letters towards the end of his life, he asked for help that never came. Even when Elizabeth promised to

---

[11] See below, Chapters 4–8, for notice of the Beales' children, but see esp. Chapter 8 for the 1590s. On Beale and marriage, see Hubert Languet to Philip Sidney, 8 January 1578, in Roger Kuin (ed.), *The Correspondence of Sir Philip Sidney*, 2 vols (Oxford, 2012), 2.804–8; and Chapter 5, n. 41. For updated discussions, see Leah Astbury, 'When a Woman Hates her Husband: Love, Sex and Fruitful Marriages in Early Modern England', *Gender & History*, 32 (2020), 523–41; Leah Astbury, 'Being Well, Looking Ill: Childbirth and the Return to Health in Seventeenth-century England', *Social History of Medicine*, 30 (2017), 500–19; with a slightly earlier chronology, Vanessa Harding, 'Families in Later Medieval London: Sex, Marriage and Mortality', in Elizabeth A. New and Christian Steer (eds), *Medieval Londoners: Essays to Mark the Eightieth Birthday of Caroline M. Barron* (London, 2019), 11–36.

assist his family—in recognition of his services as a commissioner to discuss a peace treaty with Spanish representatives at Boulogne—the support never materialized. In his final years Beale's lifelong insecurity and feeling that he was left out in the cold were more obviously justified. He admitted in the 1580s that his nature was 'perhappes to bruske and playne', perhaps to be rash and complain. Camden's characterization of Beale as vehement and bitter might have been based on his own interactions with Beale or on rumours from others in the 1590s regarding his conflicts with Archbishop Whitgift, but one wonders whether Beale would have agreed.

A Shallow Channel

He might have been a bitter and insecure man with particular concerns and idiosyncratic tendencies, but he was also representative of the sixteenth century. An English exile during the 1550s and intellectual wanderer of the 1560s who subsequently worked his way into government service in the 1570s, Beale put his experiences and expertise on European affairs to good use. He was not alone in having such a trajectory. Henry Killigrew, although over a decade older than Beale, gained significant military and diplomatic experience during this period, and the two men subsequently crossed paths and worked together in France and Germany before collaborating on legal issues back in London later in life. Daniel Rogers, just a few years older than Beale, was born in Wittenberg, Germany, led a successful career in diplomacy, and was well connected with many humanist intellectuals in the Low Countries and Germany, one of whom, Hubert Languet, was also a friend of Beale's. Others like Thomas Danett (the younger) and Thomas Bodley were closer in age to Beale and thus minors while in exile, but they too leveraged their international experiences to greater or lesser effect when back in England. With Beale, Danett shared deep interests in history and foreign languages, while Bodley's library eclipsed Beale's own. Still others, higher up the social and ecclesiastical ladder, like Francis Russell, earl of Bedford, and John Aylmer, bishop of London, also spent years in exile and subsequently had contact with Beale— Bedford as a future political patron, Aylmer a tutor and future adversary. Perhaps above all, and most significantly, Francis Walsingham spent an important part of his early adulthood on the European mainland, especially at the University of Padua, where he was a spokesman for the English students at the University. Beale and Walsingham do not seem to have known each other before the late 1560s, but their marriages to sisters and close collaboration first at the English embassy in Paris and then subsequently in the Privy Council was matched by a firm, fraternal friendship; indeed, Walsingham frequently referred to Beale as 'my brother'. The overseas experiences of English Protestants could be, as in these cases, for reasons of religious exile, education, or professional development, but for others the reason they crossed the seas was to fight in the wars of religion in France, the Netherlands, and the Holy Roman Empire.[15] Just as these men were all distinct from each other, with contingent concerns and diverse life trajectories based on social backgrounds and connections, so too was Beale distinct. After Queen Elizabeth I's accession in 1558, he stayed on the mainland far longer than any of them. Traveling on his own, he became increasingly self-reliant apart from his connection back in England to John Hales, his step-uncle and ersatz father (and fellow exile). Yet, collectively these people (women like Katherine Bertie [née Willoughby], duchess of Suffolk, very much included) were emblematic of the personal and intellectual contacts and movements across the Channel and North Sea during the mid sixteenth century.

Scholars of Tudor history have been attuned to international connections to varying degrees over the past few generations, but since the early 2000s an upswing has emphasized the degree to which England was not just connected to, but in some respects even dependent upon, broader European affairs. In the vanguard of this trend in Reformation history has been Diarmaid MacCulloch, whose magisterial biographies of Thomas Cranmer and Thomas Cromwell have illuminated the importance of German and Italian connections respectively. In other studies MacCulloch has taken a strong but judicious stance on how the Reformation in England took inspiration from and found common ground with the Reformations elsewhere, but he has also maintained that, just as the situation in England was in some ways *sui generis*, so too were the Reformations in German, Swiss, French, Dutch, and Danish lands; using 'the Continent' (or 'Continental') has an unhelpful, homogenizing tendency in this regard. By emphasizing influences and connections, one need not disregard distinctions and particularities. Indeed, in arguing that the Reformation in England was of its own nature, one then would need to agree that the Reformations across Europe were themselves different from each other and contingent upon local factors.[16] As with people, so with countries.

---

[15] For convenient biographical entries, see *ODNB*. The dated but convenient census remains useful: Christina Hallowell Garrett, *The Marian Exiles: A Study in the Origins of Elizabethan Puritanism* (Cambridge, 1938). On the English in Padua, see Jonathan Woolfson, *Padua and the Tudors: English Students in Italy, 1485–1603* (Cambridge, 1998); Jonathan Woolfson, 'Padua and English Students Revisited', *Renaissance Studies*, 27 (2013), 572–87; Giovanni Luigi Andrich and Biagio Brugi, *De Natione Anglica et Scota Iuristarum Universitatis Patavinae ab a. MCCXXII p. ch. n. usque ad a. MDCCXXXVIII* (Padua, 1892). For the later period and military men, see, e.g. Jason White, *Militant Protestantism and British Identity, 1603–1642* (London, 2012); David J.B. Trim, 'English Military Émigrés and the Protestant Cause in Europe, 1603–c.1640', in David Worthington (ed.), *British and Irish Emigrants and Exiles in Europe, 1603–1688* (Leiden, 2010), 237–58.

[16] Diarmaid MacCulloch, *Thomas Cranmer: A Life* (New Haven, CT, 1996); Diarmaid MacCulloch, *Thomas Cromwell*; 'Putting the English Reformation on the Map (The Prothero Lecture)', *Transactions of the Royal Historical Society*, 15 (Cambridge, 2005), 75–95; Diarmaid MacCulloch, 'Sixteenth-century English Protestantism and the Continent', in Dorothea Wendebourg (ed.), *Sister Reformations: The Reformation in Germany and in England: Symposium on the Occasion of the 450th Anniversary of the Elizabethan Settlement, September 23rd–26th, 2009 = [...]* (Tübingen, 2010), 1–14; Diarmaid MacCulloch,

Several colloquia have brought together scholars from across the UK and elsewhere to consider these questions and the ways in which ideas and developments on the European mainland affected Tudor England. The publications of these proceedings have offered snapshots of how the thinking of historians of religion (across multiple generations) has shifted since the twentieth century: as Collinson put it, '[w]e are now out of the tunnel and into sunny uplands. England is both part of a Britain whose diversity is now more amply acknowledged and a major European player at the heart of Europe'.[17] The effect of this research has been to show how various Protestant denominations and impulses had impacts, however attenuated, adapted, or appropriated, on the English Church and people. These studies have begun to inform broader analyses of the period, such that sixteenth-century England is now more fully recognized as a place that ideas from across the seas might find fertile soil and collaborative, existing beliefs and traditions.[18] Locations for tracing the movement and impact of Protestant ideas have been various, from Wittenberg and Heidelberg to Zurich and Strasbourg, but it may be suggestive to state upfront that Beale was educated formally or informally at all four of these locations in the 1550s and 1560s, and that this exposure had profound reverberations that can be seen later in his life; in this way, Beale is a prime example of those who represented a slice (or more) of Europe in England.

Studies of English Catholicism have taken a similar international turn. In fairness, the English Catholic diaspora has been on scholars' radars for a long time, with Albert Loomie focusing on connections with Spain, and John Bossy on

---

'The Church of England and International Protestantism, 1530–1570', in Anthony Milton (ed.), *The Oxford History of Anglicanism*, Vol. 1: *Reformation and Identity, c.1520–1662* (Oxford, 2017), 316–32; cf. for historiographical comment, Anthony Milton, 'Changing Historical Perspectives on the English Reformation: The Last Fifty Years', *Studies in Church History*, 49 (2013), 282–302.

[17] Polly Ha and Patrick Collinson (eds), *The Reception of Continental Reformation in Britain* (Oxford, 2010); quotation from Collinson's introduction, 'The Fog in the Channel Clears: The Rediscovery of the Continental Dimension to the British Reformations', xxxi. Wendebourg (ed.), *Sister Reformations*, was followed by *Sister Reformations II*, which emphasized ethics and the Reformation (Tübingen, 2014) and *Sister Reformations III*, which included Scotland (Tübingen, 2019). For comment on Anglo-German connections and scholarship, see David Scott Gehring, 'From the Strange Death to the Odd Afterlife of Lutheran England', *The Historical Journal*, 57 (2014), 825–44. For comment on the Reformation in England and looking east, see Polly Ha, 'Reorienting English Protestantism', *Journal of Medieval and Early Modern Studies*, 53 (2023), 1–23. The considerable scholarship bringing England closer to the mainland is too extensive to list, but see the notes and bibliographies in the works cited here. For discussion of how different generations adapted over the course of the Reformation itself, see Norman Jones, *The English Reformation: Religion and Cultural Adaption* (Oxford, 2002).

[18] Two examples focusing on England but with sensitivities to international currents are Peter Marshall, *Heretics and Believers: A History of the English Reformation* (New Haven, CT, 2017), and Lucy Wooding, *Tudor England* (New Haven, CT, 2022). The significance of the referendum in 2016 on the UK's leaving the European Union should not be lost on the directions of scholarship. See, e.g. Peter Marshall, 'Tudor Brexit: Catholics and Europe in the British and Irish Reformations', *Studies: An Irish Quarterly Review*, 106:424 (2017–18), 417–24, followed by Alec Ryrie, 'Tudor Brexit: From *Ecclesia Anglicana* to Anglicanism', 425–30.

France.[19] Migration and exile, community and identity, and collaboration and agency are vital emphases in their work as well as in that of subsequent scholars. Subsequent generations of historians have continued such lines of inquiry in Spanish, French, Irish, and other contexts, some evaluating the earlier period, others the later, and still others even pushing the epistemological boundaries of 'international' Catholicism into the 'transregional', a potentially helpful development for understandings of Protestantism, as well.[20] The recognition among modern scholars that Catholics in early modern England varied in their religious beliefs and political opinions, forged connections with other European Catholics for reasons sometimes peaceful sometimes less so, and held identities deeply indebted to experiences of mobility is starting to reflect Beale's own thinking at the time. Because his early travels in Germany and France, with pushes from one location and pulls to another, demonstrated in vivid colour the confessional conflicts of the period, Beale sometimes but not always saw the world in black and white.[21] For him, the international Protestant community was defending itself against an equally international Catholic cabal led spiritually by the pope(s) in Rome and Jesuits elsewhere but politically and militarily by King Philip of Spain and the Guise in France. Closer to home, Beale saw the principal threat in Mary Queen of Scots and her proximity to the royal succession if Elizabeth were to die childless.

As a religious exile, student, and political intelligencer abroad, when Beale returned to England he was sensitive to the immigrant communities of London and elsewhere. He engaged on different levels with Italian, French, Dutch, and

---

[19] A useful historiographical discussion is Michael Questier, 'Going Nowhere Fast? The Historiography of Catholicism in Post-Reformation Britain', *Huntington Library Quarterly*, 84 (2021), 405–31.

[20] See, e.g. Freddy Cristóbal Domínguez, *Radicals in Exile: English Catholic Books during the Reign of Philip II* (University Park, PA, 2021); Alexander Samson, *Mary and Philip: The Marriage of Tudor England and Habsburg Spain* (Manchester, 2020); Katy Gibbons, *English Catholic Exiles in Late Sixteenth-Century Paris* (Woodbridge, 2011); Alexander Soetaert, 'Catholic Refuge and the Printing Press: Catholic Exiles from England, France, and the Low Countries in the Ecclesiastical Province of Cambrai', *British Catholic History*, 34 (2019), 532–61; Alexander Soetaert and Violet Soen, 'A Catholic International or Transregional Catholicism? The Printing Press, English Catholics, and their Hosts in the Early Modern Ecclesiastical Province of Cambrai', *The Catholic Historical Review*, 106 (2020), 551–75; Tadhg Ó hAnnracháin, *Confessionalism and Mobility in Early Modern Ireland* (Oxford, 2021); Caroline Bowden and James E. Kelly (eds), *The English Convents in Exile, 1600–1800: Communities, Culture and Identity* (Farnham, 2013); James E. Kelly, *English Convents in Catholic Europe, c.1600–1800* (Cambridge, 2020); Frederick E. Smith, *Transnational Catholicism in Tudor England: Mobility, Exile, and Counter-Reformation, 1530–1580* (Oxford, 2022); and with a later chronology, Liesbeth Corens, *Confessional Mobility and English Catholics in Counter-Reformation Europe* (Oxford, 2019). A particularly rich collection of essays on community and identity across a wide geography is Yosef Kaplan (ed.), *Early Modern Ethnic and Religious Communities in Exile* (Newcastle, 2017), with John Coffey's chapter on the exile and return of English Puritans at 289–312.

[21] At other times Beale was fully aware that Catholics could vary among themselves just as Protestants did. On the dangers of confessional polarities without qualifications and contexts, see Peter Lake and Michael Questier (eds), *Conformity and Orthodoxy in the English Church, c.1560–1660* (Woodbridge, 2000); for a case study of a privy councillor, Rivkah Zim, 'Religion and the Politic Counsellor: Thomas Sackville, 1536–1608', *English Historical Review*, 122:498 (2007), 892–917.

German immigrants and merchants, sometimes regarding religion but more often concerning trade and technical knowledge (e.g. mining techniques). His papers include materials supplied by these contacts and can offer clues into the levels of political participation and utility offered by the English government to such individuals. Modern scholarship has focused not only on religious migrants to England but also on tradesmen like those Beale encountered and has illuminated the relationships between the English and the immigrants.[22] Although the vast majority of early modern Europeans might not have left their home villages, towns, or cities, the mobility of those who did is important when assessing notions of religious identities, political allegiances, and intellectual networks. Whether Protestant, Catholic, merchant, or mercenary, people who went abroad and moved in like-minded circles could have real and significant impacts in their host and home countries. In this way, communities of English people could be found in mainland Europe just as Europeans from various countries could be found in England. Beale was exactly one of those people, from his first work in Germany on the Elizabethan succession in 1563 to his final commission to Boulogne to find peace with Spain in 1600.

Diplomacy and Governance

People who acted as informal or formal intelligencers, agents, or ambassadors during the sixteenth century have garnered significant and worthy scholarly attention. As examples of mobility in action, of international theory and practice, these men and women were more than mere functionaries of the state. Those who supplied intelligence from across the seas, which could be the result of state action and institutional loyalty or private initiative and financial need, were often informally appointed and part of a wider programme of espionage orchestrated by, among others, Walsingham. While ambassadors could indeed serve as orators of their rulers and negotiate in their name according to strict instructions, they also

---

[22] Convenient collections of essays include Randolph Vigne and Charles Littleton (eds), *From Strangers to Citizens: The Integration of Immigrant Communities in Britain, Ireland, and Colonial America, 1550–1750* (Brighton, 2001), see, e.g. David J.B. Trim's chapter, 'Protestant Refugees in Elizabethan England and Confessional Conflict in France and the Netherlands, 1562–c.1610', 68–79; Nigel Goose and Liên Luu (eds), *Immigrants in Tudor and Early Stuart England* (Brighton, 2005), e.g. David J.B. Trim, 'Immigrants, the Indigenous Community and International Calvinism', 211–27. Patrick Collinson did much to get the ball rolling with 'The Elizabethan Puritans and the Foreign Reformed Churches in London', *Proceedings of the Huguenot Society of London*, 20 (1964), 528–55, and his 'England and International Calvinism, 1558–1640', in Menna Prestwich (ed.), *International Calvinism 1541–1715* (Oxford, 1985), 197–223. The major work of the 1980s, Andrew Pettegree, *Foreign Protestant Communities in Sixteenth-Century London* (Oxford, 1986), has in some ways been updated in Silke Muylaert, *Shaping the Stranger Churches: Migrants in England and the Troubles in the Netherlands, 1547–1585* (Leiden, 2020). See also, W. Mark Ormrod, 'England's Immigrants, 1330–1550: Aliens in Later Medieval and Early Tudor England', *Journal of British Studies*, 59 (2020), 245–63.

exercised degrees of agency. Sometimes they used opportunities abroad to bolster their own utility in state service and with a view to further political patronage and advancement, writing frequent and often lengthy pieces demonstrating their expertise and literary talents. The intersection and cross-fertilization of traditional diplomatic history with social and cultural history has shed light on hitherto underappreciated aspects of political culture, international relations, and the possibilities and limits of social mobility for those who served their princes abroad. In many respects, scholarship has pushed the boundaries of who constituted a diplomatic agent, what diplomatic processes and practices looked like in practice, the ways in which official diplomacy and informal cultural brokerage overlapped with espionage, and how far diplomatic contacts extended within and beyond Europe.[23] Beale's experiences before, during, and after his formal engagements as Elizabeth's representative abroad corroborate and extend these discussions. To the Dutch in 1576, the Germans in 1577, the Dutch again in 1587, and representatives of Spain in 1600, Beale served the queen in relatively traditional capacities, and his activities and ideas can be retraced in considerable detail because of his archival practices and correspondence. A man of the third- and then second-tier in the Elizabethan regime, he represents an example of cultural exchange in microcosm because of his pre-existing contacts, but his proclivity to collect, organize, and store information from various quarters for further reference was atypical and on a much larger scale than others'. Additionally, his knowledge of and facility in multiple languages—German, French, Italian, Spanish, and Latin (at least)—were atypical in one person and yet indicative of language learning

---

[23] On the multivalent nature of intelligence during the early modern period, see Ioanna Iordanou, *Venice's Secret Service: Organizing Intelligence in the Renaissance* (Oxford, 2019). On intelligence and espionage, see esp. John Cooper, *The Queen's Agent: Francis Walsingham at the Court of Elizabeth I* (London, 2011); Alford, *The Watchers*. The 'new diplomatic history' has displaced the old, and its many practitioners investigate aspects of literary culture, material culture, individual ambassadors, and beyond. A convenient summary of historiographical developments, with bibliography to 2016, is Tracey A. Sowerby, 'Early Modern Diplomatic History', *History Compass*, 14 (2016), 441–56, but on women and diplomacy, see Gemma Allen, 'The Rise of the Ambassadress: English Ambassadorial Wives and Early Modern Diplomatic Culture', *Historical Journal*, 62 (2019), 617–38; James Daybell, 'Gender, Politics and Diplomacy: Women, News and Intelligence Networks in Elizabethan England', in Robyn Adams and Rosanna Cox (eds), *Diplomacy in Early Modern Culture* (Basingstoke, 2011), 101–19. Representative of the turn are multiple edited collections: Joanna Craigwood and Tracey A. Sowerby (eds), 'English Diplomatic Relations and Literary Cultures in the Sixteenth and Seventeenth Centuries', special issue of *Huntington Library Quarterly*, 82 (2019); Joanna Craigwood and Tracey A. Sowerby (eds), *Cultures of Diplomacy and Literary Writing in the Early Modern World* (Oxford, 2019); Tracey A Sowerby and Jan Hennings (eds), *Practices of Diplomacy in the Early Modern World c.1410–1800* (London, 2017); Marika Keblusek and Badeloch Vera Noldus (eds), *Double Agents: Cultural and Political Brokerage in Early Modern Europe* (Leiden, 2011); Birgit Tremml-Werner and Dorothée Goetze (eds), 'A Multitude of Actors in Early Modern Diplomacy', a special issue of *Journal of Early Modern History*, 23 (2019); Birgit Tremml-Werner, Lisa Hellman, and Guido van Meersbergen (eds), 'Gift and Tribute in Early Modern Diplomacy: Afro-Eurasian Perspectives', a special issue of *Diplomatica*, 2 (2020); Dannielle Shaw and Matthew Woodcock (eds), 'New Explorations in Early Modern Espionage', a special issue of *History*, 108:381 (2023); Dorothée Goetze and Lena Oetzel (eds), *Early Modern European Diplomacy: A Handbook* (Berlin, 2024).

among other Elizabethans. However unusual, his individual efforts for his own personal reasons were so vast that they reflected archival management by the state.[24]

The growth and intensity of diplomatic activity across Europe during the sixteenth century led to an explosion of paperwork and, as is customary, bureaucracy. From England to Venice and Spain to Denmark, early modern states increasingly retained and organized what scholars now recognize as state papers. Although not entirely innovative, these developments contributed to the growth of the state itself and enabled successive regimes to refer more easily to its body of knowledge and intelligence regarding other powers. Venice has long been seen as the principal pioneer in this regard, but by the second half of the sixteenth century the diplomatic and governmental machinery in Spain and France had largely caught up, while the English and other Protestant powers would act similarly and of necessity during the wars of religion in France and the Netherlands. Moreover, and taking a long view, the thirst for current and valuable information evolved to include increasingly ethnographic information and spread well beyond government circles and secret archives.[25] Scholars' attention to early modern diplomacy and archival management has not been limited to the information contained in ambassadors' dispatches, as the documents themselves (as examples of material culture) have also drawn focus. The paper, handwriting, wax seals, and types of storage facilities are all now recognized as vital components of an individual writer's agency on the one hand, and broader state building on the other. The materiality of diplomacy and early modern culture extended well beyond the documentation. Gifts have been a topic of special interest to various scholars not only because of the mutual bonds and obligations associated with gift-giving, but also due to the meanings of the gifts themselves and the cultural exchanges they represented. Although at times a gift might be a relatively modest token or

---

[24] The case of Henry Unton's letterbook provides a useful context and contrast, on which, see Elizabeth Williamson, 'Diplomatic Letters as Political Literature: Copying Sir Henry Unton's Letters', *Huntington Library Quarterly*, 82 (2019), 559–78; Elizabeth Williamson, *Elizabethan Diplomacy and Epistolary Culture* (London, 2021). On languages, see John Gallagher, *Learning Languages in Early Modern England* (Oxford, 2019). In addition to Beale's self-driven learning of languages, he also supported those who taught others. See Chapter 8.

[25] On Venice, see, e.g. Iordanou, *Venice's Secret Service*; Filippo de Vivo, 'How to Read Italian *Relazioni*', *Renaissance and Reformation*, 34 (2011), 25–59; Kathryn Taylor, 'Matters Worthy of Men of State: Ethnography and Diplomatic Reporting in Sixteenth-Century Venice', *The Sixteenth Century Journal*, 51 (2020), 715–36. For wider contexts, see Isabella Lazzarini, *Communication and Conflict: Italian Diplomacy in the Early Renaissance, 1350–1520* (Oxford, 2015); Daniela Frigo (ed.), *Politics and Diplomacy in Early Modern Italy: The Structure of Diplomatic Practice, 1450–1800*, trans. Adrian Belton (Cambridge, 2000); and the chapters by Randolph C. Head, Filippo de Vivo, Jacob Soll, Arndt Brendecke, and Sundar Henny in Corens, Peters, and Walsham, *Archives and Information*. For English adaptions of the *relazione* and its relation to travel literature, see David Scott Gehring, 'Intelligence Gathering, *Relazioni*, and the *Ars Apodemica*', *Diplomacy & Statecraft*, 33 (2022), 211–32; cf. Tracey A. Sowerby, 'Francis Thynne's *Perfect Ambassadour* and the Construction of Diplomatic Thought in Elizabethan England', *Huntington Library Quarterly*, 82 (2020), 539–57. For Popper's works, see above. For wider public diffusion and reception of knowledge, see Donna A. Seger, *The Practical Renaissance: Information Culture and the Quest for Knowledge in Early Modern England, 1500–1640* (London, 2022).

gesture of goodwill, at others it might symbolize deep friendship and shared intellectual pursuits, at still others a recognition of necessity during hard times.[26] Beale was no outlier in these respects. His papers, while collected for personal as well as state purposes, furnish us with material evidence of early modern material culture by way of their watermarks, seals, folds, bindings, and, in some cases, shelfmarks. In analysing his life and thinking, the following pages mine the written information and Beale's habits in writing but they also recognize these material aspects, including the gifts Beale received. He does not appear to have been a great giver of gifts, but at various points he received, for example, books from friends abroad, a gold chain from Mary Queen of Scots, pistols from Protestant princes in Germany, and a smoked salmon from a Hanseatic merchant in London. These and other forms of gifts, because of their pervasive nature and practice, could be understood as softer but no less important forms of diplomacy than considerably less frequent formal agreements among princes. The same applies to notions of political and religious counsel in governing a realm.

Over the course of his career, Beale offered counsel in different forms and to a variety of people. His letters to powerful men like Cecil and Walsingham routinely included his recommendations couched with caveats like 'in my opinion', and his longer treatises for the same men advocated political and religious policy regarding, for example, trade and the Hanse or the reform of ecclesiastical law. Whether writing a letter or treatise, Beale knew that the information and interpretations he offered could be relayed to Elizabeth and subsequently inform official policy. Indeed, he was told so. His treatise on the office of principal secretary, written in 1592, is in some ways a handbook in this respect.[27] Beale's foundation for counsel and basis for political utility was his experience and wide learning in history and law. In the House of Commons, he was one among several MPs who advocated for parliamentary privileges and liberties based on historical precedent and statute law. He frequently cited these to support his positions. With an inside view of how Elizabeth's Privy Council worked, sometimes even sitting as principal secretary when Walsingham was away or indisposed, he understood how decisions were made and then relayed to Elizabeth. He knew of her tendencies to procrastinate and prevaricate, so he knew the importance of timing and

---

[26] On documents, see, e.g. Heather Wolfe and Peter Stallybrass, 'The Material Culture of Record-Keeping in Early Modern England', in Corens, Peters, and Walsham, *Archives and Information*, 179–208; James Daybell, *The Material Letter in Early Modern England: Manuscript Letters and the Culture and Practices of Letter-Writing, 1512–1635* (Basingstoke, 2012). On gifts, see, e.g. Felicity Heal, *The Power of Gifts: Gift Exchange in Early Modern England* (Oxford, 2014); Tobias Budke, *Die geschenkte Reformation: Bücher als Geschenke im England des 16. Jahrhunderts* (Frankfurt am Main, 2015); Jan Hennings, 'The Failed Gift: Ceremony and Gift-giving in Anglo-Russian Relations, 1660–1664', in Sowerby and Hennings, *Practices of Diplomacy*, 237–53; Tracey A. Sowerby, '"A Memorial and a Pledge of Faith": Portraiture and Early Modern Diplomatic Culture', *English Historical Review*, 129:537 (2014), 296–331; Jasmine Kilburn-Toppin, 'Gifting Cultures and Artisanal Guilds in Sixteenth- and Early Seventeenth-century London', *Historical Journal*, 60 (2017), 865–87.

[27] See Chapters 6 and 7.

packaging for offering advice. The extent to which early modern England was a 'monarchical republic' has been analysed and disputed, while the political history of the reign has turned away from an old-fashioned institutional narrative and towards an emphasis on individual agency outside the Privy Council, social connections, and court culture.[28] The longue durée has been considered and particular moments dissected, but rather than see Beale as representative of republican or monarchical tendencies, it is best to understand him as conservative by way of allegiance to his sovereign and law established but within a framework of counsel understood in a broad sense that afforded customary liberties. The grey area and developing ideas regarding 'counsel' have been subjects of interest among scholars, and here again Beale offers in the microcosm of one man an example both of how counsel could be offered by a range of people at different levels of political society and how counsel could have limited or no impact notwithstanding how vociferously it was offered.[29]

Because Beale was not part of Elizabeth's inner circle and never a privy councillor in his own right (though he came close in 1600), a considerable and insurmountable distance lay between him and his queen. Despite his protestations of duty and loyalty, he wore something of a scarlet letter for his entire career after his work to demonstrate the validity of the Grey claim to the royal succession in 1563. Having consulted civil lawyers in Germany, France, and (probably) Italy, Beale and his work on the succession were well known in the Elizabethan regime, and in consequence Elizabeth made him wait four years before he could kiss her hand in fidelity and service as a clerk of her Privy Council in the 1570s. Having proved himself capable and reliable in the late 1570s and early 1580s, Beale was reminded of the limits of her grace when he pushed too far in the Commons and

---

[28] Patrick Collinson's 'think piece' started out as his inaugural lecture as professor of modern history at the University of Sheffield in 1985. It was then expanded and later printed as 'The Monarchical Republic of Queen Elizabeth I', *Bulletin of the John Rylands University Library of Manchester*, 69 (1987), 394–424. Discussion and qualification of the idea followed years later in John F. McDiarmid (ed.), *The Monarchical Republic of Early Modern England: Essays in Response to Patrick Collinson* (Aldershot, 2007), but see also Peter Lake, 'The "Political Thought" of the "Monarchical Republic of Elizabeth I", Discovered and Anatomized', *Journal of British Studies*, 54 (2015), 257–87; Jonathan McGovern, 'Was Elizabethan England Really a Monarchical Republic?', *Historical Research*, 92:257 (2019), 515–28. Now dated but still useful is the review in Natalie Mears, 'Courts, Courtiers, and Culture in Tudor England', *The Historical Journal*, 46 (2003), 703–22; for a case study of agency outside the council, Natalie Mears, 'Counsel, Public Debate, and Queenship: John Stubbs's "The Discoverie of a Gaping Gulf", 1579', *The Historical Journal*, 44 (2001), 629–50.

[29] Jacqueline Rose, 'Kingship and Counsel in Early Modern England', *The Historical Journal*, 54 (2011), 47–71; Jacqueline Rose (ed.), *The Politics of Counsel in England and Scotland, 1286–1707* (Oxford, 2016); Joanne Paul, *Counsel and Command in Early Modern English Thought* (Cambridge, 2020); Helen Matheson-Pollock, Joanne Paul, and Catherine Fletcher (eds), *Queenship and Counsel in Early Modern Europe* (Basingstoke, 2018). On developments in the conception of counsel, and using a particularly illuminating type of source, see Jonathan McGovern, 'The Development of the Privy Council Oath in Tudor England', *Historical Research*, 93:260 (2020), 273–85; in general, see David J. Crankshaw's overview, 'The Tudor Privy Council, c.1540–1603', *State Papers Online 1509–1714*, Cengage Learning EMEA Ltd, 2009, accessible at https://www.gale.com/intl/essays/david-j-crankshaw-tudor-privy-council-c-1540-1603.

in opposition to Archbishop Whitgift. After re-rising to a position of power and respect, he again fell foul of the queen for similar reasons, and even in November 1600 his work back in 1563 was still acknowledged. One could reasonably wonder whether Beale and others similarly persistent would have pushed as hard for their causes had their sovereign not been a woman. Notions of queenship and power in England and elsewhere have earned considerable and justifiable scholarly attention, and they can be seen alongside discussions of a 'monarchical republic' in various ways. And yet, Beale's nervousness regarding Elizabeth can serve as a reminder that, however much he might disagree with his queen on matters of principle or policy, he always knew that his position, future, and family were ultimately at Elizabeth's pleasure, at her command.[30]

Europe in England

By way of his many experiences across the seas, his long career in the queen's service, and his immense learning across languages and disciplines, Robert Beale makes a case for how Europe (understood broadly and as variegated) mattered and contributed to life in Elizabethan England. He internalized aspects of international Protestantism and studied civil law; he maintained correspondence with like-minded men such as Hubert Languet and David Chytreaus; he used his understandings of foreign affairs to help shape and implement English policy. He was, intellectually at least, a European, and he was not alone. On the other side, he was very much an Englishman, especially as an MP in the House of Commons and when confronting Whitgift regarding ecclesiastical jurisdiction and law. Being one, then or now, does not preclude a person from also being the other. The contexts in which Beale can be situated are numerous and vast: historical studies, library and archive studies, law, religion, government, and counsel. To discuss every context in depth would overburden the reader's endurance, but, in the international context, the most relevant include the wars of religion and the variation among Protestants across Europe, especially in the Holy Roman Empire. A religious refugee as an adolescent and young man, Beale knew all too well the theories and practice of persecution for one's faith, and he knew better than most others how interconnected the theatres of war could be and did become. With warfare breaking out first in France and then in the Netherlands in the 1560s, the desire and need for solidarity among those opposed to Rome grew with every

---

[30] See the essays in Susan Doran and Paulina Kewes (ed.), *Doubtful and Dangerous: The Question of Succession in Late Elizabethan England* (Manchester, 2014), esp. that by Doran and Kewes on the earlier period, 20–44. On queenship more broadly, Alice Hunt and Anna Whitelock (eds), *Tudor Queenship: The Reigns of Mary and Elizabeth* (Basingstoke, 2010); Natalie Mears, *Queenship and Political Discourse in the Elizabethan Realms* (Cambridge, 2005); Charles Beem, *Queenship in Early Modern Europe* (London, 2020).

decade. Beale was often in the vanguard of those calling for a Protestant alliance and working with others to this end. As German Protestants increasingly fell into competing camps of hardline Lutherans (Gnesio-Lutherans) and comparatively moderate followers of a more Melanchthonian tradition (Philippists), convincing these groups to reconcile their differences and unite against their common enemy (Roman Catholicism) was a tall order. Nevertheless, Beale probably knew the religious fault-lines better than any other Englishman of his age, and he was at the forefront of this effort at many points of his life and career.

This book tells the story of a man of ambition who faced social and political limitations by turns with realism and idealism. He did not have all the answers or a plan, so in many respects he was vulnerable to circumstances. What he lacked in ancient family pedigree and stability in wealth he made up for in his political utility, competence, and principle. A mercer's son in London, as a child Beale could not have foreseen himself later kissing Elizabeth's hand as a clerk of her Privy Council in his thirties, having multiple homes as an MP in his forties, or negotiating peace with Spain as a commissioner in his fifties. Nevertheless, he did. The expansion of his public life is mirrored by the sources available. His early years before Queen Elizabeth's accession and his entering her service were comparatively lean; so, too, are the sources. By the 1570s, he was firmly fixed in England, his personal archive growing, his movements becoming more visible in others' materials and state papers. For the 1580s, the source material can sometimes be more onerous than illuminating, but a wide and deep approach demonstrates the manifold interests and activities that made Beale who he was. In his final decade, a lifetime of collecting books and papers is seen in his correspondence and written works. In 1601, at the end of his career and in the year of his death, one could imagine his office at his home in London as a jumbled mass of partially bound papers and books on shelves or in chests, with stacks of paper and writing materials on a cluttered desk, and works on history, law, and theology in Latin, French, Italian, Spanish, and German strewn around the room. Such was his life of international travel and polyglot learning. Patrick Collinson, towards the end of his own career, claimed that he knew little about Beale on a personal level, but he knew far more than almost anybody else. He knew, in his own words, that '[i]t is the beginning of wisdom to understand that Beale, was anything but a little Englander.'[31] With such a start, let us retrace his steps, move across the seas just as he did, and see how an Elizabethan could also be a European.

A European Elizabethan: The Life of Robert Beale, Esquire. David Scott Gohring, Oxford University Press.

---

[31] Collinson, 'Servants and Citizens', 502.

2
The Early Years

In autumn 1569 Robert Beale carried letters from Friedrich III, Elector Palatine, to Queen Elizabeth and her recent ambassador to Germany, Henry Killigrew. These letters, along with an official response from the Protestant princes of Germany regarding an alliance, were very important because of the Palatine desire to increase collaboration with England in the wake of Killigrew and Christopher Mundt's embassy to the princes to garner support for the Huguenots in France. Killigrew could not bring these messages from the Palatinate because he had left for England well before they were written. Beale was still in the Palatinate, but he was never an official part of the English embassy and had no credentials from England. Nevertheless, Friedrich noted in his letter to the queen that Beale was 'a man faithful to your majesty and rightly known to various men and to Killigrew himself', and that Beale would convey additional messages orally.[1] Given Beale's lack of any formal association with Killigrew's embassy, and due to the fact that he had never met either Friedrich or Elizabeth, Beale's acting as courier between princes may be more than a little surprising, as is Friedrich's going out of his way to name and praise a previously unknown messenger. Digging more deeply within the Elector's existing and accessible papers for 1569, however, one finds the answer in Christoph Ehem, one of Friedrich's primary councillors. Ehem had advanced Beale as a candidate to carry Friedrich's messages to the queen on account of his international contacts, long travels, and—equally if not more significantly—because he was not yet in the queen's service (but presumably ought to be, in Ehem's eyes); moreover, Ehem thought that Friedrich should cultivate a relationship by writing to Beale in the future.[2] In the subsequent months, after Beale had delivered Friedrich's messages in London, Ehem followed through by establishing a friendly correspondence with Beale,

[1] Friedrich to Elizabeth, 28 September 1569, Bodleian, Ashmole MS 1729, fols 126r–7v (item 68) (orig.); followed by Friedrich to Killigrew, same date, partially in cipher, fols 128r–31v (item 69) (orig.). Cecil's copy of Friedrich to Elizabeth, CP, 156, fol. 145r–v. Friedrich's copies, Hauptstaatsarchiv Munich, Kasten schwarz 16682, fols 456r–7r (to Elizabeth), 458r–9r (to Killigrew); printed in August Kluckhohn (ed.), *Briefe Friedrich des Frommen Kurfürsten von der Pfalz mit verwandten Schriftstücken*, 2 vols (Brunswick, 1868–72), Vol. 2, Part 1, pp. 360–3.
[2] Friedrich's council to Friedrich, 28 September 1569, Memorial on the response from the princes at Erfurt, 26 September 1569, Hauptstaatsarchiv Munich, Kasten schwarz 16682, fols 462r–4v, 509r–10v (orig., Ehem's hand); neither item is included in Kluckhohn.

and writing to William Cecil, Queen Elizabeth's principal secretary, offering his service in sending along international intelligence.[3]

From 1563 onwards, Beale's prospects for a career in the service of the English government were looking increasingly positive, but questions remain regarding how he gained the attention and confidence of those exercising the levers of political power and patronage in London. The task at hand is to address those questions by exploring Beale's early education, informal as it was, and travel, extensive as it was. Relative to Beale's later life in official government service, the early period is characterized by considerably fewer concrete sources that lead to firm conclusions, and the same is true for the rest of the 1560s. Nevertheless, by triangulating Beale's location and assessing his circles of associates—especially his family members and teachers—from his childhood to the age of about twenty-one (1562), a picture emerges of his intellectual development, his religious sensibilities, and his political as well as legal acumen.

Childhood and Exile

The clear, direct, and undeniable evidence regarding Beale's first two decades is thin. Precious little is known about his immediate family, little more about his education, and roughly the same about his residences and travels. From the scraps of evidence gathered, though, enough signposts can be recognized to connect the dots from London to Coventry, from Strasbourg to Zurich.

He was born about August/September 1541 and probably in London, where his father, also named Robert, worked as a mercer (dealer in fine textiles). The family history and connections are complex, and shadows remain, but the earliest surviving documents attesting to the younger Robert's existence are the probate records for his father, who died in 1548. In the last will and testament dated 16 September 1545, Robert (the younger) is named alongside another son, William, probably named after his grandfather. Their mother, Amy, was the brother of Richard Morison, who is named 'my brother in Lawe' and who was to receive a

---

[3] Ehem to Beale, 6 November 1570, 16 February 1571, AUL, MS 1009/2, items 27 and 28 (both orig.). Ehem's of 6 November, in response to Beale's of 8 August, brings news and conveys well wishes to Killigrew; that of 16 February does similarly. Ehem to Cecil, 5 February 1570, BL, Lansdowne MS 12, fols 57r–8v (orig.); the Lansdowne catalogue dates this letter to 1569 in error. Cf. summary of the legation of Ehem to the elector of Saxony, 1569, BL, Lansdowne MS 100, fols 179r–82r; sent along with a summary of the German princes' agreements made at Frankfurt in April 1569 (fols 171r–8v), as well as a summary of matters discussed between Johann Casimir and the elector of Saxony (fols 183r–5r). On Killigrew's mission, see E. I. Kouri, *England and the Attempts to Form a Protestant Alliance in the Late 1560s: A Case Study in European Diplomacy* (Helsinki, 1981); AGR, 35–53. On Ehem, see *DB*.

cup valued at £5, Robert the Elder 'desyrying hym to be good vnto my children'.[4] A third son, John, was possibly named after his great-grandfather and is named in a family pedigree, but he must have been born between the dating of the will in 1545 and the death of Robert (the elder) in 1548. From the brief description in the will, it appears that young Robert had a comfortable though not extravagant upbringing, but the link to Morison would become increasingly important in the coming years. We hear little more of his mother, who seems to have died by 1561 at the latest. Later references to John in the 1570s and 1580s are vague but plausible, as will be seen. Robert's brother William is the same 'William' referred to in a later letter by John Hales, whose close links to Beale will become more evident, to Robert Dudley, earl of Leicester, though no mention is made regarding John.[5] Early in the reign of Queen Elizabeth, William benefited financially from the patronage of his stepfather, Stephen Hales, when Hales presented him for the prebend of Ufton Decani, Coventry and Lichfield diocese, and he later earned the BA (1562), MA (1566), and BD (1572) at Oxford, finding further offices in the Church afterwards.[6] Members of Beale's extended family, or at least his predecessors, appear to have come from Woodbridge, in Suffolk, but he never attempted to reunite with anyone there.[7]

[4] Robert Beale the elder's last will and testament, TNA, PROB 11/32/171. Dating of Robert the younger's birth inferred from various sources, the most specific of which is Beale to Burghley, July/August 1591, BL, Lansdowne MS 68/107, fols 238r–9v, where Beale states that he is nearly fifty years old.

[5] Hales to Leicester, 28 July 1571, BL, Additional MS 32091, fols 248r–50r (orig.). Robert and William are noted to Leicester as 'your seruantes'. Beale's relationship in the early 1570s with Leicester is explored in Chapter 4. See also the discussion in Chapter 5 for the Beale brothers in Frankfurt.

[6] Stephen Hales presented William for the prebend of Ufton Decani (or Oloughton) on 24 December 1559, but William was instituted by proxy on 2 February 1561. Staffordshire Record Office, Lichfield Diocesan Records, B/A/1/15, fol. 29v. Joyce M. Horn (ed.), *Fasti Ecclesiae Anglicanae 1541–1857*, Vol. 10: *Coventry and Lichfield Diocese* (London, 2003), 67–8, noting the prebend's value of £2.13.4 in 1535. NB Two prebends of Ufton existed (Decani, Cantoris), and it remains unclear whether the prebend's value was for one or split between the two. Joseph Foster (ed.), *Alumni Oxonienses: The Members of the University of Oxford, 1500–1714* (Oxford, 1891), 95. For William's later offices as rector of West Horsley, Surrey, instituted on 3 April 1572, Hampshire Record Office, 21M65 A1/26 (Episcopal Register); as prebendary of Shalford (or Scamford), instituted on 24 January 1573, Joyce M. Horn and Derrick Sherwin Bailey (eds), *Fasti Ecclesiae Anglicanae 1541–1857*, Vol. 5: *Bath and Wells Diocese* (London, 1979), 78, Somerset Record Office, D/D/Ca 48 and D/D/B Register 15, fol. 36v; as prebendary of Middleton, installed 20 October 1573, see Joyce M. Horn (ed.), *Fasti Ecclesiae Anglicanae 1541–1857*, Vol. 2: *Chichester Diocese* (London, 1971), 45, Chichester Chapter Acts 1545–1642 (Act Book); as perpetual vicar of Godshill, Surrey, instituted 9 November 1573, Hampshire Record Office, 21M65 A1/26 (Episcopal Register). William appears to have died by 2 January 1579; Somerset Record Office, D/D/B Register 15, fol. 54v (Episcopal Register).

[7] Amy is noted as the first wife of Stephen Hales, whose second marriage to Bridget Over, of Coventry, was at some point before 1561. HoP:HoC. For the Suffolk connection, see Alexander Chalmers, *The General Biographical Dictionary: A New Edition* (London, 1812), 4.235–6; Augustine Page, *A Supplement to the Suffolk Traveller: Or Topographical and Genealogical Collections, Concerning that County* (Ipswich and London, 1844), 128. Most sources for the pedigree and line of descent note Robert's paternal grandfather as William and great-grandfather as John, who was of Woodbridge, Suffolk: BL, Harley MS 1110, fol. 102r; BL, Harley MS 1052, fol. 10v; BL, Additional MS 19117, fols 228v–9r. BL, Harley MS 1561, fol. 65r–v, notes both the grandfather and great-grandfather as named William. Charles Henry Cooper and Thompson Cooper (eds), *Athenae Cantabrigienses*

The family connection to Morison, Beale's maternal uncle, would later bring the young Beale within the sphere of influence of learned and powerful men in Strasbourg during the mid 1550s; later, in the 1570s, Francis Russell, earl of Bedford, became an influential political patron for Beale after having married Morison's widow, Bridget (daughter of John, Lord Hussey) in 1566.[8] A more immediate and more lasting impression on the young Beale came from John Hales, who became Beale's step-uncle when Amy, probably in the late 1540s, married Stephen Hales (a merchant tailor in London almost certainly known to the elder Robert) after the elder Robert's death.[9] The Hales family had a considerable if comparatively recent history in politics and law, with John's uncle, Christopher Hales serving as attorney general and master of the rolls, while others in the family, like James Hales, served as judges.[10] By the late 1540s John Hales had served the government in an official capacity under King Henry VIII and Thomas Cromwell; he had learned classical languages and law largely on his own; and he had acquired considerable lands and ecclesiastical properties in London and Warwickshire in the wake of the dissolution of the monasteries. In Coventry, where Hales had some of these properties, he established a free school and named it after Henry VIII.[11]

Although the young Robert Beale's early education in London is entirely obscure, his stepfather Stephen's family connection to the school in Coventry proved decisive for the decades ahead. That school, based at the Whitefriars monastery from 1545 to 1557, and onwards at the hospital of St John the Baptist, was known for its humanist bent in its teaching of Latin, Greek, mathematics, and music; and Hales's own religious position as a firm advocate of Protestantism ensured that its pupils would be educated in the fundamentals of the faith in opposition to Roman Catholicism. Coventry was at that time, as is well known, 'already a little English Geneva'.[12] It seems almost certain that Beale's stepfather Stephen provided the most direct means for the young Robert's maintenance while attending the free school of his step-uncle John, who in the coming years came to look after Beale; John Hales's own uncle, Christopher Hales, had looked after the young John when he was growing up in his household.[13] No evidence

(Cambridge, 1861), 2.311, offers that the paternal grandfather was named Thomas, but this is an error, as is the idea that the younger Robert ever attended Cambridge.

[8] *ODNB* for Francis Russell, 2nd earl of Bedford.
[9] *HoP:HoC* for Stephen Hales. The suggested timing in the late 1540s depends upon Beale's later recollection. See below.
[10] *ODNB* for John (d.1540?), Sir Christopher (d.1541), Sir James (d.1554), John Hales (d.1572).
[11] On the school, see A. A. C. Burton et al., *King Henry VIII School, 1545–1945* (Coventry, 1945), esp. 10–16.
[12] Patrick Collinson, 'Servants and Citizens: Robert Beale and other Elizabethans', *Historical Research*, 79:206 (2006), 502. Convenient overviews of public education and Protestant nonconformity in Coventry are available in W. B. Stephens (ed.), *A History of the County of Warwick*, Vol. 8: *The City of Coventry and Borough of Warwick* (London, 1969), 299–315, 372–82.
[13] *ODNB* for John Hales (d.1572); cf. *HoP:HoC* for Hales, John II (by 1516–72), which entry is far superior to, and corrects the errors in, Hales, John I (d.1572).

from Beale's time in Coventry survives, but his activities later in life shed some light, and suggest that he was at Hales's school by 1550 at the latest.

As Beale stated in 1590, in a letter to the archbishop of Canterbury, 'ffowrtye yeres and vpwardes I was brought vpp a scholler in the Cittie of Coventree. Sith that time I have borne a certaine affection vnto the towne, for that beinge a well-willer of learninge, it was the place where it pleased god to give me the beginninge of my vnderstandinge'; moreover, Beale continued, 'I have sundrie kindsfolkes, allyes, and frends in those parts, and the best part of the poore livinge, which the lorde hath bestowed vppon me, is in that cuntrie.'[14] Beale's affection for Coventry and his appreciation for the influence of his time there are clear, at his continued involvement in the affairs of the city further testify to this connection. The school in Coventry appears to have been appreciated by many of its former pupils— several donated books to establish an early lending library for the city—so Beale was in some respects representative of a wider intellectual debt to Hales's school. When Hales died in 1572, he left a will with precise details on what properties in and around Coventry were to go to whom, on what conditions, and in what order. Unsurprisingly, because Hales never married, much was to go to Hales's nephew, also named John; equally telling, however, was that Beale was named executor of the will.[15] Because the younger John was still a minor when his father, Christopher (another of Beale's step-uncles), died in 1573, Beale became ward for the younger John and thus had an increased interest in managing the affairs and properties, along with an annuity of £13.6.8.[16] With family connections via his stepfather, Beale may also have acquired property in Coventry during the 1570s, for in 1576 he was asked 'by my good frendes and neighbors of the citye of Coventree' to help them be appointed commissioners for the collection of the subsidy (tax) at that time.[17] Whether or not Beale had a firm stake in Coventry in 1576, during the 1580s he certainly acquired properties in Warwickshire and maintained a keen interest in the former ecclesiastical holdings in Coventry. In 1586 he had a grant of a manor in Priors Marston (south-east of Coventry), which he held until his death in 1601, and in 1587 he acquired extracts from cartularies and other monastic records relating to Coventry and Priors Marston. His detailed scribblings on these extracts show his continued involvement in local affairs, and that some

---

[14] Beale to Whitgift, 22 August 1590, BL, Additional MS 48039, fol. 74r (draft with Beale's autograph emendations); date from LPL, MS 4267, fols 3r–4v (orig.).

[15] John Hales's will, 17 December 1572, Coventry History Centre, PA244/37/7 (copy, misdated 27 December, but cf. the citation in PA1798/2). Proved probate record, 5 February 1573, TNA, PROB 11/55/54. For information on Hales's school and its early library, I am indebted to Madeleine Bracey, whose doctoral study will further illuminate the school's intellectual and public reach.

[16] Grant of wardship, 19 May 1573, TNA, C 66/1105, m. 9. Beale to Hatton, 25 November 1589, BL, Additional MS 48039, fols 63r–70r, at 63r.

[17] Beale to Mr Halye, clerk of the petty bag, 20 March 1576, TNA, SP 46/16, fols 8r–9v (orig.).

of the original documents were 'in the custody of my brother Charles Hales' (his stepbrother via Stephen) or the younger John Hales.[18]

This network of avuncular relationships via Beale's stepfather and among the Hales family was soon matched in importance via Beale's maternal uncle, Richard Morison. If Hales was in many respects a good example of an English humanist and autodidact in law and the domestic service of the crown, then Morison was an English humanist of a different sort who gained formal education at Oxford, Padua, and possibly Cambridge, and whose careers in government service included work as religious propagandist, MP, and royal ambassador.[19] The complementary skills, personalities, and educational backgrounds of Hales and Morison became ever more evident in the young Beale's experience and travels. The two men became close colleagues and friends, and in spring 1551 Hales accompanied Morison on the latter's mission as resident ambassador to the Holy Roman Emperor, Charles V, though the mission was cut short after Morison's 'preaching' to Charles on religious matters.[20] By spring 1552, Morison was back with the itinerant emperor, travelling around Austria, Germany, and the Low Countries; Hales, however, had relocated to Frankfurt with his brother, Christopher, returning to England only after the accession of Elizabeth. Morison's toings and froings between the European mainland and London continued until his final departure from England in early April 1554. Although he continued his travels from Strasbourg to Basle, Zurich, Geneva, Frankfurt, and Brussels, he settled permanently in Strasbourg in April 1555, having petitioned the city council for residence.[21]

Hales does not appear to have frequently returned to England between 1551 and winter 1558/9, save for one particularly important and suggestive period in winter 1552/3 when he served as courier for a letter from the superintendent of the Stranger Church in London, Jan Łaski, recommending Hales to the Grand Treasurer of Poland, Spytek Jordan. What Hales was hoping to secure for employment in Poland is unclear, as is what prevented Hales from delivering the letter to the Treasurer (he might only have gotten as far as Saxony), but on his planned return to England he picked up a letter from Georg Maior, the great Lutheran theologian at the University of Wittenberg, intending to deliver it to Łaski. It seems that Hales retained both of these letters, never delivering them to their

---

[18] Licence dated 2 April 1586, TNA, C 66/1283, m. 31. Cf. L. F. Salzman (ed.), *A History of the County of Warwick*, Vol. 5: *Kington Hundred* (London, 1949), 140–1. BL, Additional MS 32100, fols 12r, 57r, 80 for Beale's comments on the Hales's ownership of originals. *HoP:HoC* for Stephen Hales notes Charles as Stephen's son and heir. See Chapter 7.

[19] Tracey A. Sowerby, *Renaissance and Reform in Tudor England: The Careers of Sir Richard Morison c.1513–1556* (Oxford, 2010).

[20] *ODNB* for Sir Richard Morison.

[21] Garrett, *Marian Exiles*, 272–4 (Hales), 229–31 (Morison). On Morison's overseas activity, see Sowerby, *Renaissance and Reform*, 223–32.

addressees, and they worked their way into Beale's possession at one point or another, probably during the 1550s or 1560s.[22]

With Hales's travels hither and yon during the early 1550s, it seems probable that Beale joined Morison on the latter's last journey to the mainland in 1554, when the young Robert was about thirteen years old. The circle of English exiles in Strasbourg included Anthony Cooke and Edwin Sandys, who both petitioned the city council with Morison; John Aylmer, former tutor to Lady Jane Grey; John Cheke, the eminent humanist educator; Thomas Wrothe, a firm supporter of Edwardian Protestantism; and John Abell, a merchant banker of London with intimate connections in Strasbourg and with English exiles in multiple locations.[23] As with Beale's early years in London and Coventry, the documentary record for his time in Strasbourg is frustratingly thin, but Morison certainly settled there from April 1555, and that he secured residence and applied for citizenship of the city in September and October of that year.[24]

Establishing the dates of Morison's residence in Strasbourg is important because of Beale's own recollection decades later in 1584 when writing to William Cecil, by now Lord Burghley, about the then bishop of London, John Aylmer. He wrote:

> The Bishopp was sometyme my Scholemaster. [H]e was for a whilest in the tyme of Q. Marye at Strasburge lodged in myne vncle Morisines house, and a[f]ter I remayned with him in the house of John Abell, and frequented the Common Scholes and lectures of Peter Martyr and Sturmius.[25]

The implication of the language here is that Beale also was living in his 'vncle Morisines house', despite the official prohibition on unauthorized lodgers by the city of Strasbourg, but after Morison's death on 20 March 1556 both Beale and Aylmer moved into Abell's house.[26] Because of their financial resources, Morison

---

[22] Łaski to Jordan, 16 December 1552, Maior to Łaski, 1 March 1553, AUL, MS 1009/1, items 11, 12 (both orig.).

[23] Garrett, *Marian Exiles*, s.n.; Sowerby, *Renaissance and Reform*, 226–8, 230–2.

[24] Morison to Jean Calvin, 17 April 1555 from Strasbourg, in Hastings Robinson (ed.), *Original Letters Relative to the English Reformation: The First Portion* (Cambridge, 1846), 147. Garrett, *Marian Exiles*, 366 includes translations of the relevant entries from the protocol book in Strasbourg. Morison first stayed in Strasbourg in April and May 1554, then travelled elsewhere, then went back to Strasbourg in April 1555. Beale might have just stayed in Strasbourg with other English exiles, or he might have been part of Morison's travelling household. Either way, he recorded later in 1584 that he had been acquainted with the most famous and learned men abroad, and had observed the affairs of France and Germany, 'for the espace almost of these xxxti yeres', which places him in or about Strasbourg in 1554 or 1555. Beale's draft book for Whitgift, February/March 1584, BL, Additional MS 48039, fol. 2r.

[25] 'The answer of Robert Beale concerninge such thinges as have passed between the L. Archbishopp of Canterburye and him', 1 July 1584, 'For my L. Threr [Lord Treasurer, Burghley]', BL, Additional MS 48039, fol. 48v.

[26] *ODNB* and Sowerby, *Renaissance and Reform*, p. 238 notes 20 March for Morison's death. Contrast Garrett, *Marian Exiles*, noting 17 March.

and Abell were two of the more prominent Englishmen in Strasbourg at that time, so it seems that Beale's existence during his tender years was still relatively comfortable, notwithstanding the fact that he had only one member of his immediate family (Morison) as support in the city. As for what he learned from Aylmer's hands, Beale went on to note that, at this time, Aylmer 'redd to me and others certayne orations of Demosthenes and some Tragedyes of Euripides[,] and repeted the Logick and Rhetorick which we had learned in the scholes.'[27] Although he might not have been impressed, in retrospect, by Aylmer's teaching, the observation that Beale was one of several pupils deserves some notice, for there seems to have been a number of young hangers-on among the English exiles, and Beale may have reconnected with one of his classmates under Aylmer, Thomas Danett, in a professional capacity later in life.[28]

Beale's attending of the lectures of Peter Martyr Vermigli and Johann Sturm was more important than Aylmer's influence regarding the young Robert's future development. The Strasbourg school, or 'Gymnasium', during the 1540s and 1550s was in many respects a beacon of light for the international Protestant community. Johann Sturm was one of the most important pedagogues in the Protestant tradition during the mid sixteenth century, was responsible for establishing the Strasbourg Gymnasium in 1538, and was well connected to political leaders and theological luminaries from England, France, Germany, and Swiss lands. His diplomatic work included attempts to arrange meetings among French and German political and religious leaders, and, although his efforts to support the French Huguenots yielded little concrete benefits, he maintained a sense of idealism and optimism regarding the powers of education in the classics and a 'learned piety' that would promote a Christian life.[29] Sturm's importance and influence extended well beyond Strasbourg's environs, and his impact on the English can be seen particularly in his relationships with John Hales and Roger Ascham at this time, and in his subsequent position as Queen Elizabeth's informal agent in Germany (after the death of Christopher Mundt in 1572). As for Beale, he incorporated much of Sturm's thinking on the organization and retrieval of information in his own library of printed works and manuscripts, a political and religious archive

---

[27] 'The answer of Robert Beale', BL, Additional MS 48039, fol. 48v.
[28] Danett to Burghley, 1 May 1595, CP, 32/14 (orig.). See also Chapter 8. On Danett (d.1601?), *ODNB*; Sowerby, *Renaissance and Reform*, 231. Thomas's father, also named Thomas, was later involved in the *Tempestas Halesiana*, even delivering Beale's discourse on the matter of the Grey-Hertford marriage. Mortimer Levine, *The Early Elizabethan Succession Question 1558–1568* (Stanford, 1966), 72–3 *et passim*; Leicester and others to Cecil, with note on the examination of Hales by Dale and Wilson, 26 April 1564, BL, Harley MS 6990, item 29, fol. 62r (orig.), noting Beale as author of the work, and Danett as the bearer; cf. item 28, fol. 60r (orig.), Leicester to Cecil, same date, lamenting that Lord Grey had been so inconsiderate and foolish. See Chapter 3.
[29] On Sturm, see Lewis W. Spitz and Barbara Sher Tinsley, *Johann Sturm on Education: The Reformation and Humanist Learning* (St. Louis, MO, 1995), with a biography on 19–44; cf. the brief update in Barbara Sher Tinsley, 'Sturm, Johann', in Hans J. Hillerbrand (ed.), *The Oxford Encyclopedia of the Reformation* (Oxford, 1996); online edition.

unmatched by any other figure of Beale's stature during the sixteenth century.[30] Additionally, Beale understood in 1572 that 'her Ma[jes]ty mindeth to place Sturmius in Mountes roome', and that 'he be an honest man & for his effection to this Countrey [i.e. England] worthy of sum rewarde'. Due to Sturm's age and occupation, however, Beale thought Aylmer better suited to serve as Mundt's successor.[31] Nevertheless, in the wake of Beale's diplomatic activity in Germany in 1577, and with a view to continued Anglo-German collaboration, Beale knew Sturm to be a key ally and 'a man of greate estimacion with the chefest of [Germany]', and a correspondence between Beale and Sturm was established.[32]

Born in Florence, educated at the University of Padua, and skilled in languages including Hebrew, Peter Martyr Vermigli held several positions within the Catholic Church before fleeing across the Alps in 1542 and settling in Strasbourg at Martin Bucer's invitation.[33] After five years in Strasbourg, where Vermigli lectured on the Old and New Testaments, the archbishop of Canterbury, Thomas Cranmer, invited him to England, where he held the position of Regius Professor at Oxford until his departure after the accession of Queen Mary in 1553. An international and erudite humanist of the first order, Vermigli was well connected to a range of major Protestant figures, and his theology was firmly within the Reformed tradition. By the mid 1550s, Strasbourg's Bucerian tradition of Reformed but moderate Protestantism, which had been so congenial to Vermigli during his previous stay, had given way to a more orthodox Lutheran church leadership headed by Johannes Marbach, whose policies had the potential to sow division among Protestants in Strasbourg and beyond. Additionally, the political leadership in Strasbourg was wary of straying too far from the Lutheranism deemed official during the Interim and ultimately permitted by the Peace of

---

[30] See the discussion with regard to Sturm, Ramus, and Beale in Brewerton, 'Paper Trails', 116–18.

[31] Jean Rott and Robert Faerber, 'Un anglais à Strasbourg au milieu du XVIᵉ Siècle: John Hales, Roger Ascham, et Jean Sturm', *Études Anglaises*, 21 (1968), 381–94. Sturm's correspondence with Ascham has been edited and studied, but Sturm's wider contacts with Elizabethan England remain underappreciated. *Letters of Roger Ascham*, ed. Alvin Vos, trans. Maurice Hatch and Alvin Vos (New York, 1989). Beale's 'discourse [...] after the great murder in Paris & other places in France August 1572', BL, Cotton MS Titus. F. III, fols 302r–8v, with quotation at 308r. Burghley's copy with Beale's name struck through, CP, 246/29, fol. 10r (39r).

[32] 'Certain notes' by Beale or Daniel Rogers, with Beale's marginal notations, 1578, BL, Harley MS 1582, fols 156r–7v, with quotation on 156r. A fragment of a letter from Sturm to Beale, dated 9 October 1579, exists in AUL, MS 1009/?, item 6 (fol. 1r–v missing; only 2r remains and offers news regarding the German princes, the king of Denmark, and the king of Navarre; with 2v the address leaf). On Sturm's efforts for unity in 1577–8, see Irene Dingel, '*Caritas christiana* und Bekenntnistreue: Johannes Sturms Einsatz für die Einheit des Protestantismus in den Auseinandersetzungen um die lutherische Konkordienformel', in Matthieu Arnold (ed.), *Johannes Sturm (1507–1589): Rhetor, Pädagoge und Diplomat* (Tübingen, 2009), 375–90.

[33] On Vermigli's time in Strasbourg, see R. Gerald Hobbs, 'Strasbourg: Vermigli and the Senior School', in Torrance Kirby, Frank A. James II, and Emidio Campi (eds), *A Companion to Peter Martyr Vermigli* (Leiden, 2009), 35–69. For a short biography, see Marvin W. Anderson, 'Vermigli, Peter Martyr', in Hillerbrand, *Oxford Encyclopedia of the Reformation*.

Augsburg in 1555.[34] Back in Strasbourg from late 1553 to early or mid summer 1556, Vermigli lectured on the Old Testament book Judges to the English exiles, presumably Beale included; he also lectured on Aristotle's *Nicomachean Ethics* and later dedicated the lectures' publication to Edwin Sandys, who attended the lectures along with other exiles like John Jewel.[35] Vermigli's selection of Judges was the more significant topic, however, because it reflected the civic ideology of the city: the people are saved and governed by strong leaders guided by God, and without these magistrates the people would lapse into unfaithfulness.[36] Moreover, lecturing on Judges sent a signal to the city's leadership that, far from pushing the permitted theological boundaries, Vermigli was obedient and grateful in his position at the Strasbourg school. Given Beale's firm adherence to the established Church of England later in life, as well as his strident rejection of accusations otherwise, Vermigli's choice to lecture on Judges may well have stuck with the young Robert long after they both left Strasbourg. In fact, the lectures on Judges were published at Zurich in 1561, and it is probable that Beale owned a copy of this work.[37] Vermigli's departure for Zurich was occasioned by the invitation to lecture on Hebrew, and brought an opportunity to work and live among more like-minded friends and colleagues than Marbach.

When exactly Beale left Strasbourg for Zurich with Aylmer remains something of a mystery despite Beale's later comment to Cecil that 'when [Aylmer] departed from thence vppon some causes, which I haue hearde were reported vnto your Lordship by Sr Anthonye Cooke, I went with him to Zurick, and continewed there about a yere.'[38] If Cooke did indeed inform Cecil of Aylmer's departure, that letter has not yet been found or may no longer survive, but it seems reasonable to suggest a timing of very late 1556 or 1557 given events later in 1558.[39] The move to Zurich introduced Beale to another community of English exiles, but these religious refugees were considerably more advanced in their Protestantism than were those in Strasbourg, more inclined to Zwinglian, Bullingerian, or Calvinist theologies and ecclesiologies than those of Bucer. Vermigli's move from Strasbourg to Zurich is suggestive of his own theological preferences, but so too is the move of Aylmer and the future bishop of Salisbury under Queen Elizabeth, John Jewel,

---

[34]   Hobbs, 'Strasbourg', 55–6. On Marbach, see *DB*. On the political and religious complexities of the 1550s, see the overview in Joachim Whaley, *Germany and the Holy Roman Empire*, Vol. 1: *Maximilian I to the Peace of Westphalia 1493–1648* (Oxford, 2012), 325–54.

[35]   Hobbs, 'Strasbourg', 57–8. The dating of Vermigli's departure from Strasbourg is noted as mid-summer on p. 35 but early summer on p. 58.

[36]   Hobbs, 'Strasbourg', 57.

[37]   Published as *In Librum Judicum [...] Commentarij Doctissimi* (Zurich, 1561) (VD16 B 3038). BL, Hargrave MS 107, fol. 7v, noting 'Patri Martyris Vermilii Opera. ~~Viz Commentaria In Genesin[,] Librum Iudicum[,] Regum, In Samuelem[,] Loci Communes~~ 5 vol. Tiguri. 1569. &c.'

[38]   'The answer of Robert Beale', BL, Additional MS 48039, fol. 48v.

[39]   Cooke's surviving letters to Cecil from this period, dated 10 January 1557, 17 May 1557, 12 July 1557, and 24 January 1558, make no mention of Aylmer's departure. CP, 151/141, 2/11, 152/12, 152/6 (all orig.). Brett Usher's suggestion of 1557 is entirely reasonable. *ODNB* for Aylmer.

who moved from Strasbourg to Zurich with Vermigli, whom Jewel served as notary and to whom Jewel looked as mentor.[40] During Beale's stay in Zurich, a distance appears to have grown between the young Robert (now fifteen or sixteen years old) and his schoolmaster despite the young man's dedication and service, and Beale became increasingly reliant on others. As he later put it, 'I served him [Aylmer] as muche as anye servaunt could, and yet were all my charges borne by my frendes. [...] Sith I was xiiij or xv yeres olde he hathe had nothinge to doe with me, and it grieueth me havinge receyved so litle from him as I did[,] beinge now two & fowerty yeres olde'.[41] By this point in 1557, Beale's uncle Morison had died, while his step-uncle, John Hales, was embroiled in the religious controversies among the English community in Frankfurt. With Aylmer caring little for his pupil, Beale needed to rely on others outside his former family network, or he needed to grow increasingly self-reliant for his daily needs and continued education. The English exiles at Zurich were deeply and emotionally connected to the Reformed community of internationals under Heinrich Bullinger, as their correspondence at the time and subsequently testifies.[42] It seems that Zurich may not have been such a congenial place for the young Beale, however, for he never spoke or wrote anything further regarding Zurich later in life, nor did he ever fully espouse its religious positions or think to return to that city. While there in 1557, much must have been uncertain for the teenage Beale, bereft of any close or even extended family, and without any firm links to the community in Zurich during his year or so there. The next period in his life is even more obscure than the story thus far, but several clues suggest that Beale left Zurich either for Italy to the south or, more likely, for Germany to the north.

The Wander Years

If Beale was in Zurich for about a year, then it means that he left for somewhere else at some point in late 1557 or early 1558. More importantly, and unlike the vast majority of English in exile under Queen Mary, Beale did not return to England in haste after the accession of Elizabeth in November 1558. Rather, his years of wandering continued; his life as an exile ended, but his life as an Englishman abroad, a European, began. According to later accounts of the 1570s and 1580s, Beale and Aylmer both visited the schools and universities of Italy at some point during the 1550s, but no matriculation records or other documentation exist for Beale at the University of Padua, where many Englishmen, Francis

---

[40] *ODNB* for Jewel.   [41] 'The answer of Robert Beale', BL, Additional MS 48039, fol. 48v.
[42] The correspondence is found in the volumes published by the Parker Society during the 1840s: *Epistolae Tigurinae* (Cambridge, 1848), *Original Letters* for the reigns of Henry VIII, Edward VI, and Mary, 2 vols (Cambridge 1846–7), *The Zurich Letters* for the reign of Elizabeth (Cambridge, 1842, 1845, 1846).

Walsingham included, learned the intricacies of civil law, while the evidence for Aylmer anywhere in Italy is similarly thin.[43] The great printer, André Wechel commented in 1579, in a preface to a collection of works taken from Beale's personal library, that Beale had visited 'almost all the schools of Germany, France, and Italy', but this seems more like the type of gratuitous hyperbole one expects to find in a preface rather than it does a statement of fact. Similarly, Aylmer's own claim that he 'visit[ed] almost all Vniuersities in Italie and Germanie, hauing great conference with the most and best learned men' rings more like self-aggrandizement to intimidate theological adversaries of the 1580s than it does a true account of his activities three decades before.[44] Given Beale's estrangement from Aylmer in Zurich, it would be slightly surprising if the two continued to travel together to Italy, but, given Beale's legal expertise and knowledge of Italian affairs later in life, one could be forgiven for thinking that he had a spell at the University of Padua. As Beale himself later attested in 1584, '[t]ouching my studyes, I haue by the espace of xxvj yeres and vpwardes ben a Student of the Ciuill lawes, and longe sithe could haue taken degree, if I had thought, (as some doe) that the substaunce of learninge consistethe more in forme and title then matter.'[45] Twenty-six years before 1584 was, of course, 1558, which timing would fit well with the potential Padua explanation. For additional reasons, though, the University of Heidelberg was a more likely destination for Beale when he left Zurich.

Aylmer also left Zurich in 1558, and his confirmed activity at the newly established University of Jena in Saxony adds critical contextualization for Beale's later comments on a certain Lutheran theologian at the university. As Aylmer put it, he was at Jena to take up 'the Hebrewe lecture, which Snepphinus [Erhard Schnepf] had, [and he had been] intertained by them to read in their said vniuersity both Greeke and Latin, in the company and with the good loue and liking of those famous men, Flaccus Illyricus, Victorinus Strigellus, D. Snepphinus, called alter Luther, with diuers others'.[46] In contrast to Aylmer's claim about the Italian universities, his time at Jena is confirmed in letters from Johann Friedrich, Duke of Saxony, to John Hales on 1 January 1559, and to Queen Elizabeth on

---

[43] See Woolfson, *Padua and the Tudors*; Woolfson, 'Padua and English Students Revisited', 572–87; Andrich and Brugi, *De Natione Anglica et Scota Iuristarum Universitatis Patavinae*, esp. 31–4, 131. It is worth bearing in mind that Beale's later reports of intelligence during the 1560s deal overwhelmingly with French and German affairs, with Italian news in the State Papers Foreign Series coming to London from Italian authors in Venice and elsewhere. Following others, Taviner, 54, entertains 'the possibility that [Beale] passed through Padua in the early 1560s'.

[44] Wechel's preface to *Rerum Hispanicarvm Scriptores Aliqvot, quorum nomina versa pagina indicabit. Ex Bibliotheca clariβimi viri Dn. Roberti Beli Angli* (Frankfurt am Main, 1579) (VD16 R 1163–4), vol. 1, fol. iijr. Thomas Cooper, *An Admonition of the People of England. 1589*, ed. Edward Arber (Birmingham, 1882), 47.

[45] Beale to Whitgift, 7 May 1584, BL, Additional MS 48039, quotation at fol. 44r; copy sent to Burghley in BL, Lansdowne MS 42, fol. 184r–v, printed in John Strype, *The Life and Acts of John Whitgift*, 3 vols (Oxford, 1822), 3.91–8, at 95.

[46] Cooper, *An Admonition*, 47.

25 May 1559. In addition, Beale later targeted Aylmer as a sower of theological discord regarding *adiaphora* ('things indifferent'), noting that '[t]his controuersie of indifferent thinges of late yeres began in Germanye and hathe bene occacion of muche harme, and in the time of Q. Marye who was greater with Illyricus then the now Bishopp of London [Aylmer][?]'[47] Aylmer's recollection of having been 'intertained by them' to teach Latin and Greek, and having enjoyed the company of Schnepf, dates his arrival in Jena after the foundation of the university in February 1558 but before the Schnepf's death on 1 November 1558; the letter from Johann Friedrich to Elizabeth in late May 1559 offers the *terminus ad quem* for Aylmer's service as professor of Hebrew before his return to England. Beale's observation also pinpoints Aylmer in Jena, but it implies that Beale did not follow him there because of his dislike of Flacius's hard-line, orthodox and potentially divisive theologies, never mind Aylmer's lack of care or concern.[48]

When Beale was at Strasbourg attending the lectures of Sturm and Vermigli, and enduring the rod of Aylmer, he was also, according to his own testimony already noted ('xxvj yeres and vpwards'), a student of civil law, so reasonable questions emerge regarding at whose feet was he learning, whose lectures was he attending, and whose influence was exerted on the young Beale. The most logical answer is a Frenchman, a scholar of civil law named François Bauduin/Baudouin (*alias* Franz Balduin in German, Franciscus Baldwinus in Latin), whose relatively short tenure at Sturm's Gymnasium in Strasbourg overlapped with Beale's stay at Morison's and Abell's houses.[49] A native of Arras who had studied at the University of Leuven and taught at the University of Bourges before coming to Strasbourg, Bauduin has attracted the attention of modern scholars because, in many respects, he was a product of and represented 'the new wave of legal humanism.'[50] His understanding and teaching of civil law, following the *mos gallicus* or 'French method' rather than the *mos italicus*, took into account historical circumstances and change over time to explain how Roman law applied to Roman society, and he argued that such an understanding was vital to the correct application of law within a sixteenth-century context. Bauduin's lectures and subsequent publications on the alliance between law and history (not to be confused with

---

[47] Johann Friedrich to Hales, 1 January 1559, BL, Additional MS 15943, fols 1r–2v (orig.). Johann Friedrich to Elizabeth, 25 May 1559, TNA, SP 70/4, fol. 117r (orig.). Elizabeth to Johann Friedrich, 3 July 1559, Hauptstaatsarchiv Weimar, Ernestinisches Gesamtarchiv, Reg. D. 94, fol. 26r (orig.); NB: copies in BL, Royal MS 13, B. I, fol. 12r and elsewhere are misdated 2 July. Quotation from 'The answer of Robert Beale', BL, Additional MS 48039, fol. 55r.

[48] On Schnepf, see *DB*. On Flacius's intellectual development and in relation to Melanchthon, see Luka Ilić, *Theologian of Sin and Grace: The Process of Radicalization in the Theology of Matthias Flacius Illyricus* (Göttingen, 2014).

[49] Bauduin arrived in Strasbourg in early 1555 and left for Heidelberg at the very end of May 1556. On his time in Strasbourg and Heidelberg, see Michael Erbe, *François Bauduin (1520–1573): Biographie eines Humanisten* (Gütersloh, 1978), 80–121.

[50] Barbara Pitkin, 'Calvin's Mosaic Harmony: Biblical Exegesis and Early Modern Legal History', *Sixteenth Century Journal*, 41 (2010), 458.

legal history), thus pioneering a new methodology, became influential on a European scale. In fact, his understandings of history's value, along with his historically minded contacts in Strasbourg, drew him into a correspondence with Matthias Flacius Illyricus, whose historical project known as the *Magdeburg Centuries* incorporated the work and advice of a wide range of Protestant divines and historians (notwithstanding Flacius's own theological proclivities).[51]

By the time Bauduin was teaching in Strasbourg, his religious inclinations had moved away from endorsing Calvin (who had once housed Bauduin) and were moving firmly into a more German, a more broadly Protestant, Melanchthonian Lutheran direction. The Strasbourg of the mid 1550s, however, with Marbach and the city authorities embracing a more orthodox and restrictive sense of Lutheranism, was not congenial with Bauduin's developing religious temperament and sensibilities, which became increasingly irenic and ecumenical, culminating in his activity at the Colloquy of Poissy in 1561 when efforts to reunite Catholics and Protestants came to nothing.[52]

After the death of the Elector Palatine, Friedrich II, on 26 February 1556, a position as professor of civil law was available for Bauduin at the University of Heidelberg. Despite Sturm's enormously successful efforts to bring talented teachers to his Gymnasium, where an international audience of students could learn from many of the leading lights of Protestantism, the changing political and religious circumstances of the city made the Gymnasium less welcoming than it had been previously. Just as Vermigli, Aylmer, Beale, and others left, so did Bauduin. By 1558, when Beale would have arrived in Heidelberg from Zurich, Bauduin was firmly rooted in the university's legal faculty alongside other luminaries such as Christoph Ehem (who later recommended Beale, as we have seen), Caspar Agricola, Karl Hugel, and Wendelin Heilmann, soon to be joined by Nikolaus Cisner in autumn 1559.[53] Also by this time, the University of Heidelberg,

---

[51] On the novelty and methodology of the French legal tradition, with specific attention paid to Bauduin, see Julian H. Franklin, *Jean Bodin and the Sixteenth-Century Revolution in the Methodology of Law and History* (New York, 1963), esp. 116–36; Donald R. Kelley, *Foundations of Modern Historical Scholarship: Language, Law, and History in the French Renaissance* (New York, 1970), esp. 116–48; Donald R. Kelley, 'Historia Integra: François Baudouin and his Conception of History', *Journal of the History of Ideas*, 25 (1964), 35–57. See also Lars Boje Mortensen, 'François Bauduin's *De Institutione Historiæ* (1561): A Primary Text Behind Anders Sørensen Vedel's *De Scribenda Historia Danica* (1578)', *Symbolae Osloenses*, 73 (1998), 188–200; Gregory B. Lyon, 'Baudouin, Flacius, and the Plan for the Magdeburg Centuries', *Journal of the History of Ideas*, 64 (2003), 253–72. On Bauduin's use of evidence, see Nicholas Popper, 'An Ocean of Lies: The Problem of Historical Evidence in the Sixteenth Century', *Huntington Library Quarterly*, 74 (2011), 375–400.

[52] Donald Nugent, *Ecumenism in the Age of the Reformation: The Colloquy of Poissy* (Cambridge, MA, 1974), 24–5, 117, 177; at 221 Nugent accuses Bauduin of being 'almost chameleon-like' and suggests that Bauduin 'foreshadow[ed] a future where irenicism would become increasingly eccentric and utopian'. See also, Mario Turchetti, *Concordia o Tolleranza? François Bauduin (1520-1573) e i 'Moyenneurs'* (Milan, 1984), esp. 147–232.

[53] Erbe, *François Bauduin*, 96–7. On the confessional makeup of the university, see Charles D. Gunnoe, Jr, *Thomas Erastus and the Palatinate: A Renaissance Physician in the Second Reformation* (Leiden, 2011), 56–62.

under the auspices Ottheinrich, Elector Palatine, was becoming a home for study to multiple Englishmen.

Most significant with respect to Beale was the matriculation on 23 November 1558 of Henry Killigrew, who had previously been at Strasbourg as an associate of Anthony Cooke, and who would later become one of Beale's key colleagues later in the service of Queen Elizabeth. Killigrew did not stay within the university's environs for long because he was soon engaged in secret diplomatic negotiations for a religious and military alliance with the Elector Palatine and the duke of Württemberg.[54] Nevertheless, Killigrew appears to have gotten to know Bauduin, who also knew Cooke from their overlapping time in Strasbourg, for Bauduin wrote to Cecil testifying to his friendship with Killigrew and former knowledge of Cooke. Given his exposure to Englishmen during his time in Strasbourg and Heidelberg, Bauduin took an increasing interest in English affairs, as evident in his letter to Cecil, which noted the inclusion of a little book ('*libellum*') and his thoughts on matters sensitive to the new political situation.[55] The book sent by Bauduin might have been his recently published funeral oration for Elector Ottheinrich, who had died the previous month, but more appropriate, and of likely more interest to Cecil and others within the English regime, would have been his commentaries on civil law or, moreover, his treatment on the edicts of the ancient Roman princes regarding Christians. Bauduin also sent his thoughts on a more sensitive issue to Elizabeth in particular: the headings of a disputation he had prepared in the context of his recent lectures on the law of marriage. Given that King Henry VIII's will was clear on the matter of the royal succession, Bauduin noticed that the issue had been settled regarding Elizabeth as next in line for the throne, but Bauduin also recognized that underlying questions remained regarding the succession, as Cecil knew all too well.[56]

In the coming years, Bauduin came to know, or be known to, many different Englishmen of significant stature, such as Nicholas Throckmorton, Edmund

---

[54] Gustav Toepke (ed.), *Die Matrikel der Universität Heidelberg von 1386 bis 1662* (Heidelberg, 1886), 2.16. Killigrew's matriculation is not noted in Amos C. Miller's biography, *Sir Henry Killigrew: Elizabethan Soldier and Diplomat* (Amsterdam, 1963), though the mission is discussed on pp. 32–8. For an updated discussion of the mission and its wider importance, see *AGR*, esp. 28–30. William Cuningham, the noted physician and astrologer of Norwich, matriculated on 21 June 1559, and recorded his experience with 'D. Balduinus the Reader of the Ciuill Lector [Laws]' in his *The Cosmographical Glasse* (London, 1559) (STC 6119), 181 Toepke, *Die Matrikel*, 17.

[55] Bauduin to Cecil, 15 March 1559, TNA, SP 70/3, fols 52r–3v (orig.). Bauduin's interest in German involvement in French affairs, later in 1561, can be seen in Eduard von Kausler and Theodor Schott (eds), *Briefwechsel zwischen Christoph, Herzog von Württemberg, und Petrus Paulus Vergerius* (Tübingen, 1875), 277–80, 285.

[56] Bauduin's funeral oration for the elector was published several times, e.g. *Oratio in Fvnere Illvstriss. Principis Othonis Henrici Electoris Palatini etc. Habita XII Cal. Mar. MDLIX* (Heidelberg, 1559) (VD16 B 775). *Ad Edicta Veterum Principum Rom. de Christianis* (Basle, 1557) (VD16 B 762). On Cecil and the succession in the early years of Elizabeth's reign, see Stephen Alford, *The Early Elizabethan Polity: William Cecil and the British Succession Crisis, 1558–1569* (Cambridge, 1998).

Grindal, and John Jewel.[57] Additionally, he became more directly involved in English affairs—both he and Beale each wrote works specifically on the validity of marriages relevant to the royal succession. In fact, the '*libellum*' referred to in Bauduin's letter might have been his manuscript tract of advice for Queen Elizabeth on marriage, consanguinity, and legitimacy, a copy of which is among Beale's papers.[58] In the light of Beale's confirmed later interactions on the intricacies of marriage with legal scholars in Marburg, Cologne, and Speyer (the seat of the *Reichskammergericht*, the Imperial Chamber Court), but possibly none in Italy, the signs for Beale's legal education, however informal, point to western Germany. Also, given the fact that Bauduin and Beale subsequently corresponded directly in 1569 and 1570, the period and place for their acquaintance seems most likely to have been Heidelberg in 1558 and 1559 (though the possibility of Beale's initial exposure to Bauduin in Strasbourg in 1555/6 remains).[59]

No documentation—tax, municipal, schooling, or university—is known to exist for Beale's time in Strasbourg or Zurich, never mind Heidelberg, but our informed speculation is interrupted by the surviving evidence for his matriculation at the University of Wittenberg on 17 May 1560.[60] Why Beale decided to leave Heidelberg, if indeed that is where he was, might have been Bauduin's recommendation to seek religious knowledge and understanding at the original wellspring of the Reformation, where until 19 April 1560 Philip Melanchthon, a known friend to Bauduin, had held sway since Luther's death in 1546. An additional factor was probably John Hales's influence and experience in Wittenberg with Georg Maior, whose letter to Łaski, as we have seen, Beale seems to have received from Hales.[61] Whatever the most direct or indirect reason, Beale's choice to move east to Saxony was all the more significant because he chose the moderated Lutheranism, the Philippism, of Wittenberg over the more orthodox Lutheranism, the 'Gnesio Lutheranism' (or 'true'/'genuine' Lutheranism) of Jena.[62] Beale's later diplomatic career and religious sensibilities came to align more with the former than the latter, as will be seen.

---

[57] On Bauduin and the English, see Alexander Russell, 'The Colloquy of Poissy, François Baudouin and English Protestant Identity, 1561–1563', *Journal of Ecclesiastical History*, 65 (2014), 551–79.

[58] The manuscript tract (probably misdated to *c*.1561 in the Yelverton Catalogue) includes the 'Theses et capita disputationis' at fol. 1v: BL, Additional MS 48114, fols 54r–68v. Some material in this volume is from after 1601 and obviously not Beale's, but other materials, such as this tract, align precisely with his interests and corroborate materials elsewhere in his collections. The materials in this volume were simply bound after his death and with no obvious relation to each other.

[59] Letters of Bauduin to Beale in AUL, MS 1009/2, items 35–8 (all orig.). See also the receipt by Jacques Degaste, a merchant of London, regarding a financial transaction with Bauduin, 1 April 1561, AUL, MS 1009/1, item 18 (orig.).

[60] Karl Eduard Förstemann, et al. (eds), *Album Academiae Vitebergensis: Ältere Reihe in 3 Bänden 1502-1602* (Leipzig and Halle, 1894; repr. Aalen, 1976), 2.4. Incorrect date of 1 May in Béatrice Nicollier-de Weck, *Hubert Languet (1518–1581): Un Réseau Politique International de Melanchthon à Guillaume d'Orange* Geneva, 1995), 17.

[61] See above, n. 22.

[62] The historiography on the divisions among Lutherans, Philippists, and Reformed in the second generation of German Protestants is vast. For a thorough overview, see Irene Dingel, 'The Culture of Conflict in the Controversies Leading to the Formula of Concord (1548–1580)', in Robert Kolb (ed.),

It is impossible to know exactly how long Beale spent at the University of Wittenberg, but it is certain that while there he met one of his longest lasting and most like-minded of friends: Hubert Languet. Like many other Philippists and moderately inclined Lutherans, Languet was not immune to, or ignorant of, the political and international ramifications of religion after the Peace of Augsburg (1555) had supposedly settled the religious question in the Holy Roman Empire. A scholar, a diplomat, a man of letters, Languet was well connected to several others later known to Beale like Christopher Mundt and Daniel Rogers, both of whom had been born in Germany.[63] The surviving Beale-Languet correspondence dates from 1569 forward, but these letters attest to their previous friendship that had been rekindled during Beale's activity in Heidelberg and elsewhere in Germany in 1569 and again in 1577.[64]

By 1560, Beale's step-uncle, surrogate father, and key supporter from previous years, John Hales, had been back in England for roughly a year because he, like many others, rushed home to England after he learned of Queen Mary's death and Elizabeth's accession. Hales and others, however, clearly had not forgotten about the young Robert. The next likely confirmed location and activity for Beale—who by the early 1560s was in his early twenties, had broad international experience, and had weathered the storm of religious exile as an adolescent—is back in England. In early 1561 Beale benefited from the patronage not of John Hales but from Stephen Hales, his stepfather, who secured for Beale and his brother, William, prebends in Coventry and Lichfield diocese. These twin prebendaries of Ufton Decani (William) and Ufton Cantoris (Robert) came with incomes, so some degree of financial assistance had been secured even if Robert's future career or calling remained unclear.[65] Whether Beale set up residence

---

Lutheran Ecclesiastical Culture, 1550–1675 (Leiden, 2008), 15–64; cf. the massive and ongoing project of invaluable source editions, *Controversia et Confessio*, https://www.controversia-et-confessio.de.

[63] Mundt was officially a denizen of England, whose full Latinate surname was 'Montaborinum', which pinpoints his origins in Montabaur (between Frankfurt am Main and Cologne). See, for example, Henry VIII to Wilhelm and Ludwig, dukes of Bavaria, 20 January 1533/4, Hauptstaatsarchiv Munich, Kurbayern Äußeres Archiv MS 4515, fol. 26r–v (orig.). Rogers was an Englishman born in Wittenberg, styling himself *Albimontij Angli* in several of his poems written during the 1560s and 1570s, some of which were addressed to Languet, Sturm, and Beale himself. Huntington Library, HM 31188. On Languet generally, see Nicollier-de Weck, *Hubert Languet*; regarding Beale, Mundt, and Rogers on 226–7.

[64] BL, Egerton MS 1693 is predominantly but not exclusively Languet's letters to Beale.

[65] Robert was instituted on 1 February 1561, the day before his brother William, and installed on 25 April 1561. Staffordshire Record Office, Lichfield Diocesan Records, B/A/1/15 (Register), fol. 29v; LD30/12/10 (Miscellaneous); TNA, E 331/CoventryandLich/2; Horn, *Fasti Ecclesiae Anglicanae 1541–1857*, Vol. 10, 65, noting the valuation of the prebend as £2.13.4 in 1535. Beale is noted as without a university degree but as 'literate' or 'literatus' (in B/A/1/15), which indicates that the bishop judged the candidate to possess sufficient learning to qualify for ordination; he is also noted as 'clericus' (in E 331/CoventryandLich/2), though here 'clericus' may best be read as 'scholar' or 'student' rather than 'clergyman'. Robert might have retained this prebend at least until October 1592. Staffordshire Record Office, Lichfield Diocesan Records, LD30/2/7/96 (Miscellaneous). For Beale's brother, William's positions, see above, n. 6. Later in the 1560s and 1570s, Stephen seems to have taken a back seat to John Hales regarding the support offered to the Beale brothers, but see Chapter 4, n. 2, for an example of Stephen writing to Leicester in early 1573.

in the area or in London is unknown, but by late 1562 or early 1563, he was on the cusp of his greatest and most controversial task to date, and it is clear that Hales was at the root of it.

Necessary, Beneficial Peregrinations

By his early twenties, Beale had already lived no ordinary life. Born into a relatively comfortable life in London, his life took an early turn when he was sent to Coventry for his education due to his family connection with Hales. This link, as well as his link to Richard Morison, proved decisive after Mary's accession to the throne. Thus began Beale's travels. He was exposed to multiple communities of English exiles both young and old in Strasbourg and Zurich, and he appears to have established some friendships among these groups. More significant, though, were the international Protestants from whom he learned, however informally, and with whom he conversed. Had he not seen the value in an international education, had he not been comfortable in such environments, he would have worked his way back to England after Elizabeth's accession just as Hales and the others did—but he did not. No longer an exile, Beale chose to stay in Germany as a wandering scholar, and the impact of intellectual wandering should not be underestimated. There can be little doubt that he identified as an Englishman, given his life among the exile communities, but during his formative years he had also become a more broadly European Protestant.

Intellectually, Beale was well rounded on account of his humanist education in classical languages and literature, and due to his learning from multiple international perspectives—English, Rhenish, Swiss, and Saxon at least. These experiences help to explain Beale's later interests and activity during the later 1560s, 1570s, and beyond, when his service to the English state was due principally to his extensive expertise in international affairs—especially those of Germany. By way of religion, the environments where Beale seems to have been most comfortable were known for their moderate or even latitudinarian Protestant perspectives. Sturm's Strasbourg of the mid 1550s and Melanchthon's Wittenberg of the early 1560s were far less doctrinally or theologically rigid than Bullinger's Zurich and Flacius's Jena, and the impact of Beale's time in the former becomes easy to see in his later life. In terms of Beale's political and legal experience, as before, everything seems to have been informal. He lived as a religious exile in the Holy Roman Empire, and so was not immune to the politics of religion either in England or during and after the Interim. As will be seen, his was a detailed, precise, even persnickety mind, so it may be unsurprising that he responded well to legal study from a young age. His knowledge of international political organizations and legal traditions could only have been achieved by spending so much time away from England, and his understanding continued to flourish during the 1560s in palpable ways.

By 1563, he had grown increasingly self-reliant. Although he benefited enormously from relationships stemming from his uncle Morison and step-uncle Hales, he ultimately chose to travel on his own without clear or direct aid from family or friends. How he maintained himself, what he did for money, is unknown, but he continued to make his way in one form or another. Also, he continued to travel, but what started out as necessary travels as a child soon became beneficial peregrinations as a young man. The benefits might not have been readily apparent at the time, but soon they would be clear enough to both Beale and several others.[66]

A European Elizabethan: The Life of Robert Beale, Esquire. David Scott Gehring, Oxford University Press.
© David Scott Gehring 2024. DOI: 10.1093/9780198902942.003.0002

---

[66] Travel for the sake of informal education and future professional development later in the century became much more widespread, and the scholarship is considerable. For brief digests with reference to political utility and scholarly trends, see David Scott Gehring (ed.), *Diplomatic Intelligence on the Holy Roman Empire and Denmark during the Reigns of Elizabeth I and James VI: Three Treatises*, Royal Historical Society, Camden Fifth Series, 49 (Cambridge, 2016), 23–33; Gehring, 'Intelligence Gathering', *Diplomacy & Statecraft*, 33 (2022), 211–32.

3

Finding his Feet, Finding a Role

From 1563 to the end of 1569, Beale continued to learn from some of the most experienced and most learned men around him. As before, his education was informal, his exposure to opportunities a mix of family networks and his own initiative. Gradually, however, he sought to put his knowledge to use in written form, and he looked for ways that his expertise could bring him professional advancement through potential patrons. During these years Beale built a base of friends and colleagues in Paris and, to a more limited extent, in London. At a certain point in 1564, he felt that he had just one friend—albeit a rather important one. Still remaining in Germany and France during these years, Beale's intellectual development continued, and he began to see the webs of religion and politics in Germany, France, and the Low Countries as increasingly intertwined, even interdependent. His first task in 1563, however, was very much an English affair.

A Dangerous Assignment

Well before Lord John Grey instigated a project to validate the marriage of his niece Katherine Grey (sister to Lady Jane Grey) to Edward Seymour, earl of Hertford, thus providing a claim to the royal succession, the old professor of civil law François Bauduin had offered his thoughts on the royal succession and the legitimacy of marriage. As we have seen, in Bauduin's letter to Secretary Cecil in 1559, he had intimated as much and might have even sent the manuscript tract he had written on the matter.[1] Bauduin's continued concern for Elizabeth's position on the throne was evident in subsequent conversations with the queen's agent in Germany, Christopher Mundt, in spring 1561. Bauduin, according to Mundt, thought it was of the highest importance that Elizabeth marry and have an heir to secure the succession. Moreover, Balduin informed Mundt that the Catholic Guises in France were consulting doctors of law for their opinions on the English succession, and that he knew that neither Henry VIII's will nor a decree of Parliament could erase the inherent right of a legitimate heir to the throne, and

---

[1] See Chapter 2. On Elizabeth, marriage, and the succession, see Levine, *Early Elizabethan Succession Question*; Susan Doran, *Monarchy and Matrimony: The Courtships of Elizabeth I* (London, 1995); Susan Doran, *Elizabeth I and Her Circle* (Oxford, 2015).

that the present Queen of Scotland, Mary, was descended from the eldest daughter of Henry VII.[2] Securing a Protestant succession to continue the doctrines and theologies of the Church of England was important to Bauduin, for later, in 1561/2, he wrote and sent to Cecil a brief plan to explain and defend the order of religion in England. Upon request from Elizabeth, Bauduin would have happily fleshed out his ideas more fully because he thought his plan could serve as 'an Introduction and pattern for somme Lernid men in your [Elizabeth's] realme, to make suche an other Like Appologie for the deffence of your [Elizabeth's] formuler, which in thoppynion of manye wyse and Lernid is thought to be verie necessarie.'[3]

Bauduin's advice regarding marriage for the queen is important for a number of reasons, not the least of which is that Beale owned a copy of the discourse.[4] Despite the low likelihood that Elizabeth would have ever seen this tract of advice by an otherwise obscure professor of civil law deep within the Franco-German academic environment—if Cecil had a copy he knew better than to show it to Elizabeth because she needed no further counsel on marriage than what she was already getting—it seems highly likely that it helped Beale form his own discourses on the legitimacy of two particular marriages with direct relevance to Elizabeth's security on the throne. Bauduin starts his tract by reciting the history of King Henry VII's son Arthur's marriage to Katherine of Aragon, the death of Arthur, and the subsequent marriage between Henry VIII and Katherine. The general thrust of Bauduin's piece as a whole, however, concerns the unjust and incestuous nature of marriage within a family, and how when such a union is broken off or separated it would be unsuitable to be called divorce in the legal sense. Thus, Henry VIII's marriage to Katherine of Aragon was never, in truth, valid. Such an argument would, naturally, strengthen Elizabeth's position on the throne, and given the fact that Bauduin offered considerable support from the experiences and civil law codes of various Roman emperors, the argument would have been generally amenable to the queen had she seen it. At the same time, though, it mentioned nothing of the competing claims to the royal succession by others. That task would be taken up by Beale.

Many fervent Elizabethan Protestants had painful memories of dismay after the death of King Edward VI and the ensuing re-Catholicization of England under Mary, and these memories led to a great deal of concern about the succession if Elizabeth were to die childless. The pressure on the queen to marry, and

---

[2] Mundt to Cecil, 15 April 1561, TNA, SP 70/25, fols 53r–4v, at 53v (orig.).

[3] Throckmorton to Elizabeth, 8 January 1562, TNA, SP 70/34, fols 29r–32v, quotation at 31r (orig.). John Jewel's *Apologia Ecclesiae Anglicanae* (London, 1562) (STC 14581) was the final product suggested by Bauduin, who remained deeply interested in how Jewel's work was received and criticized by Catholics at the Council of Trent. See Middlemore to Cecil, 24 January 1563, TNA, SP 70/49, fols 105r–7v (orig.).

[4] Bauduin's treatise, BL, Additional MS 48114, fols 54r–68v.

subsequently to deliver an heir, was intense and came from multiple quarters—domestic as well as international—both in the early days of her reign and well into the 1570s.[5] If Elizabeth remained unwed, an unthinkable prospect to most Englishmen of the 1560s, she would be endangering her realm because the most logical, most direct royal successor would have been Mary Queen of Scots, a devout Catholic with firm ties to Catholic France.[6] Such a possibility brought fears of Marian England's return, so finding a way to secure a Protestant succession became increasingly important to those within the English Church and State. One possibility, indeed the only real possibility, lay in a granddaughter of Mary Tudor, the younger surviving daughter of Henry VII: Katherine Grey, the younger sister of Lady Jane Grey.

This Mary Tudor's second marriage to Charles Brandon, duke of Suffolk and intimate friend of Henry VIII, was deeply controversial because it was conducted overseas and without Henry's approval. The subsequent Suffolk claims were complicated by issues regarding the legitimacy of several further marriages.[7] Of most immediate concern in the early 1560s, however, was the clandestine marriage of Katherine and the earl of Hertford in late 1560. Under normal circumstances, an Englishman in his early twenties who had led a life thus far wandering from place to place without a real sense of direction, and without a direct connection to the blood royal, would have had nothing to do with the claims and marriages of the Greys, Hertford, or the queen of Scotland; but Beale's life thus far was not exactly normal. John Hales, Beale's step-uncle and surrogate father who had already opened so many doors for him directly or indirectly, created a new opportunity for the young Beale, one that came with significant potential dangers in a maelstrom that became known as the *Tempestas Halesiana*.[8]

The precise details of the issue are complex, but, at bottom, if the Grey-Hertford marriage was valid, and Katherine Grey's own lineage back to Henry VII was valid, then any children she bore would be legitimate claimants to the throne if Elizabeth did not produce an heir. The main rival to the throne, Mary Queen of Scots, was seen by many English Protestants, John Hales most certainly included, as disqualified from succeeding Elizabeth due to the common law prohibition against aliens inheriting property in England—never mind the whole of England. The importance of securing a Protestant succession gained further significance when the Grey-Hertford marriage was found invalid on 12 May 1562 by an ecclesiastical commission appointed on 31 January (under pressure from the queen

---

[5] Doran, *Monarchy and Matrimony*, offers the broadest survey analysing the courtships coming from various directions and with varying levels of likelihood for success.

[6] On the 1560s, see the lively if brief discussions by Simon Adams and Charlotte Bolland in Susan Doran (ed.), *Elizabeth and Mary: Royal Cousins, Rival Queens* (London, 2021), 82–95. On Mary's early life and upbringing, see Julian Goodare's entry on Mary in *ODNB*.

[7] On the legitimacy of the Suffolks, see Levine, *Early Elizabethan Succession Question*, 126–46. See the updated discussion in Doran, *Elizabeth I and Her Circle*, 43–64, with notice of Beale's role at 54.

[8] See the narrative in Levine, *Early Elizabethan Succession Question*, 62–85.

and Archbishop Parker to find as much), thus making Katherine's son, born while she was imprisoned in the Tower, illegitimate.

Hales was connected to Lord John Grey, uncle of Katherine and guardian after her parents' decease in the 1550s, who then took the lead in defending the legality of the Grey-Hertford marriage, however clandestine and ill-thought-out it was. Because the two witnesses to the marriage had since died, legal arguments needed to be marshalled, and Hales needed someone with legal training and connections on the European mainland to canvass legal opinion on the matter. Enter Beale. The language of the documentary record for the subsequent investigations suggests that Beale had been in England in late 1562 or early 1563 (possibly along with Henry Knolles, whom Elizabeth had sent on an embassy to Germany), and then was sent back to the mainland to find arguments by civil lawyers in Grey's favour regarding the legality of the marriage (just as Thomas Cranmer had been assigned by Henry VIII).[9] This was Beale's first 'job' in any real or paid sense, for his project was first encouraged by Lord Grey, and then advanced by Francis Newdigate, Hertford's stepfather. According to the documentation extant, Newdigate supplied some funds to Hales, but Hertford entered an agreement with Beale directly. Beale later complained bitterly, however, that '[w]hen I had served the Erle by the espace of 8 yeres or more with danger and charge, to defende as much as might be his pretended [i.e. intended, claimed, or argued for] mariage, I was vnhonourably and vncourteouslye, and without cause cast of[f,] contrarye to his promise (which I can shewe vnder his owne hande) to assure vnto me an annuitye of xl^{li} by the yere.'[10] Thus, given the inherent dangers of Beale's job, he was to be remunerated handsomely for the foreseeable future.

Beale wrote at least two full-length tracts in Latin to defend Hertford's position: one to affirm the legitimacy of the marriage of Mary Tudor and Charles Brandon, duke of Suffolk, without which marriage any subsequent claims would irrelevant, and another arguing for the validity of the Grey-Hertford marriage and, by implication, the legitimacy of their newborn baby and, by extension, the family's claim should Elizabeth die—as she nearly did when she contracted smallpox in October 1562.[11] The first piece constituted Beale's response to the

---

[9]   See, e.g. Francis Newdigate's confession to Thomas Mason, 2 May 1564, CP, 154/63.
[10]   Answers of Hales to the interrogatories, 25 April 1564, CP, 154/60, fol. 1r (orig.). 'The answer of Robert Beale concerninge such thinges as have passed between the L. Archbishopp of Canterburye and him', 1 July 1584, BL, Additional MS 48039, fol. 48r. Beale's targeting of Hertford here immediately precedes his rant against Aylmer on 48v. That Beale appears never to have been paid anything by Hertford may be explained by the extraordinary fine(s) levied upon the earl in Star Chamber in February 1562: £5,000 for deflowering the Lady Katherine Grey, another £5,000 for breaking out of prison to see her, and another £5,000 'itterataling' (i.e. repeating) the same. Transcript from the register of Star Chamber, Inner Temple Library, Petyt MS 538/50, fol. 123r, with note following regarding Archbishop Parker's role on 12 May 1562 in finding Hertford's marriage illicit and illegitimate.
[11]   The tracts survive in Beale's holograph with the 'manu propia' following his signature: CUL, MS Dd.iii.85, item 18 (on Suffolk's marriage), MS Ii.v.3, fols 19r–44r (on Hertford's marriage). A potential third tract, on Katherine Grey's first 'marriage' to the eldest son of the earl of Pembroke, is discussed

allegation that, because Suffolk had been married previously to his supposed marriage to Mary Tudor, and because his first wife was still alive during his second supposed marriage, any subsequent children or descendants via Mary were not lawfully born, including Katherine Grey. Beale concluded that the marriage and subsequent descendants were indeed legitimate, and he did so by marshalling no small number of arguments from civil and canon law. He naturally cited the early medieval compilation of Roman civil law, the *Corpus Iuris Civilis*, but he also cited as authorities and offered extracts from various medieval commentators like Baldus de Ubaldis (d.1400) and Francesco Zabarella (d.1417), popes who commented on aspects of relevant canon law like Alexander III (d.1181) and Celestine III (d.1198), and more recent jurists of the sixteenth century like Petrus Paulus Parisius (d.1545) and François Douaren (d.1559), a major exponent of the *mos gallicus* who taught at the University of Bourges at the same time Bauduin did.[12] As if these citations did not sufficiently demonstrate Beale's knowledge of esteemed legal authorities, he ended his treatise on the Suffolk-Tudor marriage with a quotation of gravitas from the high and late medieval collection of canon law, the *Corpus Iuris Canonici*: *veritas[,] cum non defensatur, opprimitur* ('the truth, when not defended, is overthrown').

Beale sent this work back to Hales in England, where Lord Grey and Newdigate reviewed and discussed its contents. Although Newdigate confessed he 'was nothing satisfyed' with Beale's work because he preferred to have the more pressing marriage (the Hertford-Grey marriage) vindicated, Lord Grey said 'that this [book] should serve for another purpose that John Hales eyther had done or was aboute to do, meaning the Booke of Succession'.[13] Thus, although Beale was hired by Lord Grey and Hertford to gather legal opinions in favour of Hertford's marriage to Katherine Grey, the first thing Beale set out to accomplish was to write a detailed legal opinion on the very founding of the family line so that Hales would have legal ammunition in his own work on the royal succession. The most plausible explanation for Beale's doing so is that Hales instructed him along these lines. Hales wrote his treatise in 1563 and circulated it in manuscript during the parliament then in session (January to April), with a view to influencing broader debates on excluding Mary Queen of Scots from the succession, and providing a sound legal path for a Protestant succession. In the end, Hales did not employ the legal minutiae recorded by Beale as much as he could have, however scholarly it was. Although rumours circulated that Hales was known to be saying that he

---

below. The paper used and hands found across the CUL materials demonstrate that Beale acquired his paper from the same source as did the jurists of Speyer. See n. 18.

[12] On Bauduin's many connections with Douaren, see Michael Erbe, *François Bauduin (1520–1573): Biographie eines Humanisten* (Gütersloh, 1978). Additional preparatory notes and extracts on marriage and bastardy in Beale's possession, BL, Additional MS 48066, fols 20r–75v, with note on the Suffolk marriage and the succession on 30r, 56r–v. Further works on divorce, adultery, and remarriage in Beale's archive include the two English treatises in BL, Additional MS 48030.

[13] Newdigate's confession, 2 May 1564, CP, 154/63, fol. 1v.

'found by the lawe of nature[,] Godes lawe[,] & Comon lawe, that they confessing themselves to be married were legitimi Coniunges', Hales seems to have favoured a more chronological account of Suffolk's multiple marriages and suits. Nevertheless, the possibility also remains that Beale had sent his own discourse after Hales had completed his.[14]

Beale's second work relative to the Grey-Hertford cause was a hypothetical legal case mirroring Katherine's first marriage, or supposed marriage, in 1553 to Henry Herbert (eldest son of the earl of Pembroke), both of whom were *impubes* (prepubescent). In reality, the marriage was never consummated, and Pembroke had it dissolved shortly after the wedding. Beale's full work no longer survives, but he framed the question of their marriage using the Latin pseudonyms Titius and Seia (fictitious names often used in legal examples) for two adolescents who married but then subsequently divorced without having consummated the marriage, with Seia later marrying and consummating with Sempronius (another fictitious name found in legal examples).[15] Beale received learned responses to his work from Johann Oldendorp, professor of law at the University of Marburg (the first specifically Protestant university); Jakob Omphal, jurist and lecturer at the University of Cologne with previous experience in England; and Kilian Senff (or Sinapius), Markus Ludwig Ziegler, and Georg Brunner, three jurists of the *Reichskammergericht* (Imperial Chamber Court) at Speyer. These men were no insignificant legal minds of western Germany at the time, at least one of whom was an associate of Bauduin.[16] Beale's familiarity with the *Reichskammergericht*

---

[14] Quotation from a transcript from the register of Star Chamber, Inner Temple Library, Petyt MS 538/50, fol. 123r. John Hales, *A Declaration of the Succession of the Crowne Imperiall of Ingland*, 1563, in Francis Hargrave (pseud. George Harbin), *The Hereditary Right of the Crown of England Asserted* (London, 1713), xxxviii–xlii (in the Appendix). Hales's tract, along with other arguments regarding the Suffolk marriage, discussed in Levine, *Early Elizabethan Succession Question*, 62–85, 126–37; Beale's tract noted briefly at 70. Cf. Victoria de la Torre, '"We Few of an Infinite Multitude": John Hales, Parliament, and the Gendered Politics of the Early Elizabethan Succession', *Albion*, 33 (2001), 557–82, briefly noting Beale at 577 n. 81.

[15] See the summary of the case made by Beale preceding the responses of Oldendorp and the jurists of Speyer, CUL, MS Ii.v.3, fols 1r, 8v. Cecil may have seen Beale's suggested case during the interrogations of Hales in 1564. Cecil's minute on the interrogatories for Hales, 3 May 1564, CP, 154/65. Cecil's minute also askes 'where is the answer made by the lerned men of padua to ye case', and 'who formed the other case that was sent to Italye'. These questions suggest either that Cecil thought Beale's discourse sent to jurists in Speyer was also sent to Padua, or that still another discourse by Beale was written but has not yet come to light. See also 'a case of matrimony' between Hertford and Katherine, endorsed by Cecil: Bodleian, Ashmole MS 826, fols 5r–6v. The only known corroborating evidence suggesting that Beale sent this or another discourse to Padua is his own comment nearly thirty years later that he knew the Chancellor of Poland formerly as rector at Padua. Beale to David Chytraeus, 16 April 1591, AUL, MS 1009/1, item 8. See Chapter 7.

[16] On Oldendorp, Omphal, and Brunner, see *DB*. Much less is known about Senff and Ziegler, but see respectively John L. Flood and David J. Shaw, *Johannes Sinapius (1505–1560): Hellenist and Physician in Germany and Italy* (Geneva, 1997), 102; Peter Arnold Heuser, 'Zur Bedeutung der Vor- und Nachkarrieren von Reichskammergerichts-Juristen des 16. Jahrhunderts für das Studium ihrer Rechtsauffassungen: Eine Fallstudie', in Albrecht Cordes (ed.), *Juristische Argumentation—Argumente der Juristen* (Cologne, 2006), 205. On Bauduin and Omphal, see Erbe, *François Bauduin*, 117, 215, 246; Mario Turchetti, *Concordia o Tolleranza? François Bauduin (1520–1573) e i 'Moyenneurs'*

extended further at this time, for he also collected various notes on the legal proceedings of the court at Speyer, even creating a nice title page with his own name
for his comparatively disorganized and rough-hewn observations and transcriptions that switched between Latin and German. That title page included three
taglines or mottos reflecting Beale's principles at the time and for years to come.
The Latin 'In spe & metu' demonstrated that Beale lived in both hope and fear of
things to come. The English 'Liue and Learne' suggested his dedication to a life of
experience and application. The Greek Ἀρχὴν ἁπαντῶν καὶ τέλος ποιεῖ θεόν' confirmed that he made God the beginning and end of all things. If such a title page,
signature, and notes are anything to go by, at twenty-two years old Beale was a
young man of ambition who thought—at least sometimes—in Latin and German,
not English.[17] Despite his own individual efforts, it would stretch the limits of
credulity to think that Beale would have received responses from these men at
Speyer without the benefit of an intermediary who could vouch for him and his
cause, and in this regard Bauduin is the only plausible candidate with such connections. Their responses, each of which finds in Seia's (i.e. Katherine Grey's)
favour, can be found among the materials Beale sent back to Hales and Hertford
(and see Figs 1 and 2).[18]

The most significant of Beale's works relative to the Grey-Hertford marriage,
and that to settle the issue of its legality, was his discourse sent to the jurists of
Speyer and (later) Paris. No small or hypothetical case, Beale's discourse of just
over twenty-five folios employed the same pseudonyms, Seia and Sempronius,
and set out the scenario under thirty-eight subheadings.[19] As he had done in his
treatment on the Suffolk marriage, Beale used the discourse as an opportunity to
demonstrate his knowledge and understanding of civil and canon law, citing along
the way many of the same authorities he used in his previous work, especially
Henrichus Bohicus (d.1390), but also now using the original canonist, Gratian,
other canonists like Hostiensis (Henry de Susa, d.1271) and Panormitanus
(Nicolò de' Tudeschi, d.1445), as well as more famous authors such as Church
Fathers like Chrysostom and Ambrose, and medieval theologians like Peter
Lombard and Thomas Aquinas. Beale's discourse, encyclopaedic in breadth and

(Milan, 1984), 172–3. Omphal served as courier between Hermann von Wied, deposed elector of
Cologne, and King Edward VI. See Edward to Hermann, 18 November 1550, TNA, SP 68/5, 183.

[17] Beale's notes, 1563, BL, Cotton MS Nero, B. IX, fols 4r–5r, 7r–18v. This is the earliest hard evidence of Beale's ability in Greek, but cf. Chapter 5, n. 36, which offers a suggestion for Beale's Greek in
1559. The booklist in BL, Hargrave MS 107, suggests that he later owned several titles in Greek and on
the Greek language (at, e.g. fols 16r–v, 20v, 21r–v, 25v, 28v, 48r, 50r). The origins of these sayings are
difficult to trace, but the Latin and Greek appear to be classical. The Greek proverb (verse in iambic
trimeter) could come in different forms, as was later discussed in Johannes Verweij, *Nova Via Docendi
Græca* (Amsterdam, 1691), 28, which notes the early Greek Father, Apollinaris (of Leodicea), as a
possible source. I am indebted to my colleague, Nick Wilshere, for his translation of the Greek and
suggestion regarding Verweij's work.

[18] CUL, MS Ii.v.3, fols 1r–3r (Oldendorp), 3r–6v (Omphal), 8v–15v (jurists of Speyer) (all orig.).

[19] CUL, MS Ii.v.3, fols 19r–44r (orig.).

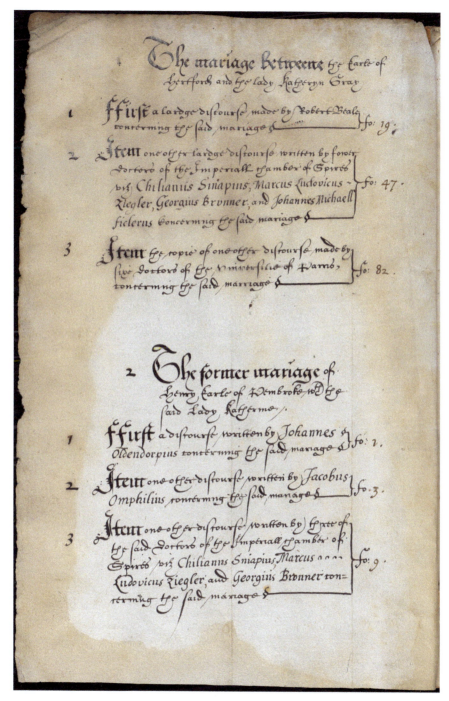

Fig. 1 List of papers relating to the earl of Hertford's marriage, 1563. CUL, MS Ii.v.3, fol. iv.

Reproduced with permission from Cambridge University Library.

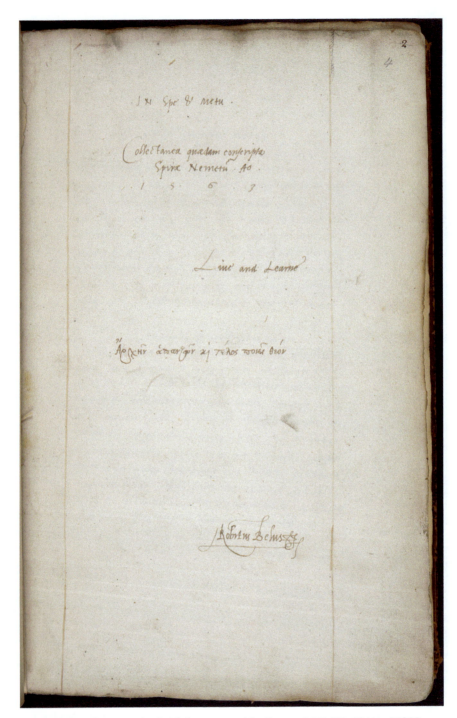

Fig. 2 Notes relating to the *Reichskammergericht*, Speyer, 1563. BL, Cotton MS Nero, B. IX, fol. 4r.

Reproduced with permission from the British Library.

astounding in depth, was once described as a *'doctissimum tractatum'* ('a most learned tract'), and one may say justifiably so given the detailed citations demonstrating that Beale had access to a considerable library of printed legal works, but one should also remember that Beale was only about twenty-two when he wrote the piece.[20] As if channelling an inner Bauduin, Beale combined a profound and detailed command of law and history when considering the questions under each subheading, and the work stands as Beale's assertion of his own abilities in law, history, and languages (Latin, Greek, and relevant vernaculars), which could serve the English government in the future. Accordingly, it would be difficult to see the work as simply a document advancing Hertford's case because Beale knew who would see it, and those men were in the position to help Beale professionally. For more immediate purposes, though, Beale received a response to his work from same jurists of the *Reichskammergericht* who had previously offered their thoughts on the Grey-Pembroke marriage, with the added help of another jurist of Speyer, Johannes Michael Fickler. The men of Speyer admitted to some extent that they had been brief in their previous treatment, so they set out a much longer, more detailed work here, longer still than Beale's. In short, Beale demonstrated the legality of the Grey-Hertford marriage, and everyone who saw his tracts knew it. The subsequent interrogations and shutting down of the matter were symptomatic of the panic caused by a potential rival claim to the succession. Although the issue did not yet come up again later in the 1560s, Beale's proving of the case was still acknowledged if ignored ('winked at') as late as 1600.[21]

Well after Beale's work in western Germany had been completed in 1563, with his own works along with the opinions of the German jurists sent back to Hales, and long after Hales and Hertford had been sent to the Tower for their conduct, Beale continued to seek legal opinion on Hertford's marriage. After he joined the English embassy in Paris, albeit in a very unofficial capacity, he requested and received the views of several professors in the faculty of canon law at the University of Paris, whose long reply Beale labelled as from 'the doctors of Parrys': Laurentius Riviere, Jacobus de la Croix, Johannes Ramatus, Petrus Pillaguetius, Martinus Gilbertus, and Prerordius Pillaguetius.[22] Their response to Beale's tract on Sempronius and Seia was dated 1 December 1564, and so it cannot be

---

[20] Thomas Tanner, *Bibliotheca Britannico-Hibernica, sive, De Scriptoribus, qui in Anglia, Scotia, et Hibernia [...] Commentarius* (London, 1748), 82. Tanner's posthumously published work notes Beale's tract as being in the library of John Moore, bishop of Norwich and later Ely, but Moore's legendary library was purchased to celebrate the coronation of King George I in 1714, and subsequently deposited in Cambridge University Library the next year. When or how Moore acquired Beale's works is unknown. The historical and antiquarian collections of Tanner, Moore's son-in-law, ended up at the Bodleian Library in Oxford, per his bequest. On Tanner and Moore, *ODNB*.

[21] Their response, CUL, MS Ii.v.3, fols 47r–76v (orig.). Relatively little is known about Fickler, but see *DB*. ? to ?, November 1600, TNA, SP 15/34, fols 77r–8r, quotation at 77v.

[22] Their response, CUL, MS Ii.v.3, fols 82r–96v. Laurentius Riviere was a deacon, Jacobus de la Croix a court official, the last four all Professor Ordinarius.

considered to be part of Hales's assignment for Beale in 1563, but Beale's sustained activity in this regard illustrates that he continued to work on Hertford's behalf because the earl's appeal to reconsider the verdict on his marriage had not yet been considered. That Beale persisted in soliciting the opinions of jurists on the European mainland lends some justification to his later complaint that he worked for the earl for several years without being properly paid.

Beale's activity in Paris aside, and notwithstanding Hertford's lack of punctual payment, Beale's involvement on behalf of Hales, Newdigate, and Lord Grey brought his name to the attention of the real power brokers in the Elizabethan regime—for better or for worse. The documents sometimes refer to Beale as Hales's 'boy' or 'the younge man', but at other times they refer to Beale by name.[23] Given the fact that many chief players within the English nobility and government were suspected of being involved in the 'conspiracy' aroused by Hales's book on the succession, it seems probable that Beale's activity would have been known to a small group of potential patrons, including Robert Dudley, earl of Leicester. Others also got wind of Beale's activity, however, some of whom were less than friendly to Hertford's cause, including the Scottish Catholic, John Leslie, whose commitment to Mary Queen of Scots was firm, and who later commented in print on Beale's activity in 1563 at 'certaine foreine Uniuersities' and with 'sundry famous learned men'.[24] With Hales effectively removed from politics from 1564 forward, Beale had lost his only means of support (from within his family or otherwise). Cecil's role in the investigations of Hales and others, and his sincere concern for the royal succession, ensured that Elizabeth's principal secretary was aware of Beale's tracts and connections among the legal minds of western Germany, and in the coming years the relationship between Cecil and Beale was both professional and friendly—but during the 1560s Cecil appears to have maintained a judicious and critical distance for the purposes of plausible deniability.[25] Beale's work regarding the succession was highly controversial because he could easily have been implicated and imprisoned like Hales and Hertford, so it was with good reason that Beale decided to stay overseas for the foreseeable future. After his work for Hertford and Hales was finished in 1563, he was again essentially left to his own devices. Given Cecil's knowledge of Beale's expertise and

[23] Newdigate's confession, 2 May 1564, CP, 154/63, fol. 1v. Answers of Hales, 25 April 1564, CP, 154/60, fol. 1r (orig.).
[24] Leicester et al. to Cecil, 26 April 1564, BL, Harley MS 6990, item 29, fol. 62r (orig.). John Leslie, *A Treatise of Treasons against Q. Elizabeth, and the Croune of England* (Leuven, 1572) (STC 7601), fols 126v–7r, quotation at 126v; cf. John Leslie, *A Table Gathered ovvt of a Boke Named A Treatise of treasons against Q. Elizabeth and the Croune of England* (Antwerp, 1572) (STC 23617.5), sig. **3r. These works appear to have been published overseas, though Leslie was in London, imprisoned for his role in the Ridolfi Plot, when he wrote them. How he became aware of Beale's activity is unknown.
[25] On Cecil's careful proceedings, see Stephen Alford, *Burghley: William Cecil at the Court of Elizabeth I* (New Haven, CT, 2008); Norman Jones, *Governing by Virtue: Lord Burghley and the Management of Elizabethan England* (Oxford, 2015).

potential value to the English crown, it seems reasonable to suggest that Cecil—indirectly, of course—pointed him in the direction of Paris.

A Base in Paris, an Eye on Germany

In 1591, Beale wrote to Cecil (then Lord Burghley) complaining about afflictions he had long suffered— 'goute and the stone'—and noting that prolonged standing caused his feet to swell. He stated also, though: 'In my youthe I tooke greate paines, and trauellinge in divers Countreyes on foote, for lacke of other habilitie.'[26] Beale's travels, indeed travails, included going from England to Strasbourg, to Zurich, to western as well as eastern Germany. In late 1562, possibly while or just before he was on assignment from Hales in western Germany, he appears to have been loosely attached to, or informally attending, the English ambassador to the German princes, Henry Knolles, whom Elizabeth sent along with Christopher Mundt to negotiate with the princes regarding aid to be sent to the Huguenots in France and a long-term alliance.[27] Beale thus learned the intricacies and practicalities of the art of diplomacy while continuing his study of civil (and canon) law. Given his time in the Holy Roman Empire, he was intimately familiar with the world of religious conflict and the need for both local and international negotiation and collaboration. In the wake of his activity for Hales and Hertford, and probably surmising correctly that he was safer overseas than back in England, Beale next made his way to the place where he was most likely to find a more secure existence. His experience and expertise to this point were largely if not exclusively in German affairs, but the English government's more sustained—indeed permanent—base on the European mainland was found west of the Empire's boundaries. From 1564 forward, Paris was to be as much a 'home' for Beale as any other place he had known, and Paris was the place where Beale would make himself increasingly valuable to the English government.[28]

Just as he could not possibly have been an official part of the Knolles/Mundt embassy in 1562, Beale was never an accredited member of the English embassy in Paris during the 1560s, despite his later remark to Cecil about 'the good will which I had to serve her Majesty's Ambassadores in ffrance sith the yere 1564[,] and in Germany as Mr Henry Knolles [and] Mr Killgrew can witnis[,] without

---

[26] Beale to Burghley, July/August 1591, BL, Lansdowne MS 68/107, fols 238r–9v, quotations at 238r–v; inconsistently transcribed in John Strype, *Annals of the Reformation and Establishment of Religion [...] a New Edition*, 4 vols (Oxford, 1824), 4.115–17, at 116; Strype renders 'trauellinge' as 'travailing', and while the experience of the former may lead to the latter, the words are distinct.

[27] *AGR*, 40–3. Beale to Burghley, 15 April 1578, BL, Lansdowne MS 27/32, fols 62r–3v (orig.).

[28] On Paris during the mid and late 1560s as a period of crisis, see Barbara B. Diefendorf, *Beneath the Cross: Catholics and Huguenots in Sixteenth-Century Paris* (Oxford, 1991), 64–84.

any charge to her Highnes'.[29] During the 1560s Beale, as a hanger on or servant at best, learned the ropes of English diplomacy by observing both extraordinary and resident ambassadors, while having no formal responsibilities of his own, and his experiences at this time left a deep impression on the twenty-something Beale. The documentary record for his time during the 1560s, as for the 1550s, is frustratingly thin, but his recollection here is worth exploration because the implications are significant regarding where he was based, what he doing, and with whom he was interacting.

Due to the centrality and permanence of the English embassy in Paris, especially when considered next to the comparatively disparate and ad hoc English activity within the Empire, Beale's decision to head west into France after completing his work for Hales and Hertford was entirely understandable (though, again, he might have been encouraged to do so). The importance of Madrid notwithstanding, the English embassy in Paris was the most important foreign post for the early Elizabethan state, so it was often staffed by the queen's most trustworthy, accomplished, and learned men.[30] Leaving aside for the moment the string of extraordinary ambassadors to France sent for specific, temporary causes, the succession of resident ambassadors bears out such an impression with a couple of notable exceptions (i.e. those who did not last very long): Nicholas Throckmorton (May 1559–February 1563), Thomas Smith (August 1562–June 1566), Thomas Hoby (April—July 1566), Hugh Fitzwilliam (chargé d'affaires, July 1566–January 1567), and Henry Norris (November 1566–March 1571).

Beale's interactions and contacts with Smith are suggested by fragments of Smith's diplomatic papers among Beale's own manuscript archive, as well as later, more explicit comments by both men. Beale owned (and sometimes annotated) some of Smith's writings from this period, as well as some predating their shared time in Paris, including manuscript versions of 'A Discourse of the common weale of this Realme of England' (more commonly *Discourse of the Commonweal*, 1549), 'A Communicacion or Discourse of the Queenes highness mariage' (more commonly 'Dialogue on the Queen's Marriage', c.1560), 'A booke touching the wages geven to the Romane souldior' (late 1562), 'Th'Estat of the realm of ffrance' (a work on tax yields in France c.1554, but copied by Beale in 1566), and the crown jewel of Smith's works—*De Republica Anglorum* (written by 1565 but printed first in 1583).[31] Beale noted at the top of his holograph copy of Smith's tax evaluation that he 'had [it] of Sr Thomas Smith in Paris anno 1566 2 May', just

[29] Beale to Burghley, 15 April 1578, BL, Lansdowne MS 27/32, fol. 63r (orig.). Contrast Taviner's argument (Chapter 3) for Beale in Paris only from 1566 onwards.

[30] A convenient summary with notice of archives, Simon Adams, 'Tudor England's Relations with France', *State Papers Online 1509–1714*, Cengage Learning EMEA Ltd, 2009; https://www.gale.com/intl/essays/simon-adams-tudor-englands-relations-france.

[31] 'A Discourse of the common weale of this Realme of England', BL, Additional MS 48047, fols 170r–226v. 'A Communicacion or Discourse of the Queenes highnes mariage', BL, Additional MS 48047, fols 96r–135r. 'A booke touching the wages geven to the Romane souldior', BL, Additional MS

before Smith's departure from the English embassy, and it seems logical that Beale acquired the other works in manuscript about this time, along with a collection of other diplomatic papers in Smith's possession.[32] This timing also suggests that Beale might have remained at the embassy in Paris while Smith followed the court's perambulation around the country.[33] Smith, having learned of the *Tempestas Halesiana* from Cecil in 1564, came to appreciate Beale's learning in civil law, especially since a major premise of *De Republica Anglorum* was to contrast the politics of the English common law with that of the Roman civil law.[34] Moreover, Beale and Smith clearly had a good relationship, for Beale collected more materials from Smith on his subsequent, ad hoc embassies to France to carry out specific negotiations regarding the return of Calais in 1567 and a potential marriage between Queen Elizabeth and Henri, duke of Anjou, in 1571. These materials were valuable to Beale because they offered up-to-date intelligence and the views from his queen and her Privy Council, but still more important to both Beale's religious sensibilities and the realm of England more largely was that, 'out of a booke of Sr Tho: Smithe', Beale secured 'A Coppye of the Deuise for alteration of religion at the first yeare of Queene Elizabethe'.[35] Beale typically said less about those he liked than about those he disliked (e.g. Bishop Aylmer and the earl of Hertford, as we have seen, or Archbishop Whitgift, as we shall see), so the value he placed in Smith and his work can be seen in his later recommendation, however qualified by the space of time, of *De Republica Anglorum* to an aspiring principal secretary for understanding the state of the realm. Conversely, it is clear that Smith thought highly of Beale as well when he offered a ringing endorsement the bearer of his letter to Cecil: '[I] pray you to remember this berer[,] Mr Beale[,] who I assure you is a rare man & of excellent giftes'.[36]

Smith vacated the Paris embassy in early summer 1566 and offered any of his servants, presumably Beale included, to his replacement, Thomas Hoby. Hoby, however, did not have the same, exceedingly productive experience as did Smith.

48047, fols 140r–65r. 'Th'Estat of the realm of ffrance', BL, Additional MS 48026, fols 29v–31v. *De Republica Anglorum*, BL, Additional MS 48047, fols 1r–50v.

[32] Memoranda of accounts for the French royal household, officials in France, expenses of Parlement, mostly in Beale's holograph, BL, Additional MS 48026, fols 10r–29r, 38r–9v, 40r–v. See also the papers not linked to Smith but relating to the conference at Bruges in 1566, some of which include Cecil's notes, in BL, Additional MS 48011, fols 1r–71v.

[33] See Smith's correspondence from various cities in *CSPF*, Vols 7 and 8.

[34] On the international dimension, especially regarding political theory, see Anne McLaren, 'Reading Sir Thomas Smith's *De Republica Anglorum* as Protestant Polemic', *The Historical Journal*, 42 (1999), 911–39.

[35] On Smith's knowledge of the Hales/Hertford fiasco, see Levine, *Early Elizabethan Succession Question*, 81; John Strype, *The Life of the Learned Sir Thomas Smith [...] a New Edition* (Oxford, 1820), 92–3. Papers of Smith's missions, BL, Additional MS 48085, fols 352r–75v. The 'Deuise', copied in a secretary hand most certainly not Beale's, BL, Additional MS 48035, fols 141r–6v.

[36] 'A Treatise of the office of a Councellor and Principall Secretarie to her Majestie', 1592, BL, Additional MS 48149, fol. 5r. Smith to Burghley, 9 March 1572, TNA, SP 70/146, fol. 55r (old foliation, 61r); *CSPF*, Vol. 17, item 444; erroneously cited in Mary Dewar, *Sir Thomas Smith: A Tudor Intellectual in Office* (London, 1964), 136.

In fact, from the very beginning, Hoby's was inauspicious. He was knighted before leaving England for France, but his party was shot at upon reaching Calais (the English flag suffered two hits), and his first meeting with the French king was hardly a smooth affair (the king having torn apart Elizabeth's letter of credence for Hoby). Then, within three short months, Hoby died on 13 July 1566 after a rapid decline.[37] One of Hoby's existing household, Hugh Fitzwilliam, served as a temporary deputy diplomat until the arrival of another formally accredited resident ambassador. The new ambassador was Henry Norris, whose arrival Beale anticipated in November 1566. Beale had learned much—directly or indirectly—from Smith between 1564 and 1566, and he seems to have agreed with Fitzwilliam's relatively strident Protestantism. To remain relevant and valuable to the new ambassador, Beale, who remained unofficially attached to the Paris embassy and not as a formal secretary, kept his eyes open and ears to the ground as an intelligencer for those higher up the chain of command.

The earliest letter known to survive from Beale to Cecil is a prime example of his activity as a gatherer of intelligence in Paris during these years, but his writing directly to Cecil in 1566 was only possible because he had previously been on Cecil's radar since the investigations of Hales in 1564 and subsequently won the confidence of Smith in Paris. Beale's language in this letter suggests that he had been writing to Secretary Cecil for some time; that he signed it 'your humble servante RB' is all the more evidence of their familiarity. Because of the breadth and depth of this letter's observations, and because it represents the earliest known direct link between Beale and the most powerful man in the English government, it is worth considering at length.[38]

Beale felt a duty 'for sondry causes' to send his missive along with Fitzwilliam on the eve of the latter's departure from Paris, but he took the opportunity to write to Cecil in glowing terms of Fitzwilliam, who 'hathe ben for his wisdom, modestye[,] and sober dealing, marvelous well liked in the ffrensh court, and amongest thother Embassadors.' Moreover, despite Fitzwilliam's having been financially hamstrung while in office, he 'hathe spared no charges nor trauell to do the queen's Majesty good service, and there ys no doubt, but that yt will turne to her Majesty's contentation & his honor.' Thinking forward, Beale added, 'I praye god that his successors, may be as able to serue there Prince and countree, in contenting these fickell hedded frensh men, as he with his greate praise hath very well performed'. The current situation in France had caused significant difficulties for the English embassy because of the 'distraction & diuision of Princes and religion', such that 'to please bothe partes' the ambassador needed to

---

[37] On Hoby, *ODNB* and Edgar Powell (ed.), *The Travels and Life of Sir Thomas Hoby, Kt. of Bisham Abbey, written by Himself* (London, 1902), with the years 1564–6 at xiii–v. On the brief tenures of Hoby and Fitzwilliam, Taviner, 71–4.

[38] Beale to Cecil, November 1566, TNA, SP 70/87/675, fols 75r–6v (orig.).

'be bothe wary, witty, and circumspect'. Although Beale praised Fitzwilliam, whose religious inclinations were more aligned with Beale's than were Norris's, Beale was a little more wary of the newcomer: 'yf Mr Norrys smack[es] after the likes [i.e. leeks] and garlik of Egipt[,] as the bruite ys here, caused by some English-frensh letters, the Admirall and hole Hugonoticall faction, which he must most stick to[,] will sone smell him out.'[39] Accordingly, Beale noted the import-ance that Norris would serve Elizabeth well by holding to the Protestant line, 'for that the Papistes and Guysardes neuer bore her Majesty any good will, but haue always sought as moche as in them was her vtter destruction, and the Protestantes will deale with none whome they suspect to be of a contrary religion'. A wavering or inconstant position on which side to support was, in Beale's view, unbecoming of an ambassador representing Elizabeth, whom the Protestants took 'to be the chiefest patrone and defendour' of their cause. Moreover, the dangerous times for religion in France 'require one bothe of great wisdom, learning, and experience for that neuer were there greater practises, deceitfuller delynges, closer workinges, then be at this present: neuer more crafty and subtle persons then those which haue the rule and goucrment of this state at this tyme'. Beale further argued for the necessity of a man of experience and 'a parfaict knowledg of this comen welth', one with the ability to discern the value and truth of some reports while seeing others as less than credible: 'what ys most likely to be white and what black'.[40] In general, Beale had some hope of Norris, but he nevertheless thought 'the wisest and politickest man in England not to[o] sufficient. Ffor he shall finde matter enoughe to cumber his brayne & employe his hole wittes'. Beale ended his letter with an encomium of Fitzwilliam, whose diligence in office was noted by others, and to whom Beale was beholden because of the 'courtesy' (i.e. financial support) shown to Beale during this period (see Fig. 3).[41]

Beale's analysis of the state of affairs in France, his description of the ideal characteristics of an English ambassador based there, and the manner in which he addressed Cecil all indicate that Beale was deeply embedded within the English embassy in Paris, and that he had earned a solid place within the circle of trust. Such a feat was remarkable given the fact that, just three years previously, he was a known overseas agent for Hales, who was at the very centre of a supposed conspiracy regarding the succession. With Smith back in England, and with Fitzwilliam now departing, however, Beale felt increasingly alone and without the practical means for subsistence or theoretical means for advancement. As he tell-ingly stated to Cecil: 'for that I haue none other frend but you'.[42]

---

[39] Beale to Cecil, November 1566, TNA, SP 70/87/675, quotations at fol. 75r (orig.).
[40] Beale to Cecil, November 1566, TNA, SP 70/87/675, quotations at fol. 75v (orig.).
[41] Beale to Cecil, November 1566, TNA, SP 70/87/675, quotations at fol. 76r (orig.). NB: The 'RB' serving as Beale's signature resembles the design of his later wax seal, as seen on the cover of this book.
[42] Beale to Cecil, November 1566, TNA, SP 70/87/675, quotations at fol. 76r (orig.).

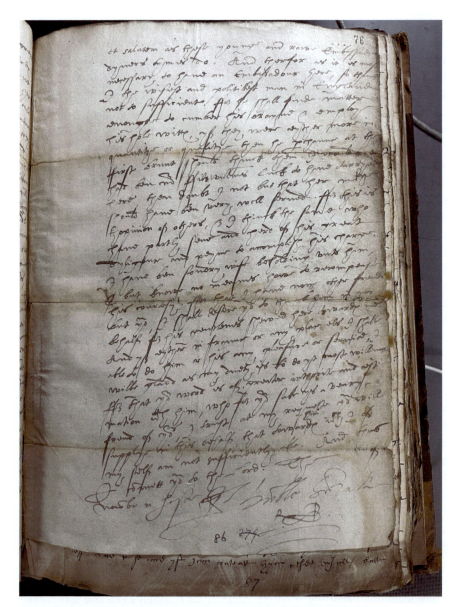

Fig. 3 Beale to William Cecil, November 1566. TNA, SP 70/87/675, fol. 76r (orig.).
Reproduced with permission from The National Archives.

Prior to Norris's employment in Paris, he had attended Elizabeth at court and his family had established themselves as loyal servants of the queen. Despite rumours to the contrary, he was known to be a strong supporter of the Protestant cause in France during the second and third wars of religion from 1567 to 1570, so much so that the French royal family did not trust him in Paris, and his post was frequently inspected by the authorities. Beale, remaining as a servant and informal intelligencer, would have recognized the sea-change in tension since the relatively halcyon days of Thomas Smith's tenure. Smith, of course, returned to France on a special embassy to try negotiating the return of Calais, and Beale did acquire copies of some of Smiths' and Norris's materials, but it does not appear that Beale and Smith were able to reunite on this occasion.[43] Others within the Paris embassy, however, included Daniel Rogers, the Wittenberg-born Marian exile who served as tutor to Norris's children and would become an important colleague of Beale regarding German and Danish policy. Apart from his teaching duties, Rogers spent much of his time during the 1560s writing poetry and getting to know many of the scholarly luminaries within the city and farther afield.[44] Outside the embassy but still in Paris were other key figures known to Beale from years past, most notably Languet as ambassador of the elector of Saxony and Bauduin as a re-converted Catholic with irenic ideals and ecumenist dreams soon to be dashed by the wars of religion.[45] In the coming years Languet became an increasingly good friend, even mentor of Beale, and the two came to share many of the same ideological positions regarding the Protestant cause as well as practical sensibilities when it came to religious diplomacy. By the second and third wars of religion in France, on the other hand, Beale and Bauduin had, despite their shared legal and historical interests, diverged in religious inclinations to a marked degree: while Bauduin sought concord and peace by way of Protestants' return to Catholicism, Beale increasingly saw the world in black and white, with forces of good defending themselves against evil oppressors. Also in Paris at this time, and of increasing importance to Beale's appreciation for printed works, was the great publisher André Wechel—a known quantity among Englishmen in Paris, and to Languet and Bauduin—who would later print a collection of Spanish works taken directly from Beale's own personal library.[46]

During the first years of the Norris embassy, Beale remained based in Paris but kept his eye out for ways to offer service by way of gathering intelligence—especially on German affairs. Some have speculated without evidence that, during his years in Paris, Beale's duties 'seem to have sometimes carried him into Germany', or that 'every now and then [he] visited the German courts'.[47] Whether

[43] BL, Additional MSS 48023, fols 340r–9r; 48024, fols 178r–213v, esp. 209v–13v.
[44] Convenient overviews of Norris and Rogers in *ODNB*. On Rogers in Paris, J. A. van Dorsten, *Poets, Patrons, and Professors: Sir Philip Sidney, Daniel Rogers, and the Leiden Humanists* (Leiden, 1962), 12–18.
[45] Nicollier-de Weck, *Hubert Languet*, 176–93. Erbe, *François Bauduin*, 122–74. On Bauduin's role in France, see Van Tol, *Germany and the French Wars of Religion*, 93, 122, 128–9 142.
[46] See above, Chapter 2, n. 44. Cf. Taviner, 64 n. 48, citing Languet's letter to Buchanan in which he also names Carolus Clusius (Charles de L'Écluse) among others as associates at Wechel's. Clusius may have been named in Beale's later work, 'the State of Germany', on which see below.
[47] 'Beale, Robert', Leslie Stephen (ed.), *Dictionary of National Biography* (London, 1885), 4.3. Kouri, *England and the Attempts to Form a Protestant Alliance*, 176, clearly following the former account.

he continued his personal travels around Germany is unknown, but it is clear enough that he had access to information, which he could then relay to London. Three examples of this practice survive; Beale sent his dispatches initially to Hales, who then relayed them to Cecil. Why Beale did not send directly to Cecil is unclear, though it may be explained by Cecil's desire for discretion or by the change within the Paris embassy. Quite simply, Beale does not seem to have gotten along with Norris as well as he had with Smith, and sending directly to Cecil would have been to bypass—thus undermining—Norris's authority.

On 18 April 1567, Beale wrote an update of 'occurences' for Hales, signing off as 'your humble seruante, Robert Beale', but his valediction and signature were later struck through rather vigorously by someone in London, as was 'Hales' on the address leaf; the scribbled 'Furbysher' over 'Hales' looks suspiciously like Cecil's hand at work and may indicate an effort by Cecil to protect Beale from the political consequences of an association with Hales. In any event, Beale began with a foreboding tone: 'Sithe Sr Thomas Smithes coming, we be all put in feare, that we shall haue warre with fraunce for the restitution of Calays, which will neuer be but by warfare.' Worse still, the French king's party, continued Beale, moved to 'flatter king Philip [of Spain] as moche as they may, hoping to haue him a frend or neuter in this cause', and in consequence, along with other reasons, the Huguenot leadership, especially Admiral Gaspard de Coligny and his brother, François d'Andelot, shared the same sentiments as the English: 'both they and we be all afraid'.[48] With one eye seeing that Catholic forces in France were making 'great preparations of horses and armes', and another eye on the Low Countries, Beale relayed a sentiment shared by many, that is, 'the Hugonots thinck that when flaundres ys ones conquered, they shall not be long in peace onles they fall out with some third, for that the king [of France] is cruelly bent against them, and will[,] as yt is thought[,] vse the king of spains force and councell therto.' After noting the pope's excommunication of the Protestant Jeanne d'Albret, Queen of Navarre, and military preparations in Swiss lands, Beale concluded by noting that the siege of Gotha in eastern Germany continued, and that ambassadors were rumoured to have been sent to Johann Friedrich, duke of Saxony, with money to help support his cause.[49] Linguistic clues like 'Gotha is still besieged' suggest that previous updates from Beale to Hales (and, indirectly, Cecil) do not survive, but it is clear from this example that Beale continued to see his role as that of informant for those higher up the political chain of command, those who could shape policy, those who might reward him for his services. Equally clear is that Beale saw the wars of religion in France and the Low Countries as intimately connected to the

---

[48]   Beale to Hales, 18 April 1567, TNA, SP 70/89, fols 161r–2v, with quotations at 161r (orig.); without author or address in *CSPF*, Vol. 8, item 1111.

[49]   Beale to Hales, 18 April 1567, TNA, SP 70/89, quotations at 161v (orig.). The siege of Gotha was a major event in the Empire, and Beale kept an eye on it later in 1569, recording an update in 'the State of Germany', on which, see below and Gehring, *Diplomatic Intelligence*, on Gotha on 76, 79–85.

wider cause of Protestants across Europe, England very much included. His dedication to, and firm advocacy for, the cause by this point must be seen as distinct from any later influence by those often seen as champions of the Protestant cause: Walsingham and Leicester. Rather, Beale's mind had been conditioned by his own exile, peregrinations, educational pursuits, and family connections via Morison and Hales. In 1566, Beale had nothing to do with Walsingham and Leicester.

The next surviving update to Hales in Beale's hand was on 16 September 1567, again with Hales's name furiously struck through in a hand suspiciously resembling Cecil's; this time Beale wisely omitted signing his name, probably because he had been told to do so. Longer than the missive of April, this letter advises of Guisard 'machinations' against the Huguenots and various movements of forces, but particularly telling in Beale's description of French news is that he has gathered three different opinions on the state of affairs. Knowing that news reports and opinions were as stable as shifting sands, and that supplying only one perspective could lead to bad policy decisions, Beale tried to collate as much information as possible before sending back to London where the powers that were could make more informed decisions.[50] He went on to describe the general sense of unease and fear among Protestants 'in this towne' (Paris) and concluded by relaying news that the counts of Egmont and Hoorn had been arrested in Brussels, '[a]nd yf things go so well forward on [the papists'] side as they hope, fraunce can not be in quiet long.'[51] Again, Beale's principal news came from Paris and wider France, but he sought news from farther afield because he understood that what happened in Paris was connected to what happened in Brussels, what in France to what in the Low Countries.

The third surviving update by Beale is dated 15 January 1568, and, again, remained unsigned. The first and final folios have been lost, but one can reasonably suppose that the first subjects addressed in the letter were, as before, affairs immediate to Paris, and that it was sent to Hales and by association Cecil. Despite the pages lacking, this account is far and away the longest of Beale's three. In what remains, Beale comments on the embassy of Thomas Radcliffe, earl of Sussex, to Vienna regarding the ongoing marriage negotiations between Elizabeth and Charles, archduke of Austria, noting that expectations had 'couled, and thought here not like to go forward.'[52] More worthy of report, however, was that Beale's hope for the Huguenots was waning, and he thought

---

[50] Beale to Hales, 16 September 1567, TNA, SP 70/94, fols 35r–6v, at 35r (orig.); calendared without attribution to Beale, mistaking Hales's name for 'W. Haddon', CSPF, Vol. 8, item 1692. Lack of clear information and the abundance of rumour were key themes of reports sent from the English embassy at Paris. See, for example, Fitzwilliam to Cecil, 19 October 1566, TNA, SP 70/86, fols 123r–5v (orig.).

[51] Beale to Hales, 16 September 1567, TNA, SP 70/94, fols 35v–6r (orig.).

[52] Beale to Hales?, 15 January 1568, TNA, SP 70/96, fols 65r–6v, at 65r (orig.); without attribution in CSPF, Vol. 8, item 1947. On the negotiations, the treatment in Susan Doran, 'Religion and Politics at the Court of Elizabeth I: The Habsburg Marriage Negotiations of 1559–1567', The English Historical Review, 104:413 (1989), 908–26, is best compared with the detailed study using archives in Austria

[a] good peace were most necessary for bothe parts, *sine vincant, sine vincatur*
[without defeating, without being defeated], the realme is spoiled and vndon.
[...] And yt is to be feared lest the king of spaine at the last become master of
them bothe, who ys only author and contynewere of all this mischief: whew
other princes should also haue some regard, lest in tyme he attempt the like in
other places.

Beale's foresight here regarding Spanish involvement in the French wars of religion is significant, but so too was his recommendation that the Huguenots 'ioyne
with the Prince of Orange and other of the lowe country against the Spainiards, to
obtene like liberty of religion'.[53]

Also, due to his experience in Germany, Beale commented on German involvement in support of the Huguenots, however limited it may have been, noting also
that the king of France was 'content to admitt [the Elector Palatine] arbiter of the
hole cauce' in France.[54] Among the German princes, the electors of the Palatinate
and Saxony were the most powerful and influential on the side of the French
Protestants, Beale recognized, and he saw value in the duke of Württemberg, who
relayed to the other princes information regarding potential harm to Protestants
and 'publisheth in every corner'. As for the rest, in Beale's view, they 'be *plane
tepidi* [clearly lukewarm], for that to say the truthe, there ys at this present no
feruor or constancy of relligion almost left in Germany. They suffer them selfs to
be eluded by [their] good Emperor, and mony is theyr only god'. Indeed, Beale
continued by pointing out those German princes who served the kings of France
and Spain as pensioners loath to lose their pensions (Johann Wilhelm, duke of
Saxony-Weimar; Eric, duke of Brunswick). Due to what appeared to be 'the general danger of the ruyne of relligion in Christendom', Beale's tone was downtrodden regarding the prospects of Protestants in Paris and elsewhere.[55] His solution
moving forward, and given the fact that England was under threat from Catholics
looking to overthrow the state, was that, '[a]s the papists haue theiyr ligue, so
were yt not amiss that the princes protestants for theyr defence had the like';
moreover, '[i]t wold do some good to [instill] feare [in] thother [side], in shewing
they had no default of corage'. Nevertheless, he admitted that the 'princes agre not
very well about relligion', offering the example of the dukes of Württemberg and
Zweibrücken as opposed to the Elector Palatine, and noting further that the lesser
princes 'are poore and of small authority, and they all suffer them selfs to be fedd

and Germany, Kurt Diemer, 'Die Heiratsverhandlungen zwischen Königin Elisabeth I. von England
und Erzherzog Karl von Innerösterreich 1558–1570', PhD thesis, University of Tübingen, 1969.

[53] Beale to Hales?, 15 January 1568, TNA, SP 70/96, fol. 65v (orig.).

[54] Beale to Hales?, 15 January 1568, TNA, SP 70/96, fol. 65v (orig.). On German involvement in
France during these years, see Van Tol, *Germany and the French Wars of Religion*; Jonas van Tol,
'Religion or Rebellion? Justifying the French Wars of Religion and Dutch Revolt to German
Protestants', *The Sixteenth Century Journal*, 51 (2020), 445–64.

[55] Beale to Hales?, 15 January 1568, TNA, SP 70/96, fol. 66r (orig.).

with faire wordes, and neuer will preuent the danger tyll the fire come to theyr owne houses.'[56]

Beale concluded with a few comments on the Turkish threat and the Muscovites' activity in the eastern Baltic and Poland, though he admitted that his intelligence on Denmark and Sweden was thin at the moment. The central thrust of these three updates, and probably any that do not survive, however, was that the troubles of the Huguenots in France were not isolated but rather were part of a wider international programme spearheaded by Philip, king of Spain, and the pope in Rome. Situated directly in the epicentre of intelligence gathering for European Protestants during the second and third wars of religion in France, Beale was keenly and fearfully aware of the threats to international Protestantism, but he nevertheless continued to hope. In consequence, his previous allegiance to a broad rather than narrow Protestant Church—the Bucerian tradition in Strasbourg or the Philippism of Wittenberg and Heidelberg over the strictures of Zurich or the Gnesio-Lutheranism of Jena—fed directly into his call for religious alliance across France, the Low Countries, Germany, and, indeed, England.[57] By 1568, Beale's intellectual pedigree largely stemmed from Germanic origins; his informal diplomatic experience included his shadowing of both ambassadors extraordinary (Knolles) and resident (Smith, Hoby, Fitzwilliam as chargé d'affaires, and Norris); and his detailed knowledge and developed understanding of international politics and religion was principally focused on French and German affairs. In July 1568, an opportunity started to open when the Elector Palatine, Friedrich III, laid plans for an embassy to Queen Elizabeth to encourage her to send a representative to Germany with a view to providing aid to Protestants in France and building a Protestant league.[58]

In response, Elizabeth sent that diplomatic veteran of ten years previously in Germany, Henry Killigrew, to discuss both the immediate issue of funding an army to be sent into France under Friedrich's second son, Johann Casimir, and a long-term resolution for a Protestant league. The practical and theoretical difficulties experienced by Killigrew on his way to Hamburg, then to Heidelberg, back to Hamburg, then to Dresden, and back to England have been surveyed and exhaustively detailed, but Beale's involvement has not.[59] Shortly after the Palatine embassy to London in December 1568, he probably learned from Norris of the English plans to send an embassy to Heidelberg; Norris had been corresponding

---

[56] Beale to Hales?, 15 January 1568, TNA, SP 70/96, fol. 66v (orig.).

[57] Jewel's *Apologia* and other strands in the Elizabethan Church espoused similarly inclusive ideas. For discussion, see Diarmaid MacCulloch, 'The Latitude of the Church of England', in Kenneth Fincham and Peter Lake (eds), *Religious Politics in Post-Reformation England* (Woodbridge, 2006), 41–59.

[58] Friedrich to Elizabeth, 12 July 1568, BL, Cotton MS Vespasian, F. III, fol. 148r (orig.). Report on a council meeting, 14 July 1568, in Kluckhohn, *Briefe Friedrich des Frommen*, Vol. 2, Part 1, pp. 234–5.

[59] Miller, *Sir Henry Killigrew*, 101–22. Kouri, *England and the Attempts*, esp. 86–132. On Beale's role, preliminary thoughts were offered in Gehring, *Diplomatic Intelligence*.

with those back in England on the Palatine negotiations.[60] Whether via Norris or his own channels of information from Germany, Beale knew that the upcoming English embassy to Germany was exactly what he had previously hoped and called for.

Before Killigrew reached Heidelberg on 31 March 1569, Beale had been there for probably more than a month. Equally important was the fact that a friend of Languet, Louis Frennes, Seigneur de Lumbres (or Lambres), knew that Beale was there and sent him a letter dated 11 February from Frankfurt.[61] Lumbres, a paid agent of William of Orange and who had been in Heidelberg previously in 1568, was also working along the same lines as Killigrew would. Because both Killigrew and various Germans thought Lumbres was actually a Huguenot, the confessional conflicts in France and the Netherlands became increasingly blurred on the one hand but less important on the other because many—Beale very much included— saw the individual areas of battle as parts of a greater theatre of war. Probably rather comfortable in a place he knew formerly, Beale remained in Heidelberg through April, and it is clear that he and Lumbres built up something of a relationship in correspondence between Heidelberg and Frankfurt because Lumbres thanked Beale for various favours in a letter of 17 April.[62]

Also in Frankfurt was Languet, who wrote to Beale on 21 May with a full update of intelligence on French and Dutch affairs (including the death of the prince of Condé), the duke of Zweibrücken's military aid to the Huguenots, the anticipated arrival of the English fleet in Hamburg, and the recently agreed (if temporary) peace between Denmark and Sweden. Some of this information came from Lodovico Guicciardini, who had recently published a description of the Low Countries, and whom Languet thought was known to Beale ('*quem puto tibi notum*'). Languet relayed that he had recently met in Mainz with Killigrew, who then continued north to Hamburg to meet the fleet, and that Lumbres had recently left Hamburg after having been with Killigrew. Equally if not more important than the content of the letter, however, was that Languet addressed his letter to Beale in '*Heidelbergae apud clariss. Dn Doct Zanchium*', that is at the home of Girolamo Zanchi, the renowned and Reformed Italian minister who had taken up a position as Professor of Theology at the University of Heidelberg in January 1568 (see Fig. 4).[63]

---

[60] *AGR*, 176 n. 44.

[61] Lumbres to Beale, 11 February 1569, AUL, MS 1009/1, item 22, noting Languet (orig.). On Languet and Lumbres, Nicollier-de Weck, *Hubert Languet*, 225 n. 72. On Lumbres's activities, Kouri, *England and the Attempts*, 43–4, 91, 105.

[62] Lumbres to Beale, 17 April 1569, BYU, MS 457, item 1 (orig.). Lumbres was also in contact with Killigrew, but the latter makes no reference to Beale in his correspondence with Cecil in TNA, SP 70 or to Leicester in Magdalen College, Cambridge, MS PL 2503, 257–63, 279, 281–3, 293–7, 331 (all orig.).

[63] Languet to Beale, 21 May 1569, BL, Egerton MS 1693, fol. 3r–v (orig.); date of 'duod. Cal. Jun. 1569' rendered accurately in Nicollier-de Weck, *Hubert Languet*, 531, erroneously as 12 June in Taviner, 65. On Zanchi's difficulties in Strasbourg, see James M. Kittleson, 'Marbach vs. Zanchi: The Resolution of Controversy in Late Reformation Strasbourg', *Sixteenth Century Journal*, 8 (1977), 31–44; for a brief biography, Otto Gründler, 'Zanchi, Girolamo', in Hillerbrand, *Oxford Encyclopedia of the Reformation*.

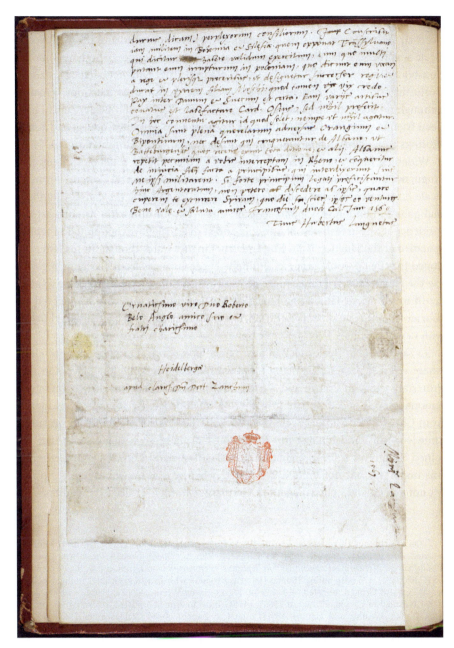

Fig. 4 Hubert Languet to Beale, 21 May 1569. BL, Egerton MS 1693, fol. 3v (orig.).
Reproduced with permission from the British Library.

Zanchi had studied under Peter Martyr Vermigli in Lucca as a child and had been an instructor at Sturm's Gymnasium in Strasbourg during the very years Beale was there. Additionally, Zanchi was known to Languet, who had come to Strasbourg in winter 1562–3, so it seems plausible that Languet had suggested to Beale that he stay at Zanchi's house given the personal connections. Finally, although no previous link has been found between Zanchi and Beale, Zanchi had been friends with Thomas Wrothe and Anthony Cooke in Strasbourg, had some dealings with Henry Knolles, and had corresponded with Edmund Grindal.[64]

Widening Beale's network of contacts still further, in June Odet de Coligny, the Huguenot former cardinal de Châtillon and brother of Admiral Coligny, wrote to Beale having heard from Lumbres of Beale's desire to serve the cause. Châtillon had gone to London in 1568 to seek aid directly from Elizabeth; he soon set up residence at Sheen just west of London, and early in 1569 was appointed as representative of the Huguenots in England. Looking forward, though, in his letter he hoped that Beale would serve as an intelligencer for news from Germany regarding the Huguenots or France more generally. Additionally, he asked Beale to give credit to Monsieur Guillaume Stuart de Vézines, the bearer, who had served as courier from the Huguenots to Elizabeth earlier that year and later supplied Beale with news from elsewhere.[65]

To say the least, Beale's lack of any official position in Paris, London, or elsewhere did not prevent his being a known quantity to some key players in the Protestant cause in France and western Germany, and this was due to his international travels and expertise in gathering intelligence. By summer 1569, apart from Christopher Mundt, Beale was probably the English asset with the greatest knowledge of—and interest in—Protestant Germany, so it made sense that he joined Killigrew's train in Heidelberg. Beale's first-hand knowledge of Germany was important but not unique. No matter what he did, he would never replace Mundt as England's official agent in Germany. Mundt's service extended back to

[64] On Zanchi and Languet, Nicollier-de Weck, *Hubert Languet*, 150, 225–7. Zanchi to Knolles, undated but probably August 1564, in Girolamo Zanchi, *Opera Omnia Theologica: Opervm Theologicorvm D Hieronymi Zanchii, Tomus Septimus, Epistolarvm Libri Dvo* (Geneva, 1619) (possibly USTC 6700274), 125 (also noting Thomas Heton as a friend), with Zanchi to Grindal, noting Knolles, at 124–5; cf. to Grindal, undated, 133, 139–40 (again noting Wrothe, Cooke, Heton, and Knolles), 140–1 (Grindal to Zanchi, 23 August 1563), 141 (Grindal to Zanchi, undated, returning salutations from Cooke, Wrothe, and Heton), 159 (Languet to Zanchi, dated 27 December 1562), 167–8 (to Walsingham, 14 September 1581), 181 (to John Jewel, 11 September 1571).
[65] Châtillon to Beale, 10 June 1569, BL, Egerton MS 1693, fol. 4r–v (orig.). On the Cardinal, see E. G. Atkinson, 'The Cardinal of Châtillon in England, 1568–71', *Proceedings of the Huguenot Society of London*, 3, for 1888–92 (London, 1892), 172–285, on the letter to Beale at 225. Vézines noted as the bearer in letters to Elizabeth from the queen of Navarre, prince of Navarre, and Admiral Coligny, 1–2 February 1569, *CSPF*, Vol. 9, items 92–4. Vézines to Beale, 20 September 1569, BL, Additional MS 5935, fol. 64r–v. On Vézines's activity at this time, Hugues Daussy, 'London, Nerve Centre of the Huguenot Diplomatic Network in the Later Sixteenth Century', in Vivienne Larminie (ed.), *Huguenot Networks, 1560–1780: The Interactions and Impact of a Protestant Minority in Europe* (New York, 2018), 29–40, at 34.

the reign of Henry VIII and he was a known, trusted entity to the German princes. At best, while Mundt lived, Beale could hope that his own intelligence reports could supplement Mundt's during the sometimes long gaps between the latter's reports.[66] In any event, from Heidelberg, Beale and Killigrew's train travelled to Dresden to meet with August, elector of Saxony, to continue negotiations. Even though Beale was again not included in any official documentation or credence from Elizabeth, he gained an insider's view of both the Palatine and Saxon electoral residences and courts. Reminiscent of his activity in 1563, as if Beale was looking ahead and with a view to securing a position within the English government, he wrote a discourse that summer and autumn entitled 'the State of Germany'.[67]

This work offered an overview of the political and administrative structures in the Holy Roman Empire such as the system of spiritual and temporal electors and the powers of the free cities, but it also named princes, noted sources of revenue, and included a lengthy transcription of an earlier printed work itemizing the contributions of princes and free cities to the war effort against the Turk. In many respects, the work resembles the form and outline of an Italian *relazione*, which classic diplomatic document Beale knew (or came to know) very well. Indeed, he collected several *relazioni*, some of which predate 'the State of Germany' and focus on England in particular.[68] Of particular focus in the treatise are Heidelberg and Dresden, not only because Friedrich III and August were the most powerful secular electors in the Empire, but also since Beale was a familiar entity in Heidelberg and could shadow Killigrew in Dresden. Several details from Beale's treatise are worth pointing out because they illuminate his experience and thinking at the time.

On the religion practised in Germany, Beale noted that there were Catholics, Lutherans, and 'Calvinists' 'as they terme it'. He clearly inclined more towards the Reformed situation in the Palatinate than the Lutheranism found elsewhere, and he even made a favourable comparison between Queen Elizabeth's Church and

---

[66] On Mundt, with an emphasis on his earlier career, see Esther Hildebrandt, 'Christopher Mont: Anglo-German Diplomat', *Sixteenth Century Journal*, 15 (1984), 281–92; on a later moment in 1566, Jonas Bechtold, 'Divergierende Formalitätszuschreibungen und die Skalierbarkeit (in)formeller Akteure der Diplomatie: Christopher Mundt als englischer Gesandter am Reichstag 1566', *Frühneuzeit-Info*, 33 (2022), 17–31.

[67] Included in Gehring, *Diplomatic Intelligence*, 51–108, with discussion of authorship, 11–16; with appendix on *Türkenhilfe*, 219–51.

[68] On 'the State of Germany' as a *relazione*, Gehring, *Diplomatic Intelligence*, 34–9. Beale's collection of *relazioni*, BL, Additional MS 48080, with examples from 1569 or earlier at fols 107r–33v, 171r–90v, 271r–83v, 285r–95v. The first two examples Beale acquired from Petruccio Ubaldini in or after 1587, while the third and fourth might have been acquired earlier. Either way, the structure and style of 'the State of Germany' strongly suggest Beale's familiarity with the genre of *relazioni* by 1569. On Ubaldini, see Chapter 6. The regional and local knowledge Beale included was vast and spread across considerable lands, confessions, and personalities. For convenience, see the modern reference work, Anton Schindling and Walter Ziegler (eds), *Die Territorien des Reichs im Zeitalter der Reformation und Konfessionalisierung: Land und Konfession 1500–1650*, 7 vols (Münster, 1989–97).

Friedrich's reformation of the Palatinate: 'The gospell is sinceerelie preached, Images, and other superstitious Ceremonies (which the Lutherans throughout all Germany besides yet vse[)], were Abollished, and the Sacramentes aswell Mynistred, as presentlie in the Church of England.'[69] In addition, Beale's differentiations between different groups of Lutherans was telling and harked back to his earlier years and association with Hales and Aylmer because he contrasted the hard-line attitudes of Gnesio-Lutherans like Matthias Flacius Illyricus and others at Jena (on, e.g. salvation, works, and *adiaphora*) with those of Philippists like Georg Maior and others at Wittenberg.[70] Beale's observations on judicial practice and 'civilians' (i.e. civil lawyers), especially at Heidelberg and in the *Reichskammergericht* at Speyer, reflected his own learning and experience.[71] His assessments of Friedrich and August were often minute and demonstrated the fact that he had significant levels of private access, including admission into the mines of Saxony and August's armoury (the means and display of the elector's wealth). For example, Beale descended into a mine on 21 June 1569 with Killigrew and Christoph Ehem, the councillor of Elector Friedrich, and recorded the technological knowledge in practice that he witnessed. Given Beale's later discourse for Thomas Smith on the mining works in northern England, and his recommendation of German techniques used in Saxony, his experience with Killigrew and Ehem was significant at the time and for the future.[72] Finally, and just as he had in his letter of 15 January 1568, Beale noted certain Lutheran princes who sided with the Spanish and French kings 'against them of the Religion', and again he singled out Johann Wilhelm of Saxony-Weimar's activity 'in the second Civill Warres in ffraunce'.[73]

Such a lengthy, detailed assessment on the political and religious situation in Germany was unprecedented in England, notwithstanding Roger Ascham's work written as a series of intelligence reports during the 1550s and later published about 1570.[74] No previous agent or ambassador, formal or informal, had assembled a snapshot like Beale's, nor would any in the future for decades to come. Like his discourses on the Suffolk and Hertford marriages, 'the State of Germany' was an exercise demonstrating depth of knowledge and breadth of understanding across a range of issues relevant to English policy both domestic and foreign.

---

[69] 'The State of Germany', *Diplomatic Intelligence*, ed. Gehring, 66–7.

[70] 'The State of Germany', 104–5, on religion more generally, 98–106.

[71] 'The State of Germany', 59–60, 87, 95–6. Beale's notes, 1563, BL, Cotton MS Nero, B. IX, fols 4r–5r, 7r–18v.

[72] 'The State of Germany', 63–8 (on Friedrich), 76–9 (on August), 71–6 (on mining and the armoury), 72–4 (on the Freiberg mine). Beale's discourse on mines for Smith, 1573, BL, Additional MS 48020, fols 259r–62r.

[73] 'The State of Germany', 100–1; cf. Beale to Hales?, 15 January 1568, TNA, SP 70/96, fols 65r–6v, at 66r (orig.). On Johann Wilhelm's principles in siding with the French king, see Van Tol, *Germany and the French Wars of Religion*, 207–14.

[74] On the relationship between Ascham's *A Report and Discourse* and Beale's 'state of Germany', see Gehring, *Diplomatic Intelligence*, 24–5.

In 1563, Beale's primary audience consisted of Hertford, Grey, and Hales; and despite the fact that he accomplished his task with clarity and celerity, he was never fully compensated for his troubles. In 1569, however, Beale's primary audience was undoubtedly William Cecil, whom Beale once thought was his only friend, to whom he had written updates previously, and on whom he came to rely. The motivation is clear because such an exposition of Beale's powers of observation and intelligence gathering was of significant value to the English government, so Beale's ultimate goal in writing 'the State of Germany' was, without question, to gain more secure and formal employment within the Elizabethan regime. The work was, in effect, his pitch to Cecil, who subsequently recognized the enormous value of such a synoptic discourse written by those who travelled across the seas. When, in January 1571, Cecil offered travel advice to the young Edward Manners, earl of Rutland, he directed him to record the same types of features in France as had Beale in Germany.[75]

By September 1569, Beale was again in the Palatinate with Ehem, while Killigrew was back in England. As noted previously, Beale was nominated by Ehem to carry the missives from Elector Friedrich to London, but one can now see why. Beale proved himself worthy that summer. He clearly had facility in all of the necessary languages (German, French, Latin), and he had learned the practice of diplomacy by shadowing ambassadors: Knolles in 1562, Smith and others from 1564 to 1568, and Killigrew and Ehem in 1569. Back in England in October, Beale's life would soon change significantly and irrevocably. He remained in correspondence with Ehem and Châtillon (and the cardinal's servant or secretary, a certain Dupin or de Pin) in the immediate aftermath of his return to London, possibly even staying at the house of William Paulet, marquess of Winchester and lord treasurer, because he did not have a place of his own or family on which to rely.[76] Unsurprisingly, he also stayed in touch with Languet, who wrote updates from Frankfurt and Speyer with news on German affairs, including theological disputes concerning Flacius in Saxony, signing off as 'yours most affectionate' ('*Tuj amantissimus*').[77] Regarding his move from Paris, via Germany, to London, Beale's friend in Paris John Herbert wrote to London in August 1570 with an

---

[75] Cecil to Rutland, 20 January 1571, TNA, SP 12/77/6, draft in a poor state, printed in Sarah Warneke, *Images of the Educational Traveller in Early Modern England* (Leiden, 1994), 295–8. Beale and Rutland later became close. See Chapter 6. For other travellers' reports later in the reign, such as those by Stephen Powle, see Popper, *Specter of the Archive*, ch. 1. For such reports and their relation to other genres, Gehring, 'Intelligence Gathering', 211–32.

[76] Châtillon to Beale, 2 February 1570, AUL, MS 1009/2, item 16 (orig.), noting also a letter from Strasbourg from Mundt. Dupin to Beale, 22 February 1570 (from Sheen), AUL, MS 1009/2, item 45 (orig.). Dupin's activity noted in Atkinson, 'Cardinal of Châtillon in England', 240, 258; CSPF, Vol. 9, items 423, 1705, 1835; Vol. 10, item 499. Dupin addressed his letter to Beale 'de la maison de Monsieur le grand tresorier'. Cf. Beale's copies of some of Winchester's materials, BL, Additional MS 48007, fols 10v–11r, 167v, 174v–5r.

[77] Languet to Beale, 27 March (sexto Calend. April) 1570, 5 November (Nonis Nouemb.) 1570, BL, Egerton MS 1693, fols 5r–v, 6r–v (both orig.).

update on the state of the Huguenots in France and the duke of Alba's activity in the Low Countries. Herbert also recorded 'what diligence I haue vsed in solliciting your affaires', notwithstanding his difficulty in speaking with the wife of François Bauduin on Beale's behalf, 'but nothing makes me so much to wondre as that D. [François] Baldwyn caryed such parcells of your stuffe as he had at Paris, as they once confessed the tronck to be half full, to Angiers, considering the charges of conveyeing the same to and fro, yf he meane to restore the sayed parcells.' Herbert added that he had lost Beale's maps, and that he was unable to purchase the new book of Abraham Ortelius (i.e. his monumental atlas, *Theatrum Orbis Terrarum*) due to the high price.[78] Thus Beale's activity in Germany and journey to London, in so far as he hoped it would open new doors of opportunity, cost him because he lost some of the materials in his evolving archive of political papers and books. Beale's materials must have been recognizably valuable for, after all, why else would Bauduin have paid to have them moved long distances across France? How many of Beale's parcels Bauduin took is unknown, as are their size and contents, but at one point Bauduin did admit to Beale that Beale's papers were in his possession. Little remains of what was probably a fairly large and long-standing correspondence. From what we can tell, though, in 1569 Bauduin moved from Paris via Besançon (eastern France) in summer to Angers (western France) in the autumn, and during his journey he was clearly unaware of Beale's exact whereabouts, sending for example his letters of 15 September 1569 and 23 February 1570 from Angers to Beale in Paris at the lodgings of Herbert, 'gentilhome Anglois'.[79] Beale's correspondence with Bauduin at this time brought other Englishmen into the mix, such as a certain Mr George Paindavaine and Thomas Wrothe, who had been at Strasbourg during the mid 1550s with Beale, Cooke, and the others. No other links have yet come to light between Beale and Wrothe, whose life after returning to England in winter 1558–9 was characterized by his role as MP and his being something of a specialist on Germany.[80]

---

[78] Herbert to Beale, 9 August 1570, AUL, MS 1009/2, item 22, quotations at 1r (orig.). Herbert later led an embassy to the Netherlands in 1576 (preceding Beale's own) and joined Beale as clerk of the Privy Council in 1590 and as commissioner to treat with Spain in 1600. See Chapter 8 and *ODNB*, *HoP:HoC*, and Gary McClellan Bell, 'The Men and their Rewards in Elizabethan Diplomatic Service, 1558–1585', PhD thesis, University of California, Los Angeles, 1974, 273–9, which includes notice of Herbert's time in France during the 1560s while the entries in the *ODNB* and *HoP:HoC* do not.

[79] Bauduin to Beale, 15 September 1569, 23 February 1570, AUL, MS 1009/2, items 37, 36 (both orig.); Bauduin's admission, 'voz papiers chez moy', at item 36, fol. 1v. On Bauduin's final years, Erbe, *François Bauduin*, 175–85.

[80] Bauduin to Beale, 8 April 1570, 4 July 1570, AUL, MS 1009/2, items 35, 38 (both orig.), the former with reference to both Paindavaine and Wrothe, the latter with reference to both along with a quittance for Bauduin and 'Mr George Paindavaine' dated 25 October 1558 and an additional note on Bauduin's wife in Heidelberg. On Wrothe, Garrett, *Marian Exiles*, 344–6; *HoP:HoC*.

Looking Back, Looking Forward

Beale's experience from 1563 to 1569 and later was an ever-expanding plot of travel and potential opportunity in which he was often frustrated and let down by others but also proved himself to be remarkably adaptive and self-reliant. The cast of characters during these years (as well as the years ahead) included some recurring figures—Englishmen like Henry Killigrew, Frenchmen like Bauduin, Germans like Sturm, and Frenchmen in Germany like Languet. In winter 1569–70, Beale was roughly twenty-nine years old and was well schooled and experienced in law, politics, and religion on many levels. He could look back on his life to that point with a sense of accomplishment in qualitative terms but not yet in quantitative terms by way of real job security or financial comfort. Granted, in 1561 he had been instituted as prebend of Ufton Cantoris in Coventry and Lichfield diocese with a valuation of £2. 13. 4., but there is no way of knowing how or whether Beale had access to that comparatively minor income.[81] His adult life thus far had been spent almost exclusively in the Holy Roman Empire and France, and by working outward from the exposure provided previously by Morison and Hales, he had been able to build an extended network of associates and friends who could keep him informed of matters elsewhere.

Many of Beale's contacts continued to provide streams of intelligence and friendly connections for years to come. On a personal level, he was indebted to those who showed him kindness and offered him shelter during the lean years between 1554 and 1570, so when he recalled these experiences later in life, he did so because these people and places continued to matter to him. On an intellectual level, Beale was a European Protestant. His schooling started at the grammar school established by Hales in Coventry, but then it continued at Sturm's in Strasbourg and with others in Zurich, Wittenberg, and—almost certainly—Heidelberg. His was a technical and specific mind, but he could also step back from the minutiae to see the broader picture, to get a sense of why the details mattered. His writings both short and long testify as much. By way of religion, he was anti-Catholic first because of his exile under Queen Mary but then, more importantly, because he understood Catholic attacks on Protestants to be connected parts of a wider plan to exterminate those of 'the true religion'. Securing a Protestant succession should Elizabeth die childless was vital to Beale's personal wellbeing as well as the broader Protestant International, as was the security of Protestants in France and the Low Countries. Religion and politics were inseparable during this age, as the first historian of the Reformation, Johann Sleidan, knew all too well and whose great work was translated into English soon after its initial publication at Strasbourg: 'And in describing matters of Religion, I might

---

[81] See Chapter 2, n. 65.

not omitte politique causes. For [...] they came in maner always together, and especially in our tyme they could not be separated.' Beale cited Sleidan's history of the Reformation in 'the State of Germany' and appears to have owned a copy (possibly first edition). More personally, he also knew all about the politics of religion, having fled from England, moved from Strasbourg to Zurich, wandered from western Germany to Saxony, and settled for a time in Paris.[82] Beale's attention to politics in a broad sense was very much a product of his education in civil law, and his legal acumen was not to be underestimated by those who saw his works of 1563 and 1569—including Cecil.

In the wake of his activity with Killigrew in 1569, Beale finally earned a more formal place within the English government in 1570, and his network of powerful friends and associates in England widened. He also joined the ranks of those who cut their teeth in service abroad and accordingly proved their worth to those back in England. Others like Killigrew and Rogers had similar early career paths and would, in time, run parallel in some ways with Beale. It is no surprise that, given their shared experiences, in the coming years Beale considered them both friends, as we shall see. During the 1570s, Beale's continued relationship with Cecil and his new relationships with men like Walsingham and Leicester would take him to new heights. 1570, therefore, represents a real turning point in Beale's life, a point of no return, after which his life of obscurity was a thing of the past, but that past was worth remembering for its continued value in the present and future.

A European Elizabethan: The Life of Robert Beale, Esquire. David Scott Gehring, Oxford University Press.
© David Scott Gehring 2024. DOI: 10.1093/9780198902942.003.0003

---

[82] Johann Sleidan, *A Famovse Cronicle of oure Time, called Sleidanes Commentaries*, trans. John Daus (London, 1560 (STC 19848), fol. [cccclxxiv]). 'The State of Germany', 85. BL, Hargrave MS 107, fol. 12v, noting an edition of 1555 printed at Strasbourg.

4
To Paris and Back—Again

In 1570 there was no way that Robert Beale could have known what the future would bring for his personal or professional life, but the decades to come were a logical consequence of his experience thus far. As a child and teenager, he had benefited from his extended family contacts, and during his twenties he had enjoyed the assistance and favour of some influential people in English government and society, most notably his step-uncle, John Hales. His informal and insecure work—if it can even be called such—for English ambassadors in Paris between 1564 and 1568 coincided with the ever-increasing temperature of religious conflict in France and the Netherlands. That Beale had the knowledge, contacts, and ability in 1569 to take advantage of Henry Killigrew's embassy to the German princes is testament to Beale's resourcefulness as well as his recognition that his expertise (documented most significantly in 'the State of Germany') was valuable to the Elizabethan government. Nevertheless, in early 1570 and for most of the year, it seems that Beale's career was still very much uncertain.

Upon his return to London, he could not have been sure that any of his English family or friends were going to be of much assistance. On account of the *Tempestas Halesiana* of 1563–4, Hales had been under house arrest since his release from the Tower in 1565, and he was never to return to royal favour. Beale's brother, William, had remained in England and pursued his studies at Oxford while Robert was in Germany and France during the 1560s; he also collected an income similar to Robert's as prebend in Coventry and Lichfield diocese.[1] Just as Robert had, William benefited from Hales's patronage as evident in Hales's desire expressed to Robert Dudley, earl of Leicester, in 1571 that William be made a canon in Oxford because Hales 'wolde [gladly] haue hym contynue his studie'.[2] Whether the Beale brothers ever significantly re-connected during the 1570s or later is unclear. Given William's career trajectory in the Church of England, especially in 1572–3 when he gained several new rural offices (and incomes), in contrast to Robert's career in foreign affairs and government intelligence, it is unlikely

---

[1] On Hales, *ODNB*. On William and the prebends, Chapter 2, nn. 6, 65.

[2] Hales to Leicester, 28 July 1571, BL, Additional MS 32091, fol. 249v (orig.). Stephen Hales, the Beale brothers' stepfather, was also in contact with Leicester, though the only known example of correspondence is about property in Coventry rather than the Beales. Hales to Leicester, 5 March 1573, Longleat, Dudley MS II, fol. 133r–v (orig.). I am grateful to Simon Adams for bringing this letter to my attention and for sending me his transcription before I was able to consult the letter myself; it is not recorded in the associated calendar of the Dudley Papers at Longleat.

that Robert sought to benefit from William's calling, though William might have accompanied Robert on the latter's mission to Germany in 1577; then again, it might have been the youngest brother, John.[3] As for Beale's only 'frend' in London during the mid to late 1560s, at least according to his own account, William Cecil was without question the most powerful man in Elizabethan England, but Beale could not have expected to have the principal secretary's ear and access to his purse. After all, at nearly thirty years old in 1570, Robert was starting to grow long in the tooth but was still a small fish in a big pond.

In the subsequent years, though, new political patrons and family members came into his life. He had previously come to Leicester's notice in 1564 due to his writings on the legitimacy of the earl of Hertford's marriage (and, in consequence, on the claim to the succession), but Leicester and Beale appear to have become closer during the early 1570s.[4] Also, Francis Walsingham, whose life before 1570 is just as obscure as Beale's, became in the 1570s Beale's professional mentor and religious *confrère*. The fact that Francis and Robert married sisters (Ursula and Edith St Barbe, respectively) made the two men brothers-in-law, but while Francis's marriage with Ursula is known to have been from 1566, when Beale was based in Paris, the date of Robert's marriage to Edith is unknown.[5] By working with English friends and colleagues old and new, and by using his network of international contacts, Beale during the early and mid 1570s would come to the very doorstep of the political elite in Elizabethan England. From a relative nobody who, if anything, had come under suspicion for his research into the royal succession, Beale rose to considerable ranks in both domestic and foreign service.

Back to Paris

Beale was a major part of Walsingham's household during the latter's tenure as resident ambassador in Paris from winter 1570/1 until Beale's departure in March 1572. The official residence was on the left (south) bank of the Seine and in the university district of St Germain, a central area for international Protestants at

---

[3] The timing of William Beale's additional four offices in the Church (April 1572 to November 1573) suggests that Robert's role in the government during these years may have helped William. Queen Elizabeth presented William to the prebendary of Shalford (or Scamford), Wells cathedral, on 17 December 1572. TNA, C 66/1105, m. 29. See also Chapter 2, n. 6. On the potential for their being together in Frankfurt, see Chapter 5.

[4] Leicester, William North?, and John Mason? to William Cecil, 26 April 1564, BL, Harley MS 6990, fol. 62r (orig.). Hertford subsequently sought Leicester's favour in his pursuit of his marriage's validation: Hertford to Leicester, 30 December 1565, Magdalen College, Cambridge, MS PL 2502, 497 (orig.).

[5] See below but contrast Collinson, 'Servants and Citizens', 503, which offers 1566 for the year of Beale's marriage (the year of Walsingham's marriage to Ursula) but without evidence. Taviner, 67, surmises 'sometime in the mid 1560's' but similarly without evidence.

this time.[6] Walsingham, Beale, and the rest of the diplomatic entourage departed from London on 29 December 1570, and it is clear from Walsingham's personal journal and correspondence during this period that Beale soon reconnected with several acquaintances and friends, and that he served as a courier and general agent or representative for Walsingham.[7] Within the first few months, Beale was again running in the same circles and meeting with Henry Norris, Daniel Rogers, Henry Killigrew, Odet de Coligny (the Huguenot former cardinal de Châtillon), and his old friend Hubert Languet. In fact, at various points in 1571, Languet, as the ambassador of the elector of Saxony at Paris, came for dinner at the English embassy.[8] Beale was not simply meeting up with old friends, however, for Walsingham trusted him in highly sensitive environments and with confidential information intended for the negotiation (in secret) of an Anglo-French alliance founded on a marriage between Queen Elizabeth and 'Monsieur', Henri, duke of Anjou, the future King Henri III. Less than one month into his time in Paris, Beale was sent by Walsingham to the French court at the residence known as 'Madrill', two miles outside Paris, as Walsingham put it, 'to aduertise the King and Queen mother from me'.[9] As one of Walsingham's general and informal servants, rather than in the capacity of a formal secretary, Beale was entrusted by the English ambassador to perform significant tasks requiring diplomatic and linguistic skills uncommonly possessed by those outside the usual diplomatic corps of people like Norris, Killigrew, and Thomas Smith.[10]

---

[6] Walsingham remained resident until May 1573. The scholarship and sources for this period are vast and will be noted below only as immediately relevant. A useful if dated narrative is Read, *Mr Secretary Walsingham*, 1.80–262. For marriage negotiations in 1570–2 in general, Doran, *Monarchy and Matrimony*, 99–129. See also the discussion of the residence in Taviner, 89–90 n. 52.

[7] Walsingham's Journal, TNA, PRO 30/5/5, edited with significant omissions in Charles Trice Martin (ed.), *The Camden Miscellany, Volume the Sixth [...] Journal of Sir Francis Walsingham from December 1570 to April 1583. From the Original Manuscript in the Possession of Lieut.-Colonel Carew* (London, 1870/1). Much of the relevant correspondence is found across the TNA, SP 70 series, various vols in BL, Cotton (e.g. Caligula, E. VI; Vespasian, F. VI), and among Burghley's papers in BL, Lansdowne, and CP. A convenient if imperfect collection used by historians for centuries is Dudley Digges (ed.), *The Compleat Ambassador, or, Two Treaties of the Intended Marriage of Qu: Elizabeth [...] Comprised in Letters of Negotiation of Sir Francis Walsingham, her Resident in France* (London, 1655). The volume providing the text for Digges's printed work is discussed by Jason Powell, who assesses over two dozen manuscript copies with part of or the whole text of the printed work of 1655. Jason Powell, 'Building Paper Embassies: A Prehistory of *The Compleat Ambassador*', *The Journal of Medieval and Early Modern Studies*, 50 (2020), 541–64. Beale owned one such volume with some but not all the material (BL, Additional MS 48046). Cited here and below is TCD, MS 706, which clarifies some awkward phrasing and details lacking in Digges but does not include the later material for 1581; the Dublin volume appears to be contemporary to Walsingham's tenure in Paris and is preferred over Digges. Cf. but use with caution, Gary M. Bell, *A Handlist of British Diplomatic Representatives 1509–1688* (London, 1990), 90–1.

[8] Walsingham's Journal, TNA, PRO 30/5/5, fols 2v, 7v, 8v. On Languet in Paris, with passing reference to Beale in 1571, Nicollier-de Weck, *Hubert Languet*, 247–61.

[9] Walsingham to Cecil, 1 February 1571, TNA, SP 70/116, fol. 54r (orig.).

[10] Although many scholars over the years have thought Beale to have been Walsingham's secretary in Paris during this time, presumably owing to the high-level access he had, Taviner has argued convincingly that Beale was in fact a lower-level servant. Taviner, 79–85. As will be seen below, Leicester addressed Beale as Walsingham's 'attendant'.

Walsingham's confidence in Beale regarding matters of state was shared by those who had known him previously, such as Hales and Cecil, and it extended to others. Unsurprisingly, Beale's spell in Paris was not sedentary. On 23 February 1571, barely a month after arriving with Walsingham at the embassy, Beale was sent back to London as courier of Walsingham's letters to Leicester, Cecil, other government figures, and—adding a significant personal touch—Walsingham's wife Ursula. In his letter to Cecil, Walsingham made special note of 'this bearer who hathe ordre from me to commvnicate vnto you matters bothe of wayght and secreacye'.[11] On 1 March Beale delivered this oral message to Cecil (elevated to Baron Burghley on 25 February), and it is suggestive of the top-level nature of this information that Burghley wrote on that date to Walsingham that with 'thinges as are of moment' he 'emparted them to her Majestie'. Within a couple of days, Beale was heading back to Paris with written and oral messages from Burghley and others, but all the more significant was that, on 10 March, Elizabeth wrote to Walsingham regarding the matter of sending aid to the Huguenot stronghold of La Rochelle, 'whereof you gave knowledge by Beale'.[12] About a month later, Beale served again in April as a courier of written and oral messages between Walsingham and Burghley, Elizabeth, and others.[13] His service as an intermediary here should not be reduced to that of a mere messenger, for the levels of trust and, indeed, like-mindedness in the political and religious agenda were essential prerequisites for the job, and Beale's previous informal associations with the English ambassadors at the Paris post laid much of that groundwork.[14]

A suggestive example of the trust placed in, and political access granted to, Beale at this time came from Burghley's pen when he closed a letter to Walsingham on 14 April as follows: 'I need not write more, because this bearer[,] Mr Beale, is soe sufficient[,] to whome I have alsoe shewed some of our occurrentes'.[15] Beale's time in London with key players in the government was clearly well spent, with the result that his abilities and potential value to the state were increasingly recognized. On at least one of these trips back to England, Beale almost certainly met with Leicester, and it appears that the two men had, by this point, established a significant level of friendship and intimacy even if Beale was not directly employed by Leicester. In early July 1571, Leicester wrote an illuminating letter to Beale in which he commented on many of Beale's activities earlier that year.

[11] Walsingham to Burghley, 23 February 1571, TNA, SP 70/116, fol. 105v (orig.). Walsingham's Journal, TNA, PRO 30/5/5, fol. 3v. Cf. Walsingham to Burghley, 5 March 1571, TNA, SP 70/117, fol. 6r (orig.).

[12] Burghley to Walsingham, 1 and 3 March 1571, TCD, MS 706, fols 92r–v, 95v–100r (quotation from 92r). Elizabeth to Walsingham, 10 March 1571, TCD, MS 706, fol. 103r.

[13] Beale was sent to England on 5 April 1571, arriving back in Paris on the 18th. Walsingham's Journal, TNA, PRO 30/5/5, fol. 5v.

[14] On Walsingham's network of agents and intelligencers later in the reign, see Alford, *The Watchers*.

[15] Burghley to Walsingham, 14 April 1571, TCD, MS 706, fol. 145v. NB: Elizabeth refers to the bearer as 'Robert Beale' in full in hers to Walsingham the previous day, fol. 144r–v; draft in Burghley's hand dated 12 April leaves a large blank space before 'Beale': TNA, SP 70/117, fol. 119r.

Entirely in Leicester's hand, the letter was addressed 'To my frend Robert Beale attendant on the Q. majesties Embassador in fraunce'.[16]

'Beale', he began, 'I thank you veary hartely for your lardge and good discours you haue wryten to me[,] and that you so franckley vtter your opinione aswell touching the cause of Monsieur'. Although Beale's 'lardge and good discours' has not yet been found among Leicester's papers, and its central subject is unknown, it probably discussed the current situation regarding the French wars of religion with reference to the German embassy led by Languet, and it presumably included discussion of the prospects of Elizabeth's match with Anjou.[17] At the very least, Leicester's reference to it serves as additional evidence that Beale continued to offer (with good reason) his unsolicited intelligence and unfiltered opinions to those in positions of power who shaped policy. Beale's thoughts were apparently not limited to foreign affairs, for Leicester continued in his letter to address 'some other matters at home in the clergye that you founde fault withall'. Here Beale was entering dangerous territory because getting involved in the ongoing disputes within the Church of England could get him into serious trouble and potentially cause him to run afoul of Queen Elizabeth over such differences that, as Leicester put it, were just 'tryfles'. Leicester's concern here was to downplay differences among English Protestants, especially those who opposed the bishops regarding *adiaphora* (things indifferent), 'for vndowdtedly I find no more hate or dyspleasure almost betwene papyst & protestant than ys now in many places betwene many of our owen Religion'.[18] The hierarchical relationship between Lord Leicester and his 'frend' Beale becomes clear in the tone of the letter's more godly statements in the context of what became the admonition controversy: 'For the dyfference ys not in doctryne, but in cerymony, and as the one must only by tried by the right touch stone[,] in dede so theother hath more lyberty, for as yt ys more temporall, so ys yt more Indyfferent'.[19] Leicester's intent to caution Beale gained further clarity:

---

[16] Leicester to Beale, 7 July 1571, BL, Egerton MS 1693, fols 9r–10r (orig.), misdated 1572 in Beale's own endorsement. Hales later that month referred to Beale and his brother William as Leicester's 'seruantes'. See above, n. 2.

[17] On Leicester's papers and their dispersal, see the works of Simon Adams: 'The Lauderdale Papers, 1561–1570: The Maitland of Lethington State Papers and the Leicester Correspondence', *Scottish Historical Review*, 67 (1988), 28–55; Simon Adams, 'Two "Missing" Lauderdale Letters: Queen Mary to Robert Dudley, Earl of Leicester, 5 June 1567 and Thomas Randolph and Francis Russell, Earl of Bedford to Leicester, 23 November 1564', *Scottish Historical Review*, 70 (1991), 55–7; Simon Adams, 'The Papers of Robert Dudley, Earl of Leicester, I: The Browne-Evelyn Collection', *Archives*, 20 (1992), 63–85; Simon Adams, 'The Papers of Robert Dudley, Earl of Leicester, II: The Atye-Cotton Collection', *Archives*, 20 (1993), 131–44; Simon Adams, 'The Papers of Robert Dudley, Earl of Leicester, III: The Countess of Leicester's Collection', *Archives*, 22 (1996), 1–26; Simon Adams, *Household Accounts and Disbursement Books of Robert Dudley, Earl of Leicester*, Camden Fifth Series, Vol. 6 (Cambridge, 1995).

[18] Leicester to Beale, 7 July 1571, BL, Egerton MS 1693, fol. 9r (orig.).

[19] Leicester to Beale, 7 July 1571, BL, Egerton MS 1693, fol. 9v (orig.). Differences among England's Puritans and the established Church were not just about ceremonies, for in 1572 that 'admonition controversy' as initiated by Puritans gained greater steam in their full-scale questioning of the ecclesiastical structure of the Church, favouring instead a presbyterian system. See Peter Lake, *Anglicans and*

And hereto I suppose we may and ought to apply ourselues to that lawfull obedyence that we owe to our magistrate, which sewrly in causes Indyfferent I am perswaded we ar. [A]nd I could neuer yet hear any reasone that could make me think otherwayse of these comon quarrels in our church but that they wer for matters simply Indyfferent & nothing concernes doctryne, and therfore ought they to be concluded in our obedynce to the magistrate.[20]

With a solid nod to 'do not question your obedience to the queen' aimed squarely at Beale regarding the ceremonies of the Church, Leicester here privately tried to help keep Beale out of trouble. After all, Leicester knew that Beale had been deeply involved in the Hertford/Grey/succession fiasco back in 1563, so it was important to keep him within Elizabeth's good graces. In closing, Leicester's care for Beale rings both sincere and concerned:

Prais you when you haue cause to wryte at lardge of your affayres ther, to esthew asmuch as you can to enter into any cause that concerns this matter of ours at home[,] I mene touching our byshoppes estate of Religyon[,] in sort to myslyk them [...And if you do write about an issue concerning the Church,] lett yt be only of that matter to my self, for that I doe vse to shew your dyscourses to her majestie, who lyketh very well of them [...] this frendly I advyse you[,] knowing you wyll take yt well, & I meane for your best. So fare well good Beale[,] with all my hart [...] your loving frend, R. Leycester.[21]

Beale took this advice seriously. For the next decade and more, he attempted to remain within the queen's favour by staying out of domestic religious affairs.[22] Additionally, during the 1570s Beale increasingly took to heart Leicester's concern for uniting Protestants across Europe in their cause against Roman Catholicism (see Fig. 5).

Leicester cared not only for Beale but also for his brother, William; as Leicester put it in his postscript, 'your brother was with me yesterday & ys well, & I think remaynes with me a while here.' Additionally, Leicester later helped to further William's ecclesiastical career by obtaining an advowson from the queen to present

---

Puritans? Presbyterianism and English Conformist Thought from Whitgift to Hooker (London, 1988), 13–70; Robert Harkins, 'Calvinism, Anti-Calvinism, and the Admonition Controversy in Elizabethan England', in Bruce Gordon and Carl R. Trueman (eds), The Oxford Handbook of Calvin and Calvinism (Oxford, 2021), 141–54. See also Beale's copies of letters to Leicester regarding the vestment controversy: Member(?) of the University of Oxford to Leicester, January 1565; James Pilkington, Bishop of Durham, to Leicester, 25 October 1564, BL, Additional MS 48064, fols 171r–4v.

[20] Leicester to Beale, 7 July 1571, BL, Egerton MS 1693, fol. 10r (orig.).
[21] Leicester to Beale, 7 July 1571, BL, Egerton MS 1693, fol. 10r (orig.).
[22] On the lingering impact of Beale's work for Hertford, see below. On his later clash with the archbishop of Canterbury, John Whitgift, see Chapter 6. On the final straw with Whitgift, see Chapter 8.

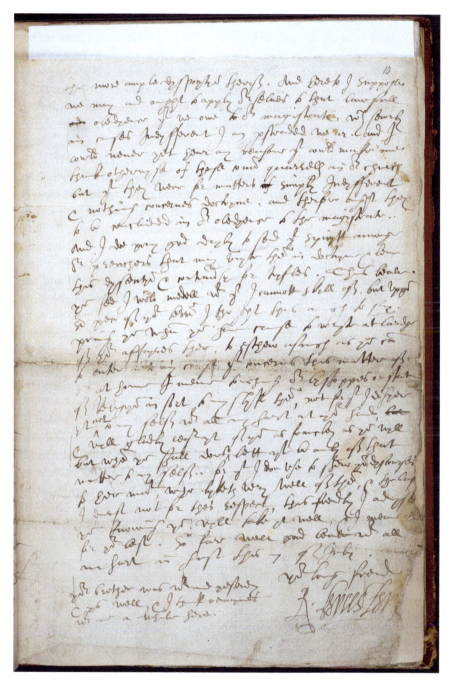

Fig. 5 Earl of Leicester to Beale, 7 July 1571. BL, Egerton MS 1693, fol. 10r.
Reproduced with permission from the British Library.

William to a prebend at Christ Church, Oxford, just as Hales had requested.[23] As for Robert, Leicester appears to have been working behind the scenes on his behalf, for as Hales wrote, 'it maye pleace you to geue me leaue to renewe myn olde sute for these two yong men Robert & William Bele, that it will pleace you to place Robert, where her Majestie[,] at your sute[,] determyned.'[24] For what exact role Leicester had advocated is unknown, but it would be reasonable to suppose that, when Beale made his next trip to England as courier from France, he would soon find out.

That position, however, lay in the future. For now, in 1571 and early 1572, Beale was still attending Walsingham at the embassy in Paris and joining him to travel to the French court in various locations around northern France. He was part of a household interacting on a daily basis with French officials both within France and based in England, like Châtillon and his servant Dupin (or de Pin), and with several other like-minded English Protestants of the more advanced sort, some of whom Beale had known for many years, like Killigrew, Rogers, and Thomas Danett (who continued to serve as courier between England and the mainland).[25] Beale also continued to look east for developments in the Holy Roman Empire, as evident in his correspondence with Christoph Ehem, council-lor of Friedrich III, Elector Palatine, and Languet, ambassador for August, elector of Saxony, both of whom sent him general news and political intelligence.[26] In addition, Palatine contacts directly with the English in Paris by way of Friedrich's correspondence with Walsingham, and in the form of the elector's servant, Johannes Junius, provided still further exposure to the wider ramifications of the French wars of religion, Anglo-French negotiations, and the royal succession in England. Beale's role in Anglo-German relations while in Walsingham's embassy can be seen, for example, in his writing from Blois to Friedrich on Walsingham's behalf (and sending via Junius) regarding Protestant alliance building in October 1571. In fact, Beale was writing relatively frequently for Walsingham either in early drafts or in finished, final letters.[27] Because Burghley and, indeed, Elizabeth recognized Beale's importance to English operations in France, notwithstanding

[23] Leicester's advowson for William, BL, Cotton Charter XV, 42, which notes William Beale as a 'clerico', which here is best read as 'clergyman' rather than 'scholar' or 'student'; contrast Chapter 2, n. 65. Leicester had been Chancellor of the University of Oxford since his election on 31 December 1564. *ODNB*. See also Chapter 2, n. 6.

[24] Hales to Leicester, 28 July 1571, BL, Additional MS 32091, fol. 249v (orig.).

[25] Walsingham's journal and correspondence show the variety of interaction with these and many other figures, such as Peter Ramus, who visited Walsingham on 19 December 1571. TNA, PRO 30/5/5, fol. 11v; cf. fols 5v, 7r for Dupin's service as courier between Paris and London in spring 1571. On Châtillon and Dupin, see Chapter 3, n. 76.

[26] Ehem to Beale, 16 February 1571, AUL, MS 1009/2, item 28 (orig.). Languet to Beale, 28 June 1571, BL, Egerton MS 1693, fol. 8r (orig.).

[27] Walsingham to Burghley, 7 October 1571, TCD, MS 706, fol. 248r–v. [Walsingham] to Friedrich, 5 October 1571, TNA, SP 70/120, fol. 62r. Final letters in Beale's hand: Walsingham to Burghley, 30 July, 12 August, 16 September 1571, TNA, SP 70/119, fols 49r–50v, 90r–3v (both orig.); TNA, SP 70/120, fols 47r–9v (orig.).

the fact that he was not a formal secretary but rather a personal and intimate friend and servant, the queen even authorized Walsingham to appoint Beale as the ersatz English ambassador in Paris during a period of Walsingham's absence in autumn 1571. When Beale learned of this potentiality, he wrote to Burghley begging that he be excused from taking the role due to his inability and lack of financial resources, pleading with Burghley to ensure 'that so great a burden be not layd apon so vnsufficient a parsons necke'.[28] This would not be the last time Beale was suggested for a major position as substitute for Walsingham. Moreover, and giving a rare glimpse into his personal life, Beale noted to Burghley that he was 'fully minded at Mychelmas [29 September] to repaire homewardes to setle my self, & see whether at lengthe after so longe & yet vnprofitable travaile, I might obtayne somwhat towardes a poore lyving.' Along these lines, Beale hoped that Burghley's favour would help him secure stable employment, particularly due to 'that good opinion which your Lordship seamed to have conceaved of me before my departure' from England.[29] Here one finds Beale's longing for a more settled life but without reference to an existing wife or children. Such a family would need to wait; he still had work to do in the international context.

Mary Queen of Scots and Other Interests

Although the prospect for a marriage between Elizabeth and Henri, duke of Anjou, petered out in summer 1571 because of Henri's insistence on practising his Catholic faith (the English would have none of it), the ever-looming issue of the royal succession was front-and-centre after the uncovering of the Ridolfi plot that same summer. In short, the Florentine banker, Roberto Ridolfi, had organized a significant international effort including the king of Spain, the pope, and the duke of Norfolk to assassinate Elizabeth, and then to place Mary Queen of Scots on the English throne.[30] The plan included a Spanish invasion of England from the Netherlands while assuming that English Catholics would rise up in significant numbers against Elizabeth, but at the centre of the whole scheme was Mary with the support of her chief counsellor and ambassador, John Leslie, bishop of Ross.

---

[28] Burghley to Walsingham, 2 September 1571, TCD, MS 706, fol. 231v. Beale to Burghley, 15 September 1571, TNA, SP 70/120, fol. 45r–v, quotation at 45r (orig.).
[29] Beale to Burghley, 15 September 1571, TNA, SP 70/120, fol. 45v (orig.).
[30] On the Ridolfi plot from a broadly international perspective but with emphasis on the Spanish, Geoffrey Parker, 'The Place of Tudor England in the Messianic Vision of Philip II of Spain', *Transactions of the Royal Historical Society*, 12 (2002), 167–221, esp. 189–206; cf. Geoffrey Parker, *Imprudent King: A New Life of Philip II* (New Haven, CT, 2014), 205–7. On Beale and Mary, particularly for the 1580s, see Chapter 6 and Patricia Basing, 'Robert Beale and the Queen of Scots', *British Library Journal*, 20 (1994), 65–82.

Beale's concern regarding the succession dated from 1563 at the latest, but his burgeoning personal archive of manuscripts and printed books gained significant material regarding Mary and Leslie from the 1570s forward. The earliest datable comes from about 1571, and predictably comes in the hand of John Hales. When exactly Beale acquired Hales's notes on a printed work by Leslie (arguing for the right of Mary in the English succession) is difficult to tell, but it seems reasonable to estimate the second half of 1571 due to Beale's own notes on Hales's. Given Hales's previous activity strongly denouncing Mary's cause in this regard, it is unsurprising to know that he continued to critique Leslie's arguments in her favour.[31] In the context of the Ridolfi plot in 1571, and Mary's role in it, a new sense of vitriol ran through many who had long opposed her. Beale was no exception, for just as he had written various 'discourses' for Hales, Cecil, and Leicester, some of which worked their way into Elizabeth's hands, in December 1571 Beale penned his thoughts on the various possible relationships between France and England, and Mary with either country, directing his scorn squarely at the Queen of Scots.[32] In short, Beale countered the idea that, from the French perspective, an alliance between France and Mary was to be favoured over an Anglo-French pact. Although the Anjou marriage negotiations had collapsed, and so a marriage alliance was, for now, out of the question, a broader political accord between England and France would ensure that Mary was relatively isolated moving into 1572.

Beale claimed that his 'pamflett' was not intended for wider dissemination than Killigrew (acting English ambassador in France while Walsingham was in ill health) or perhaps a few others due to the circumstances in which he wrote it. Killigrew, though, thought highly of the work and enclosed it in his own letter to Burghley on 3 December. Given the fact that many of Beale's previous and unsolicited writings had worked their ways up to the highest levels, his self-deprecation rings like humanist but hollow rhetoric. The pamphlet, written in a polished and formal secretary hand, took the form of a position paper laying out arguments why the king of France should ally with the cause of Mary Queen of Scots, followed by counter-arguments. For example, in response to the argument that, on account of Mary's previous marriage to the French king's brother (Francis II), France was bound in honour to her, Beale noted that Mary, 'who by prostitutinge and advylinge the honor of ffraunce, deserveth yt not.'[33] In response to the notion that subjects are not to rise up against and depose their divinely appointed monarchs, Beale observed that several other queens in France and elsewhere had been

---

[31] Notes by Hales, c.1570/1, BL, Additional MS 48043, fols 65r–81r, with Beale's note at 72r; cf. fol. 10v, where Beale notes the dating of the published version of Leslie's book, on which, see below. On Leslie's knowledge of Beale's work for Hertford, see Chapter 3.

[32] Beale's pamphlet, followed by Beale to Burghley, 3 December 1571, TNA, SP 70/121, fols 48r–51v (fair copy), 52r–3r (orig.); Killigrew's letter of the same date enclosing the pamphlet precedes it on fols 45r–6v (orig.). For a gripping if brief account of the Ridolfi Plot, see Alford, *The Watchers*, 127–9, followed by a treatment of Beale's tract after the St Bartholomew's Day massacre, on which, see below.

[33] Beale's pamphlet, TNA, SP 70/121, fol. 48r.

justly punished for their tyranny, and here Mary was hardly innocent in her behaviour in Scotland. Along these lines, Beale even recommended that 'some of [George] Buchanans litle latyn bookes' detailing Mary's treachery be 'presented to the kinge, and likewise to some of the noblemen of his cownsell'.[34] In other responses, Beale marshalled his extensive knowledge of political history in France, Spain, Italy, the Low Countries, the Holy Roman Empire, and even Denmark to argue against Mary's position at every turn. The many examples from the medieval and more recent past showed that, due to Mary's domestic affairs as well as her conspiracies against Elizabeth, there were plenty of lessons to be learned and precedents on which to rely for recommending against an alliance with Mary Queen of Scots. Rather, Mary ought to have been punished as others had been. Beale thought that Elizabeth was possibly being overlenient when he wrote that '[c]ertainelie histories declare that in like cases other princes seekinge the mainetenaunce of their estate, and contynuaunce of quiet in their realmes and countreys[,] haue vsed greater seuerity' against such threats to the crown,

> [b]ut the Queenes Majestie beinge a moste gracious and pitifull prince forget-tynge all former quarells of vsurpacion of titles and armes, which might iustly haue moved her to some revenge[,] hath so honorably vsed the Queene of Scottes, and sought her reconciliacion with her subiectes, her libertie and advauncement so much as none could do more.[35]

Despite Mary's conspiring with the Spanish and others against Elizabeth, Beale noted his own sovereign's continued moderation in response by simply restrain-ing the Scottish queen's liberty of movement. In sum, Beale's pamphlet read as an admonition to King Charles IX not to associate with Mary, but rather to join in 'perfect league and amity' with England, 'and to confirme with [Elizabeth] the younge kinge of Scottes governement'.[36]

Because Beale had intended, or so he claimed in his letter to Burghley, that his 'pamflett' serve Killigrew as a reply to the French king ('in case he insisted moche in the recommendacion of the Queen of Scottes cause'), Beale 'thought good to adde [a] fewe lynes' to explain his position more clearly for Burghley in particu-lar. After all, his pamphlet in its first draft could have been 'enlarged with more examples & commen places' were he not 'destitute of tyme, bokes, & other neces-saryes'. Beale claimed not to have written anything against Mary in malice or par-tiality; as he said, 'in deade I have no cause, having byn on the contraryside for my long & faithfull service vnkindly recompensed, to my great hinderance & almost

[34] Beale's pamphlet, TNA, SP 70/121, fol. 49v. On Buchanan's works, see below.
[35] Beale's pamphlet, TNA, SP 70/121, fol. 50v.
[36] Beale's pamphlet, TNA, SP 70/121, fol. 51v. On Mary's captivity in the early 1570s, see dated but still useful narrative in John Daniel Leader, *Mary Queen of Scots in Captivity: A Narrative of Events* (Sheffield, 1880).

vtter vndoing'.[37] Beale cast aside this thin veil of impartiality, however, in later parts of his letter when he considered what might 'redounde' to and benefit his prince and country:

> And therfore hertofore I have alwayes thought, & yet thinck the Queen of Scottes to be [a] pernitious & viperous enemy to the Queen Majestys estate, & [I] never could be perswaded that by lenitye & honorable vsage she or any of her rablement could be wonne to be her maiestys good frynds & subiectes. [...] Therfor I thinck, now considering [Mary's] dangerous practises, that yt behoveth & that of necessity the Queen's Majesty for the safty & assurance of her owne person & realme, seke meanes to disgrace her in asmoche as her majesty iustly may.

This was sharp language for a mere attendant of the English ambassador in Paris, even if he had significant experience and was accordingly of significant value to the English state. Bearing in mind the fact that his strident opinions on religion and politics could land him in hot water, as Leicester had recently reminded him, Beale asked Burghley to take his letter in confidence according to his 'accustomed curtesy', for Beale had 'byn the bolder, assuring my self that not only your lordship will accept this in good parte, but also extend apon occasion your laufull favor towardes me, where & whensoever I shall have neade of the same.'[38]

Beale asserted that his thinking on Mary had been consistent over the years prior to his writing his pamphlet. Back in 1563, his role as legal scholar and surveyor of jurists' opinions in the Empire and France brought him directly into contact with the succession, albeit by examining the validity of a Protestant claim rather than, as Hales aimed at the same time, by denouncing the claim of a foreigner, Mary, to inherit the English crown. Nevertheless, Beale's activity was obviously intended to verify the Hertford/Grey claim and, in the process, act as a bulwark against any competing claim coming from north of the Scottish Borders. Following Mary's deposition and flight into England in 1568 after the murder of her husband, Henry Stewart, Lord Darnley, and marriage to James Hepburn, earl of Bothwell, English suspicions of Mary as a potential enemy grew all the more.[39] Beale's service and travels in France and Germany during these years, though, would have made it relatively difficult for him to remain fully abreast of the situation. Hales, however, may provide the missing link.

Beale would have learned much from Hales's aforementioned personal notes on a published work written by John Leslie, bishop of Ross and primary advocate for Mary Queen of Scots. Leslie's book argued for the right of Mary to the English

---

[37]   Beale to Burghley, 3 December 1571, TNA, SP 70/121, fol. 52r (orig.).
[38]   Beale to Burghley, 3 December 1571, TNA, SP 70/121, fols 52v–53r (orig.).
[39]   On the murder of Darnley, marriage to Bothwell, and flight from Scotland, *ODNB*.

succession, defending her honour in the process. It was printed at Rheims in 1569 and Liège in 1571, but in Beale's manuscript copy he noted that Leslie's work was first 'published in writing' (i.e. circulated in manuscript copies) in 1569.[40] It is entirely possible that Beale's copy was originally Hales's because the latter's notes on the work follow in the same volume, where he observed the work's publication in Liège. Hales's primary interest in evaluating Scottish claims was legal—by what law the matter of the English succession should be decided, where and by whom it should be tried, and whether Mary or any others had any right or claim.[41] In response to Leslie's points, Hales employed arguments from precedent in statute law, international law (*ius gentium*), and various medieval scholars like Ranulf de Glanvill, Gerald of Wales, and John Fortescue to make his case that Mary had no right or claim to the English throne. In many respects, therefore, Hales was reciting and updating the arguments he had made previously to exclude foreigners, especially Mary, from the succession, but here was a set of his thoughts directly at Beale's disposal in 1571.[42] By rehearsing Leslie's arguments, and then countering them in great legal detail, Hales's work made for potentially dull reading for some, but it was familiar territory for Beale and would prove grist to his mill in the years to come. Thus, from a particularly legal and English perspective, Beale's opposition in 1571 to Mary Queen of Scots was long in gestation and thanks, in large part, to his first significant patron—Hales.

Yet there is also reason to believe that Beale's dislike for Mary was further confirmed and strengthened as her role in the Ridolfi Plot became clearer, and after he read works on Mary by George Buchanan, political theorist and tutor to the young Scottish king, James VI. Here one notices the beginnings of Beale's general interest in Scottish affairs, particularly Buchanan's works in the context of broader discussions of subjects' rights in opposition to tyrannical rule. It seems that Beale had in mind two of Buchanan's 'litle latyn bookes' to be sent to the French king and nobility in December 1571, both of which he probably owned. One was the *detectio* or history of Mary's role in the murder of Darnley as well as her conspiracy and marriage with Bothwell back in 1567, while the other was the *actio* or speech advocating for the prosecution against Mary. These books were known to others in 1568–9 and constituted parts of the later whole published at London in 1571.[43] Moreover, there seem to have been multiple books in Latin written by

---

[40] Beale's note and title of the work precede Leslie's work in a formal secretary hand: BL, Additional MS 48043, fols 10v, 11r–55v. Internal evidence suggests that Beale acquired this material in or shortly after 1571. Leslie's work, *A defence of the honour of the Right High, Right Mighty, and Noble Princesse, Marie Queene of Scotlande* (1569) (STC 15505), renamed slightly in 1571 (STC 15506).

[41] Hales's notes, BL, Additional MS 48043, fols 65r–67r, 72r–81r, with summary questions at 65r, and heading in Hales's hand at 72r where Beale observed accordingly: 'Mr John Hales his hand'.

[42] On the *Tempestas Halesiana* in Parliament and beyond, see Chapter 3.

[43] *De Maria Scotorum Regina totaque eius contra Regem coniuratione, foedo cum Bothuelio adulterio, nefaria in maritum crudelitate & rabie, horrendo insuper & deterrimo eiusdem parricidio: plena & tragica plane historia* (London, 1571) (STC 3978; English translation of 1571, STC 3981).

Buchanan at this time because of his role in the investigations into Darnley's murder. That Beale was aware of Buchanan (and knowledgeable regarding his books) is less surprising when their mutual friend in Paris is recognized: Languet.[44] Equally if not more important for the years to come, in reading Buchanan's works arguing vociferously against the Catholic Mary's cause, and for the cause of the Protestant Scottish lords, Beale was exposed to current political resistance theory and its link to religious causes. On a broader level, from 1571 forward Beale appears to have started his collection of materials relating to Mary, Leslie, and Scottish law.[45] His recommendation to Burghley in December 1571 that Buchanan's works be distributed at the French court appears to have been taken on board because soon the finished product, *De Maria Scotorum Regina*, was translated into French for distribution in France. Additionally, in July 1572, another copy of Beale's pamphlet was made for reference and distribution back in London, this at the same time as Beale's political elevation into the Elizabethan regime.[46]

By winter 1571/2, Beale's initial expertise in German affairs had grown to include matters relating to France and, by extension but also in relation to the English royal succession, Scotland. While based in Paris or following the court around northern France, Beale kept himself busy by gaining whatever useful information he could from whomever he could—French, English, German, or otherwise. For example, back in 1569, when he explored a mine in Saxony with Killigrew, Beale became interested in mining techniques and minerals more generally. In 1571, when he had the opportunity to learn about the alloys involved in French coinage, he met with and received notes directly from the noted antiquary, historian, and President of the Chamber (or Court) of Currency, Claude Fauchet. In the coming years, Beale's interest and expertise in mining continued.[47] At the same time, though, he was clearly running out of enthusiasm for a life of

---

I. D. McFarlane, *Buchanan* (Oxford, 1981), 324–7, 340–8. 'Buchanani (Georgi) Actio in Mariam Scotorum Reginam' and 'Detectio' published in London, BL, Hargrave MS 107, fols 30r, 35v. NB: McFarlane discusses the 'Actio contra Mariam', not 'in Mariam'.

[44] Nicollier-de Weck, *Hubert Languet*, 104, 442–4.

[45] See esp. Beale's copy of Buchanan's *De Jure Regni apud Scotos* and French tracts on resistance in BL, Additional MS 48043, fols 123r–52v, 175r–225r. Based on a close comparison of paper stocks across Beale's archive, Taviner, 262–3 suggests winter 1577/8 for when Beale acquired his copy of *De Jure Regni apud Scotos*. Other relevant papers acquired by Beale during the 1570s and later are found in BL, Additional MSS 48027, 48048, 48088, 48098. Beale probably also owned the printed edition of *De Jure Regni apud Scotos* (1583): BL, Hargrave MS 107, fol. 19v.

[46] BL, Cotton MS Caligula, C. III, fols 412r–14r. McFarlane, *Buchanan*, 340 n. 51; 348 n. 70 relies on the *CSP* vols for *Foreign* and *Scotland* (for the SP 70/121 and Cotton versions, respectively), but appears not to have made the connection that the manuscripts behind the calendar entries are copies with only minor differences between the two. Neither version is in Beale's hand.

[47] BL, Additional MS 48047, fols 234r–5v. Beale gained a quarter share of the Company of Mineral and Battery works in 1582. M. B. Donald, *Elizabethan Monopolies: The History of the Company of Mineral and Battery Works from 1565 to 1604* (Edinburgh, 1961), 73; cf. 133, 189. See also Chapter 6. On Fauchet's role, alongside François Bauduin and others, in the development of French historical scholarship, see Donald R. Kelley, *Foundations of Modern Historical Scholarship: Language, Law, and History in the French Renaissance* (New York, 1970), 245–9, 263, 266, 277, 280–1, 292–5.

peregrination. His complaints to Burghley in September and December 1571 regarding his weariness and longing for a settled life and position were sincere and understandable. His desire for a more stable and secure life probably intensified over the course of his time in France (he had not been back to England since his return to Paris on 18 April), but he soon got his chance.[48]

By early March 1572, both Beale and Walsingham were looking to leave France and return to England. Like Beale, Walsingham was open with Burghley on the matter, stating plainly that, although his health had returned, the financial burdens of serving as ambassador were increasingly crushing his personal coffers.[49] On 9 March, Beale left Blois, south-west of Paris, as bearer of Walsingham's letter to Burghley in which Walsingham made a strong case for an alliance with the German Protestant princes. As a counter-league to the Catholic League, this alliance was, in Walsingham's view, all the more necessary and potentially possible due to his recent correspondence with Friedrich III, Elector Palatine, and his recent discussions with the elector's servant, Johannes Junius. Because of Beale's experience and expertise in such efforts with the German princes, Walsingham's choice of him as bearer of the letter and fuller report to Burghley made sense.[50]

By late March, it was increasingly unlikely that Beale would be returning to France anytime soon. As Elizabeth explained to Walsingham, ongoing negotiations with the French ambassador in London regarding an Anglo-French alliance (which, ideally, would draw in the Protestant princes in Germany, Scandinavia, and elsewhere) meant that the queen intended to 'staye the retourne of Beale, vnto you'.[51] A potential delay in Elizabeth's letter reaching Walsingham meant that his colleague, Thomas Smith, also in Blois with Walsingham to negotiate, became progressively disturbed that Beale had not yet returned by Palm Sunday

---

[48] Taviner, 87–8 supposes that Beale was the bearer of Walsingham's letter to Burghley on 19 January 1572 (TNA, SP 70/122, fol. 97r (orig.)), in which Walsingham states that 'this bearer my brother in lawe' was knowledgeable of Walsingham's dire financial situation due to the charges incurred by his 'byll of espyall'. Such a supposition would, therefore, have Beale married by this time, but it is far more likely that the bearer was Walsingham's brother-in-law, William Dodington, whom Walsingham names in the first line of the letter, and whom Walsingham desired to acquaint Burghley with the financial situation. Dodington's name occurs frequently in Walsingham's journal as a familiar correspondent. On Dodington, who married Walsingham's sister, Christiana, between 1569 and 1572, see HoP:HoC and ODNB (for Francis Walsingham). Walsingham's journal, TNA, PRO 30/5/5, unfortunately cuts off at 17 January 1572 on fol. 12r, resuming on 21 December 1573 on fol. 36r. The question of when Beale marries Edith St Barbe, sister of Ursula, is explored below.

[49] Walsingham to Burghley, 2–3 March 1572, TNA, SP 70/123, fols 3r–6v (orig.)

[50] Walsingham to Burghley, n.d. but 8 March 1572, TCD, MS 706, fols 307v–11v, with note on Beale as courier at 310r; NB n.d. in The Compleat Ambassador. Address leaf noting 8 March, TNA, SP 70/123, fol. 11r–v (orig.). Although Walsingham's letter is dated 8 March, Beale did not leave Blois until the next day as bearer also of Smith's letter dated that morning. Walsingham to Friedrich, 29 December 1571, discussing Elizabeth and Mary, Anglo-French rapprochement, and the Anglo-German alliance, printed in Kluckhohn, Briefe Friedrich des Frommen, Vol. 2, Part 1, 442–4.

[51] Elizabeth to Walsingham, 20 March 1572, TCD, MS 706, fols 319r–22v, quotation at 322r; cf. to the same effect, Elizabeth to Smith and Walsingham, 20 March 1572, BL, Cotton MS Caligula, C. III, fols 257r–8v, quotation at 258v.

(30 March) or Good Friday (4 April).[52] Smith was upset that Beale had not yet returned, but then again he probably could not have blamed Elizabeth and Burghley for keeping him in England. After all, Smith previously begged Burghley 'to remember' Beale, 'a rare man & of excellent giftes'.[53] Although Beale's exact activities at this time are not clear, he was probably relieved to be back in London and hopeful for steady—even sedentary—employment at the hands of Burghley, Leicester, or anybody else for that matter. The coming months, however, proved to be both a tumultuous time in Elizabethan politics and the beginning of a long and fruitful period of state employment for Beale.

London (and France), 1572

Beale's arrival in London shortly before the opening of the first session of Elizabeth's fourth parliament (8 May to 30 June 1572) ensured that he would be surrounded by discussions about the Ridolfi Plot and the conspiracy of Norfolk and Mary Queen of Scots. Indeed, the primary purpose of this parliament was to secure Elizabeth's safety and punish the offenders according to law; this would not be the last time a parliament was called in response to a Catholic threat.[54] Although Beale does not appear to have had any formal role in these parliamentary debates and developments, in time he collected a vast amount of material not only from the parliament of 1572 but also that of 1571, in session from 2 April to 29 May, precisely when he was in London as the bearer of letters from Walsingham, and when Burghley had given Beale access to 'some of our occurrentes'.[55] Given his experience and expertise in civil law in the Holy Roman Empire and Paris, it is unsurprising that Beale took a significant interest in collecting and learning what he could of English law from these two parliamentary meetings. In fact, from this point forward, Beale's interest in English history and legal traditions, as well as his habits in collecting material for his personal archive, moved into high gear. If he

---

[52] Smith to Burghley, 30 March 1572, TNA, SP 70/123, fol. 32r (orig.); 4 April 1572, TCD, MS 706, fols 351r–2r.

[53] Smith to Burghley, 9 March 1572, TNA, SP 70/146, fol. 55r (old foliation, 61r), noting Beale as 'this berer'.

[54] For a narrative, see Neale, *Elizabeth I and Her Parliaments, 1559–1581*, 241–312. For documents, T. E. Hartley (ed.), *Proceedings in the Parliaments of Elizabeth I*, Vol. I: *1558–1581* (Leicester, 1981), 259–418.

[55] Beale's papers included multiple manuscript versions of John Hooker's *Order and Usage*, on which see Vernon F. Snow (ed.), *Parliament in Elizabethan England: John Hooker's 'Order and Usage'* (New Haven, CT, 1977), esp. 96–7; BL, Additional MSS 48020, fols 26r–52v; 48025, fols 154r–61v; 48110, fols 2r–42r. Thomas Norton's collection of papers on these parliaments came to Beale in 1584: BL, Additional MS 48023, fols 117r–62r; on Norton's papers in Beale's possession, see Chapter 7. Cf. BL, Additional MSS 48098, 48049, fols 74r–103v, 249r–50v. See also above, n. 15. Beale later in 1576 sat for Totnes, Devon, in the second session of Elizabeth's fourth parliament, which episode is explored below.

had previously kept his papers and books in parcels and trunks, as noted in 1570 by his friend, John Herbert, he would soon need more and bigger containers.[56] Regarding the parliamentary concerns at the time, the House of Commons' strong resolution to execute Norfolk for treason, and to urge the same for Mary, would certainly have seemed justified to Beale and solidified his thinking for years to come regarding the threat to Elizabeth's person caused by Mary and her conspirators both within and beyond England's borders.

As the political maelstrom calmed in late June and early July, Beale's life changed dramatically, irrevocably, and (as he would have thought) for the better. On 8 July 1572, Beale took the oath to become a clerk of the Privy Council, and he was noted as an esquire—a gentleman or one with the right to bear arms. Beale's coat of arms dated to the time of his great-grandfather, William, and included a gold chevron with black stars, three gold griffins on a black background, and, as crest, a black and red unicorn with a gold mane, horn, and beard; the griffin, according to heraldic tradition, signified watchfulness, which only seems appropriate in Beale's case.[57]

From that day forward in 1572, his focus on English domestic affairs became of equal if not greater significance than his interest in foreign affairs, but his previous expertise and continued contacts would be counted on for the rest of his life. Roughly a week before Beale took the oath, for example, Walsingham wrote to Leicester highlighting that Beale was to give the earl a full report of the situation in France vis-à-vis the situation in Flanders and the potential for an alliance with the German princes, noting also the role played by Johannes Junius and the Elector Palatine; all of this talk, of course, was for the sake of the international Protestant cause.[58] In London, though, Beale's point of view—literally—became that of an insider with deep knowledge looking at the wars of religion in France and the Netherlands from across the Channel rather than from a position embedded within. He would remain in England for nearly four years before his next trip to the mainland—the longest stretch of time in England since his childhood.

---

[56] See Chapter 3, n. 78.

[57] Privy Council register for 24 May 1570 to March 1576, TNA, PC 2/10, 106; John Roche Dasent (ed.), *Acts of the Privy Council of England*, Vol. 8: *1571–1575* (London, 1894), 78–9 transcribes the oath. Beale's coat of arms is reproduced with colour coding ('s' for sable/black, 'o' for or/gold) alongside a family tree noting some but not all of his children (Francis, Margaret, Katherine, and Elizabeth): BL, Harley MS 1561, fol. 65r. These arms without the crest are included in the coat still visible and retaining some elements of colour on Edith's funerary monument, c.1628, in the church of St Michael and All Angels, Eastington, Gloucestershire. Edith's coat combined (marshalled) Beale's coat on the dexter half, with those of her father, Henry St Barbe of Somerset on the sinister. The comparatively plain coat of arms affiliated with the Beale family of Shropshire at BL, Additional MS 48025, fol. 200v, is not relevant.

[58] Walsingham to Leicester, 2 July 1572, TCD, MS 706, fols 382v–3r; cf. Walsingham to Burghley, 12 July 1572, TNA, SP 70/124, fol. 54r–v but missing first leaf (orig.), enclosing Ehem to Junius, fol. 56r–v. See also Friedrich to Junius (in Paris), June 1572, printed in Kluckhohn, *Briefe Friedrich des Frommen*, Vol. 2, Part 1, 467–8.

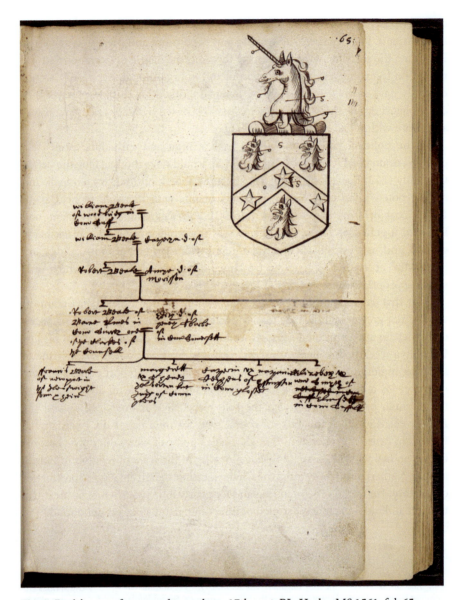

Fig. 6 Beale's coat of arms and genealogy, 17th cent. BL, Harley MS 1561, fol. 65r.
Reproduced with permission from the British Library.

Old habits die hard. Beale was still very concerned about foreign affairs, and, less than two months after he took the oath in London, the St Bartholomew's Day massacre in Paris shocked Europe in late August 1572. Shaken from any remaining sense of security after the Peace of Saint-Germain a year earlier, Protestants across Europe were enraged by the organized and orchestrated assassination of the Huguenot champion, Admiral Coligny, along with several thousand others in

Paris and, subsequently, in twelve other cities.[59] For Beale and so many others, the massacres represented a watershed moment for religious identity and political action. Given his years in Paris, it is not surprising that Beale was keenly interested in the events in France; nor is it surprising that he still had contacts (starting with Walsingham, now firmly back in Paris) to relay accurate and up-to-date information. To be sure, Walsingham relayed what information he had from royal and other French sources, noting also that he had heard that the Protestant princes of Germany 'awake, and marvelouselye stomacke this late crueltye, and doe thinke that the daunger there will reach to themselves yf they doe not seek to prevent it'. It appears that Beale had additional informants, though, so that the fullest and most significant English reaction to the St Bartholomew's Day massacres in Paris and elsewhere ultimately came from Beale's hand in London, and it was addressed specifically to Beale's primary target for such works of intelligence going back several years—William Cecil, Lord Burghley.[60] This work was not, in the end, an account of the violence in France but rather a plan for how England could avoid the same by working with religious allies and defending itself against enemies. It laid bare Beale's state of mind at the time—and for years to come—and so is worth detailed analysis.

Beale began by observing that Burghley had to this point accepted Beale's letters 'in good parte' and by hoping that this longer work would be received similarly. He noted 'the daungere of the Queenes Majesties estate and such remedies as seme to me requisite', and urged that his purpose in writing was not any private gain or hatred towards anyone, but rather that he was 'only forced thereto by an

---

[59] On the situation in Paris, see Diefendorf, *Beneath the Cross*, esp. 76–106. On the provincial cities, Philip Benedict, 'The Saint Bartholomew's Massacres in the Provinces', *Historical Journal*, 21 (1978), 205–25. For a broader survey, Mack P. Holt, *The French Wars of Religion, 1562–1629*, 2nd edn (Cambridge, 2005). For some of the international reaction, Robert M. Kingdon, *Myths about the St. Bartholomew's Day Massacres 1572–1576* (Cambridge, MA, 1988).

[60] See Walsingham's correspondence with Burghley and the recently installed principal secretary Thomas Smith, in TNA, SP 70/125, BL, Cotton MS Vespasian, F. VI, and *Compleat Ambassador*, 238–46; quotation from Walsingham to Smith, 16 September 1572, TCD, MS 706, fol. 430r-v (*Compleat Ambassador*, 245). Discussion in Read, *Mr Secretary Walsingham*, 1.198–262. Beale received at least five different accounts, lists, and letters in Latin and French describing aspects of the massacres either in whole or in part: BL, Additional MSS 48118, fols 211r–16r, 224r–6v, 236r–8v, 242r–8v; 48126, fols 101r–3v. Beale's discourse in his draft, BL, Additional MS 48049, fols 340r–57r; fair copy with title, 'A discourse of Mr Beales after the great murder in Paris & other places in France August 1572', BL, Cotton MS Titus, F. III, fols 302r–8v; Burghley's own final version with title 'A Mr Beales discourse after the greate murder in Paris and other places in ffraunce in August 1572', with Burghley's endorsement, 'What perill may come to England', CP, 246/29 (orig.), retaining some of the marginal comments in Beale's draft omitted in the Cotton copy. The finished product in the Cecil Papers is unattributed in *Calendar of the Cecil Papers in Hatfield House*, Vol. 13: *Addenda* (London, 1915), 112, though admittedly 'Mr Beales' is most vigorously struck through. Potential direct or indirect informants from Paris included Languet and the mutual friend, André Wechel. See Chapter 3. Scholars have long assumed without evidence that Beale was a witness to the massacre in Paris and wrote his discourse there (e.g. *ODNB*), but Beale uses the word 'here' to refer to England, and it is highly unlikely that he would be back in Paris so soon after becoming a clerk of the Privy Council. A tantalizing possibility for Beale's location in Paris after the massacre is offered in Cooper, *Queen's Agent*, 96–8.

earnest zeale to thadvauncement and maintenaunce of trew religon[,] the preservacion and continewance of her highnes royall person and dignitie[,] & the libertie of this our poore Countrey'.[61] Accordingly, from this work one gets a good sense of Beale's thinking in the wake of the massacres and after reading various reports directly from France. Rather than seeing the massacres as a series of events isolated in a national context, Beale saw 'theis late horrible accidentes in ffraunce' as part of a wider 'coniuration of the Counsell of Trent to roote out all such as[,] contrarie to the popes tradicions[,] make profession of Christes Gospell'. While Catholic powers, by way of various treaties and dissimulations, had prevented Elizabeth, the Protestant princes of Germany, and Protestants in France from providing sufficient plans to defend themselves previously, Beale thought 'yt time and more then tyme for vs to awake out of our dead sleepe & take heede lest like mischefes as haue alreadye ouerwhelmed our brethern and neighboures in ffraunce and fflaundres embrace vs'.[62] Beale widened the international context further by discussing the (perceived) conspiracies between the Holy Roman Emperor and Spanish and French royal families regarding the Polish succession, while noting that the pretended French efforts for Anjou to accede to the throne of the Polish-Lithuanian Commonwealth were 'a devise to blind ours and the Germans eyes'.[63] Moreover, and bringing matters closer to home, Beale supposed—based on reports from the mainland—that Catholic marriage alliances would include Anjou 'matched with the queen of Scottes[,] which matter hath bene longe a brewinge[,] wherof Mr Walsingham more then a twelve month sith advertised her Majestie'.[64] As proof that an Anjou/Mary marriage was a threat to English security, 'they iointlye minde the conquest of this Islande [...] [a]nd as the booke printed not longe sith in Liege for the defence of the Scotish queenes title affirmeth that she hath an interest in this Crowne'. Beale's reference here to the book written by John Leslie, bishop of Ross, and published at Liége in 1571 further testifies to the fact that Beale saw the world of religious conflict not in an isolated or insular fashion but rather as an intimately connected network or web, with conspiratorial Catholics looking to suppress, extirpate, or exterminate those 'of the true religion' no matter where they lived—France, Flanders, or England.[65] The shift of focus to Mary Queen of Scots continued in Beale's discourse when he observed that, although Mary could pursue the English throne by way of her

---

[61] Beale's discourse, CP, 246/29, fol. 1r (alternative foliation, 30r).

[62] Beale's discourse, CP, 246/29, fol. 1r–v (30r–v).

[63] Beale's discourse, CP, 246/29, fol. 1v (30v). Henri, duke of Anjou, eventually became king of Poland-Lithuania in 1573 before becoming king of France in 1575. See Norman Davies, *God's Playground: A History of Poland*, Vol. 1: *The Origins to 1795*, rev. edn (Oxford, 2005), 312–17.

[64] Beale's discourse, CP, 246/29, fol. 1v–2r (30v–31r).

[65] Beale's discourse, CP, 246/29, fol. 2r (31r); cf. fol. 5r–v (34r–v). On Ross, and on Hales's notes on the work in defence of Mary Queen of Scots, see above. Beale also noted a book published in Scotland in 1567 offering prophesies that England would be conquered 'as I remember [...] by those whome we esteemed the vilest people of all'. This work has not yet been traced.

claim to the succession, she would prefer to take England by conquest in league with Anjou and other international Catholics and, in so doing, follow through on the papal bull of 1570 (*Regnans in Excelsis*), which stated that Elizabeth was a schismatic and usurper.[66] Beale's discourse also demonstrated his legal knowledge in marital affairs by dispelling the argument that, because Mary had previously been married to Henri's brother (Francis), she could not legally marry Henri; papal dispensations, Beale pointed out, had long provided the means to such arrangements, though he remained conspicuously silent regarding Henry VIII's marriage with Katherine of Aragon.

The international repercussions of the massacres in Paris and elsewhere hit Beale hard. Having spent the vast majority of his adult life in a range of settings on the mainland, he was very much a broadly European Englishman who saw the interconnected nature of Spanish, French, Scottish, Imperial, and papal machinations (as he understood them). To be sure, in his words, 'Spaine is malitious and will be for many causes revenged. ffrom the ffrench kinge[,] whoe so commonly hath deceaved thexpectacion of all men[,] no more good can be looked for then from an other Nero'. Then again, Beale saved his greatest vitriol for Mary. Indeed, 'the chiefest mischef is to be feared inwardly, I meane the facton of the queene of Scottes and papestes in this realme' who 'haue intelligence to and fro with our ennemies'. In sum, Beale feared a two-pronged attack by Catholic powers from abroad and within England itself—from 'many of the puisantest princes of Europe' in collaboration with English Catholic 'rebells' within England and supported by those English abroad—'as thaccustomed manner of exiles is to egge them on'. Beale's comment on English exiles encouraging rebellion within England is directed here at Catholics, but the sentiment applied just as much to Protestants during the reign of Queen Mary, when he himself was in exile. More to the point in 1572, at the centre of the plot would be Mary Queen of Scots, 'whoe by her doinges seameth as muche spanish as french', and 'will be a meanes to continew good vnitie' alongside the Catholic religion that 'shall knitt the knott of this concorde'.[67]

Beale's fear was all the more heightened because, as he put it, England had 'no parfect amitie[,] frendship[,] or intelligence with any', Scotland and Ireland either standing aside in one case or even receiving aid in rebellion against English forces in another. Regarding other potential allies across the Protestant world, '[t]he Princes of Germany we care not for, Sweden graunteth letters of Mar[qu]e, Denmarke is indifferent and ready to enclyne to the greater parte'. Moreover, one of Elizabeth's pensioners, the duke of Holstein, had changed sides and had served

[66] On *Regnans*, see Aislinn Muller, *The Excommunication of Elizabeth I: Faith, Politics, and Resistance in Post-Reformation England, 1570-1603* (Leiden, 2020), with reference to Beale and Mary at 134.
[67] Beale's discourse, CP, 246/29, fols 3r, 4r–v, 5r (32r, 33r–v, 34r).

the Spanish duke of Alba for several years, Beale noting also in detail Holstein's activities to take the city of Hamburg for Alba.[68]

To secure the realm, Beale returned to the issue that originally brought his name to Burghley's attention, and which probably caused him to stay overseas longer than he otherwise would have during the 1560s—the succession. Wary to delve deeply into the matter because 'yt passeth to farr my capacitie', he generally urged that Elizabeth marry sooner rather than later for her own safety as well as that of her realm.[69] Here Beale was, of course, fully aware of the most recent marriage negotiations with Henri, duke of Anjou, but now he pushed for Elizabeth to marry to ensure a thoroughly Protestant succession rather than anything that could be seen as lukewarm or contrary to the Protestant cause. In a similarly strident fashion, Beale thought the time for half-measures regarding Mary had long passed:

> And amongst theis [our enemies] chefest heddes must be removid[.] I meane the queene of Scottes whoe[,] as she hath ben the principall cause of the ruine of the two realmes of ffraunce and Scotland[,] hath partly played the like parte here[.] All wisemen generally thoroughe out Europe cannot sufficiently marvell of her Majesties over mild dealinge with her in norishinge in her owne bosome so pestiferous a viper as hath already gon about the destruction of her highnes person and estate, hath empoysonned and alienated the hartes of diuers of the subiectes of this land and so contineweth daily. [Therefore, Catholic practices against England will] continew vnles this realme and the world be ridd of so wicked a fury. She hath deserved yt[,] and how iustly her Majestie may proceade to thexecucion was declared by thadvise and consent of her hole parliament.[70]

Thus, although Beale had not participated in the parliamentary proceedings of spring 1572, he was well aware of and agreed wholeheartedly with that parliament's decisions. If, for whatever reason, Mary were eventually to be released from her captivity, Beale remembered 'a sainge of Suetonius that such as cam from prison or exile afterwardes to thEmperiall dignitie proved ordinarily great tyranntes: and whether we ought to conceaue the like feare of this woman now lett all likelyhoodes iudge.'[71]

---

[68] Beale's discourse, CP, 246/29, fol. 4v (33v). Beale's most recent informant regarding Holstein's activities for Alba was probably Ehem, who wrote on exactly these developments to his colleague of the Elector Palatine, Johannes Junius, on 27 June 1572. In Junius's absence the letter was to be delivered to Walsingham. A copy of that letter was then sent with Walsingham's to Burghley on 12 July. TNA, SP 70/124, fols 54r–55v (orig.), 56r–57v.

[69] Beale's discourse, CP, 246/29, fol. 6r (35r).

[70] Beale's discourse, CP, 246/29, fol. 7r (36r). Cf. Beale's description of Mary in his letter of 3 December 1571: '[a] pernitious & viperous enemy to the Queene Majestys estate'. See above, p. 80.

[71] Beale's discourse, CP, 246/29, fol. 8r (37r).

In calling for 'the death of that Jezabell' Mary, Beale here unapologetically nailed his colours to the mast.[72] If he had been cautious in the past, and some like Leicester would say that he had not been cautious enough, the uncovering of the Ridolfi Plot and Parliament's recommendations against Mary fully convinced Beale that he could be more vocal about the Queen of Scots as the most proximate, most dangerous head of the Catholic hydra. In the coming years Mary became increasingly significant to Beale's professional life, but in the short term Beale hoped that England would increase its efforts in gathering intelligence. Hitherto, the parsimonious nature of official intelligence gathering by the Elizabethan state had frustrated Beale in more ways than one, and here his frustration was palpable: 'I pray god yt be not in savinge a penny to spend a pound'.[73] Moving forward, Beale advocated reaching out again to the Protestant princes of Germany who now, in light of the massacres in France, were more likely to respond positively to calls for alliance with England. Moreover, such a 'good amitie' with them would cause the German princes to stand in awe of Queen Elizabeth as the unquestioned leader of European Protestantism, and after all, the number of potential allies on the mainland looked to be dwindling: 'as thinges stand Germany only remaineth from whence any fidelitie or goodnes can be looked for'.[74] In drawing his 'discourse' to a close, Beale detailed some of the ongoing internal politics of the Holy Roman Empire, noting along the way his own previous conversations with 'diuers Counsallors of the chiefest protestaunt princes in Germany', and he called for a replacement for the recently deceased Christopher Mundt, that long-serving English agent in Germany going back to the reign of Henry VIII. This person would, in Beale's view, be sent to deal with the Protestant princes of Germany as well as the kings of Denmark and Sweden to establish 'sum good amitie[,] intelligence[,] and league of mutual defence'.[75] Beale's recommendation was John Alymer, bishop of London and erstwhile tutor whose rod Beale had not forgotten. He was probably thinking that it was best not to have the two of them in London at the same time.[76]

Yes, Beale was back in London, but his knowledge and expertise were to be the hallmark of his future career, and echoes of his previous experience would come again and again in the 1570s and until his death in 1601. He remained in contact with several correspondents, many of whom offered intelligence not otherwise available to the English regime, and he served as an intermediary between foreigners in England and the English state. Now in a position to convey such

---

[72] Beale's discourse, CP, 246/29, fol. 8v (37v).   [73] Beale's discourse, CP, 246/29, fol. 8v (37v).
[74] Beale's discourse, CP, 246/29, fol. 9r–v (38r–v). See also, Van Tol, *Germany and the French Wars of Religion*, 225–36, esp. 229–32.
[75] Beale's discourse, CP, 246/29, fols 9v–10r (38v–39r). On Mundt's service during the reign of Elizabeth, see *AGR* and Chapter 3, n. 66.
[76] See also Chapter 2.

information more regularly and easily to Burghley and others, Beale was in a salaried position with the potential for soft power and influence in policy. With an income of £50 per year for the rest of his life (paid irregularly at first but later in even quarterly instalments), Beale also had reason to believe he had greater financial security than he had ever known.[77]

Clerk of the Privy Council, and Marriage and Children, 1572–6

Beale's career before his becoming a clerk of the Privy Council was a product of his international travels, learning, and contacts. It seems most likely that Leicester had suggested Beale's name to Elizabeth for this position, as Hales had observed a year previously.[78] Given Beale's by now years-long relationship with Burghley, the lord treasurer would only have agreed with the placement on account of Beale's attention to detail and obedient service. As for Walsingham, he probably was happy to see Beale being retained in London, for, after all, Beale made no secret of his longing to return to England from France. Despite such patrons and allies in high places, and notwithstanding Beale's written works that found their way to Elizabeth, it would be another four years before, as Beale later recalled, he 'could be admitted to kisse her Majesties handes, by reason of some misconceipte about the Erle of Hartfordes matters'.[79] Thus, the work Beale had put in nearly a decade before on behalf of Hertford and Lord Grey to establish the validity of the earl's marriage and claim to the succession had cost him dearly, and it goes some

---

[77] Correspondence with Languet continued to offer news and updates from across Europe, as did that with Anthoine Olivier regarding Dutch affairs: BL, Egerton MS 1693, fol. 11r–v (orig.); BYU, MS 457, item 3 (orig.). On Beale's role as intermediary, for example, for Louis Frennes, Seigneur de Lumbres, an agent of William of Orange and mutual friend of Languet (see Chapter 3), see Smith to Burghley, 2 June 1573, BL, Lansdowne MS 18, fol. 12r (orig.), misdated by Smith as 1563 but correctly identified as 1573 in Thomas Wright (ed.), *Queen Elizabeth and Her Times*, Vol. 1 (London, 1838), 480–1. Beale's salary is noted in the associated undated patent, TNA, C 66/1090, m. 25. The Exchequer's Issue Book for 1572–3 (TNA, E 403/2261, unfoliated) does not include Beale's name and payments where it should. That for 1573–4 (TNA, E 403/2262, unfoliated) includes one payment of £25 followed by two of £12 and 10 shillings; that for 1575–6 (TNA, E 403/2263, unfoliated) includes the same, plus an extra fourth payment of £12. For payments of 1576–7 and subsequently (TNA, E 403/2264, unfoliated, onwards), Beale received regular payments of £12 and 10 shillings. Although the letters patent are undated in TNA, C 66/1090, m. 25, the Issue Book for 1596 notes that his letters patent were dated 4 August 14 Eliz. (1572): TNA, E 403/2281, unfoliated.

[78] See above, n. 24. On the roles performed by the clerks of the Council, and the types of men who served, see Vaughan, 'The Clerks of the Tudor Privy Council, c.1540–1603'; F. J. Platt, 'The Elizabethan Clerk of the Privy Council', *Journal of the Rocky Mountain Medieval and Renaissance Association*, 3 (1982), 123–42. On the membership of the Privy Council at this time, see Michael Barraclough Pulman, *The Elizabethan Privy Council in the Fifteen-seventies* (Berkeley, CA, 1979). Both Vaughan and Platt discuss Beale, but a more dedicated discussion in a literary and archival context is Brewerton, 'Paper Trails: Re-reading Robert Beale as Clerk to the Elizabethan Privy Council'.

[79] Beale to Burghley, 16 October 1592, BL, Lansdowne MS 72/73, fol. 197r (orig.). Also, despite his services in the years ahead, Beale appears never to have exchanged gifts on New Year's Day with the queen. See Chapter 8, n. 3.

way to explain why Beale had not held a more prominent and formal role in the English embassy in Paris between 1564 and 1572. Then again, he had been suggested as Walsingham's replacement during his illness in autumn 1571, only for the interim post to go to Killigrew. Among others, Hales was, of course, imprisoned and never came back to the queen's favour, so it should not be surprising that Beale's implication also caused Elizabeth to exercise some degree of cautious distance. That Hertford's case was still very much a sensitive matter is clear in a letter from Matthew Parker, archbishop of Canterbury, to Burghley in early 1574, when he noted with extreme caution that Burghley had requested certain relevant materials but also that he (Parker) did not want the matter opened again.[80]

Yet Beale had a job to do, so he set upon his new task working alongside Edmund Tremayne, the senior clerk of the two. Other notable clerks with whom Beale would work in the future included Thomas Wilkes, William Waad, and Daniel Rogers. Within a matter of months, he started assembling a 'formulary' or 'precedent book' that included extracts from various letters sent out in the name of the Privy Council. The book was very much Beale's own working compilation serving a utilitarian purpose, a practical workbook for generating the Council's paperwork—from letters to individual noblemen, ambassadors, and princes, to passports, commissions, warrants, and other official orders. Beale wrote on the cover of this volume '1572 Robert Beale', perhaps pleased with himself that he had attained a position of such rich access to official documentation, for the compilation demonstrates that a considerable amount of sensitive information was made available to him so he could learn how to write documents in the Council's name.[81] In the years to come he continued to add more and more to this volume, with additional headings for different types of documents, so the volume now looks like a patchwork but very useful reference tool. In 1575, probably unsatisfied with the rough nature of the work, he assembled a new volume, writing inside the front cover that 'This Booke of Presidents and letters was gathered in the yeare of our Lord god 1575 [...] by me Robert Beale then one of ye clercks of her Majesties most honorable privye councell', followed by his signature in a bold, formal style.[82] As with his previous formulary, Beale continued to add to this volume (until the mid 1580s), and one finds not only his own hand, scribbling extracts and phrases, but other, more secretarial hands also employed for transcription. The longest section by far in this second volume, however, included diplomatic instructions for ambassadors as well as various memorials and letters

---

[80] Parker to Burghley, 9 March 1574, CP, 159/85 (orig.). See also Chapter 8, n. 2.

[81] BL, Additional MS 48150. Beale's spelling of his surname on the cover appears first to have been 'Bele' but then with an 'a' inserted awkwardly between the first 'e' and the 'l'. Given that 'Bele' frequently occurred as a spelling earlier in life, but not later, he may have inserted the 'a' some time later. Cf. the title page of sorts for Beale's notes regarding the processes of the *Reichskammergericht*, 1563, BL, Cotton MS Nero, B. IX, fol. 4r.

[82] BL, Additional MS 48018, with the oath of a clerk of the Privy Council at fol. 4r.

to and from those sent abroad or, of particular interest to Beale, to Mary Queen of Scots during the 1560s. In fact, in a copy of Killigrew's instructions when he was sent to Mary in 1566, next to a section noting 'a certeine booke' written three years previously against the Queen of Scots 'by one of the parliament house' without permission, Beale wrote in the margin 'oh poore John Hales'.[83] Killigrew's instructions for later missions also relevant to Beale follow, such as those for his mission to the Elector Palatine in Germany in 1569, and to France to replace Walsingham during the latter's illness. Additionally, it looks as though Beale made use of Walsingham's letterbook of 1571–2 or at least some of the items copied therein.[84]

These two formularies for a clerk of the Privy Council indicate Beale's access and activity. He was now located at the centre of power in Elizabethan England and became involved in various processes and events, such as accompanying the queen on her progress to Canterbury in 1573, along with many others in Elizabeth's retinue. Beale's exact role during these two weeks (3–16 September) remains unknown, but appears that he went out of his way to help smooth any rough edges because the Chamberlain's accounts for Canterbury record that he was paid 10 shillings 'for paynes by hym taken for the Cytie'.[85] During the mid 1570s he continued to acquire more and more materials for his personal reference archive, and in this way he was very much ahead of his time in collecting, organizing, and storing personal and state papers for later use.[86] In Beale's written works one can see how interconnected he understood Europe to be during the wars of religion; in his archive one can see how he prepared accordingly. He had long collected materials regarding German and French affairs, but now he widened his view to take account of English trade relations with the Hanse in northern Germany, with the Dutch, Spanish, and Muscovites, while also considering Scotland in its own right apart from Mary Queen of Scots' doings.[87] His collecting

---

[83] BL, Additional MS 48018, fols 431r–563v, quotation at fol. 502r.

[84] BL, Additional MS 48018, fols 509r–28v. The British Library's catalogue description for this volume notes that Beale 'made use of the collection attributed to Sir Dudley Digges and published as *The Compleat Ambassador*', but Digges's work was published in 1655, long after Beale's death. It is currently unknown whether and when Beale would have had access to either the copybook now in Dublin, another copybook, or the individual originals sent to their addressees—or all three. Beale's formulary, BL, Additional MS 48018, includes relevant material but was compiled in and after 1575. See Powell, 'Building Paper Embassies'.

[85] Relevant section of Chamberlain's accounts in Elizabeth Goldring, Faith Eales, Elizabeth Clarke, Jayne Elisabeth Archer (eds), *John Nichols's The Progresses and Public Processions of Queen Elizabeth I: A New Edition of the Early Modern Sources*, Vol. 2: *1572–1578* (Oxford, 2014), 84, but see also p. 80 n. 169.

[86] Arnold Hunt discusses Beale's innovatory role and significance in 'Early Modern Secretary', 105–30, esp. 118–28. See also Introduction.

[87] On English trade with the Hanse, BL, Additional MSS 48084, fols 12r–17v; 48010, fols 398r–414v (possibly collected later). On the Dutch, see, e.g. BL, Additional MSS 48007, fols 323r–63v; 48014, fols 20r–74v. On Spain, BL, Additional MS 48116, fols 29r–v, 32r–v, 40r–3v, 45r–v, 50r–v. On Muscovy, BL, Additional MS 48020, fols 330r–2r. On Scotland, its nobility and genealogy, and law, see, e.g. BL, Additional MSS 48049, fols 104r–v, 120r–2v, 329r–32v; 48032–3.

trade-related items made sense because of the centuries-old relationships in this regard and the ongoing negotiations (which ultimately became testy in the case of the Hanse in particular), but Beale's interest in Scottish genealogy was pointed—it all had to do with the succession in Scotland and, potentially, in England. The timing here is significant, too, because in September 1575 Beale personally met the Queen of Scots for the first time at Sheffield Castle. At an especially tense moment due to Elizabeth's refusal to allow the French ambassador, Monsieur de la Mothe Fenelon, to see Mary, Beale accompanied (apparently looking after) the ambassador's nephews and steward on their trip to see Mary, but Beale also delivered what he later called a 'token' gift from Elizabeth to the Queen of Scots, and informed her keeper, George Talbot, earl of Shrewsbury, that funding for her allowance was to be reduced significantly. In fact, the gift was hardly a token; it was described in the inventory of Mary's possessions after her death as 'A Jewell of gold made in the forme of a rocke, all set with diamonds and Rubies'.[88] Whatever Beale had previously written in such strident terms about Mary, he appears to have swallowed his pride and maintained a professional sense of decorum. Indeed, Mary seems to have taken sufficient liking of him to bestow her own gift upon him—a gold chain, which he later needed to sell when in dire financial straits.[89] Beale would not see Mary again for another six years, but as an indication of his ever-expanding network of contacts, in 1575 Alexander Hay sent to Beale a genealogy of Scottish kings from Robert Bruce to James VI. Hay had borne witness against Mary in 1568, was a capable administrator in the Scottish government, and during the mid 1570s was Director of the Chancery and Keeper of the Quarter Seal in Edinburgh; Hay knew what he was doing.[90]

Spain was of particular interest to Beale and not simply because of the wars in the Netherlands. English relations with Spain had long been seen as integral to broader strategies across western and central Europe, especially since the reign of Henry VII, so his personal archive of trade agreements and related materials

[88] Earl of Shrewsbury to Elizabeth, 24 September 1575, LPL, MS 3206, fol. 745r (very rough draft noting the change in funding). Beale summarized his first and subsequent 'missions' to Sheffield in a later letter to Walsingham, 26 September 1586, BL, Cotton MS Caligula, C. IX, at fol. 446v (orig.), recording 'I then had no especiall message to deliuer vnto her, but onlie a token from her majestie.' Beale's role in delivering this item is noted in the margin of the inventory, TNA, SP 53/21, fol. 42r. For the French ambassador's frustration, see his correspondence with Leicester and Walsingham on 20 September 1575, CSPF, IX, items 362–3. For brief recognition of Beale's activity, Leader, *Mary Queen of Scots in Captivity*, 364.

[89] Gold chain noted as sold for £65 in Beale's tabulation of costs incurred for his embassy to the princes of Germany in 1577: Beale's recollections and itemizations of costs for Burghley, 1578(?), BL, Lansdowne MS 51/26, fol. 54r. See Chapter 5, nn. 1–2.

[90] Beale noted his receipt of the genealogy from 'Mr Alexander Haye' on 13 October 1575. BL, Additional MS 48049, fol. 104v. Compare Beale's later comment on Hay that he 'was honest, but not of the quickest witt, brought vp in [Mary's] tyme vnder Liddington, and one that knoweth the course of thinges well, and could say many thinges in her defence yf he would'. Beale to Walsingham, 17 November 1581, TNA, SP 53/11, item 68, fol. 2r–v (orig.). Beale's 'freindship and guidwill' with Hay appears to have faded, so that Hay later remarked that it has been 'very lang sen I hard any thing from yow': Hay to Beale, 8 October 1593, AUL, MS 1009/2, item 48 (orig.). On Hay (d.1594), see *ODNB*.

constituted a major resource to which he could turn when necessary. Moreover, as the perceived threat of Spanish invasion grew during these years, it became increasingly important to prepare the English coastline accordingly, and here one can see Beale's retaining of draft letters from the Privy Council as part of this concern.[91] With remarkable foresight, he also became more and more aware of the evolving situation in Ireland, where English attempts to subjugate the population had stalled, and where English fears of Spanish invasion took special hold. The materials relative to Ireland in Beale's archive, many of which are heavily annotated in his hand, detail the lands and geographic practicalities, the intra-Irish factional divisions and disputes among the Irish and Anglo-Irish, as well as the multiple attempts by the English government to 'reform' English governance or suppress Irish dissent. Some of these materials came indirectly from Henry Sidney, who served as lord deputy of Ireland between 1566 and 1571, and again from 1575 to 1578, but others came directly, it seems, from Edmund Tremayne, the clerk senior to Beale, who had visited Ireland in 1569 and 1573 and written multiple reports for the English government.[92] Beale's was no idle interest in Ireland, for he put his knowledge to use later in 1578 when he wrote yet another detailed 'discourse' with his own endorsement: 'Appon Consultacion for ye new establishment in Irland 1578. this discours was given by Robert Beale to Mr Vicechamberlayn [Christopher Hatton]'.[93] Although it is unclear whether Hatton asked for Beale's opinion (after all, his knowledge was derived not from his own first-hand experience but from others' accounts), his ability and confidence in offering his opinion in the discourse testifies both to his access to historical, legal, and current information, and to his soft power potentially to influence English policy in Ireland. By this point, Beale had mastered the arts of gathering intelligence from multiple sources and perspectives, then assembling that information into a systematic analysis of the various political positions, offering in the end his own solution to the problem. His unsolicited written works might have been at points ill-advised in their being too strident, but there is no question that Beale's mind and work habits were efficient, thorough, and forward-looking.

To be sure, Beale's career in government service was in the ascendant during the mid 1570s. He had benefited from the patronage and assistance of some of the most powerful men in the realm; he had secured a long-term administrative position at the heart of government; he had earned a good salary. Now in his early

[91] BL, Additional MSS 48000; 48063, fols 261r–4v; cf. 48062, fols 408r–9v; 48088, fols 14r–15v. On English trade with Spain, and the 16th-c. development of the Spanish Company, see Pauline Croft (ed.), *The Spanish Company* (London, 1973), vii–xxix.
[92] BL, Additional MSS 48015, 48017. On Sidney and Tremayne, *ODNB*. David Heffernan, *Debating Tudor Policy in Sixteenth-Century Ireland: 'Reform' Treatises and Political Discourse* (Manchester, 2018), xxi, 3, 16 describe Beale as Walsingham's 'understudy' and offer Walsingham as Beale's source for Irish material.
[93] 'Touchinge the plott for Ireland', 1578, BL, Additional MS 48017, fols 200r–7r. For discussion of this tract on 'coign and livery', see Chapter 6.

thirties, though, his personal life was changing, too. John Hales, Beale's step-uncle who had provided support and in some respects saw him through the lean years of the early and mid 1560s, had not been as visible a factor in Beale's life since his return to England in 1572. Hales had, of course, advocated for Beale and his brother, William, in 1571, and it may be that Hales had something indirectly to do with the brothers' respective careers. Hales, though, died in late December 1572, leaving no children but naming Beale as executor of his will dated shortly before.[94] In consequence, 'for his paynes therein' he was compensated with a lump sum of 100 marks (£66.13.4), a considerable sum well exceeding his new yearly salary as clerk of the Privy Council. Thus, in losing his most significant early supporter and substitute father figure, Beale gained significantly by way of a financial windfall; because of his new role and need to live in London, Hales's largesse was timely. Beale was also soon assigned the wardship of the younger John Hales (the nephew), a responsibility that included looking after not only the youngster but also the considerable lands bequeathed to him in Warwickshire and Coventry. For his duties to the family, Beale received an annuity of £13.6.8 from May 1573 until the younger John reached majority, and the child may well have lived in London with Beale during this time. It appears that the child's education (which included lessons in French) was entrusted to the Dutch humanist Jacobus Regius, who had been in Coventry for the previous couple of years but had recently relocated to London.[95]

Even more significant than Beale's caring for Hales's nephew, which was in many ways reciprocal to how Hales had cared for the young Robert, was the fact that by August 1574 he had married Edith St Barbe, daughter of Henry St Barbe and sister to Ursula St Barbe, the wife of Walsingham. Due to their close professional relationship and daily proximity during their time in France, Beale and Walsingham had gotten to know each other very well and, as others have pointed out, their ideological outlooks on the European situation were essentially mirror images.[96] The precise dating of Beale's marriage is unknown, but certain termini exist: Walsingham had married Ursula in 1566, and he referred to Beale as his 'my brother Beale' by 27 August 1574 at the latest.[97] Unfortunately, no records of the marriage have been found among the parish registers associated with Beale, but it

[94] John Hales's will, 17 December 1572, Coventry History Centre, PA244/37/7 (copy, misdated 27 December, but cf. the citation in PA1798/2). Proved probate record, 5 February 1573, TNA, PROB 11/55/54. Beale's brother, William, is not named in Hales's will.

[95] Grant of wardship, 19 May 1573, TNA, C 66/1105, m. 9. Regius to Beale, 4 September 1573, AUL, MS 1009/2, item 46 (orig.), noting the role of a certain Peter, most likely the same Peter named in Hales's will as his servant. On Regius, see P.J. Blok and P.C. Molhuysen (eds), *Nieuw Nederlandsch Biografisch Woordenboek*, Part 4 (Leiden, 1918), cols 1130–2; available online at https://www.dbnl.org/tekst/molh003nieu00_01/.

[96] Taviner, esp. Chapters 3–5.

[97] *ODNB* for Walsingham. Walsingham's journal, TNA, PRO 30/5/5, fol. 44v. See above, n. 48, for another brother-in-law.

seems unlikely that he would have married Edith while in Germany or France during the 1560s, or in France again in 1571–2. No evidence suggests that he married in 1570 while in London between these periods. The most plausible explanation, unless further evidence comes to light, is that he and Edith exchanged vows at some point between Beale's return to England in spring 1572 and Walsingham's reference in summer 1574. Whether they exchanged rings at this time is unknown, but Beale later declared that the wedding ring 'cam from Popery', who had 'taken [it] from Pagans'. During this time Beale most certainly had his hands full, possibly even looking after the younger John Hales in a very direct sense, so he could have used Edith's help. That Beale's own first child, Francis, was not born until December 1577 might have been a consequence of that wardship and is evidence of the relatively late start for Beale as a traditional 'family man' in his mid to late thirties. That Francis was baptized in the parish of Allhallows, London Wall, suggests that Beale was living in the London neigh-bourhood he would call home for the rest of his life; that he was almost certainly named after his uncle and senior godfather, Walsingham, demonstrates the close family bonds created during the 1570s.[98]

Parliament, 1576

London was fast becoming Beale's home, just as it had been when he was a child before heading to Coventry. His personal life was based principally in the capital for decades to come, as was his professional life in government service, which became increasingly multifaceted and valued by others. During the first session of Elizabeth's parliament of 1572, Beale was in London and attuned to the debates and developments regarding Mary Queen of Scots; during its second session from 8 February to 15 March 1576, he was in the House of Commons. His sitting for the borough of Totnes, Devon, may at first seem strange given the fact that Beale had never once been there or knew any of its particular concerns, but all is explained by the involvement of Francis Russell, earl of Bedford. The Russell family had exercised considerable patronage and would continue to dominate in the

---

[98] On Beale and wedding rings, Beale's book for Whitgift, 1584, BL, Additional MS 48039, fols 37v–8r. Francis was baptized on 27 December 1577. The first daughter, Ursula, was baptized 17 January 1579 and equally certainly named after the child's aunt and senior godmother, Walsingham's wife. Edward Basil Jupp and R. Hovenden (eds), *The Registers of Christenings Marriages and Burials in the Parish of Allhallows London Wall within the City of London from the Year of Our Lord 1559 to 1675* (London, 1878), 10–11. On names and godparentage, I am most grateful to Emily Chambers for passing along her knowledge, but see also Will Coster, *Baptism and Spiritual Kinship in Early Modern England* (Aldershot, 2002), 167–91, esp. 175–6. Stow's *Svrvay of London* (London, 1598, 1603) (STC 23341, 23343) noted Beale's recently built house on what is now St Mary Axe 'ouer against' London Wall, 110 (1598), 147–8 (1603). See Chapter 8. Walsingham's daughter Mary was baptized in 1572 in Allhallows, London Wall, and he is named as a resident of the same parish later in the 1570s, but Walsingham's *ODNB* entry notes his London residence as Seething Lane in Allhallows, Barking, near the Tower, from the 1560s forward. Jupp and Hovenden, *The Registers*, 7. LMA, P69/ALH6/MS05090, fol. 41v.

West Country parliamentary seats, and in the 1570s Bedford's influence can be seen in the Puritans and Puritan sympathizers who sat for the areas under his control. Under normal circumstances, the MP who sat for the first session in 1572 would have continued to sit in 1576, but that man, Robert Monson, had become a judge during the interim, so a by-election gave Bedford the opportunity to choose his man anew.[99] Bedford could have, of course, chosen nearly anyone, but he had been loosely connected to Beale since 1566 having married Bridget, the widow of Beale's uncle Richard Morison. Thus, via Beale's aunt Bridget, Bedford and Beale were distant family even if not blood related. Given Beale's role as a clerk of the Privy Council, which included Bedford, the two men had had the opportunity to get to know each other in a more personal manner more recently, as well. In a similar vein, Beale's later working relationship with the earl of Shrewsbury is illuminated by his work for the Privy Council during the mid 1570s.[100]

Beale was, to say the least, active in this parliament. He served on committees concerning ports, cloth, benefit of clergy, and goldsmiths. Men from Beale's distant and more recent past, as well as his future, were also engaged on the same committees, including Edmund Tremayne (ports), Thomas Danett (benefit of clergy, goldsmiths), and Thomas Norton (ports, cloth, goldsmiths).[101] For an organized and experienced administrator like Beale, such committee work was routine, even if it was Beale's first time as an MP, but his watching and participating in the process of a bill becoming law would have been particularly appealing to his legal mind. Long had he read deeply in civil and canon law, long had he incorporated legal decisions in his writings, but never before had he seen how laws were made. Yet this session of parliament was not only a theatre for legislation but also a means for both Houses to petition Queen Elizabeth regarding religious causes, and here one can see Beale's Protestant pedigree and ideological inclinations coming to the fore. Very much a junior MP (just as he was a junior clerk), Beale was not involved in the writing of the petition, but he most certainly agreed with its central thrust and appeal: 'a broadly-based, moderate anti-clericalism, and it emphasized the advantages for the civil government which

---

[99] On Bedford's influence, see J. E. Neale, *The Elizabethan House of Commons*, rev. edn (Harmondsworth, 1963), 188–92. On Totnes, see *HoP:HoC*. On the session more generally, see Neale, *Elizabeth I and her Parliaments*, 313–68. The entry for Beale in the copy of Leslie Stephen (ed.), *Dictionary of National Biography* (London, 1885), 4.3–7, in the BL Manuscripts reading room, includes a reader's erroneous suggestion that Beale entered the Commons in 1574.

[100] *ODNB* for Francis Russell, 2nd earl of Bedford. Leicester to Shrewsbury, 3 February 1573, LPL, MS 3197, fol. 53r (orig.). Shrewsbury to Elizabeth, 24 September 1575, LPL, MS 3206, fol. 745r. Pulman, *Elizabethan Privy Council*, 17–51.

[101] For an overview of Beale's parliamentary service, *HoP:HoC*. For the committee work, *Journal of the House of Commons*, Vol. 1: *1547–1629* (London, 1802), 105–6, 111–12, 114–15. The third and final session of this parliament met January to March 1581, when Beale was again active on various committees. Simonds D'Ewes, *A Compleat Journal of the Notes, Speeches and Debates, both of the House of Lords and House of Commons Throughout the whole Reign of Queen Elizabeth, Of Glorious Memory* (London, 1693), 236–65, adds nothing of significance regarding Beale's activity.

would flow from a healthy, preaching Church'.[102] The petition was judiciously cautious in its call for reformation of abuses within the Church, and here Beale would easily have contrasted its call for reformation with that of the 'admonition controversy' some years before.[103] Moreover, Beale's lack of direct involvement might have been due to Leicester's previous advice about staying out of such discussions. Nevertheless, the parliamentary petition was strident in its vitriol for schismatics, heretics, and the 'increase of obstinate papistes' within England obedient to the pope in Rome. An indication that Beale took seriously this parliamentary initiative, a perfect intersection of politics and religion, is a copy of the petition and Elizabeth's response among his papers related to this Parliament, some of which he later acquired directly from Walsingham.[104]

The Road Ahead

Beale's life between 1570 and early 1576 foreshadowed the next twenty-five years until his death in 1601. He continued his work overseas on diplomatic assignments; he secured further patronage and job security in London; he benefited from extended familial relationships while building a family of his own. An overarching theme thus far has been how Beale's early life in Coventry, Germany, and France shaped his ideological outlook in religion and politics, and one can see how his working relationships with like-minded men such as Walsingham, Leicester, and Burghley only confirmed his earlier views. One major part of his early life, however, was forever lost at this time: John Hales. As a father figure during the 1550s and 1560s, Hales had been working for Beale (and his brother, William) behind the scenes. The extent to which Hales was directly responsible for Beale's name becoming increasingly familiar to Burghley and Leicester cannot be known precisely, but it is fair to say that, without Hales, Beale would never have climbed the ladder of government office to become a clerk of the Privy Council in 1572 shortly before Hales's death. At the same time, it is equally reasonable to point out that Burghley and Leicester provided the necessary next step during the early 1570s. Only after having worked closely with Walsingham in France in 1571–2 does Beale become closely identifiable as an administrative and religious *confrère* with the future principal secretary. Their later relationship and reinforcing ideologies, however, need to be understood as the result of their independent but similar experiences during their twenties and thirties, and due to their minds of extraordinary intellect conditioned by their environments.

---

[102] Hartley, *Proceedings*, 1.422; petition and Elizabeth's reply, 445–7.
[103] On which, see above, n. 19.
[104] BL, Additional MS 48064, fols 188r–200v, with petition and response on 191v–3v. These materials appear to have been acquired in or after the final session of this parliament in 1581, during which Walsingham conferred with the bishops on religious matters.

In the coming years, Beale would become increasingly involved with Mary Queen of Scots and more concerned about the state of religion in England. His position at the heart of the Elizabethan government would continue, thus ensuring his immersion in domestic affairs and paperwork, but if one eye was focused on particularly English issues and developments, then the other was fixated on the wider European theatre and the survival of international Protestantism in France, the Netherlands, and elsewhere. That should be no surprise; such a bifurcated but intertwined perspective resembled his life as a whole. Soon after the parliamentary session of 1576 ended in March, with significant administrative and legislative business complete, Beale learned that he would soon be heading across the Channel again—this time on official business and with instructions as a formal ambassador.

A European Elizabethan: The Life of Robert Beale, Esquire. David Scott Gehring, Oxford University Press.
© David Scott Gehring 2024. DOI: 10.1093/9780198902942.003.0004

5

Diplomatic Interlude

In April 1576 Robert Beale crossed the North Sea for the first time in roughly four years; in 1577 he did so again on his second embassy in as many years. Since his taking the oath to become a clerk of the Privy Council, Beale's life in London had been sedate and safe if compared to the decades before 1572. A confluence of developments and attitudes within the Privy Council, Parliament, and the Netherlands in early 1576, however, meant that Beale's experience and expertise would be called upon in a very official capacity. The next year, a series of events in Protestant Germany brought Beale back to some of the people and lands he had previously known so well. Crossing the seas and serving as Her Majesty's representative was not for the faint of heart or light of pocket. As Beale later recalled regarding the mission of 1576, he was in 'danger of drowning, and taking by the Spaniardes, who laie at Bruers hauen [Brouwershaven, Zeeland], wherby I ventured to passe', and he 'tooke paines to goe it a foote' between Middelburg and Flushing (Vlissingen, a distance of over four miles) for his negotiations. Although he had a daily allowance of 40 shillings, his extraordinary costs added up significantly, and from the start, he incurred charges of £15 for his initial crossing of the North Sea (paid by his wife, Edith).[1] Worse still, during his crossing in 1577, Beale was wounded when his company fell victim to pirates and 'were spoiled of 250li at the least, in readie money, besides all our apparell and other furniture[,] wherof 150li was mine owne'. Despite his thrift and 'daies of my bare dietts', Beale incurred significant debts because of payments for transportation, horses, and various other costs during his embassy of, according to his own calculation, 1400 English miles 'at the least'. The experience of piracy left a lasting impression, for Beale preferred in the future that he 'wold not be in like danger to be assalted and so violently taken, hurt, kept vnder hatches, menaced with killing & drowning

---

[1] Beale's recollections and itemizations of costs for Burghley, 1578(?), BL, Lansdowne MS 51/26, fols 53r–4v, quotation at 53r; inclusion among Burghley's papers for 1586 suggests dating for that year, but internal evidence more convincingly suggests 1578; incomplete transcription dated erroneously to 1591 in Strype, *Annals of the Reformation*, 4.115–17. Cf. Beale's lengthy complaint about his charges not being reimbursed in Beale to Burghley, 15 April 1578, BL, Lansdowne MS 27/32, fols 62r–3v (orig.); incompletely transcribed in Strype, *Annals*, 4.117–19. A more positive view regarding payments to Elizabeth's ambassadors is Gary Bell, 'Elizabethan Diplomatic Compensation: Its Nature and Variety', *Journal of British Studies*, 20 (1981), 1–25; at 10–11 Bell observes the full payment to Beale after his return in July 1576, and at 25 he notes the gift to Beale of cash from the duke of Brunswick in 1577 (see below, n. 2), but in the latter mission Beale was still short.

[...] & after left without bread, drink, money or other furneture to the mercy of the wide seas'.[2]

Beale's service as Elizabeth's formal ambassador to the Dutch in 1576 and the Germans in 1577 did not come out of nowhere, and it should not be surprising all things considered. In many ways, he was the exact man for the job in both cases, but, then again, he was one of several ambassadors in each case. During the parliamentary session of early 1576, when he was active on several committees and witness to an increasingly strong position taken by advocates of an unyielding Protestantism in the face of Catholic aggression, foreign policy issues were taken up by the House of Commons. As a prerogative of the queen, foreign policy was more an issue for the Privy Council and rarely discussed in the Commons. Given Beale's position as clerk of the Council, and now in the Commons, he had an ear in each. In this parliament, an increasing fear for Dutch Protestants was coupled with an anti-Catholic sentiment that saw Spain as the principal threat to Protestant Europe. The Dutch, desperate for assistance in late 1575, sought protection from Elizabeth, and, if unavailable, from Henri III, king of France. Fear of French control of the Netherlands and the potential for a Franco-Spanish alliance drove some MPs in the Commons to take a strong position for intervention; Elizabeth and Burghley were less certain.[3] The perennial English concern to ensure neither France nor Spain became too powerful added strength to the argument that the Dutch Protestants needed assistance, and the arrival in London of Philip of Marnix, lord of St Aldegonde, a veteran of the Protestant cause, only added more. In late 1575 and early 1576, Spain's financial situation was parlous and on the precipice of default, but the attempt to split the neighbouring rebellious provinces of Zeeland and Holland was considered worth the effort. At the time of Beale's mission, only the town of Zierikzee remained in the Dutch rebels' hands, though a month-long siege by the Spanish was wearing it down. As Geoffrey Parker has observed, both sides agreed 'that the fate of the whole revolt rested upon the outcome of that siege. If Zierikzee fell, the rebellious provinces would be cut in two and [the Dutch] position would be far weaker; if Zierikzee

---

[2] Beale's recollections, BL, Lansdowne MS 51/26, fols 53r–v; Beale mentioned these losses in his letter to Burghley, in which he also noted that, to raise funds for his journey before departing, he sold the gold chain given to him by Mary Queen of Scots for £65 (fol. 54r). His wounding is mentioned only in Beale to Burghley, 24 April 1595, BL, Lansdowne MS 79/80, fols 192r–5v, at 192v (orig.). The lasting impression is in Beale to Burghley, 15 April 1578, BL, Lansdowne MS 27/32, fol. 62v (orig.). Beale continued to seek Burghley's assistance in getting reimbursement for several years. See, e.g. Beale to Burghley, 30 July 1582, CP, 162/47 (orig.), which notes at 2v the 'extraordinary liberality' offered by the princes of Germany to Beale, e.g. the £340 from the duke and duchess of Brunswick recorded in his recollections at 54v.

[3] A sound discussion of the issues is Glyn Parry, 'Foreign Policy and the Parliament of 1576', *Parliamentary History*, 34 (2015), 62–89.

could be saved, [Dutch] credibility in the eyes of foreign rulers, and particularly those of Queen Elizabeth, would be decisively strengthened.'[4]

In any event, Beale's embassy from April to July 1576 was not to sign a defensive pact or build any sort of religious alliance. The immediate concerns were more mundane. First, Dutch seamen out of Flushing had seized Lucretia d'Affaytadi, daughter of a wealthy Italian merchant, and fiancée of the Portuguese ambassador in England, Francesco Giraldi. She was sailing under an English flag, so the affront to Elizabeth was serious. A tit-for-tat followed, with Dutch ships seized and stayed at Falmouth, Cornwall, while English ships were similarly captured and retained at Flushing. The final wound to the queen's honour occurred in April when Edward de Vere, earl of Oxford, was taken and stripped to his shirt while attempting to cross the Channel back to England after a year's travel in France and Italy.[5] The insults to the Portuguese ambassador and Oxford aside, the jeopardizing of English commercial enterprise was serious because the Merchant Adventurers, as well as the budding Spanish Company, were vital to the English economy and, by association, Elizabeth's treasury.[6] Accordingly, to repair the damage done, a concerted and sustained effort extended from England by way of individual embassies by John Herbert (Beale's old friend), William Davison (a close future colleague), and William Winter (Elizabeth's vice admiral whose esteemed naval service had extended back to the reign of Henry VIII and who joined Beale in June). Additionally, Daniel Rogers supplied information throughout much of 1575–6 and negotiated alongside Beale.[7] Like Herbert, Beale was a sensible candidate as ambassador because of his proficiency in multiple languages and his legal knowledge and expertise; having the patronage of Burghley, Leicester, and Walsingham, could not have hurt his candidacy either. Beale, though, would have internalized the gravity of the religious situation perhaps more than the others—save Rogers—because of his previous experience in the Holy Roman Empire and France. While economic and political causes nearly brought Elizabeth to loggerheads with William the Silent, prince of Orange, the real danger underlying it all—as Beale knew all too well—was the potential fracture of solidarity among Protestants across Europe. So, the two separate realms of

---

[4] On Marnix, see Monique Weis, 'Philip of Marnix and "International Protestantism": The Fears and Hopes of a Dutch Refugee in the 1570s', *Reformation & Renaissance Review*, 11 (2009), 203–20, esp. 212–16; Aloïs Gerlo and Rudolf De Smet (eds), *Marnixi Epistulae: De briefwisseling van Marnix van Sint Aldegonde: Een kritische uitgave, Pars I (1558–1576)* (Brussels, 1990). On the state of the war, see Geoffrey Parker, *The Dutch Revolt: Revised Edition* (London, 1988), 156–78, on Zierikzee, 167–8, quotation, 168. Cf. Jonathan Israel, *The Dutch Republic: Its Rise, Greatness, and Fall 1477–1806* (paperback with corrections, Oxford, 1998) 184–5.

[5] For brief summaries and details of these events, see: Read, *Mr Secretary Walsingham* 1.327–8; Conyers Read, *Lord Burghley and Queen Elizabeth* (London, 1960), 173–4; Wallace T. MacCaffrey, *Queen Elizabeth and the Making of Policy, 1572–1588* (Princeton, NJ, 1981), 206–7. A fuller exposition with reference to Beale's involvement is Taviner, 157–67.

[6] On the potentially awkward position of the Spanish Company, see Croft, *Spanish Company* (London, 1973), vii–xxix.

[7] Use with caution Bell, *Handlist of British Diplomatic Representatives 1509–1688*, 183–5. See esp. *ODNB* for Herbert and Rogers in 1576.

the secular and the sacred were necessarily intermingled and mutually dependant causes in the interest of a broad, collaborative network among Protestants to withstand Catholic aggression coming from France, Spain, or elsewhere. Moreover, Beale was particularly good at recognizing the interconnected nature of religion and politics across international boundaries, according to his own account in April 1578, and he thought that Burghley was hard pressed to find one 'at home & abroad of better estimation' than himself. Also, although he had always behaved well while abroad, he knew that, because these ventures were in the queen's name, 'it behoved me to kepe sum better countenance [bearing/behaviour] then hertofore I did'.[8] In April 1576, when preparing for his first mission as the queen's formal ambassador in his own right (not as a mere hanger-on or informant), his understandings of diplomacy and diplomatics came together because of his need to negotiate on an international level with a European prince at his court, and because of his critical analysis of the documentation produced by these negotiations. Given his by-now established habits of collecting, collating, and copying paperwork of all sorts, a reasonably full record of Beale's activity emerges.[9]

Zeeland, 1576

Beale was entrusted to settle a major controversy with a religious ally in the prince of Orange, and for a man who had previously never served as ambassador, his official instructions showed a notable level of trust. The final version of his instructions dated 17 April, which he kept in his own collections and included a final paragraph not found in other versions, informed him that he was to meet directly with the prince or the governors of Zeeland to secure the release of English ships from Flushing in exchange for the release of Dutch ships at Falmouth.[10]

---

[8] Beale to Burghley, 15 April 1578, BL, Lansdowne MS 27/32, fol. 63r (orig.). Beale took particular care in this letter to call upon Burghley's memory and high opinion of Beale, hoping that the Lord Treasurer did not think less of him in light of the charges he incurred during the two embassies of 1576 and 1577. He noted 'to remember his chiefest helpe & comfort at your lordship's handes' (63v).

[9] By relying principally on the State Papers in the old Public Record Office (now TNA), which do not shed very much light in this instance, Read, MacCaffrey, and others could only see part of the situation; John Roche Dasent (ed.), *Acts of the Privy Council of England*, Vol. 9: *1575–1577* (London, 1894), 102–3, 130, 138, 145, 151–2, 68, 222, 234 adds little. Taviner went further and saw farther, but the account here brings together all materials known, highlighting Beale's own letters now at Brigham Young University as well as his (very intentional) personal collections and copies among the Yelverton MSS and elsewhere.

[10] Beale's instructions, 17 April 1576, BL, Additional MS 48116, fol. 11r–v (orig.); copies omitting the final paragraph and dated 16 April, TNA, SP 70/138, fol. 46r–v (printed in J. M. B. C. Kervyn de Lettenhove (ed.), *Relations Politiques des Pays-Bas et de L'Angleterre, sous le règne de Philippe II* (Brussels, 1889), 8.339–41); BL, Cotton MS Galba, C. V, fols 271r–2r; copies in BL, Sloane MS 2442, Egerton MS 2790, and Lansdowne MS 155 derive from either the SP 70 version or the Cotton version. The final draft's final paragraph was inserted in a different hand from the main body of the instructions, noting Beale's flexibility in discretion a second time. Cf. Note of things to be declared by [Mr Beale] to the Prince of Orange, 21 April 1576, TNA, SP 70/138, fol. 62r–v, which specifies the merchants and vessels involved.

Officially, the instructions said nothing of an informal religious association or alliance, though a not-so-subtle hint was included that Elizabeth could turn away from the Dutch if she were not satisfied, leaving them prey to Spanish attacks. Beale's natural inclination was to find a settlement with a common enemy of Catholic Spain, and he would have found it comforting that he was assigned to use his own discretion 'accordingly as you shall fynd the State of thinges there at your arryvall', deciding for himself whether to visit the prince or the governors first. As with any official embassy, Beale carried a good deal of other paperwork, including letters addressed to him personally and those for the Dutch. Among these other papers one finds why Beale took a personal interest in finding a way forward with England's co-religionists in the Netherlands.

First, the letter written to the prince of Orange by Walsingham, Leicester, Burghley, and Thomas Radcliffe, earl of Sussex, (all of whom signed Beale's instructions and supported the Protestant cause) urged the prince to remedy the situation and thus to avoid bringing the cause of religion into 'scandale et décadence'.[11] Burghley, who appears to have taken a back seat to others during the preparation of the embassy, wrote to Walsingham offering his own opinion that 'Mr beale is wise, and I pray hym[,] if my name be of any vallew, to vse it to ye place' because of his personal interest in the earl of Oxford's cause.[12] Beale also received letters addressed specifically to him (though sent after he had left London on 18 April). Edward Horsey, a military man and previous ambassador, sought Beale's assistance for the restitution of his neighbour's goods (John March, one of the victims of Flushing piracy, it seems).[13] Similarly, John Hastings, a relation of Henry Hastings, earl of Huntingdon, wrote on behalf of his own neighbour, the merchant Peter Geydon, noting also the prince of Orange's virtues, hoping for 'his good successe' and the 'consequence of the establishment of religion', and extending his best wishes to a number of key Dutchmen, Marnix of Aldegonde included.[14] Huntingdon himself, also a signatory to Beale's instructions, wrote on behalf of Geydon, but conveying significantly more. As an advocate of Protestantism both in England and abroad, the earl was glad that Beale was chosen as ambassador to the prince, who sought 'ye aduauncement of ye gospell', whom 'all good persons wylle fauor, and assyste hym with theare prayer, tho they can not ayde hym with worldly power'. Like Beale, Huntingdon saw the fate of the Protestant Netherlands as tied to that of England, urging Beale to convince the prince that order be taken 'that flushynge may bee freed from that slaunder which seemyth in manye partes of thys realme to bee spredde of yt. At which owre papystes do not a lyttell reioyse, and take[,] as they thynke[,]

[11] TNA, SP 70/138, fol. 44; transcribed in Lettenhove, *Relations Politiques*, 341–2.
[12] Burghley to Walsingham, 16 April 1576, TNA, SP 70/138, fol. 42r–v, quotation at 42v (orig.).
[13] Horsey to Beale, 19 April 1576, BL, Egerton MS 1694, fol. 5r (orig.).
[14] John Hastings to Beale, 20 April 1576, BL, Egerton MS 1694, fol. 8r (orig.).

no smalle cause of aduauntage agaynste ye professors of ye gospell'.[15] It seems that several merchants sought Beale's direct assistance, with Walsingham and even Elizabeth urging Beale on behalf of an individual man. Beale's personal connections to London and its mercantile community are here evident, and they continued to grow in the coming decades. When on 2 May at Middelburg Beale received Walsingham's brief and otherwise ordinary letter (written from the court at Whitehall), the first words he read would most certainly have touched: 'Brother Beale'.[16] Another letter written from court on the same day, and similarly unexciting in appearance, serves to highlight Beale's international connections within London. Although Herbert was sent in March to retrieve the fiancée of the Portuguese ambassador, Giraldi, the ambassador wrote directly to Beale (with Walsingham's permission) seeking Beale's assistance for several Italian merchants, and to his own secretary, Julio Busini, in a similar position as the English in Flushing.[17]

Even before Beale reached Zeeland in late April, the multiplicity and variety of those trusting in, and writing to, him at this time demonstrate that, although he was not a top-tier member of the Elizabethan government or London society, he was known well by several people of note and power—locally and internationally. He was recognized as a man of sincere religion and adamantly opposed to Catholicism, and one who inspired many to believe that he could get things done. Upon his arrival in Middelburg, he got to work.

The organizational habits learned during previous decades bore fruit during the mission of 1576, a fine example of which is Beale's collection of documents from late April and May.[18] Forming something of a loose schedule of events, these papers, which include original, sealed Dutch views as well as Beale's copies of English demands, detail the general and particular grievances aired to the prince of Orange and Dutch officers of the admiralty, with responses from the Dutch. The documents themselves read as little more than frustrated negotiations, but the manner in which Beale kept them, and his marginal annotations, show that he recognized the significance of his mission both at the time to his government (the collection of originals with his notes) and for his own, potentially long-term career in Her Majesty's service (his own copies of everything). To be sure, Beale's habits in generating and keeping paperwork for a later date demonstrate not only a detailed mind working in the present but also a methodical intellect taking a long view and knowing that documentary trails provide markers of one's conduct

[15] Huntingdon to Beale, 19 April 1576, BL, Egerton MS 1694, fol. 6r (orig.).
[16] Walsingham to Beale, 22 April 1576, BL, Egerton MS 1694, fol. 10r (orig.).
[17] Giraldi to Beale, 22 April 1576, BYU, MS 457, item 4 (orig.), misdated to 6 April in the BYU catalogue; Beale's copy, BL, Additional MS 48149, fol. 103r–v. Cf. Giraldi's later letters to Busini on 1 June, BL, Egerton MS 1694, fol. 16v; and to Walsingham on 2 June, BYU, MS 457, item 11 (orig.).
[18] Demands general and particular, responses, offer, other papers, dated 27 April to 18 May, BL, Additional MS 14028, fols 2r–14r (orig. and copies); Beale's additional copies, BL, Additional MS 48149, fols 215r–33v, noted by the BL's catalogue as 'annotated by Beale so as to form a journal of his mission'.

and ability, and evidence for legal proceedings. This collection is not in the form of a journal of each day's events like Walsingham's while in Paris, but then again Beale was not serving as a resident ambassador (a job he had refused previously). Rather, his compilation of the documents themselves served as a different form of the ambassador's letterbook, an example of which he would have known from his time in Walsingham's household in Paris.[19]

On the same day Beale received Walsingham's letter (2 May), he responded with a lengthy account of his proceedings thus far.[20] After starting his letter with a tone of familiarity for his brother-in-law, Beale detailed his activity and negotiations since his arrival on Easter Sunday (22 April), noting that the Dutch claimed to stay not just English ships but all ships no matter their flags because of their battle for Zierikzee, and lest the Spanish receive crucial supplies to be used against the Dutch. Beale questioned 'by what lawe or pretext' the Dutch acted, but the tone of his letter tends to increase in a frustrating tone, deeming them 'so vnreasonable and insolent' that 'I wold to god I had broken a lymme, when I was first named to this service'. The trying experience in Middelburg and Flushing was already wearing on Beale, it seems, for he wrote, in closing the letter, that he was to head that afternoon to Holland by way of Brouwershaven, which had recently been taken by the Spanish: 'where the lord send me better successe, and a spedye retorne home.'[21] Beale seems to have made the journey without issue to William the Silent at Delft, for he met with the prince and Daniel Rogers there on 5 May.[22] As happened frequently at the time, delays in the post between the Netherlands and England meant that Beale penned another letter on 21 May before he heard back from Walsingham regarding his missive of 2 May. Here again Beale noted the delays in his negotiations caused by the battle for Zierikzee, as well as the Dutch need to seek external aid, 'seing her majesty hath refused them: And that is as I well perceave ffraunce'. Given the circumstances, Beale acknowledged that his mission was an uphill battle, but as he observed to Walsingham, 'I do the best I can, as shall more particularly appeare when I shall cum [home] my self'. Making matters worse, he had been in extreme pain of late due to a toothache. If Beale had previously hoped for a broken limb to prevent his serving as ambassador, now he was enduring the torments of a toothache while in the field. No wonder he wanted to return home to his wife.[23]

By the time of his next update to Walsingham on 29 May, Beale had finally received word from London on 26 May. In one letter, Burghley, Sussex, Leicester,

[19] Walsingham's journal, TNA, PRO 30/5/5. Walsingham's letterbook, TCD, MS 706 (among other copybooks). See Chapter 4, n. 7.

[20] Beale to Walsingham, 2 May 1576, BYU, MS 457, item 5 (orig.).

[21] Beale to Walsingham, 2 May 1576, BYU, MS 457, item 5, fols 4r, 5r–v (orig.).

[22] Rogers's journal of occurrents, January to July 1576, TNA, SP 70/134, fol. 250v (orig.).

[23] Beale to Walsingham, 21 May 1576, BYU, MS 457, item 7 (orig.), quotations from fols 1v, 2r. The toothache also appears to have kept him from enjoying dinner with the prince of Orange and Daniel Rogers on 18 May. Rogers's journal, TNA, SP 70/134, fol. 251r.

and Walsingham authorized him via 'some further Instructions' to tell the Dutch
that their ships in Falmouth would be released on condition that the English ships
were similarly released. More importantly, they recognized that the potentially
long intervals between the arrivals of Beale's letters meant—and here reflecting
their confidence in him—that 'so shall yt be necessarie that in your dealinges in
these matters you vse all diligence, discrecion and good dexteritie that may bringe
this cause to such a good end'.[24] This somewhat reassuring but ultimately ano-
dyne message contrasted with Walsingham's own message to Beale written and
received on the same days. Here Beale learned of the view in London, which
Walsingham himself vouched to be true, that, unless the Flushingers were
'redvsed to som resonable order, and to forbeare to ovtrage her majesty's svbiects',
rather than continue 'ther former evyll vsage by arrest and others wyse, yt is fvlly
resolved that we shall ioyne with the King of Spayne ageynst them'.[25] Between the
two letters received on 26 May, Beale was reminded of his flexibility in exercising
discretion, and of the gravity of the situation—that is that the unity (real or perceived) of the Protestant cause against Spain depended upon anti-Catholic allies
overcoming comparatively petty differences. In short, again, he was reminded of
the dangers posed by disunity among Protestants.

In late May, Beale wrote again to Walsingham of his hope for Dutch success in
relieving Zierikzee, noting also that if the Spanish were to continue to hold, all
intercourse between Zeeland and Holland would be cut off and 'all will in short
tyme go to wrack'. The Dutch military activities against Spain, with the assistance
of two companies of English forces, were significantly more pressing than were
their negotiations with Beale, but as he said previously and would again, 'I do
what I can (god ys my witnes) to get an answer, and to be despatched'.[26] Beale's
hopes for a speedy return to England were given some justification when
the prince of Orange and Marnix named him as bearer of their letters to Elizabeth,
Burghley, Walsingham, and others; finally, it would have seemed to Beale, he
had something of substance to convey back to London.[27] As events unfolded,

[24] Burghley, Sussex, Leicester, and Walsingham to Beale, 11 May 1576, BYU, MS 457, item 6,
quotations from fol. 1r–v (orig.). Beale's copy, incorrectly dated 20 May, BL, Additional MS 48149,
fols 83r–6r.

[25] Walsingham to Beale, 11 May 1576, BL, Egerton MS 1694, fol. 3r (orig.); misdated in
Walsingham's own hand to 1575. Cf. Walsingham to Beale, 28 May 1576, BL, Egerton MS 1694, fols
12r–3v (orig. with Beale's endorsement of receipt on 1 June).

[26] Beale to Walsingham, 29 May 1576, BYU, MS 457, item 9, fol. 1v (orig.). On English forces serv
ing in the Netherlands before Elizabeth openly committed in 1585, see David J. B. Trim, 'Fighting
"Jacob's Wars": The Employment of English and Welsh Mercenaries in the European Wars of Religion:
France and the Netherlands, 1562–1610', PhD thesis, King's College, University of London, 2002, with
notice of the English companies and Zierikzee, 319–20, 405.

[27] Letters dated 31 May 1576, TNA, SP 70/138, fols 145r–58v (orig.); the prince of Orange and
Marnix name Beale as bearer, and the letters are endorsed 'Mr Beale' and 'By Mr Beale' on the address
leaves; cf. Gerlo and De Smet, *Marnixi Epistulae*, 276–8 for Marnix's letter. Just four days previously, the
Privy Council had written to Beale instructing him, despite his desires for a speedy return to London,
to stay in the Netherlands until his objective was achieved. Privy Council to Beale, 27 May 1576, TNA,

the frustrated negotiations were matched by Beale's disappointment that he would need to stay in Middelburg, whence he wrote again to Walsingham and Burghley on 4 and 5 June, acknowledging his instructions to remain there until his mission was completed.[28] Growing weary of what seemed an endless series of toings-and-froings, delays, and bland affirmations of good will from both sides, Beale would remain in Zeeland for nearly another eight weeks.

Word from home soon came. With a tone of genuine familiarity, Thomas Castelyn, a mutual friend of Beale and Walsingham, informed that Mrs Beale, Edith, was in good health, as were Walsingham and his wife Ursula, Edith's sister. Castelyn had heard from Edith about Beale's previous toothache, though he hoped the pain had long passed. Similarly, Francis Mylles, secretary to Walsingham, wrote to Beale enclosing a letter and a blank paper at the request of Edith. Mylles, like others, hoped 'in private respect for your reterne, to the ioy of all yours here and of Mrs Beale especially', who had run 'owt of charitie' and grown impatient with the merchants whose problems had caused Beale's long absence.[29] Although Beale's own letters to Edith, Castelyn, or Mylles have not survived (or are yet to be located), Beale almost certainly wrote to his wife frequently while abroad, probably as often as he did to Walsingham or Burghley.

As usual, Walsingham and Elizabeth's Privy Council kept Beale informed, Walsingham noting his own concern for the prince of Orange, the beleaguered state of Zierikzee, and the potential ruin of the Protestant cause in the Netherlands.[30] As June wore on, Beale continued to exercise his characteristic industry, reporting to Walsingham and others on military movements, the prince of Orange, and mentioning other personalities of note, such as Floris van Pallandt, count of Culemborg, who offered the most courtesy to Beale, and, 'although he be not the depest man[,] yet ys veary honest & best affected to her majesty, and nothing ffrensh.'[31] Beale's previous refrains continued regarding his hope for the good success for Zierikzee and regarding the delays in communication due to the contrary winds preventing passage west to England from Zeeland. Pleading with his

SP 70/138, fol. 131. See also Walsingham to Beale, 28 May 1576, BL, Egerton MS 1694, fol. 12r–v (orig.), noting the opinion of Johann Casimir, Count Palatine of the Rhine, that the Dutch, having no relief from France and drawing the hatred of England, can only see their own ruin at hand; address leaf notes the letter as received 1 June.

[28] Beale to Walsingham, 4 June, BL, Additional MS 5935, fols 26r–7r. Beale to Burghley, 5 June 1576, BL, Cotton MS Galba, C. V, fols 254r–5v (orig.).

[29] Castelyn to Beale, 4 June 1576, BL, Egerton MS 1694, fol. 18r (orig.). Mylles to Beale, 18 June 1576, BL, Egerton MS 1694, fol. 19r (orig.).

[30] Walsingham to Beale, 3 June 1576, BL, Egerton MS 1694, fols 14r–15v (orig.); extract in BL, Additional MS 48149, fol. 26r, incorrectly dated in the Yelverton catalogue to 3 April. Privy Council to Beale, 9 June 1576, BYU MS 457, item 12 (orig.); copy incorrectly dated 10 June, BL, Additional MS 48149, fols 29r–30r.

[31] Beale to Walsingham, 10 June 1576, BYU, MS 457, item 13, quotation at 2v (orig.); copy in BL, Additional MS 48149, fols 33r–6v. Beale noted that Culemborg 'meaneth (as he saieth) shortly to retire into Germany' seeing how things were in the Netherlands. Cf. Rogers's observations on Culemborg in the journal entries for 7 May and 7 June, TNA, SP 70/134, fols 250v, 253v.

brother-in-law in a tone more frank than his letters to others (save Burghley), Beale tried to excuse himself of any charges of not being as attentive as he was expected to be: 'I have vsed the best diligence & expedition I possibly could. But must attend the lordes leysure.'[32]

By late June, William Winter joined Beale as Elizabeth's ambassador with fresh instructions for negotiating with the prince of Orange to release English ships, punish the offenders, and settle matters for good (by persuasion or, failing that, stealth).[33] Winter was to work with Beale and remind the prince that it was important to settle these differences among religious allies for the sake of the prince's own cause against Spain, but, as Walsingham had previously observed in his own missives to Beale, Elizabeth would ultimately side with Philip of Spain against the Dutch if her demands were not satisfied in Zeeland. To find agreement, ultimately the prince was able to secure a loan from the Merchant Adventurers, orders were secured for the release of the stayed ships, and Beale was back in London on 25 July after roughly fifteen weeks abroad in Elizabeth's name.[34]

During that time, he had earnestly sought to resolve disputes that he understood as minor when compared to the larger dangers facing the cause of Dutch Protestants against Catholic oppression. He had worked again with his like-minded compatriot, Daniel Rogers, whose friendship Beale appreciated and reciprocated, and whose international contacts and experience were just as extensive as Beale's (if not more so). Although his letters back to England did not mention his collaboration with Rogers, the two worked closely together and dined with the prince of Orange (and the count of Culemborg) on multiple occasions in May and June.[35] By this point, Rogers had established broad connections among the Dutch and served as an informant for the English government in both official and informal capacities. About this time, manifestations of the friendship between Beale and Rogers can be seen in the verses penned by Rogers, who styled himself an Englishman 'Albimontij' (of Wittenberg), having been born there in 1538; the

---

[32] Beale to Walsingham, 13 June 1576, BYU, MS 457, item 15, quotation at 2r (orig.). Beale also noted the difficulties experienced by Rogers when, due to contrary winds, he needed to land in Flanders, travel via Antwerp, and only then get to Middelburg.

[33] Winter's instructions, 19 June 1576, BL, Additional MS 48023, fols 330r–5r (Beale's copy, endorsed in his hand at 339v); TNA, SP 70/138, fols 193r–200v (earlier draft with Burghley's emendations).

[34] Agreement with the prince, signed by Winter and Beale, 21 July 1576, BL, Cotton MS Galba, C. V, fols 287r–8r; Beale's copies of earlier draft of an accord offered by the prince, BL, Additional MSS 14028, fol. 20r; 48149, fol. 48r–v. Beale's return noted as three days before the Spanish ambassador's letter dated 28 July 1576, Martin A. S. Hume (ed.), *Calendar of State Papers, Spain (Simancas)*, Vol. 2: *1568–1579* (London, 1894), item 448. Beale later referred to these fifteen weeks in BL, Lansdowne MS 51/26, fols 53r–4v. Beale retained the draft copy of the Privy Council's order to release the Dutch ships from Falmouth: BL, Stowe MS 163, fol. 28r–v. The council register, TNA, PC 2/11, 56, offers the date of 29 July 1576 but records only a brief minute for this letter.

[35] Rogers's journal, TNA, SP 70/134, with May and June at fols 249v–54v.

two also exchanged books as gifts, possibly going as far back as 1559.[36] Rogers and Beale shared similar experiences and interests: they had both studied at Wittenberg for a time, had befriended Hubert Languet, and combined scholarly pursuits with diplomatic experience.[37] The mission of 1576, it turned out, was not an opportunity lost on Beale to solidify and expand his circle of close associates, colleagues, and contacts.

In many respects, Beale's engagement with internationally inclined Englishmen and the international community abroad had been reinvigorated, but then again he had remained connected with old friends while in London, too. A good example of such a friendship was Beale's with René Hennequin, a French politician and legal officer (Maître des Requêtes), whose letter of 22 July Beale received in London shortly after his return from Zeeland. Beale and Hennequin had previously become friends at the house of François Bauduin, presumably in Paris, and shared similar literary interests and, in the course of their correspondence, memories. Because Beale had lost his books from those days (carried away by Bauduin), including an early manuscript copy of Jean du Tillet's history of France, Hennequin had another copy produced and sent to Beale. When the book was eventually printed in Latin at André Wechel's press in Frankfurt am Main, the publisher sent him a copy along with some other works.[38] In this way, during the 1570s, Beale's previous life as a single man travelling around Germany and France, with little or only informal support or financing but with an ever-widening network of friends and like-minded associates, came back to him, but now he was a married man with secure employment as a clerk of the Privy Council, experience in the House of Commons, and even service as Elizabeth's ambassador. His professional life had changed enormously since the beginnings of his friendship with Hennequin at Bauduin's, but his personal life had also changed since his last extended stay abroad: he had a wife in Edith and family of in-laws in the Walsinghams.[39]

[36] Rogers's book of poetry, Huntington Library, HM 31188, with examples from the early and mid 1570s dedicated to Beale at fols 85v, 104r, 116v, 184v, 188v, 216v, 228v, 234r, 301r. Beale's gift 'to his dearest friend' ('*amico suo charissimo*'), *Arati Solensis Phænomena, et Prognostica, Interpretius, M. Tullio Cicerone* (Paris, 1559) (USTC 750689), bound with other works owned by Rogers, Bodleian, Savile T. 10. Rogers supplied Beale with George Buchanan's *De Jure Regni apud Scotos*, which Taviner reasonably dates to 1577/8. Taviner, 257–63.

[37] For a brief biography of Rogers, *ODNB*; for these years among the Dutch, J.A. van Dorsten, *Poets, Patrons, and Professors: Sir Philip Sidney, Daniel Rogers, and the Leiden Humanists* (Leiden, 1962), 33–47.

[38] Hennequin to Beale, 1 August, 23 September 1575, 3 January, 22 July 1576, AUL, MS 1009/2, items 31, 32, 29, 30 (all orig.). Wechel to Beale, Easter 1579, AUL, MS 1009/2, item 53 (orig.). The work by Tillet, *Commentariorum [...] de rebus Gallicis libri duo* (Frankfurt am Main, 1579) (VD16 D 3066), was included in BL, Hargrave, MS 107, fol. 25r. On Beale's loss of books due to Bauduin's taking them, see Chapter 3. Other works from Wechel's press about this time, listed in BL, Hargrave, MS 107, fol. 25r under the same shelfmark (O. 11.), and probably sent to Beale in the same package, include the Danish history of Saxo Grammaticus (VD16 S 2050), local Saxon history (VD16 W 3696), the French history of Gaguin (VD16 G 44), and Sleidan's translations of various French histories (VD16 C 4637). Wechel's letter to Beale noted the inclusion of Tommaso Fazello's work on Sicilian history (VD16 F672), which also came from Wechel's press and is suggestive of Beale's interests in Italian history.

[39] During his absence, Edmund Tremayne remained as the sole clerk of the Privy Council, complaining to Beale on 21 June, 'I am driven to write all thes dispatches with myne hand, to the grete iniurie of my blynd eyes.' BYU, MS 457, item 14 (orig.).

Back in London, Beale would have just over a year before his next mission overseas as Elizabeth's ambassador. Zierikzee had fallen to Spanish forces who subsequently mutinied for lack of pay, but the situation in the Netherlands remained unstable and uncertain. Although the documentary record becomes thin during these months, Beale appears to have remained busy trying to pick up the pieces after the agreement with the prince of Orange fell through because the English continued to stay Dutch shipping.[40] One can safely assume, however, that he was happy to be with Edith again, away from the danger of Spanish capture, his toothache long behind him. In or about March 1577, Edith became pregnant with their first child, soon to be named Francis, and Beale soon gained a reputation of sorts for advising that one cannot live a happy life in celibacy or unmarried.[41] During Edith's second trimester, though, he was sent abroad to lands and men he had known well from previous years. Beale would miss the birth of his first child.

Germany, 1577

Beale's second mission as Queen Elizabeth's ambassador was very different from his first. Rather than repair commercial relations with the Dutch, with religious unity against Spain only in the background, the mission of 1577 was explicitly about quelling theological disputes among those opposed to Rome and forging an articulated alliance between England and the Protestant princes of the Holy Roman Empire. Theological differences among Protestants in the Empire had existed for several decades, and although the Peace of Augsburg in 1555 had supposedly settled the question among Lutherans, divisions remained and deepened. By the mid 1570s, some Lutherans were now no longer shunning fellow Protestants but rather condemning them in the Formula of Concord (1577, later incorporated in the *Book of Concord*, 1580). Beale had noticed the fractures and factions among German Protestants (Lutheran or otherwise) back in the 1560s, putting his observations into writing for Cecil most fully in 'the State of Germany' (1569), but now his knowledge and contacts were being put to use by the English government. As was recognized by Germans themselves, Beale was sent to Germany because

---

[40] Beale's copy of a letter to JPs of Cornwall regarding the release of Dutch ships, 29 July 1576, BL, Egerton MS 1694, fol. 20r. For Dutch reactions to Elizabeth's reneging on the agreement, see the prince of Orange to Elizabeth, Walsingham, and Sussex, 23 August 1576, *CSPF*, vol. 11, items 883–5; cf. Marnix to Walsingham, 24 August, item 887.

[41] Languet to Philip Sidney, 8 January 1578, in Roger Kuin (ed.), *The Correspondence of Sir Philip Sidney*, 2 vols (Oxford, 2012), 2.804–8; Kuin renders the Latin '*Belum, qui non putat quemquam posse beate & fœliciter vitam in celibatu transigere*' as 'Beale [...] who does not believe that anyone can live his whole life blessedly and happily as a bachelor' but may not recognize the context of Beale's recent firstborn child. The Latin '*celibatu*' can be interpreted as 'celibacy', 'bachelorhood', or 'single life'. Compare Languet to Sidney, 2 May 1578, in which Sidney is reminded of Beale's praise of marriage, in Kuin, *Correspondence*, 2.839–42.

he spoke German well and was well disposed to the country.[42] In this way, Beale was far better prepared and suited for the mission to Germany than he had been for his previous to Zeeland, where he had little to no previous experience (notwithstanding his knowledge of international law and trade in a general sense). Certain parallels with his mission to Zeeland existed, however, because Beale was not the first sent to Germany in 1577. Earlier that year, Philip Sidney had met with various princes to sound the potential for religious alliance, and Daniel Rogers had gone a step further by bringing the articles or 'heads' of the alliance for the princes to consider, this while Daniel's brother, Dr John Rogers, was doing similarly with agents of Frederik II, king of Denmark. Beale's mission represented the capstone of this activity, and, as in the previous year, he worked closely with Rogers during the second half of 1577. Taken together, these embassies represented a major effort by the English government to reconcile differences among German Protestants and enter into a formal agreement with them to help defend their religious brethren elsewhere. Additionally, Beale's old friend, Languet, became a potential link between Sidney and Beale, offering counsel for the young poet courtier by suggesting Beale's example in various ways.[43]

Relative to Beale's personal life, which included a loving and pregnant wife, the mission could have come at a better time. Beale had complained about how long his service in Zeeland had taken (fifteen weeks), but now Edith was pregnant for the first time, it seems, and Beale was about to go away for an indeterminant amount of time (in the end, it was just over five months). If, for reasons of his private life, Beale did not want to go to Germany, then, for reasons of his public devotion to international and religious causes, he knew that he had to go. One may be forgiven for thinking that he was the perfect man to serve as Elizabeth's formal ambassador to the German princes at a time of potentially irreparable damage not only within the Holy Roman Empire but also to international Protestant causes in France, the Netherlands, and elsewhere if and when necessary. Admittedly, the threat posed by sixth war of religion in France (March to September 1577) was largely past by the time Beale arrived in Germany, and the Pacification of Ghent had provided some degree of breathing space for Dutch Protestants in Holland and Zeeland in 1577. Even so, reconciling German Protestants in late 1577 could, it was hoped, ensure greater Protestant solidarity if

---

[42] For the Formula and its contexts, see Robert Kolb and Timothy J. Wengert (eds), *The Book of Concord: The Confessions of the Evangelical Lutheran Church* (Minneapolis, MN, 2000); Robert Kolb and James A. Nestingen (eds), *Sources and Contexts of the Book of Concord* (Minneapolis, MN, 2001); special issue of *The Sixteenth Century Journal* to mark the quatercentenary of the Formula, 'The Formula of Concord: Quadricentennial Essays', 8:4 (1977). On Beale's German, Morris Zimmerman to Heinrich Suderman, 24 August 1577, abstract in Konstantin Höhlbaum (ed.), *Kölner Inventar, 2. Band: 1572–1591* (Leipzig, 1903), 122.

[43] *AGR*, 55–79, characterizes Beale's mission as 'the maturation' of English policy towards the German princes but does not delve into Beale's personal experience during these months. Taviner has almost nothing to say about the mission in 1577. On Languet's thoughts for Sidney, see n. 41 and below.

conflicts were renewed in these theatres. With his long-established commitment to, and understanding of, a broad-based Protestantism, Beale crossed the seas once again, this time with formal diplomatic instructions and Elizabeth's official letters to nine princes of the Empire, plus one for Anna, electress of Saxony, for good measure and to try swaying August, elector of Saxony, if diplomatic overtures proved unsuccessful. As he had done in 1576, Beale made sure to retain the originals or copies of whatever he could to continue building his portfolio of diplomatic service in Her Majesty's name.[44]

Having left London about midnight on 25 August, Beale was in Bruges on 31 August, though his crossing was anything but uneventful as he relayed to William Davison (then in Brussels) and others. In short, and as he had previously known of others' experiences, Beale fell victim to pirates, losing what seems to have been nearly everything he had apart from his paperwork—money, clothes, and anything of conspicuous value.[45] Although little more than some mangled apparel was eventually recovered from Beale's assailants, who apparently sailed under commission from the prince of Condé, Beale appointed a factor of the Merchant Adventurers in Middelburg, Thomas Cartwright, to pursue the matter on his behalf in his absence; this would not be the last time Beale's and Cartwright's paths would cross. After passing through Antwerp, and meeting with Landgrave Wilhelm of Hesse (presumably at Marburg or Kassel), Beale proceeded to Frankfurt, where he and Rogers established a centre of operations and residence. Here Beale reunited with old friends like Languet and Wechel (at whose house Languet was staying), while hearing the fates of acquaintances from his previous times in the Palatinate, such as Christoph Ehem, who had helped promote and advance Beale's career back in 1569.[46] Beale appears to have been torn between seeing those from his formative years, especially Languet, serving his sovereign

---

[44] Beale's instructions, 21 August 1577, BL, Additional MS 48085, fol. 3r–v (orig.); this volume, along with BL, Additional MS 48128, offers a rich trove of material and demonstrates Beale's efforts. Elizabeth to Julius, Duke of Brunswick; Wilhelm, Landgrave of Hesse; August, Elector of Saxony; Anna, Electress of Saxony; Ludwig, Elector Palatine; Johann Casimir, Count Palatine; Ludwig, Duke of Württemberg; Johann Georg (misnamed Georg Joachim in TNA copy but correctly identified in Beale's copy), Elector of Brandenburg; Georg Friedrich, Margrave of Brandenburg; Karl, Margrave of Baden; all dated 21 August 1577, BL, Additional MS 48128, fols 151r–5v (Beale's copies); Walsingham's letterbook, TNA, SP 104/163, fols 28r–32v, 28r noting the date and time of Beale's departure. Originals: Hauptstaatsarchiv Hannover, Cal. Br. 21, Nr 362, fol. 1r; Staatsarchiv Marburg, Bestand 4, Abteilung I, Nr 82, fol. 51r–v; Hauptstaatsarchiv Dresden, GR, Loc. 7278/1, fols 241r–v, 244r; Hauptstaatsarchiv Stuttgart, Bestand A 114, Bü. 8.

[45] Beale to Davison, 31 August 1577, TNA, SP 83/2, fol. 130r–v (orig.). Leicester to Davison, 2 September 1577, TNA, SP 83/2, fol. 149r (orig.). Thomas Cartwright to Beale, 7 September 1577, BYU, MS 457, item 16 (orig.). Beale to Walsingham, 8 September 1577, TNA, SP 81/1, fols 39r–41v (orig.); BL, Additional MS 48149, fols 37r–8v (copy). The news spread quickly in London, even among the Germans: Zimmerman to Suderman, 31 August 1577, abstract in Höhlbaum, *Kölner Inventar*, 2.123.

[46] See the lengthy update in Beale to Walsingham, 21 September 1577, TNA, SP 81/1, fols 45r–8v (orig.), which notes that Beale stayed at the house of a certain Monsieur Swartz in Frankfurt. For Languet at Wechel's, Rogers to Walsingham, 10 October 1577, TNA, SP 81/1, fols 79r–80v, at 79r (orig.). On Ehem, see above. In Frankfurt Beale also appears to have befriended, if he had not previously, Johannes von Glauburg.

on an important mission, and getting back home to Edith: after less than a month away from his wife, Beale wrote to Walsingham that 'for many causes I wold be assone [as soon] at home as conveniently might be.'[47]

Beale's reunion with Languet was about more than just having a stable address to which post could be sent while he travelled around Germany. Their friendship was genuine, and Languet's assessment of Beale's character is here worth considering. As Languet had previously informed Sidney, Beale was a man of significant intelligence and learning, and for Languet it was joyous to see Beale 'matured in dignity, prudence and experience, yet humble in the face of the Court's vanities and unchanged towards his friends. [...] I have never known a man who knows so much that I do not but would dearly love to.' Indeed, Languet implored Sidney:

> frequent Master Beale as much as possible and consult him about your affairs. [...] I cannot admire him enough. He has derived a great deal of sagacity from his age and experience: at least his spirit has contracted no stain at all in Court: for I see him so much a stranger to all deceit and pretense that I believe he could not even imagine flattering anyone.[48]

Beale, in Languet's eyes at the very least, was a plain dealer, comparatively direct in speech and avoiding the epicurean luxuries and conspicuous consumption of an early modern court and capital city. The lessons and habits of the lean years back in the 1550s and 1560s appear to have combined with Beale's austere and religious sensibilities later identified as 'Puritan'. The renewed correspondence between Beale and Languet after the former's return to England in early 1578 testifies to the fact that their friendship and admiration was not one-sided, as does the fact that Beale appears to have tried to get Languet a formal position as Elizabeth's agent in Germany along the lines of Johann Sturm's and, before him, Christopher Mundt's.[49]

Friendly reunions aside, Beale had work to do. On the one hand, he was to prevent any potentially damaging rhetoric coming out of an assembly organized by the Count Palatine, Johann Casimir, in Frankfurt, where those condemned by hardline, Gnesio-Lutherans in Saxony were looking to issue a statement of

---

[47] Beale to Walsingham, 21 September 1577, TNA, SP 81/1, fol. 48v (orig.).

[48] Languet to Sidney, 10 March 1575, in Kuin, *Correspondence*, 1.403–6. Quotations from Languet to Sidney, 9 October 1577, 15 February 1578, in Kuin, *Correspondence*, 2.770–3, 809–13.

[49] Letters from Languet to Beale in BL, Egerton MS 1693 (all orig.), fols 16r–33v are entirely from 1578, with later letters later in the volume. Letters from this period from Beale to Languet are difficult to locate, but internal evidence in Languet's demonstrate the two-way correspondence. Beale's only letter to Languet yet located was written on 23 January 1579 during the visit of Johann Casimir to London for his installation into the Order of the Garter. Bibliothèque Nationale de France, Latin MS 8583, fol. 158r (orig.). For the suggestion of Languet as agent, see Walsingham to Beale, 2 November 1577, TNA, SP 81/1, fols 103r–4r. While Sturm was yet living, Walsingham thought Elizabeth could hardly be persuaded to provide for another agent, notwithstanding even Leicester's persuasions. Sturm lived for another dozen years until 1589.

international solidarity in opposition to the exclusivist, politically explosive Formula of Concord.[50] Daniel Rogers was pressed by the assembly to add his signature to their petition to the electors of Saxony and Brandenburg, but he declined to subscribe to the statement because his charge from Elizabeth did not include such authority; additionally, Beale persuaded him not to sign even as a witness.[51] Rogers appears to have been the primary face of the English at the assembly in Frankfurt, but Beale was the systematic thinker behind the scenes. Among other papers from this mission, in Beale's personal archive are found a record of the assembly's proceedings and copies of the petition sent to the electors, and it appears that Beale may have used his knowledge of these activities when composing the oration he would later give before various princes or send in writing to those he could not see personally. The oration written by Beale, as he noted to Ludwig, Elector Palatine, was to be esteemed by the princes as if it came directly from Elizabeth's own person, and it emphasized the need for Protestant unity despite its variety and in accord with Paul's observation that the Holy Spirit distributes different gifts to different people (1 Corinthians 12).[52] After helping to check the potential for further conflict in Frankfurt, Beale was instructed to dissuade the Lutheran princes from endorsing the Formula of Concord, which condemned Protestant Churches outside a relatively narrowly understood Lutheranism, while persuading them to join a defensive alliance with Queen Elizabeth. Beale's efforts in this regard took him from Frankfurt to Heidelberg and Neustadt in the Palatinate, back to Hesse with the Landgrave, over to Erfurt and Dippoldiswalde in Saxony, and back to western Germany again. For those princes to whom Beale could not travel for reasons of expedition, such as the duke of Württemberg and elector and margrave of Brandenburg, Beale sent messages via courier that he would otherwise have delivered personally. Bearing in mind Beale's desire to return home and his wounding and significant loss due to pirates, cutting short his already very lengthy journey offered only slight relief.

Over the course of Beale's mission of optimistic highs for religious alliance and pessimistic lows due to theological intransigence, Beale reflected upon his previous time in Germany, and used his experience to his advantage. For example,

---

[50] See above, n. 42.

[51] See Rogers's account in his two letters dated 10 October 1577 to Walsingham, TNA, SP 81/1, fols 77r–8v, 79r–80v (both orig.). See also, *AGR*, 69–71.

[52] Papers relating to the Frankfurt assembly, including the letter of introduction for the messenger, Paul Knibbe (Paulus Knibbius), and the petition to the electors of Saxony and Brandenburg, both dated 24 September 1577, BL, Additional MS 48085, fols 34r–40r. Rough draft of Beale's oration, BL, Additional MS 48085, fols 61r–70r; copy, TNA, SP 81/1, fols 59r–64v. Originals and forwarded copies (noted as 'Werbung' in German archives) at Hauptstaatsarchiv Dresden, Staatsarchiv Marburg, Hauptstaatsarchiv Stuttgart, Hauptstaatsarchiv Hannover, Geheimes Staatsarchiv Preußischer Kulturbesitz; see *AGR*, 184–5 nn. 57, 60, 62, 67. The heads of the league, *Capita Foederis*, were distributed with written copies of Beale's oration. On Beale's oration and Elizabeth's person, see Beale to Walsingham, 11 October 1577, TNA, SP 81/1, fols 85r–9r, at 86r (orig.).

when in late September he discussed matters with Ludwig, Elector Palatine, he realized that Ludwig did not understand Latin very well, so Beale also tried in French and, after learning that Ludwig had only little skill in that language, Beale finally spoke in 'Dutch [German] as well as I could'.[53] Also, when thinking about the likelihood of getting the Protestant princes to join an alliance, Beale recalled the previous difficulties in such a project, noting 'as I remember in Sleydan they refused before the Protestantes warres, to enter into anye league with protestantes Cantons of the Heluetian[s]'. Beale's recalling Sleidan here testifies to the import-ance he placed in the history he had previously cited in 1569 and probably had on his bookshelf.[54] Having been despoiled at the outset of his voyage, literally losing his shirts and his cash, Beale informed Lord Treasurer Burghley that his financial need was a source of significant stress and compounded by 'thinges beinge growen to the double price of that they were at other times of my beinge here'. Beale's immediate costs while trekking around Germany as Elizabeth's ambassa-dor were only the start of it, for, as he noted to Burghley, he was also responsible for paying the dues (£40) relating to his wardship of John Hales's lands; because he wanted to prevent any 'process' against himself or the lands, he asked Burghley to arrange a deferral until a later date.[55]

Despite the importance of Beale's mission to the public cause of international Protestantism, however it accorded with his own experience and religious out-look, Beale's private family life was probably never far from his mind. His brother, William, had taken on several roles within the Church of England by 1577, and although it is unlikely that William had accompanied Beale on this mission for an as-yet-unknown reason, Daniel Rogers noted to Walsingham that 'Mr Beales brother' had left Frankfurt with a certain John Furrier in early October, possibly as couriers. Another possibility is that, while William remained in England tend-ing his flocks, Beale's youngest brother, John, might have been part of the diplo-matic entourage in Frankfurt, just as Robert had been in Paris during the 1560s.[56] Which brother was in Germany with Beale may not matter as much as the facts that one of them was there, that Walsingham as Beale's brother-in-law knew (and probably supported it), and that one of Beale's brothers was seeing him in action and in lands Robert had known previously. If Beale was even remotely taking a

[53]   Beale to Walsingham, 11 October 1577, TNA, SP 81/1, fol. 85v (orig.). Beale's collection of papers from this period includes a considerable amount of correspondence from the princes in German, which meant that he (or another) would need to translate that material into either Latin or English for others, like Elizabeth or Burghley, to read. Beale's speaking German with a prince of the Empire after not having been in Germany for several years is testimony to his previous facility in the 1560s, and his notes on the *Reichskammergericht* in 1563 demonstrate his facility in switching between Latin and German at that time. BL, Cotton MS Nero, B. IX, fols 4r–5r, 7r–18v. Also, see above, n. 42.

[54]   Beale to Walsingham, 11 October 1577, TNA, SP 81/1, fol. 87r (orig.). See Chapter 3, n. 82.

[55]   Beale to Burghley, 11 October 1577, TNA, SP 81/1, fol. 90r–v (orig.).

[56]   Rogers to Walsingham, 13 October 1577, TNA, SP 81/1/, fols 92r–3v, at 92r (orig.). On William and Robert, see Chapter 2. On John and a potential second experience as a member of Robert's diplo-matic entourage, see Chapter 7.

brother under his wing, he was also thinking about the next generation of Beales, for by late autumn Edith was well into her third trimester of pregnancy. During his journey from one prince's court to another in Germany, Beale had no convenient opportunity to learn of Edith's progress, and it seems probable that he first learned of Edith's giving birth to his firstborn son when in the Low Countries on his return journey in January 1578. Davison, still serving as Elizabeth's ambassador there, received news from Thomas Randolph in London that 'Mrs Bele is brought a bedde of a Sone[,] no smale comforte to the mother and grat yoye I am sure to ye father when he[,] to whom I praye you deliver this letter[,] as I hope [hears] of the good newes he shall receave of his wyffes happie deliverance.'[57]

If Beale received joy at this news on his way through the Low Countries, he met with frustration when trying to cross the Channel. In late January Beale received Randolph's letter from Davison bearing the good news from London, but he also relayed back from Antwerp to Davison his own difficulties in getting compensation from the Dutch government for the acts of piracy committed against him—despite charging Cartwright to look into his case while he was away in Germany. The hanging of three or four of the offenders was, to Beale, insufficient, especially because he knew that he may bear some financial responsibility for the losses and the consequent loans he needed to take on. Beale clearly kept a close eye on how much he needed to front financially, as his later accounts for Burghley illustrate.[58] Adding fuel to Beale's frustration was the fact that the Dutch prevented him from crossing the seas back to England without the proper paperwork relating to the security measures he had put in place after being robbed. As he again relayed to Davison in the hope that he would assist in the matter, Beale had acquired significant weaponry in Germany 'for my more assurance in the voiage which I have made'. Beale felt justifiably vulnerable, so he purchased harquebuses (long guns) and dags (pistols) for the sake of security, but it seems that additional weapons were given to Beale as gifts 'by sondry noblemen & gentes of those partes', and he was loath to leave them behind. Although Beale did not specify from whom he received gifts of German guns, one may bear in mind that he had once toured the elector of Saxony's armoury, one of the finest not only in the Empire but potentially in all of Europe.[59] (If necessary, he could obviously sell the weaponry when back in England to help recoup his financial losses.)

---

[57] Randolph to Davison, 29 December 1577, TNA, SP 83/4, fol. 56r–v (orig.). The baby boy was baptized on 27 December and named Francis, almost certainly after Walsingham, his uncle and senior godfather. See Chapter 4, n. 98. Jupp and Hovenden, *The Registers*, 10.

[58] Beale to Davison, 25 January 1578, TNA, SP 83/5, fol. 27r–v (orig.). For Beale's accounting, see above, n. 1.

[59] Beale to Davison, 26 January 1578, TNA, SP 83/5, fol. 28(bis)r (orig.); Beale also noted that Davison should be good to his old friend, Pietro Bizzarri, on whom, see Chapter 6. On the armoury of Dresden, see Chapter 3. Other princes, such as the duke of Brunswick and landgrave of Hesse, supplied Beale with much needed cash, hence Beale's noting the 'extraordinary liberality' in his letter to Burghley in 1582. CP, 162/47 (orig.).

One way or another, with or without the firearms, Beale finally got back to London on 29 January after five months away on a very difficult, seemingly impossible diplomatic mission to quell theological discord among German Protestants while securing a religious and military alliance with the princes. Some may see Beale's (and others') efforts as a failure because the Formula of Concord proceeded, gained significant support among Lutherans, and the process of con-fessionalization hardened in the Empire. This was not the first time Elizabeth had made the attempt, and not the first time Beale had been implicated in such an endeavour, so he knew from the outset that he faced an uphill battle. Measures of the success achieved by Beale and Rogers, whose efforts in this regard are not to be discounted, need not be absolute, for their missions did in fact bear significant fruit at the time and in the time to come. Rogers himself believed in mid October that 'Mr Beale his cominge will dooe good'.[60] From others' perspectives, Beale's return was noted 'out of Germanie, where he hath not frutelessly laboured in her Majesties name, as may appear by Dathenus letters & Languets, and other'.[61] Along with Languet in Frankfurt, Dathenus (Pieter Datheen) had been one of the two Dutch Reformed representatives (with Johannes Junius) at Johann Casimir's assembly, so he would have had first-hand knowledge of Beale's activities. In the months and years immediately following the mission, Beale's continued and expanded circle of correspondents kept him informed of theological develop-ments and shifting fault lines among the Protestant princes of Germany. If Beale had been, alongside Rogers, Queen Elizabeth's most knowledgeable servant regarding politics and religion in Germany before 1577, he was now also the best connected—and both the English and Germans knew it. Various Germans wrote to Beale as a like-minded friend and as a potential patron or assistant for young Germans wishing to come to England or already there.[62] Beale's position as a de facto secretary for German affairs was thus assured in the years that followed, and, as it happened, for the rest of his life Beale was looked to by others for all

---

[60] Contrast the tone of failure in W. B. Patterson, 'The Anglican Reaction', in L. W. Spitz and W. Lohff (eds), *Discord, Dialogue, and Concord: Studies in the Lutheran Reformation's Formula of Concord* (Philadelphia, PA, 1977), 150–65, with a measured notion of success in *AGR*, 74–9. Rogers to Walsingham, 13 October 1577, TNA, SP 81/1, fols 92r–3r, at 92v–3r (orig.).

[61] News of the Battle of Gemblours, etc., 3 February 1578, TNA, SP 104/163, fol. 106v (orig.). The hand is that of Laurence Tomson, Walsingham's secretary; Beale returned on 29 January, Rogers doing so four days previously along with an ambassador from Johann Casimir, Peter Beutterich.

[62] Significant princes writing to Beale included Johann Casimir, Count Palatine (AUL, MS 1009/2, items 7–8 (both orig.)); Wilhelm, Landgrave of Hesse (AUL, MS 1009/2, items 2, 4 (both orig.)); Julius, Duke of Brunswick (AUL, MS 1009/2, items 9–10 (both orig.)). Others writing in friendship, on behalf of others, or seeking aid themselves, included Hieronymous Schlick (AUL, MS 1009/2, item 44 [orig.]); Johannes von Glauburg (AUL, MS 1009/2, items 23–6 (all orig.)); Wolfgang Musculus (AUL, MS 1009/2, items 17–18 (both orig.)); Johann Sturm (AUL, MS 1009/2, item 6 (orig.)); Jacobus Telones (AUL, MS 1009/2, items 39–42 (all orig.)). For Languet, see above, nn. 48–9. Despite Languet's frequent overtures to Philip Sidney to seek out and befriend Beale, the two men do not appear to have become close. Reasons why may include Beale's unfamiliarity with and distaste for life at court, or perhaps Beale's increasing concern for his family life after the birth of his son, Francis. Beale did, however, later correspond in 1595 with Robert Sidney, Philip's brother. See Chapter 8.

manner of advice on Germany—theological developments among theologians, political among princes, and commercial among the merchants of the Hanseatic League and in the Steelyard of London.

An International Life, Settling Down

Beale had become comparatively comfortable and secure in London from 1572 to 1576. With relatively assured employment as clerk of Elizabeth's Privy Council, with increased responsibilities as ward for John Hales's nephew (and lands), and with his wife, Edith, Beale might have thought in early 1576 that his years of overseas travel were only in his past. His personal archival practices during these years suggest that he was planning for a long career in domestic government service. Those years spent in the Holy Roman Empire and France, however, were the reason he had gained such comfort and security. He had expertise and relevant languages in the religious and political affairs among Protestant co-religionists and political allies across the Channel, and this knowledge was key to his role in London within the machine room of government because of the informal advice and intelligence channels he could offer. His missions to the Low Countries in 1576 and Germany in 1577 accordingly come as no surprise. In both cases he served as one of several ambassadors sent by Elizabeth, and so he may seem on the surface to have been merely an additional cog in the diplomatic wheel of representatives, just as replaceable as the others. In truth, his skill in law and commercial affairs enabled him to navigate and negotiate with the Dutch in ways that, for example, Daniel Rogers—despite his wide contacts among Dutch literati—could not. Similarly, his deep understanding of the complicated world of religion and politics in the Empire empowered him to speak with authority and in German among the princes of the Empire in ways that even Philip Sidney—a prince himself as son of a viceroy—could not.[63] Whether Beale realized it or not, he was vital to both the formulation in London and the execution abroad of Elizabethan foreign policy.

His previous experience abroad gave him the requisite knowledge, but his own intellectual and archival habits of copying and keeping paperwork during these missions provided his long-term understanding across the 1570s, 1580s, and 1590s. Those habits, along with the modern historian's luck in archival survival, suggest that Beale, as a private person, knew the value of a private archive to the running of the state that did not yet have an organized and accessible state paper office. These practices also suggest a sense of personal insecurity in Beale because

---

[63] The classic treatment of Sidney during these years remains James B. Osborn, *Young Philip Sidney, 1572–1577* (New Haven, CT,1972), but see also Robert E. Stillman, *Philip Sidney and the Poetics of Renaissance Cosmopolitanism* (Aldershot, 2008).

his employment at the queen's wish was precarious due to his association with the *Tempestas Halesiana* back in 1563–4. Discussing the succession, even by implication, was dangerous business, after all. By building up his archive of information to be deployed in Her Majesty's service, Beale was essentially looking to bolster his own credentials, to make himself invaluable to Walsingham, Burghley, and—by extension—Elizabeth.[64] The strategy, it turns out, worked.

If Beale knew that he needed to serve as ambassador in these instances, that did not mean that he wanted the job in either case. While overseas, on multiple occasions in his letters back to Walsingham he made plain his longing to return home to London. After his return, he was similarly direct with Burghley about how financially disastrous these missions were for him on a personal level. During these missions, Edith was left at home, possibly looking after Hales's nephew. In light of Languet's comments to Sidney about Beale's taste for the married, non-celibate life, Beale probably did not want to leave her side. He most certainly did not want to leave her in August 1577 when she was pregnant; missing the birth of their son Francis in December would have been a bitter pill to swallow, too. Concerns for his family may help to explain why, after his return in late January 1578, he did not go abroad again for nearly a decade, when he went to the Netherlands to work with another old friend and veteran of diplomatic service, Henry Killigrew. In the intervening period, Edith would be pregnant several more times, giving birth to Ursula in January 1579, Bridget in June 1581, Margaret in April 1583, and Katherine in February 1588.[65] In consequence, Beale had some very real and immediate family responsibilities in London to which he needed to attend. These children were all baptized in Allhallows London Wall, where Walsingham's daughter, Mary, had also been baptized in 1572, so Beale's budding immediate family also had its extended relations in the neighbourhood. In these years and for the foreseeable future, he appears to have endeavoured to remain comparatively safe and secure with his family and work in London, well distant from Spanish attacks in the Low Countries, from French or Flemish depredations on the way there.[66] Yet, Beale could be at home and continue his international correspondence, bolstering his intimate knowledge of foreign affairs more generally as they applied to the English state—and Church. And so he did.

A European Elizabethan: The Life of Robert Beale, Esquire. David Scott Gehring, Oxford University Press.
© David Scott Gehring 2024. DOI: 10.1093/9780198902942.003.0005

[64] On Beale and other private persons in a wider national context, see Popper, 'Information State', 503–35, and the discussion in Chapter 1.

[65] Jupp and Hovenden, *The Registers*, 11–12, 18. Ursula was most likely named after her aunt and senior godmother, Ursula Walsingham. See Chapter 4, n. 98. Unknown, unnamed children who died at birth remain obscure. For an example, see Chapter 6.

[66] On Walsingham's daughter Mary, see Chapter 4, n. 98. Beale was right to be wary. Rogers was captured in 1580 and imprisoned for four years in the Low Countries. *ODNB*; *AGR*, 82–3.

6

A Busy Man

Between 1578 and 1585, Robert Beale's family circle grew just as his professional responsibilities expanded. This period has been rightly recognized as the apogee of Beale's political power and influence, especially given the relative decline of his role within the machinery of Elizabethan government during the 1590s.[1] His tendencies to collect, copy, and collate paperwork from various quarters and on a wide variety of subjects—habits picked up during the 1560s and formalized during the 1570s—intensified considerably during the 1580s. As a result, his personal archive swelled dramatically. As in the case of others who produced and retained masses of paperwork, notably Francis Walsingham, Beale the man during these years can sometimes be difficult to see.[2] Notwithstanding the problems in teasing out his personal life, some clues do emerge about the man ever behind the scenes in Elizabethan political life to this point. Additionally, although the voluminous material collected by Beale can sometimes diverge into arcane and disparate topics, a clear and expansive view of his professional life comes into finer focus.

Beale's wife Edith had several more children during these years, all of whom save one were baptized at Allhallows London Wall. This location suggests that his main residence remained within the City to ensure close proximity to the power brokers in the Privy Council, but it also ensured that he could easily attend the court via the Thames at Elizabeth's palaces of Greenwich and Hampton Court. During these years he spent more and more time at his other residence in Barnes, in Surrey, west of the City, very close to Walsingham's second home at Barn Elms. In 1579 Walsingham acquired the lease of the manor of Barn Elms from Elizabeth in recognition of his services, while Beale probably acquired his own home in Barnes shortly afterwards. Thus, the brothers-in-law Beale and Walsingham continued their close relationship not only in profession but also in personal life; after all, Francis and Ursula Walsingham were almost certainly the senior godparents for Beale's first and second children, Francis and Ursula.[3] As seen in his

---

[1] Taviner, 151, 153.

[2] See the comment by Read in his *Mr Secretary Walsingham*, 1.vii; cf. the sympathetic comment but in some ways richer account in *ODNB*.

[3] On Walsingham and Barn Elms, see Read, *Mr Secretary Walsingham*, 3.430–2, noting also that the area around London Wall was 'a rather distinguished neighbourhood' (431). Beale's daughter, Bridget, who died as an infant, was buried at St Mary's, Barnes, in 1581, which suggests that he had acquired his home by that time, and Beale signed some of his correspondence from Barnes from this point forward. Surrey History Centre, P6/1/1, fol. 43v; on dating, see below, n. 68. Beale's residence at Barnes during the 1580s is not known with certainty, but it probably was not yet Milbourne House, for

correspondence, Beale also remained under the wing of William Cecil, Lord Burghley, and his collaboration and friendship with Henry Killigrew increased over the years, with the latter present and attesting when Beale's 'Image was was [*sic*] dedicated to god by the congregation[,] Mr Secretary [again] being godfather and Mrs Barett godmother through my wyffes great weaknes'.[4] New colleagues and friends also entered the scene during the early 1580s in consequence of Beale's unexpected rise into the upper echelons of the Elizabethan political world. Close personal and professional relations appear to have developed with Edward Manners, earl of Rutland (d.1587); George Talbot, earl of Shrewsbury (d.1590); and Walter Mildmay (d.1589), the latter of whom served with Beale and Shrewsbury when negotiating with Mary Queen of Scots, and who commented privately to Walsingham regarding his friendship with Beale.[5] Beale's relationship with Rutland might have been bolstered by simple practicalities: he probably stayed at Rutland's seat, Belvoir Castle, when travelling between London and Sheffield (where Mary was detained) because it was along the Great North Road between Grantham and Newark. These budding, maturing, and established relationships aside, Beale, if he is to be believed, also experienced the sometimes dire financial, material, and physical consequences of such a life. To Burghley and others in high places he frequently complained of his poverty, begging for reimbursement for his previous personal outlays and consideration of his learning and services, and signing off his letters by noting his 'poore house in London'.[6] To friends of more modest means, such as William Davison, Beale could complain 'from my house at Barnes' of his 'sore eyes' and ailing hands that prevented him from his daily duties at court, for that, 'in trothe *neque oculus neque manus facere*

---

which he later acquired a formal lease, along with 116.5 acres of land, in 1592. See the Chapter 7, n. 3, and the materials relating to Milbourne house, especially the extracts from the Cartwright muniments at Aynhoe, C(A)2274, Northamptonshire Record Office, in the Richmond Local Studies Library. On the godparents and names, see Chapter 4, n. 98.

[4] Killigrew to William Davison, 29 December 1580, TNA, SP 15/27/2, fol. 129r (orig.). Killigrew wrote from London, so baptism there is probable even though Beale's child is unnoticed in the parish registers for Allhallows London Wall. The child might have been named Frances, and so named after her godfather, but died very young. The first child baptized at St Mary's, Barnes, was Elizabeth on 25 October 1584. Surrey History Centre, P6/1/1, fol. 4v. See also the later genealogy, BL, Additional MS 19117, fols 228v–9r; 'Francisca' was also named on her mother, Edith's funerary monument at Eastington, Gloucestershire, observed in Ralph Bigland, *Historical Monumental and Genealogical Collections, Relative to the County of Gloucester* (London, 1791), 1.540; the monument still exists at St Michael and All Angels Church. Mrs Barett remains obscure. That Killigrew's wife was the intended godmother demonstrates the close relationship between Beale and Killigrew by this point.

[5] Mildmay to Walsingham, 4 June 1583, TNA, SP 53/12, fol. 75v (orig.). When exactly Beale first met Rutland is unclear, but an intermediary might well have been Burghley, who advised the earl in 1571 regarding the benefits and purposes of international travel shortly after Beale had written his account of Germany for Burghley's use. Cecil to Rutland, 20 January 1571, TNA, SP 12/77/6, draft in a poor state, printed in Warneke, *Images of the Educational Traveller*, 295–8.

[6] See, e.g. Beale to Archbishop Whitgift, 7 May 1584, BL, Additional MS 48039, fol. 45v; cf. Burghley's copy with 'at' for 'in', BL, Lansdowne MS 42, fols 181r–4v. This letter is discussed more fully below.

officium suum possunt.[7] Such ailments aside, one may hope that Beale was able to take advantage of the spoils of his position, one of which was that he could receive gifts from those looking to grease the wheels of negotiation. When an envoy from the Hanseatic League later sought Beale's assistance, for example, he sent to Beale a smoked salmon as a gift from his homeland.[8] Whether Beale enjoyed the salmon remains unknown, but such a dish on the family table cannot have gone unappreciated.

The complexities of Beale's home life—multiple residences, children, close family and friends—were in some ways the consequence of, and reflected in, his professional activities at the time. Indeed, his long-time Italian friend, Pietro Bizzarri, wrote of Beale's kindness and the confidence he had not only in Beale but also his 'most noble kin'.[9] As had been the case previously, Beale's roles in government focused primarily on foreign affairs and legal questions, but they also expanded to include matters that blurred the lines between foreign and domestic. Such was the time when, especially during the 1580s, occurrents beyond the seas came to influence, even dominate, the affairs of state at home.

Acting like a Principal Secretary

Walsingham had been serving as either sole or joint principal secretary since December 1573; he worked first with Thomas Smith until 1576, and then with Thomas Wilson from 1577. Wilson had performed well as a diplomatic specialist in the Low Countries before his appointment but would not serve abroad again before his death in 1581. Walsingham, however, led embassies to the Low Countries in 1578 (June to October), France in 1581 (July to September), and Scotland in 1583 (August to October). Scholars have disagreed slightly on what role, exactly, Beale played on these three occasions, but the lack of consensus is probably appropriate given that Beale himself, some years later, was vague on the matter: 'Twice or thrice I haue ben commaunded to attend in Courte, in the tyme of the absence of her Majesties late Secretary [Walsingham]'.[10] During the first,

---

[7] Beale to Davison, 8 July 1585, TNA, SP 12/180, fol. 35r (orig.) (italics added). Significantly, this letter was written not in Beale's holograph but rather by a secretary.

[8] Joannes Schulte (Johann/John Schultz) to Beale, 14 November 1585, TNA, SP 82/2, fol. 75v (orig.). On Schulte's mission at this time, see Beale's copies of various relevant papers in BL, Additional MS 48009, fols 321r–67v; and Chapter 7.

[9] Bizzarri to Beale, 12/22 October 1583, TNA, SP 83/20, fol. 52r (orig.). *CSPF*, vol. 18, item 161, renders '*suo nobilissimo Parentato*' as 'your noble family', but the English 'kin' more accurately reflects both close family and extended relations, which in this case would certainly include Walsingham and, previously, Hales.

[10] Beale to Burghley, 24 April 1595, BL, Lansdowne MS 79, fol. 192v (orig.). On Wilson's and Walsingham's embassies and lives, see Bell, *Handlist of British Diplomatic Representatives 1509–1688*, and *ODNB*. The original entry for Beale in the *Dictionary of National Biography* (London, 1885) 4.3–7, notes that '[d]uring Walsingham's absence in the Netherlands in the summer of 1578 Beale acted as

Wilson remained behind as the sole principal secretary in a formal sense, but it seems that Beale also acted in an informal capacity as a secondary (not primary or principal) secretary. In summer 1578, Wilson had been on the job for less than a year before Walsingham left to meet with Spanish authorities in the Low Countries, so it seems plausible that he could have used advice from someone already well acquainted with the practices and procedures of the secretaryship and Privy Council. Between Walsingham's return from the Low Countries and his embassy to France in July 1581, Wilson's health declined significantly, resulting in his own death just two months before Walsingham departed for Paris. Accordingly, a significant gap needed to be filled, and again a logical explanation is that Beale quietly and informally filled the space during Walsingham's absence, but the relevant volumes detailing the business of the Privy Council appear to note that Beale was not consistently attending such meetings but rather was part of a team interrogating the Jesuit, Edmund Campion.[11] Although Beale's acting as an informal advisor to the principal secretary or as a secondary secretary is plausible in 1578 and 1581, however hypothetical some scholars' inferences, Beale's service as the sole principal secretary during Walsingham's mission to Scotland in 1583 is considerably easier to trace.

Shortly before his departure north, Walsingham wrote to Burghley from Barn Elms with his thoughts regarding the potential for Anglo-Scottish amity in a broad sense, and for good relations between Elizabeth and James VI in particular. In a postscript Walsingham noted that John Somers had been the first choice to fill in as principal secretary, but due to Somers' finding 'him selfe vnapt for the servyce', Walsingham thought 'no other wyll be found more apt for the place then

secretary of state, as also in 1581 and 1583, on occasion of Walsingham's missions to France and Scotland in those years' (p. 4). Conyers Read, possibly following the *DNB* but not documenting the assertion in 1925, claimed that Beale 'more than once took Walsingham's place as Principal Secretary when he was away from England' in *Mr Secretary Walsingham*, 1.423. Most recently, Gary Bell repeated the claim again for all three years' embassies in the *ODNB* article on Beale published in print in 2004 and through the online versions updated in 2008, 2011, and 2015. Taviner, 150, remained cautious by noting simply that Wilson acted alone in 1578 and 1581, but that Beale most certainly served in Walsingham's stead in 1583. Wilson, however, could not have acted alone in summer 1581 because he had died on 20 May. On clerks of the Privy Council acting as principal secretary, see F.J. Platt, 'The Elizabethan Clerk of the Privy Council', *Journal of the Rocky Mountain Medieval and Renaissance Association*, 3 (1982), 139.

[11] Beale's hand occurs sporadically inserting later notes in the register, but his activity regarding Campion is clear: TNA, PC 2/13, 467, 483-4, 490-1, 494. Thorough searches in the state papers collections (TNA, BL, CP) and Beale's private papers for this period yield nothing concrete regarding his potential services as secretary. Walsingham's own journal for December 1570 to April 1583 (TNA, PRO 30/5/5) has significant omissions during the periods of his embassies in 1578 and 1581. Scholars have long recognized the limitations of the Privy Council registers; the monumental effort and edition by David Crankshaw offers a corrective for one volume: *Proceedings of the Privy Council of Queen Elizabeth I, 1582-1583*, 3 vols (Woodbridge, forthcoming); that volume, for 29 June 1582 to 20 June 1583, was taken to Spain centuries ago and is now recognized as Bibliotheca Nacional de España, Madrid, MSS 3821. The volume does not illuminate Beale's role more than any other volume does, but I am nevertheless grateful to Timothy Crowley for sending me an electronic version of the manuscript.

this bearer my brother Beale, yf her majestye shall allowe thereof'.[12] That Elizabeth did indeed permit Beale to take his brother-in-law's place is evident in Beale's own holograph letter to the earl of Rutland in recognition of the earl's previous favour shown. Beale here offered an update on the Low Countries, France, and Mary Queen of Scots, noting also 'the little leisure that I have to write, being forced alone to supplye Mr Secretaryes roome, and myne ordinary place'; the secretary's 'roome' can be understood as 'place' in the abstract (as in 'occupation'), but it also reflects the idea that Beale was actually in Walsingham's office in his home on Seething Lane.[13] Until Walsingham's return from Edinburgh, Beale acted as principal secretary, receiving intelligence from quarters domestic and foreign, relaying information and updates as required. Having been in the shadow, as it were, of the principal secretaries and Privy Council since 1572, thus over a decade, and having continually solidified his position as a specialist in legal and international causes for nearly a decade longer still, Beale was as well suited as anyone could be at the time. With Walsingham's support, and presumably Burghley's given their close relationship, Beale must have been a relatively easy choice despite his proclivity to complain about his personal finances and his increasing tendency to disagree with the ecclesiastical establishment. He must have done a satisfactory job as stand-in secretary, for in February 1584, when Walsingham had fallen ill, Beale again occupied Walsingham's 'roome' (and argued with Whitgift, as will be seen).[14]

Years later in 1592, when the secretaryship had become vacant after Walsingham's death in April 1590, Beale wrote what is now his most recognizable and most famous treatise.[15] By this point Beale had observed Walsingham in action for roughly seventeen years and had served as clerk of the Privy Council for even longer. Also a product of his own experience during the early 1580s,

[12] Walsingham to Burghley, 6 August 1583, BL, Harley MS 6993, fol. 54v (orig.). On Somers, see Bell, *Handlist of British Diplomatic Representatives 1509–1688*, and Bell, 'Men and their Rewards in Elizabethan Diplomatic Service, 1558–1585', 420–7.

[13] Beale to Rutland, 12 September 1583, Belvoir Castle, MS VI, under misdating of 12 September 1582, fol. 1r (orig.); following an error in a later endorsement on the address leaf, the *Historical Manuscripts Commission Twelfth Report*, Appendix, Part IV: *The Manuscripts of His Grace the Duke of Rutland, G.C.B., Preserved at Belvoir Castle*, Vol. 1 (London, 1888), 140, similarly misdates this letter to 1582. See also Beale to Rutland, 18 September and 18 December 1581, Belvoir Castle, MS V, under dates (orig.); in the earlier letter Beale notes his gratitude to the earl for his sending a case of dags (pistols). Walsingham's journal for 25 March 1583 to 3 December 1584 is comparatively lacking for early August to late October 1583, when Beale was serving in his stead: BL, Harley MS 6035, fols 241–91. Cooper, *Queen's Agent*, 167.

[14] Nicholas Faunt to Anthony Bacon, 28 February 1584, LPL, MS 647, fol. 136r, left margin (orig.) On Whitgift, see below.

[15] 'A Treatise of the Office of a Councellor and Principall Secretary to her Majestie', BL, Additional MS 48149, fols 3v–9v; transcribed reliably in Read, *Mr Secretary Walsingham*, 1.423–43. Cf. the similar treatise of the same year written by Walsingham's secretary: Charles Hughes (ed.), 'Nicholas Faunt's Discourse Touching the Office of the Principal Secretary of Estate, &c. 1592', *English Historical Review*, 20 (1905), 499–508. For discussion, see Popper, 'Information State', 503–35; Andreani, *Elizabethan Secretariat*, 34–42 et passim.

the work offers a mature, generally measured, and enormously experienced view of the practices and material required for the successful principal secretary. Beale here laid out the types of books and intelligence, the ways of managing subordinates, and the administrative habits to be sought and cultivated. He encouraged an aspiring secretary to own and consult Thomas Smith's *Commonwealth*, Abraham Ortelius's atlas, maps of England, and Venetian *relazioni*; that Beale himself owned most if not all of these items is not lost on the reader. He noted that Walsingham had agents in over forty locations paid from Elizabeth's or his own purse, but he also cautioned against the liberality of this example; after all, Beale himself could do no such thing. Public records, Beale wrote, should be kept in a place for others to consult, especially those new to state service who needed to learn on the job; his own archive was a model in the making. Understandably, he frequently used the first person 'I' and examples from his own experience to highlight his close proximity to the office. For a man possessing only a very limited taste of the daily life of a principal secretary in his own right, he had been a keen onlooker from afar during the secretaryship of William Cecil before his elevation as Lord Burghley, and subsequently became an intimate observer from inside the engine room of Elizabethan government both in the Privy Council and in the House of Commons. His practices of gathering intelligence combined with his synthesizing such material in various memoranda and treaties to create a holistic view of various issues and situations. His vast network of friends, colleagues, and correspondents at various social strata (from merchants to lords) provided for Beale a wide range of perspectives that he could call upon and incorporate in his professional life. In short, although he had only served as principal secretary in an ersatz capacity and for a very brief period (or three at the most), Beale could act like a principal secretary by way of his practices intellectual, administrative, and diplomatic (in all senses of the word).

Between 1578 and 1585, Beale's collecting and copying of material significantly increased the size of his personal archive of books and manuscripts. Printed works acquired at this time by Beale can be inferred from references within his papers and notes but also from the later catalogue of books in the Yelverton Collection, where his activity and contacts offer strong or at least plausible connections and ownership.[16] His long-standing interest in and dedication to histories, commentaries, and international events are borne out in the booklist of items published at this time, and many of the works were written or supplied by Beale's known contacts. For example, his old friend André Wechel was a publisher in Frankfurt am Main and sent Beale various histories by Philippe de Commines, Jean Froissard, Robert Gaguin, and Saxo Grammaticus, as well as the commentary by Jean du Tillet on French affairs; it will be recalled that Wechel also published

---

[16] BL, Hargrave MS 107. For additional discussion, see Chapter 1.

an anthology of Beale's own books on Spanish affairs and history.[17] Beale's Italian connections and interests are evident in the booklist by way of his friend Bizzarri's histories of the wars against the Turks (1573) and of Genoa (1579), the great Francesco Guicciardini's history of Italy (1580), and his associate Petruccio Ubaldini's life of Charlemagne (1581).[18] Other works of significant interest to Beale and demonstrating his vast knowledge at this time include John Leslie's history of Scotland (1578), a harmony of confessions of faith among Reformed Churches (1581), Torquato Tasso's work on the ambassador (1582), David Chytraeus's works on the history of the Confession of Augsburg (1582) and on the state of the churches in the east (1583), George Buchanan's works on Scotland, including *De Jure Regni apud Scotos* (1583), and the works of Jan Hus and Jerome of Prague (1583).[19] Books of domestic importance appearing in the list, and of specific interest to Beale, were Burghley's work on the execution of justice (1584), Thomas Smith's on the commonwealth of England (1584), and David Powel's on the history of Wales (1584).[20]

In Beale's manuscript archive, his personal copies of material from others increased significantly at this time, but Beale did not always return what he borrowed. His own contacts and links in Germany and France ensured that he did not need to borrow from others for those lands. For Denmark to the north, though, he had comparatively less access, and so, in addition to his own papers on Danish affairs, he acquired materials, made his own copies, and added annotations and headings for his own later reference.[21] On Wales and Ireland, little suggests that he had any particularly reliable personal conduits, but his position as clerk of the Privy Council ensured that he had a general view of letters and materials sent by Henry Sidney, lord deputy of Ireland (and father of Philip Sidney). As with the material pertaining to Denmark, Beale amassed copies in the late 1570s and 1580s, organized them neatly into volumes, and annotated them for later reference as needed.[22] So too regarding material on Scottish history and legal matters, which he collected and collated accordingly, adding notes for future reference again and again.[23] Within these and other papers, he sometimes specified where or from whom he had acquired the material. In a domestic context, he received highly significant material

---

[17] BL, Hargrave MS 107, fol. 25r; these works are all grouped together. On Wechel and these works, see Chapter 5.

[18] BL, Hargrave MS 107, fols 24v, 34r, 36v, 32v. At some point after 1587, Ubaldini supplied Beale with several Venetian *relazioni* copied in his own hand. BL, Additional MS 48080, items 3–11. Beale also appears to have owned later printed works of history by Ubaldini on England and Scotland. BL, Hargrave MS 107, fols 22r, 26v, 32r.

[19] BL, Hargrave MS 107, fols 27v, 10r, 39r, 10r, 16v, 19v, 7v.

[20] BL, Hargrave MS 107, fols 40r, 32r, 28v. On Smith, see above, Chapter 3. On Wales, see below.

[21] Some of the material in BL, Additional MSS 48001 and 48152 explicitly relates to the missions to Denmark and the Holy Roman Empire in 1577, but much also relates to embassies in the early 1580s.

[22] BL, Additional MSS 48015, 48017. On the volumes of the Yelverton collection and when they were collected, collated, and bound (either during Beale's time or afterwards), see the main introduction to the catalogue in hardcopy.

[23] BL, Additional MSS 48027, 48032–3.

from the martyrologist John Foxe on the proposed reform of ecclesiastical law during the Henrician Reformation. Similarly, he arranged for copies from a series of proposals raised between 1575 and 1581 on further reform of the Church of England; within his own copies he carefully noted which of these proposals he had taken from a book of Walsingham's.[24] The reform of Church canon and, by extension, jurisdiction, was a very sensitive issue for Beale during the early 1580s, as the archbishop of Canterbury, John Whitgift, would soon learn.

Alongside his increasingly large library and archive, Beale found himself drafting and amending official letters and ambassadors' instructions. In 1577 he had offered his suggestions and slight emendations regarding the intended alliance between England and the Protestant princes of Germany; given his unparalleled expertise on the Holy Roman Empire at that time, it is unsurprising that his ideas were adopted and put into action. Subsequently, though, his knowledge and assistance were sought regarding Denmark as well, for in 1583, when he served as principal secretary in Walsingham's absence, he corrected Elizabeth's letters patent to clarify an Anglo-Danish treaty relating to trade in the Baltic; as evidence that his advice mattered, these suggestions were incorporated into the final version sent to Denmark.[25] About this same time, he also amended multiple versions of draft instructions for Edward Stafford, then preparing to leave England as resident ambassador in France.[26] Moving forward, recognition of Beale's expertise and value extended even further. When, for example, Elizabeth wrote to the Doge in Venice regarding duties and imposts on Venetian merchants in England, and on English merchants in Venetian territories, Beale amended an early draft of the letter not only stylistically but also substantively. Unsurprisingly, his emendations were adopted in a later draft and then in the final version sent to Venice.[27]

---

[24] BL, Additional MS 48040, fols 13r–104v, with Beale's note reading 'of Mr John Foxe' at 13r. BL, Additional MS 48064, fols 188r–200v, with Beale's note regarding Walsingham's book at 188r, 189r 193v, 198v; the third item Beale noted to have been 'made by D[r John] Hamond'. More broadly, it seems that many of Beale's copies across his archive came from originals (or copies of the originals) now in the Cotton collection, which includes much of Walsingham's papers. Beale noted the dispersal of Walsingham's papers in his treatise on the office of the principal secretary (Read, *Mr Secretary Walsingham*, 1.431), but an effort to trace the dispersal has been made by Hsuan-Ying Tu in 'The Dispersal of Francis Walsingham's Papers', *The Sixteenth Century Journal*, 50:2 (2019), 471–92, which originated in 'The Pursuit of God's Glory: Francis Walsingham's Espionage in Elizabethan Politics, 1568–1588', unpublished PhD thesis, University of York, 2012, 17–42. As discussed in Chapter 7, the papers of Thomas Norton did not enter Beale's hands until 1586 at the earliest. See Taviner, 244–79.
[25] Letters patent of Elizabeth, 12/22 October 1583, BL, Additional MS 48152, fols 41r–4v (with Beale's amendments); TNA, SP 75/1, fol. 93r–v (final version); Rigsarkivet, TKUA, SD, England, AI, 1 (final letter sent, calendared briefly in *Report of the Deputy Keeper of Public Records*, 45th report, App. II, 25, with additional relevant materials in TKUA, SD, England, AII, 9).
[26] Stafford's instructions, September 1583, BL, Additional MS 48152, fols 286r–92v; TNA, SP 78/10, item 42. On Stafford's dealings while in France, see Mitchell Leimon and Geoffrey Parker, 'Treason and Plot in Elizabethan Diplomacy: The "Fame of Sir Edward Stafford" Reconsidered', *English Historical Review*, 111:444 (1996), 1134–58.
[27] Elizabeth to the 'Signoria' of Venice, 12/22 March 1585, BL, Additional MS 48126, fols 187r–8v (draft with Beale's suggestions); TNA, SP 99/1, fols 44r–7v (final draft); letter as sent calendared in Horatio F. Brown (ed.), *Calendar of State Papers Relating to English Affairs in the Archives of Venice, Volume 8, 1581–1591* (London, 1894), item 265.

As with the outbox, as it were, so with the inbox: Beale was often called upon to translate or decipher letters arriving from overseas for the Privy Council or Elizabeth herself. Among his own papers, his translations into English of French material regarding the wars of religion in 1575–6 suggest that he intended his translations for use by another person, but later in the decade and into the 1580s it becomes clear that his work in translation and deciphering was required and requested.[28] After his diplomatic mission in 1577, copies of internal correspondence (in German) among the German princes regarding the Formula of Concord were received and endorsed by Beale, with some materials translated into Latin for easier reading by those unable to read German. Beale's resourcefulness and reputation for translating German materials was endorsed by Daniel Rogers, who in 1579 noted to Walsingham that 'Mr Beale his dutchman' could translate additional German correspondence into Latin or English for the secretary. Due to his experience and the lack of an alternative candidate, Beale was, for all intents and purposes, Elizabeth's de facto secretary for German affairs.[29] Beale's linguistic talents extended beyond conventional European languages like German, French, and Italian, for he also appears to have been involved in deciphering potentially dangerous messages sent securely back to England by English agents abroad— Henry Cobham in France and Daniel Rogers in captivity in the Low Countries.[30]

Given the reference materials at his disposal, and his access to sensitive intelligence via the Privy Council, Beale continued to pen the same sort of discourses, summaries, and working thought-pieces as he had previously. Although his earlier works and letters of the 1560s and early 1570s had the principal aims of securing the attention and patronage of John Hales and, above all, William Cecil, Beale's literary output of the late 1570s forward continued to emphasize his international perspective and legal acumen, but they also took on an increasingly practical purpose—to inform those in government who decided policy. The volume and nature of Beale's correspondence alone attest to the ways in which he sought to advise. His expertise remained principally in foreign affairs and the law, but his view was always to demonstrate how developments and personalities abroad could affect England for good or ill. In addition to sharing his thoughts in his comparatively brief letters, Beale's longer writings demonstrated his fuller

---

[28] Beale's autograph translations regarding the French wars of religion, BL, Additional MS 48152, fols 141r–4r.

[29] e.g. German copy and Latin translation of the German Electors' letter to other princes, 10 September 1579, TNA, SP 81/1, fols 182r–93v. Rogers to Walsingham, 6 April 1578, TNA, SP 81/1, fols 134r–5v, quotation at 134v (orig.).

[30] Cobham to Walsingham, passage deciphered, 17 October 1582, TNA, SP 78/8, fol. 171 (item 75) and preceding unfoliated/unpaginated item; Cobham to Walsingham, deciphered, early February 1583, TNA, SP 78/9, fol. 49r (item 23). Rogers to Walsingham, partially deciphered, 24 October 1582, TNA, SP 81/2, fol. 104r (item 46a). On the use of ciphers and with reference to relevant scholarship, see William H. Sherman, 'Decoding Early Modern Cryptography', *Huntington Library Quarterly*, 82 (2019), 31–19.

views and enabled him to justify his positions before his intended audience, who invariably included Walsingham, Burghley, and others on the Privy Council.

In a slight departure from his usual geographical interests, in 1578 Beale wrote a treatise on Ireland, in his own words, 'uppon Consultation for ye newe establishment in Irland 1578. this discours was given by Robert Beale to Mr vicechamberlayn' (i.e. Christopher Hatton). This consultation appears to have involved several interested parties and generated and corroborated several discourses by others, including Thomas Ratcliffe, earl of Sussex; Nicholas White, master of the rolls in Ireland; John Chaloner, secretary for Ireland; and Sir Nicholas Malby, president of Connacht.[31] In short, Beale understood that the government hoped to establish in Ireland 'trewe religion, justice [...] Englishe manere and Ciuilitie, [and] [t]o haue the Countreye better inhabited[,] builded[,] and manured'.[32] To ensure a more uniform obedience to Elizabeth, Beale argued that suppressing the use of Irish 'coign and livery' (oppressive exactions from a lord's tenantry to that lord) was particularly important because it was, in his view, 'th'onlye cause of all disordere'.[33] Subsequently and characteristically, he addressed the difficult consequences to law, order, and justice in such a system where the powerful do as they please without regard for others. Citing legal precedents from the reigns of Edward III, Henry VI, Henry VII, Elizabeth, and from the Statutes of Kilkenny (1367) in particular, Beale made the case that the Irish had been in violation of laws to which they had long been subject regarding the suppression of coign and livery, adding 'I haue read that an Erle of desmonde was beheaded as a traitor for vsing the same'.[34] Clear in the discourse is Beale's deep research on multiple sides of various issues, his engagement with Irish terms for key social figures and ideas, and his ability to anticipate counter-arguments; such, after all, had been his linguistic and legal training, however on-the-job it had been. Another focus of the discourse was to reinvigorate the Irish husbandman to increase agricultural productivity and, in consequence, revenues for Elizabeth. Noting that 'in the Romane common wealthe, that when the Romane coulde in time of warre be a souldior & and time of peace retorne to his former trade & calling, so longe was that

---

[31] BL, Additional MS 48017, fols 200r–7r, with quotation in Beale's hand in the margin of 200r. The text is in a neat secretary hand but with occasional interventions by Beale (e.g. at fol. 205v and at the very end, 207r). Beale owned and annotated the discourses by those named here: BL, Additional MS 48015, fols 291v–306v. Additional discussion of Beale's use of such tracts, and the flaws in Beale's own, in Popper, *Specter of the Archive*, ch. 1.

[32] BL, Additional MS 48017, fol. 200r.

[33] BL, Additional MS 48017, fol. 200v. For discussion and transcriptions on the subject at the time, see David Heffernan, 'Six Tracts on "Coign and Livery"', *c.*1568–78', *Analecta Hibernica*, 45 (2014), 1, 3–33; David Heffernan, *'Reform' Treatises on Tudor Ireland, 1537–1599* (Dublin, 2016); Heffernan, *Debating Tudor Policy in Sixteenth-Century Ireland*.

[34] BL, Additional MS 48017, fol. 201r; Beale noted in particular 10 Hen. VI c.3, 10 Hen. VII c.18 and 19, and 11 Eliz. c.7. Later in the discourse 33 Hen. VI c.3 and the Statutes of Kilkenny are called upon, 204r. Beale's numbering for statutes remains obscure and frequently disagrees with *The Statutes of the Realm*. In any event, his discussion of the Statutes of Kilkenny takes precedence.

Common weathe well gouerned. But when the souldior began to doe nothing els but make profession of souldiorshipe then grewe all disorders'.[35] Aside from references to ancient Rome, Beale, despite the fact that he had never actually been to Ireland, also demonstrated his knowledge of medieval and recent Irish history by way of his learning and citing specific examples and genealogies among the rivalling aristocracy and major landowners across a wide geography—from the Pale around Dublin to the county palatine of Tipperary. Moreover, his understanding of the roles and significance of, and contempt for, the Old English in Ireland is on display at various points, particularly when he echoed the Statutes of Kilkenny that the Old English 'indeede manye times proue worse then Irishe: as maye be said of the Geraldines heretofore and not longe sithe of the Butlers and James ffitzmoris which rebellions are maintained by this Coine and liuerye'.[36] Beale's tone in writing is firm and convincing when advocating measures to suppress coign and livery by the Irish, but he also characteristically ensured that his personal views were recognized by using the phrase 'in my opinion', and he indicated his learning, particularly at the end of his discourse where he compared the bringing of order in Ireland to that 'As happened heretofore in the reducing of Wales, which at the first was (as Cambrensis writeth) soch as Irland nowe ys'.[37]

The breadth and depth of the discourse on Ireland, both looking back to be historically informed and looking forward to inform policy, illustrated how Beale could gather a large if sometimes dated body of source material on a subject regarding which he had previously little knowledge, and then turn his research into a persuasive treatise to be consulted by those who could use it when making government policy. He wrote the discourse on Ireland shortly before the Second Desmond Rebellion broke out in 1579, but roughly a year later he was directly involved in the rallying of English forces, most notably writing to the dean of St Paul's Cathedral, Alexander Nowell, regarding the need for the dean to supply horsemen.[38] Given his prior and continual expertise in German affairs, though, unsurprisingly the bulk of Beale's attention in foreign policy matters remained focused on the Holy Roman Empire and, increasingly, how the Hanseatic League of merchants and towns related to English endeavours and concerns. He wrote several detailed and useful pieces, especially after his successful return in early 1578 from his mission to the German Protestant princes. A taste of his thinking at that time can be seen in his analysis of, as he put it, '*Incommodae Locutiones*

---

[35] BL, Additional MS 48017, fol. 202v,   [36] BL, Additional MS 48017, fol. 206r.
[37] BL, Additional MS 48017, fol. 207r, in Beale's hand. Beale's collection of extracts from Gerald of Wales, again in his own hand, in BL, Additional MS 48015, fols 1r–4r (on the topography of Wales), 20r–2v (on Ireland); with these extracts are Beale's collections of other historical notes and transcriptions of various statutes, including those cited in the discourse, most notably from the Statutes of Kilkenny at 30r–1v. Other material in MS 48015 dating from the 1570s also lays out Beale's organization and research.
[38] Beale to Nowell, 6 and 10 October 1580 (3 letters), LMA, CLC/313/P/036/MS25202, fols 5r–10v (orig.).

Vbiquistarum', in which he dissected the works of Johann Brenz and Jakob Andreae.[39] Investigating the locations of the heavens and earth, the resurrection of the body, role of angels, and the divisibility and supposed ubiquity of Christ, Beale's brief work appears not to have been intended for any particular person, and it may have remained solely in the version extant in his own collections. Nevertheless, his detailed knowledge of fine theological distinctions and intra-Protestant strife in the Empire would, in time, become increasingly useful in a context closer to home.

Beale's interest in the Hanseatic League, particularly due to their proximity in London's Steelyard and the importance of their towns to English trade, began in the early 1570s but gained considerable steam later in the decade and into the next, especially after the expiration of privileges enjoyed by English merchants at Hamburg in 1577.[40] Among his papers exist several treatises of varying lengths either written directly or annotated and amended heavily by Beale. Early examples of his thinking can be seen in his annotations to a copy of a brief discourse on the Hanse, which concludes that, although previously the English had needed the Hanse and merchants of the Steelyard to furnish England with imports, by 1578 English merchants could do the same in their own ships and to their own profit. Moreover, because the privileges enjoyed by the Hanse in London were no longer similarly enjoyed by the English in the Hanse towns, the situation was uneven and needed redressing.[41] A similar piece from 1578 advocating the cancellation of the privileges enjoyed in the Steelyard, if they were not reciprocated for English merchants in northern Germany, corroborated Beale's thinking here on legal grounds. These two comparatively short works on what the English perceived to be injustices in treatment of the Hanse by the English, and of the Merchant Adventurers by the Germans, found much larger and detailed expression in a third work, two copies of which survive in one volume owned by Beale.[42]

This work was, as Beale called it, 'A Collection, touching matters in variance between the Merchants Aduenturers and the Stiliarde'.[43] By bringing together several different issues, the work showed how widely Beale understood the problems

[39]   BL, Additional MS 48085, fols 290r–5r (text in fine secretary hand with Beale's emendations and additions).

[40]   See Beale's collection of papers relevant to the cancellation and subsequent negotiations, BL, Additional MS 48010, fols 423–91. For a long chronological survey, see T. H. Lloyd, *England and the German Hanse, 1157–1611: A Study of their Trade and Commercial Diplomacy* (Cambridge, 1991), with discussion of the negotiations in and after 1577 at 320–5. From the English side, with more of a social history perspective, see Thomas Leng, *Fellowship and Freedom: The Merchant Adventurers and the Restructuring of English Commerce, 1582–1700* (Oxford, 2020).

[41]   BL, Additional MS 48019, fols 120v–6v.

[42]   BL, Additional MS 48115, fols 92r–7r; longer works, 118r–33v, 142r–60r.

[43]   BL, Additional MS 48115, fol. 142r (title in Beale's hand); the title for the other version, 118r, is in a fine secretary hand. The version on fols 118r–33r is written throughout in the same secretary hand, save Beale's 'And by what right' (130r), but it incorporates some of Beale's changes found in his own hand in 142r–60r. For present purposes the earlier version with more of Beale's annotations is favoured.

and merits of England's relationship with the Hanse, and how far back the inter-national agreements reached. The by-now usual breadth and depth of his legal knowledge and historical insight were on full display, but he also offered some first-person clues regarding his access and methods. For example, in his marginal comments he wrote that he had himself seen the contracts discussed and was not relying solely on hearsay or biased testimony from the English merchants. He noted that the alderman of the Steelyard, possibly Mauritz Timmerman, had shown Beale 'a writing, and sayeth that the meaning of them of Hamburg was to haue the words of the denuntiation made to ye merchantes Aduenturers vnder-stode according to ye treaty of vtrecht', which marked the end of a conflict between England and the Hanse that provided the Germans with security in the Steelyard much to the chagrin of the Merchant Adventurers.[44] In sum, and reflect-ing his balanced view of the problems and vying perspectives, Beale concluded as usual on legal grounds that 'It appereth by the fourth article of the treaty of vtre-cht, that there shold haue ben sum further consideracion & restoration of thes libertyes on both sides; which I find not don as I have before declared: which hath byn the cause of all the controversyes that haue arrisen'.[45]

Difficulties between the Hanse and Merchant Adventurers regarding each oth-er's trading privileges continued well into the 1580s and beyond, so Beale remained well attuned and informed over the years, and not just on the Hanse. Indeed, he seems to have been aware of pressure applied by the Merchant Adventurers on the Privy Council in the form of bribery to get the most favourable outcome possible; more telling, though, is that Beale may have even relayed this information in confidence to Adam Wachendorf, the secretary of the Steelyard, who then passed this information from 'Dr Beale' to others; the German's assump-tion that Beale was a doctor reflected a commonly held tendency overseas to ele-vate Beale beyond his station.[46] Before working on another discourse about the Steelyard at some point after 1582, he received a list of all the Hanse towns, organ-ized into their respective geographies, from Thomas Russell, the deputy governor of the Eastland Company, which had been chartered in 1579.[47] The work written after 1582, like those preceding it, was a combination of a fine secretary hand and Beale's own emendations, but it also built upon those works because it

[44] BL, Additional MS 48115, fols 148r–v. On Beale's knowledge of the alderman's role about this time, see BL, Additional MS 48010, fols 445r, 476v–8r. On the Treaty of Utrecht (1474), see T. H. Lloyd, 'A Reconsideration of Two Anglo-Hanseatic Treaties of the Fifteenth Century', *English Historical Review*, 102:45 (1987), 916–33.

[45] BL, Additional MS 48115, fol. 160r (Beale's hand). Beale's contact with the alderman continued into the 1580s as the controversies dragged on. See, e.g. Beale to Walsingham, 8 October 1581, TNA, SP 12/150, fols 68r–9v (orig.).

[46] Wachendorf to Suderman, 17 February 1582, abstract in Konstantin Höhlbaum (ed.), *Kölner Inventar*, 2. Band: *1572–1591* (Leipzig, 1903), 227.

[47] On the Eastland Company, see Henryk Zins, trans. H.C. Stevens, *England and the Baltic in the Elizabethan Era* (Manchester, 1972), 54–133, with notice of Russell's significance at 100 *et passim*.

incorporated some of the previous text; yet, again, it remains only in draft among Beale's other papers on the Hanse, so the intended audience is obscure. As before, the views of both sides and legal processes were considered, with Beale suggesting that both the Merchant Adventurers and Hanse should regain the privileges previously enjoyed. It is difficult to ascertain with certainty the degree to which these pieces on the Hanse and Steelyard were formally the work of Beale alone because of the multiple hands involved. At the very least, though, he collected and read vast amounts of information about the situation from a variety of viewpoints, and he engaged with the issues by way of his emendations and additions. As will be seen, he closely followed and participated in these negotiations in the years to come, relaying information to Walsingham and Burghley as events unfolded, even corresponding with a major humanist and historian of the Hanse, David Chytraeus, one of the theologians previously responsible for the intra-Protestant fracture following the Lutheran Formula of Concord.[48]

By way of his administrative habits in amassing a well-organized reference library and archive, coupled with his respected legal knowledge and skills in historical research, and complemented by his literary abilities when offering an easily digestible synthesis of complex issues, Beale was fully able—and willing—to act as principal secretary if called upon. By 1578, he had first observed Walsingham at work as the premier English ambassador overseas and then as principal secretary (sole and as one of two). As with Beale's legal training, notwithstanding whatever informal education he had gained at Heidelberg, so too with his life in the administration of government—it was all on-the-job training. Such was admittedly the case for all Elizabethan administrators. Professionally, these years represented the climax of Beale's career because, with Walsingham in place, Beale could realistically climb no higher than he already was. On the side, in the early 1580s he became involved with the Council of the North, which eventually brought some additional salary even if it meant, in theory, that he might need to travel. This role in the north was almost certainly tied to his activity at that time in Sheffield with Mary Queen of Scots. Additionally, he served as deputy to the governor of the Company of Mines Royal (the governor was, conveniently, Walsingham) from about 1580, and, according to his later account, Beale 'kept the books without one pennye allowaunce [...] And it is well knowen, that my labor herin hathe bene more then of anye other, so as I haue not ben altogether an vnprofitable drone'. The next year he became a shareholder of the Company of Mineral and Battery Works, which had seceded from the Mines Royal in the

---

[48] For material relevant to later in the 1580s, BL, Additional MS 48115. Long treatise on the Hanse in 1586, annotated by Beale as in the past, BL, Additional MS 48011, fols 82r–164v. BL, Additional MSS 48009–10 include papers extending from the 13th c. to 1587, much of which was the source material for Beale's knowledge. Beale to Walsingham, 29 August 1585, TNA, SP 12/181, fols 230r–2v (orig.). Beale's copy of 'Hansae Teutonicae Delineatio', ascribed to Chytraeus, after 1581, BL, Additional MS 48115, fols 80r–5v. On Beale's later correspondence with Chytraeus, see Chapter 8.

1560s. His interest and expertise in mining and related technologies stemmed from his activity in 1569 and was conveniently documented for Cecil and Smith shortly afterwards. An additional indication of Beale's rise and specialisms was his involvement in the importation of steel from beyond the seas. By early 1582 he was internationally recognized as one knowledgeable in such affairs, and on 22 December of the same year he was granted the sole licence to import steel from 'all and euerye the partes beyond the seas' into England, a monopoly of 'the whole traffique trade and merchaundise of the said steele' that could prove lucrative over the twelve years of the licence.[49] These positions reflected Beale's stature and conveyed some additional esteem. Firmly planted in England during these years, busying himself in the daily occurrents of the Privy Council, Beale also kept at least one eye looking out across the seas. While Irish affairs and negotiations with the Hanse were clearly of importance on the domestic side of matters of state, so too were events in France, the Netherlands, and Germany during the early and mid 1580s. Naturally, Beale had a lot to say on those matters, too.

Across the Seas

After his return to London from his mission of 1577–8, Beale remained well-informed on how theological polemics among German Protestants continued to jeopardize the solidarity necessary to withstand Catholic aggression in France and the Netherlands. He understood the particularities of the French and Dutch contexts, not least through his own observations in the former and negotiations in the latter, but he also recognized that the Protestants of the Empire and Denmark also had critical roles to play. In correspondence with his old friend, Hubert Languet, and a comparatively new ally, Landgrave Wilhelm of Hesse, Beale received updates on how many and which princes were rejecting the Lutheran Formula (and *Book*) of Concord, which had caused such discord among Protestants across German, Swiss, Danish, Dutch, and French lands (see Fig. 7).[50]

---

[49] On Beale and the Council of the North, see below. On his work with the Mines Royal, see Beale to Burghley, 24 April 1595, BL, Lansdowne MS 79, fol. 193v, with quotation and further examples of how Beale assisted the company (orig.). Beale received a quarter of a share of the Company of Mineral and Battery Works on 15 January 1582 from William Burd, who also served as the treasurer of the Mines Royal. Donald, *Elizabethan Monopolies*, 73, 53; cf. Beale's activity for the company with Julius Caesar in the 1590s, 133, 189. For his activity in the late 1560s and early 1570s, see Chapters 3 and 4. Claude Nau to Beale, 8 April 1582, Newberry Library, Case MS 5089 (orig.). For the grant, TNA, C 66/1224, mm. 4–6; for this licence Beale was not required to pay any fine or fee to the Queen's hanaper for its sealing.

[50] Languet to Beale, 20 January, 14 February, 31 March, 2 May, 16 July, 25 August, 22 September, 23 October 1578; 20 April, 21 November 1579; 20 February 1580, 12 March 1581, 15 February, 22 April 1581, BL, Egerton MS 1693, fols 16r, 19r–v, 21r–2r, 23r–v, 25r–v, 28r–v, 30r–v, 32r 34r, 37r–v, 39r–v, 42r–v, 46r, 48r–v (all orig.). Wilhelm to Beale, 20 September 1579, BL, Egerton MS 1693, fols 35r–6r (orig.). Wilhelm to Beale, 15 January 1581, AUL, MS 1009/2, item 2 (orig.). Cf. Antoine des Traos (secretary to Wilhelm) to Beale, 13 July 1581, AUL, MS 1009/2, item 5 (orig.); Johannes von Glauburg

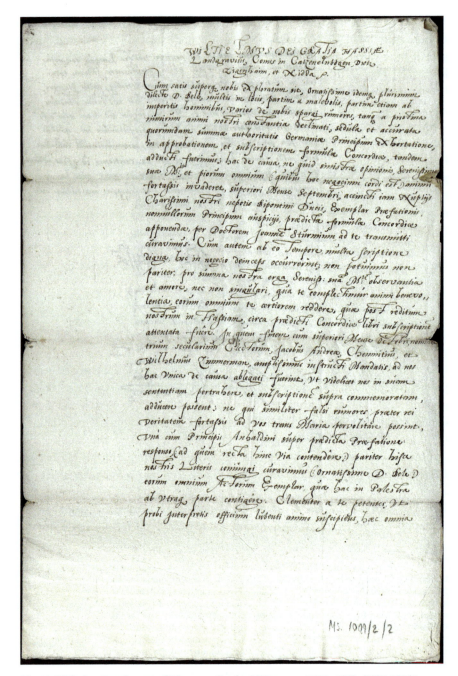

Fig. 7 Wilhelm, Landgrave of Hesse, to Beale, 15 January 1581. AUL, MS 1009/2, item 2, fol. 1r (orig.), in University of Aberdeen Museums and Special Collections, is licenced under CC By 4.0.

As in his fuller and more formal discourses, Beale's correspondence and activities indicate the integrated nature of his worldview. So broad were his activity and vision that he engaged with the Spanish ambassador, Bernardino de Mendoza, regarding both the piracy by Francis Drake along the coast of South America and the threat posed by Mary Queen of Scots to England.[51] Beale's recognition of the importance of the American land masses in 1583 is seen in his hosting of John Dee and Adrian Gilbert, along with Walsingham, for the purposes of a secret discussion about the north-west passage and relevant maps and rutters. He followed up by acquiring Dee's holograph manuscript treatise, 'Of Famous and Rich Discoveries' (which he only returned in 1591), and it appears that in the intervening years Beale and Dee became relatively good friends, and Dee entertained Beale and Edith for dinner at his home.[52] Drake's plundering of distant coasts and Dee's ambitions in mystical lands were relevant to Beale's domestic concerns in anti-Spanish policy and fostering new trade routes, but still more important were English efforts to collaborate with those opposed to Rome throughout Europe and to protect a broad community of religious brethren fighting for a common cause.

As Beale had tried in 1577, so too did Jacques de Ségur-Pardaillan, ambassador from the king of Navarre to the German princes, in 1583–4. Alongside attempting to reconcile differences among Protestants and establish a defensive alliance, Ségur was to convince the princes to assist Gebhard Truchsess, archbishop of Cologne (one of the seven electors of the Empire), who had recently converted to Protestantism and consequently lost his seat. Before heading into the thickets of religion and politics in the Empire, though, Ségur went to London, where he received the blessings of the English government and met with Beale specifically to discuss how best to approach the mission.[53] Beale received a copy of Ségur's instructions (dated at Nérac on 15 July 1583), and the Navarrese implored Beale in September regarding the need for Elizabeth to use her influence among the king of Denmark and the princes of Germany; the inclusion of the Danish angle was particularly telling because Navarre's ambassador in Denmark, Charles de Dançay, soon wrote to Beale along the same lines, emphasizing the 'fraternele amytie et bonne Intelligence' that had for so long been between England and Denmark, and seeking aid in the attempt to curb the 'ambitieux[,] superbes[,]

---

to Beale, 26 March 1581, AUL, MS 1009/2, item 24 (orig.); the Protestant electors to the city council of Cologne, 27 August 1582, endorsed by Beale as 'Aduertisementes out of Germany', BL, Additional MS 48115, fols 27r–30v. On Languet and Wilhelm, see Chapter 5.

[51] Memorial of answers by Mendoza to the speech delivered him by Beale, 29 October 1580, TNA, SP 94/1, item 57 (Beale's hand). Materials regarding Beale, Mendoza, and Mary Queen of Scots, 1582–4, Martin A. S. Hume (ed.), *Calendar of State Papers, Spain (Simancas), Volume 3, 1580–1586* (London, 1896), items 195, 211, 213, 334–5, 337, 346, 366.

[52] James Orchard Halliwell (ed.), *The Private Diary of Dr John Dee* (London, 1842), 18, 38, 46. Dee's 'Of Famous and Rich Discoveries' (1577), BL, Cotton MS Vitellius, C. VII, fols 26r–269v. On Dee more broadly, see Glyn Parry, *The Arch-Conjuror of England* (New Haven, CT, 2011), on Beale at 152–3, 170.

[53] Ségur's mission in the context of English efforts is discussed in *AGR*, 92–7.

et seditieux Theologiens' in Germany.[54] The confidence of Ségur and Dançay in Beale's knowledge of Germany and general ability to help the cause was better placed on the German than Danish side. Curiously, soon Beale found himself amending an early draft of Elizabeth's missive to King Frederik II of Denmark regarding trading privileges, though he made no reference to Navarre.[55] The omission is slightly surprising because the futures and fates of France and the Netherlands were very much occupying Beale's mind and time between August and October 1583, when he served as principal secretary and received intelligence from those abroad, especially George Gilpin, Henry Cobham, and Bizzarri. The integrated nature of Beale's understanding of English support for the causes in France and the Netherlands can be seen in a letter by Beale to Burghley about this time, and the additional dimension of Cologne came to the fore in his 'Discovrse towchinge ye present troubles in Germany', which Beale conveniently dated to 'when Mr Davison was sent into Holland to the Elector of Colleyn'.[56] In short, Beale advocated significant military action to support the archbishop of Cologne as well as Protestants in the Netherlands. Fighting for their faith, in Beale's view, was wholly within the legal bounds of the Empire, so he also pushed for an embassy to be sent to the emperor to justify these actions.

After Ségur's return to England, and thence back to the king of Navarre, plans were soon put in motion for yet another English embassy to Germany and Denmark to sound the alarums of what many perceived to be imminent defeat for the Protestants. With good reason did Ségur assume that Beale would be nominated to serve as Elizabeth's ambassador; in consultation with others, Beale himself even advised Burghley on the need to send a man into Germany, especially to England's longest-serving religious and military ally, Duke Johann Casimir of the Palatinate, whose solidarity with Elizabeth had been evident when he was installed into the Order of the Garter in 1579. In the event, Beale successfully avoided another long journey away from Edith and the children, but he did inform the eventual ambassador (Thomas Bodley) on how best to approach the mission, with specific attention paid to Julius, duke of Brunswick.[57] Thus, in the

---

[54] Ségur's instructions endorsed by Beale, BL, Additional MS 48126, fols 143–7v. Séégur to Beale, 3 September 1583, BYU, MS 457, item 19 (orig.); copy in BL, Additional MS 48149, fol. 146r–v; cf. Ségur's later correspondence to Beale of 5 January 1585 and 10 August 1587, BL, Additional MS 48127, fols 121r*, 122r (both orig.). Dançay to Beale, 18 December 1583, BYU, MS 457, item 20 (orig.); copy in BL, Additional MS 48149, fols 160r–1r.

[55] Heads of a letter from Elizabeth to Frederik, October 1583, BL, Additional MS 48126, fols 116r–17r.

[56] A convenient survey of the 'inbox' from abroad can be seen in CSPF. Beale to Burghley, 5 September 1583, BL, Lansdowne MS 39, item 36 (orig.). Beale's discourse, October 1584, BL, Additional MS 48126, fols 58r–61v; cf. a different, brief set of Beale's ideas in 1584, TNA, SP 83/23, fol. 237r–v.

[57] Ségur to Beale, 5 January 1585, BL, Additional MS 48127, fol. 121r* (orig.). Ségur to Walsingham, 4/14 March 1585, TNA, SP 78/14, fol. 39r (orig.). Consultation for the realms of France and Scotland, 27 March 1585, CP, 163/76 (notes in Burghley's hand). Beale's notes for Bodley's instructions, April 1585, TNA, SP 81/2, fols 174r–5v. On Johann Casimir's installation, see AGR, 77.

short space of 1578 to 1585, Beale's web of correspondents continued to expand, as did his access to Walsingham's own network of intelligencers abroad.[58] Back in the 1560s, Beale's correspondence and discourses tended to lean in a slightly theoretical direction, working with very concrete information and research but nevertheless hypothesizing on the threats posed to Protestantism and the subsequent outcomes if support were not provided by England and Germany. During the 1580s, though, his previous theories increasingly seemed to become reality, and Beale was right in the middle of the decision-making process. As ever, though, he understood Spanish hegemony, Huguenot insecurity, and vacillation by both English and German leaders as linked to equally large if not larger problems within England itself: Mary Queen of Scots.

Closer to Home—Sheffield

Between the early 1570s and early 1580s, Beale's opinion of Mary Queen of Scots did not change much. His view of Mary as a pernicious viper—pestiferous, even—who posed a real and direct threat to Queen Elizabeth's safety continued, though his understanding of Scottish history and politics gained greater depth as the years rolled by.[59] Beale had first come to the attention of Cecil and others due to his work in understanding the gravity of and genealogies involved in the royal succession, and this with a comparatively positive view to providing a securely Protestant candidate if Elizabeth did not provide an heir in the customary manner. These deliberately constructive efforts, however much they cost Hales in consequence, gave way to a more negative view among many in the English regime who sought to exclude the primary threat to what they held dear—a Protestant succession.[60] Beale, because of his legal knowledge and understanding of the situation in Scotland as it related to broader European developments, was well suited during the 1580s to serve as an advisor on how Elizabeth could deal with the viper caged in Sheffield Castle. Mary had been under house arrest and under the custody of George Talbot, earl of Shrewsbury, since 1569 with only

---

[58] Beale later cautioned in his work on the office of the principal secretary against having too many agents and secretaries, which could and did get very expensive for Walsingham. See Alford, *The Watchers*.

[59] On the earlier period, see above, esp. Chapter 4.

[60] Taviner, 185–213 discusses Beale, Mary, the succession, and the 'exclusion' crisis between the early 1570s and 1586 but swiftly moves past the missions of 1581–4. Patricia Basing's discussion and edition of six letters from 1583–4 offer a better understanding of Beale's role during these years, but the focus remains on the broader religious and political issues rather than on Beale himself. 'Robert Beale and the Queen of Scots', *British Library Journal*, 20 (1994), 65–82. For a survey of Mary's time (January 1569 to December 1584) under the supervision of George Talbot, earl of Shrewsbury, see Leader, *Mary Queen of Scots in Captivity*. On Mary more generally, see Retha M. Warnicke, *Mary Queen of* Scots (London, 2006); cf. Julian Goodare's article in the *ODNB* that offers a discussion incorporating various historians' views.

limited freedom to visit Buxton, in Derbyshire, in the hope that its spa would aid her declining health.

Notwithstanding his consistent aversion to further diplomatic service, Beale travelled to Sheffield for the purpose of negotiating with Mary on several occasions between late 1581 and mid 1584. His usual complaints continued, and he clearly did not like to be away from Edith and their young children for long spells, but he understood the significance of these missions because they represented an effort to keep a close eye on Mary and ensure direct lines of communication. Beale might well have acquiesced in these instances because, after all, if he had to be involved in any diplomatic negotiations, he certainly preferred them to be conducted in England rather than abroad. As one would expect, his letters and reports from Sheffield offer voluminous intelligence on Mary, her correspondents, and affairs among the Scottish nobility and on King James VI, and in this regard Beale was simply doing a good job for Walsingham and his sovereign. One can also see among these papers how he needed to swallow his pride and maintain a dispassionate and diplomatic distance when speaking directly with Mary in the interest of cordial relations and a possible treaty between Elizabeth, Mary, and James.[61]

Keeping a cool head when speaking with Mary would have been a significant challenge for Beale because of his recent interrogations of those also at the centre of the Catholic threat against Elizabeth. In late 1580 and late summer 1581, he was directly involved in the examinations of Catholic sympathizers and priests, including the Jesuit, Edmund Campion, at the Tower. Along with John Hammond and Thomas Norton, Beale was instructed to get to the bottom of the international and domestic threat to Protestantism in England posed by Campion, and the interrogators were authorized, if necessary, to use torture (the rack among much else). Beale's involvement in these examinations was undoubtedly due to his fervent anti-Catholicism and knowledge of English law, but he appears to have been averse to using torture as a method of persuasion. By no means lenient regarding the threat to Elizabeth and the regime, Beale, it seems, preferred to work within the bounds of decency even if others leaned otherwise. As Archbishop Whitgift later remarked, Beale condemned 'racking of grievous offenders, as being cruel, barbarous, contrary to law, and unto the liberty of English subjects'. Regarding Campion in particular, Beale wrote to Rutland shortly before his departure for Sheffield that, in a dismissive tone, 'in my simple [humble] opinion he shewed him self only to be a good Oratour, and a very

---

[61] The principal source for most general information has been and remains the relevant volumes of the *Calendar[s] of State Papers, Scotland* and the manuscripts calendared therein from TNA and the BL. Additional useful information from the materials of Mary herself has long been available in the multi-volume Alexandre Labanoff (ed.), *Lettres, instructions et mémoires de Marie Stuart, Reine d'Écosse* (Paris; London, 1844–52). Taviner and Basing have used Beale's own collections and copies, particularly BL, Additional MS 48049.

simple [without craft or subtlety] schollar & devyne otherwayes'.[62] If Beale thought Campion a relative simpleton, in Mary he had an altogether more crafty adversary.

The first of Beale's trips to Sheffield Castle during the 1580s was in November 1581, when Elizabeth sent him to Mary with formal instructions regarding the title of James VI as king of Scotland, Mary's intelligence with other princes, and her continued detention under Shrewsbury; a consistent thread in Beale's instructions was Mary's poor behaviour, such as her conspiring with others in pursuit of the English throne, and its consequences. Compared to his trip to see Mary in 1575, these trips were of a different order of magnitude. In short, he was to inform Mary that she needed to tone down her demands and know her role relative to Elizabeth.[63] These instructions were in response to Mary's request to Elizabeth that the latter send a representative to Sheffield to hear her complaints, but, in the little more than three weeks Beale spent with the queen of Scots, it became apparent that he did not enjoy his time with her and longed to return to London. He may not have been entirely healthy before his departure from London, as Walsingham relayed to Elizabeth that Beale needed an extra two or three days before leaving 'by reason of the in[-]dysposytion of your [i.e. Beale's] bodye' (a recurrent theme). After his arrival at Sheffield, a series of letters from Beale to Walsingham laid bare his frustrations.[64] The first of his missives was a lengthy

---

[62] Beale was involved in the searching of Richard Stanyhurst's house and later examination, as he described letters to Leicester on 28 August and 26 November 1580. TNA, SP 12/141, fols 102r–3v (orig.), SP 12/144, fol. 76r–v (orig.); cf. the large network of Catholic threats at home and abroad in Beale's extracts from the examination of the Jesuit John Hart in December 1580, BL, Additional MS 48035, fols 179r–82v. Beale's involvement in the examinations of Campion in July and August 1581, TNA, PC 2/13, 467, 483–4, 490–1, 494. Whitgift's quotation from his schedule of Beale's misdemeanours, 1585, printed in John Strype, *The Life and Acts of John Whitgift*, 3 vols (Oxford, 1822), 1.401. Beale's quotation from Beale to Rutland, 18 September 1581, Belvoir Castle, MS V, under date, fol. 1r (orig.); the word 'simple' carries a wide range of meanings, many of which can be applied here. The connection between Stanyhurst (or Stanihurst) and Campion is that the latter had lived in the former's house in Dublin during the 1570s. *ODNB*. On Campion, see Thomas M. McCoog (ed.), *The Reckoned Expense: Edmund Campion and the Early English Jesuits: Essays in Celebration of the First Centenary of Campion Hall, Oxford (1896–1996)* (Woodbridge, 1996); for the primary sources from the Catholic perspective, James V. Holleran (ed.), *A Jesuit Challenge: Edmund Campion's Debates at the Tower of London in 1581* (New York, 1999); Alford, *The Watchers*, 108–12.

[63] Beale's instructions, early November 1581, TNA, SP 53/11, item 63. Mary's enciphered correspondence with Michel de Castelnau, seigneur de La Mauvissière, the French ambassador in London, in late October and early November, demonstrates that she expected Beale's arrival. See the abstracts and discussion in George Lasry, Norbert Biermann, and Satoshi Tomokiyo, 'Deciphering Mary Stuart's Lost Letters from 1578–1584', *Cryptologia*, 47:2 (February, 2023), 46–7; https://doi.org/10.108 0/01611194.2022.2160677.

[64] Walsingham to Beale, 14 November 1581, BL, Egerton MS 1693, fols 52r–3v (orig.), quotation at 52r, where Walsingham also observes that Beale did not want to stay in Sheffield long. Beale's 'indisposition of health' (illness) was also the reason why Elizabeth, despite her initial desires, did not later send him to Scotland with articles of a league with James VI. Walsingham to Edward Wotton, 11 June 1585, TNA, SP 52/37, item 61, with quotation at 172. Beale to Walsingham, 14 November (3 letters), 16, 17, 23, 24, 28 November 1581, TNA, SP 53/11, items 64–71 (all orig.). Cf. Beale's copies and related documents in BL, Egerton 1693, fols 52r–3v; BL, Additional MS 14028, fols 36r–46v; BL, Additional MSS 48027, fols 224r–9v, 48049, fols 240r–4v.

and full report on his first few days since he had arrived on 11 November. Marshalling his detailed knowledge of the English and Scottish successions and genealogies, as well as his expertise in history, Beale was quick to beat back the assertions made by John Leslie, bishop of Ross, who had 'by printed books and genealogies verie presumptuouslie taken vppon him to avouche that [the right of succession] belonged vnto her'. Rather, Beale noted, the English Parliament would judge whether Mary or her son had any legitimate claim to be Elizabeth's successor.[65] Mary had been pressing for Elizabeth to send a representative to James for the purposes of a mutual understanding if not alliance between the three monarchs of two countries. In addition to Beale's view that matters of the succession were entirely an English affair, while matters of James's right and title as king were entirely Scottish, for his part Beale wanted nothing to do with such discussions either at Sheffield Castle or in Edinburgh. What he put comparatively delicately in his initial letter to Walsingham after having been at Sheffield just a few days, 'hitherto this Countrey framethe not well with me', he put more bluntly later that afternoon in his second and third letters of 14 November due to the associated costs, dangers, and displeasures: 'For I neither like of the matter nor persons whith whom I shall hav to deale'.[66]

At this time Mary was seriously ill and nearly confined to her bedroom. She frequently requested permission to get out for fresh air in the countryside, an appeal to which Beale was not necessarily opposed, and Beale offered what religious counsel he could as a matter of decency but within the limits of his instructions. According to Shrewsbury, Mary had been more seriously ill in previous years and might have been putting on an act because she knew Beale was reporting directly to Walsingham and Elizabeth. On the other hand, though, Beale sympathized with Mary and tended to agree that a physician should attend to her. Indeed, Beale reported on 23 November of his eery discussion with Mary in her bedchamber without any light, for the candles had been blown out just before he entered the room. In a potentially surprising manner, he seems to have espoused a humanitarian concern for the woman he had previously characterized as a viper, but, then again, as best he could Beale exercised diplomatic caution among those looking to deceive him. Growing increasingly weary regarding his financial estate and accumulating debts, and not wishing to leave his wife and children beggars were he sent to Scotland, Beale requested that, despite Shrewsbury's fine entertainments, he be permitted to return to London. Again, perhaps in sympathy with Mary, Beale appears to have become slightly ill, for as he confided in a postscript intended for Walsingham's eyes alone, 'I do not much complaine, and yet in troth, although my enterteinment be most honorable, have I not ben

---

[65] Beale to Walsingham, 14 November 1581, TNA, SP 53/11, item 64, fol. 5v (orig.). On Leslie, see Chapter 4, and Margaret J. Beckett, 'Counsellor, Conspirator, Polemicist, Historian: John Lesley, Bishop of Ross 1527–96', *Scottish Church History*, 39 (2009), 1–22.

[66] Beale to Walsingham, 14 November 1581, TNA, SP 53/11, item 66, fol. 1v (orig.).

well in health since I cam into these countryes and therfore am desirous to be the sooner released.'[67] With Mary's health in question and negotiations at an impasse on all fronts, Beale nevertheless told her that she would be treated well at Sheffield, and she took this assurance as sincere. Beale left Sheffield Castle on 4 December with a personal memorial from Mary and a list of her demands and 'sayings', to which Beale added his own notes of advice and interpretation for Walsingham. With his newborn daughter Bridget having only arrived in June, one can imagine that Beale looked forward to getting home quickly, and Edith might have appreciated the help. Nevertheless, Beale kept Shrewsbury informed from London, even purchasing for the earl the best maps and descriptions of the region's counties that could be had.[68]

More than a year would pass before Beale ventured again to Sheffield, but his expertise and role were not forgotten. Mary's secretary, Claude Nau, wrote on Mary's behalf to Beale in March 1582, as did Mary directly a month later—again requesting him to continue negotiating for her liberty in exchange for assurances to Elizabeth, while tempting him with future rewards.[69] Additionally, Beale's relationship and, indeed, friendship with Shrewsbury continued in correspondence regarding Mary's situation and the earl's request for additional resources to fund Mary's household and diet. Beale was adamant that he had done as much as he could to find a resolution, noting to his 'frend' Shrewsbury in April that 'howsoever things may hereafter happen to fall out, I have dealt uprightly [...] and, for my poor credit's sake [...] I can say no more, but remit the matter unto the Lord'. As if the earl had forgotten the point, in June Beale again put his faith in God 'that I may be an instrument to do some good; and, forasmuch as I am in hope that there will some good success ensure, I shall pray.'[70] Although he might not

---

[67] Beale to Walsingham, 17, 23, and 24 November 1581, TNA, SP 53/11, items 68–70 (all orig.), quotation from item 70, fol. 1v. Contrast Beale's admission three years later that he was, in fact, a bit of a complainer; see below.

[68] Mary's memorial for Beale, 4 December 1581, TNA, SP 53/11, item 73 (orig. in Claude Nau's hand and endorsed by Beale as delivered on his date of departure). Mary's demands with Beale's notes, 3 December 1581, TNA, SP 53/11, item 72; cf. Burghley's copy, CP, 162/93. Mary to Castelnau, 9 January 1582, Lasry et al., 'Deciphering Mary Stuart's Lost Letters', 47. Bridget, the Beales' newborn child, was baptized on 11 June 1581. She may have been named after Richard Morison's wife, and therefore Beale's aunt, Bridget, or after an as-yet unidentified godmother. Jupp and Hovenden, *The Registers*, 11. The young Bridget appears to have died within months and was buried at St Mary's, Barnes. Surrey History Centre, P6/1/1, fol. 43v (with probable error in recording 1580 for 1581). It remains unclear whether the Beales had any servants at this time. Their previous, a certain 'Cuthberd Deytton', had died of jaundice in July 1580. Jupp and Hovenden, *The Registers*, 91. Beale to Shrewsbury, 28 December 1581, AUL, MS 1009/1, items 23, 29 (draft in two parts).

[69] Nau to Beale, 7 March 1582, BL, Egerton MS 1693, fols 64r–5v (orig.). Mary to Beale, 16 April 1582, TNA, SP 53/12, item 7. Mary to Castelnau, 7 April 1582, Lasry et al., 'Deciphering Mary Stuart's Lost Letters', 49–50.

[70] Beale to Shrewsbury, 2 April 1582 (two letters), Edmund Lodge (ed.), *Illustrations of British History* (Howard Papers), 3 vols, 2nd edn (London, 1838), 2.208–18, with quotations at 210, 217. Cf. Beale to Shrewsbury, 28 June 1582, LPL, MS 3198, fol. 166r–v (orig.); Shrewsbury to Thomas Baldwin, 10 February 1582, LPL, MS 3198, fol. 120r (orig.), noting 'my frend mr bele'; cf. the other letters from Shrewsbury to Baldwin noting Beale in this volume and dated 23 November 1581, 1 December 1581, 14 May 1582.

have enjoyed all of his time at Sheffield Castle with Shrewsbury, Nau, and Mary, he clearly made a good impression as someone both knowledgeable in Scottish and French affairs and competent as an administrator and servant of Queen Elizabeth. His abilities in these regards, along with his continual claims of poverty, may have contributed to the beginning of his involvement with the Council of the North (based at York) that November when Henry Hastings, earl of Huntingdon, was sent the commission as lord president of the Council. Beale was named, along with several others, to assist Huntingdon in the furtherance of justice. Although it remains unclear what role if any Beale played in the immediate wake of that commission in winter 1582/3, he was formally named as secretary to the Council of the North at York later in the 1580s even though it could prove difficult to serve *in situ* while continuing as clerk of the queen's Privy Council; indeed, the use of a sufficient deputy at York was noted in the letters patent. With another later serving as Beale's deputy and actually doing the work of the secretary, at least Beale could draw the same profits and emoluments as had his predecessor.[71]

In response to Mary's pressing demands, and despite his own wishes, Beale was sent back to Sheffield in April and again in May 1583. As he had previously for missions of significant importance in 1576 and 1577, he retained his original instructions dated 6 April 1583 and copies of all relevant correspondence and memoranda; as before, his reasons for doing so were clearly to ensure that he had an easily accessible reference archive on which he could later call should the need arise.[72] Beale's mission began upon his arrival at Sheffield on 12 April and was to respond to Mary's continued requests for liberty but also to discuss her complicity in threats against Elizabeth. The core of his mission was at odds with Mary's former gratitude and positive opinion expressed towards him regarding his sincerity in negotiating, so the continued loggerheads were foreseeable. Beale and Shrewsbury informed Mary that they knew she had referred to Queen Elizabeth as a 'Tirant[,] Antichrist, [and] a faithless vsurper' and sought, with the assistance of Catholic powers overseas, to displace Elizabeth on the English throne. About this time, Beale might have also heard a particularly salacious account of Mary's conduct after the murder of her second husband, Henry, Lord Darnley, in 1567.[73]

[71] Commission to Huntingdon, 21 November 1582, TNA, SP 15/27, fols 205r–8r, with Beale named at 205v. Beale later became secretary and keeper of the signet in the north via a grant, initially for life, dated 20 October 1586, but later cancelled and surrendered on 29 August 1589; a yearly fee or salary is not noted. Letters patent, TNA, C 66/1271, m. 25. R.R. Reid, *The King's Council in the North* (London, 1921), 254–5, 379, 489. See also Beale's own later materials of *c.*1596 relating to the secretaryship: CP, 185/141; BL, Additional MS 48152, fols 205r–12r. See also Chapter 7.

[72] Beale and Shrewsbury's instructions, 6 April 1583, BL, Additional MS 48049, fols 210r–19v (orig.); copies of correspondence and relevant papers, some of which in Nau's hand, 173r–89r, 199r–208v, 261r–2v, 292r–3v, 298r–301v.

[73] Mary to Castelnau, 15 January 1583, Lasry et al., 'Deciphering Mary Stuart's Lost Letters', 60. Shrewsbury and Beale to Elizabeth, 16 April 1583, TNA, SP 53/12, item 51 (orig.), with quotation at 354. At some point after March 1588, Beale recorded the story as told by Archibald Douglas, a

As one might have expected, Mary's responses to Beale were completely frustrating. She openly offered all the assurances to Elizabeth for which one could ask, but she also worked behind the scenes conniving with others against Elizabeth. Beale vented privately to Walsingham in a separate letter dated the same day, noting again Mary's 'wylynes' but also observing that he had accomplished his charge; moreover, in his view there was little further point in his being at Sheffield because his and Shrewsbury's discussions with Mary, Nau, and others had been conducted entirely in English rather than French, which the earl did not understand. Had their discussions been in French, Beale's involvement would have been necessary, but seeing as all was in English, Beale asked Walsingham to recall him back to London, especially bearing in mind 'my wiffes estate [and] some other particular causes that require my beinge at home'.[74] Walsingham would have known that Edith's condition at the time was potentially tender since she was about to give birth to another child (to be named Margaret).[75] The apparent futility of working with Mary, as well as the necessity of Beale's return for personal affairs, sufficiently convinced Elizabeth to recall him, as Walsingham informed him in a letter dated 21 April, which Beale received by 26 April. Before he could leave Sheffield, though, Nau wanted to speak privately with him in the gardens of the castle for advice on what Mary could do, especially given Beale's wide-ranging perspective considering affairs in Scotland, France, and England. Thus, since Beale wanted his own personal copies of the paperwork, which Nau could supply, as much as Nau wanted counsel in return, Beale did not get home to London until early May in the end, and so, again, he missed the birth of his child.[76]

Much to his dismay, Beale was despatched again by the end of the month. He was not alone this time because Walter Mildmay formally represented Elizabeth on this occasion and carried official letters of credit to negotiate a treaty with Mary. Although Beale's name was included in a draft of the instructions dated 24 May, he was relieved of formal duties on the final instructions dated 27 May; his informal services were still to be called upon, however, because Mildmay

conspirator in Darnley's murder but at Elizabeth's court and in Walsingham's service in 1583. According to Douglas, Mary and several other women danced naked, trimmed their pubic hair, and mingled the trimmings in puddings then served to men who became ill, including John Ballendine, 'called Justice Clerk', who 'toke the same to be the cause of his bane or infection'. Beale's 'Notes of ye Evill demeanour of ye Scotish Quen after ye death of the L. Darnley', after March 1588, BL, Additional MS 48027, fol. 78r; in addition to Douglas's report, Beale included other accounts by or regarding Henry Killigrew, Nicholas Throckmorton, and Daniel Rogers. Notice of Douglas's account (but with inaccurate citation) in John Bossy, *Under the Molehill: An Elizabethan Spy Story* (New Haven, CT, 2001), 58.
[74] Beale to Walsingham, 16 April 1583, TNA, SP 53/12, item 53 (orig.).
[75] Jupp and Hovenden, *The Registers*, 12. Margaret was baptized on 24 April.
[76] Walsingham to Shrewsbury, 21 April 1583, TNA, SP 53/12, item 55. Shrewsbury and Beale to Walsingham, 26 April 1583, TNA, SP 53/12, item 59 (orig.). Mary also recognized the futility of these discussions in hers to Castelnau, 16 April 1583, Lasry et al., 'Deciphering Mary Stuart's Lost Letters', 66–8. Beale appears to have left Sheffield on Monday, 29 April. Nau's autograph memorandum for Beale, on behalf of Mary, was dated 28 April. BL, Additional MS 48049, fol. 301r–v (orig.); see Basing, 'Robert Beale'.

would need his advice and assistance.[77] True to form, Beale's previous experience and services were valued by Mildmay, who reported to Walsingham, '[o]f Mr Beale I need to say nothing, you know hym better than I. To Her Majestie he is a good servaunt, and to me a good frend for his advise which I could by no meanes lacke'.[78] Before long and because the treaty had been called off, Beale was sent back to London from Sheffield with both written and oral communications from Mary to Elizabeth, reflecting the fact that, while Mildmay was Elizabeth's formal representative, Beale was still entrusted with intimate messages. A comparatively quick trip on this occasion (in Sheffield for less than three weeks) was much to Beale's delight—Mildmay had noticed that Beale wanted to return home as quickly as possible and had been ill at ease.[79] Upon his return to London Beale's spirits might have risen when spending time with Edith and the children, but by mid August he had taken the reins as acting principal secretary while Walsingham was in Scotland. Encumbered formally with the weight of the office and the volume of paperwork involved, but still thinking about the negotiations the previous May, Beale wrote to Shrewsbury from Elizabeth's palace at Oatlands, west of London: 'I wold to god that [the negotiation] of your Lordship and Sir Walter Mildemaye, had taken better successe, for then in my simple opinion many inconveniences might have ben prevented and redressed, which I thinck will enssewe, and be veary dangerous yea remedilesse'. With a tone of resignation and comparative poverty next to a peer of the realm: 'Although I be no great dealer in the matters of this world, yet shall I be gladd to do your Lordship any service that I shalbe able, as one that doth acknowledge him self so bound. [...] I have prepared a box of aloes for your Lordship, but as yet I have not had any convenient meanes to send the same'.[80] As for his efforts with Mildmay, Beale was frustrated that Mary's proposals to Elizabeth were rejected yet again: 'I wold to god that [her] offers unto my Lord of Shrewsbury and Sir Walter Mildemay had ben better accepted. for then in myne opinion a great part of these mischiefes had ben prevented'.[81] By this point, any positivity or optimism Beale could muster was running thin, never mind his energy levels.

Beale's final trip to Sheffield in May 1584 to establish a treaty with Mary lasted about as long as that of 1583 and produced just as little. It may be significant,

[77] Shrewsbury and Mildmay's instructions, 24 and 27 May 1583, Mildmay's credence, 27 May 1583, TNA, SP 53/12, items 64–6.

[78] Mildmay to Walsingham, 4 June 1583, TNA, SP 53/12, fol. 75v (orig.).

[79] Mildmay to Walsingham, 11 June, Shrewsbury and Mildmay to Walsingham, 15 June 1583, TNA, SP 53/12 items 77–8 (both orig.). Cf. Shrewsbury and Mildmay to Elizabeth, 17 June 1583, TNA, SP 53/12, item 81 (orig.), noting Beale as the bearer; Mildmay to Walsingham, same day, TNA, SP 53/12, items 82–4 (all orig.).

[80] Beale to Shrewsbury, 27 August 1583, Longleat, Talbot MS I, fol. 109r–v (orig.).

[81] Beale to Rutland, 12 September 1583, Belvoir Castle, MS VI, under misdating of 12 September 1582 (orig.). Mary's initial and apparently not unpleasant meeting with Beale and Mildmay on 1 June included Beale's recommendation of a certain 'book of flowers' for Mary, for which she then instructed Castelnau to pay in cash, though her tone turned negative later that month. Letters of 1 and 15 June 1583, Lasry et al., 'Deciphering Mary Stuart's Lost Letters', 74–6.

however, that, given his previous experience and the trust placed in him by Elizabeth after his service as her principal secretary in Walsingham's absence, neither Mildmay nor Shrewsbury were named in the formal written instructions, and Elizabeth had given specific oral instructions to Beale directly. Also, just as Mary had previously thought well of Beale, so too had she recently confirmed that she remembered his good services; thus, it seems that Beale might have borne the distinction of being respected by both queens. As before, he collected originals and copies of relevant papers from this mission, such as it was, for further reference should a three-way treaty among Elizabeth, Mary, and James ever come to pass. For his own part, he genuinely hoped that it would, because the assurances to Elizabeth would guarantee her safety from intrigues and threats from Catholics domestic or foreign who pinned their hopes on Mary as a Catholic queen of England.[82] Before his departure from Sheffield in late May, Beale reported on more personal matters at Sheffield Castle among differences between the earl of Shrewsbury and his son, reportedly caused by the earl's wife, Bess of Hardwick, and the family dynamics more generally. That Beale had a personal interest in these family dynamics was curious but genuine, for as he stated to Rutland, 'I have a regard to the maintenanc of the house and shalbe gladd to do any good office'. Beale's inside knowledge of such intimate affairs and his reporting to others indicate the levels of access and trust he had gained by this point, as well as his confidence in his position.[83] Indeed, Beale had grown very confident on account of his professional advancement and personal connections. He had served his sovereign in discussions with foreign powers and as clerk of her Privy Council; he had held private conference with her on multiple occasions, even sitting as her principal secretary in a formal sense. His longest standing patron, Burghley, continued alongside Walsingham, Beale's brother-in-law who protected and provided opportunities for him in various ways. Politically, Beale was informed, reliable, and trusted on affairs both foreign and domestic—and he knew it. By way of religious causes, though, his direct engagement with the direction of Church of England was comparatively thin, until Archbishop Whitgift, that is.

Closer to Home—Lambeth

A long series of events led to Beale's journey in early May 1584 up the Thames to Lambeth Palace, home of the archbishop of Canterbury, John Whitgift. On one

---

[82] Mary to Castelnau, 3 September 1583, Lasry et al., 'Deciphering Mary Stuart's Lost Letters', 77–8. Beale's instructions, 4 May 1584, BL, Additional MS 48049, fols 220r–3v (orig.); copies of correspondence, 224r–9v. Shrewsbury and Beale to Walsingham, 16 May 1584, TNA, SP 53/13, pp. 71–82 (orig.). Beale to Walsingham, 17 May 1584, TNA, SP 53/13, pp. 83–6 (orig.).
[83] Beale to Walsingham, 17 May 1584, TNA, SP 53/13, pp. 83–6 (orig.). Beale to Rutland, 23 May 1584, Belvoir Castle, MS VII, under date, quotation at fol. 2v (orig.).

hand, he was preparing for his upcoming trip to Sheffield to discuss matters relating to Elizabeth's security on the throne and Mary's request for liberty to travel freely, but on the other he had been deeply engaged in disputes among some ministers of the Church and their leadership in Canterbury as well as London, where Beale's former tutor, John Aylmer, was bishop. In their calls for addressing religious concerns of reform and countering the Catholic threat, the parliamentary sessions of 1576 and 1581, at which Beale served on various committees, provided some of the fuel on which Beale would draw in early 1584 and again later that year in Elizabeth's fifth parliament, which assembled in November. The death of the previous archbishop, Edmund Grindal, in July 1583, after a tumultuous tenure during which he supported the moderate Puritan party much to the frustration of Elizabeth, opened the door to a more strident sense of discipline and uniformity coming from the upper levels of the Church. Beale appears to have held Grindal in some esteem regarding his desire for further reform and a preaching ministry, but Whitgift, who had previously been bishop of Worcester and from whom Beale had initially expected some degree of moderation regarding Puritanism, was primed for his task, and in some respects Aylmer and others had already gotten the ball rolling.[84]

Well before Whitgift's attempts at enforcing uniformity in late 1583 and 1584 by way of a set of articles to which all clergy were to subscribe, Aylmer's own activity to rein in and control those whom Grindal protected and enabled had come to Beale's attention. A particularly illuminating view into how Beale positioned himself can be seen in a letter in his collections from Aylmer to Walsingham in early 1583. How exactly this letter came to Beale's possession is unclear, but Walsingham might well have simply shared it with him because of their mutual religious sympathies. The bishop wrote to endorse one appointed clergyman, but he railed against another, Thomas Barber, a preacher at St Mary le Bow, London. Barber had been something of an itinerant preacher, Aylmer claimed, and was 'suche a depravor of the ministers that I maye not suffer hym in yt, specially being such as are as good and better than hym selfe'. Beale took issue with Aylmer's claim that his ministers' preaching was as good as or better than

---

For Beale's service in the session of 1576, see Chapter 4. For his activity in 1581 regarding cloth, Arthur Hall's book, the Family of Love, and attorneys, *Journal of the House of Commons: Vol. 1, 1547–1629* (London, 1802), 122–3, 127–8, 130. Beale's relationship with Grindal appears to have been almost non-existent save for the latter's reference to a letter 'written at great length' from Beale, to which Grindal intended to respond. Grindal to Walsingham, 17 July 1582, TNA, SP 12/154, fol. 106r (orig.). See also, though, Beale's copy of Grindal's 'Orders for reformacion of the abuses about the learned exercyses and conferences of the ministers of the Churche', autumn 1576, BL, Additional MS 48064, fols 197v–198r, which Beale noted as 'This was subscribed with Archbishopp Grindalls own hand'. On Grindal, see Collinson, *Archbishop Grindal*. On Whitgift's early activity as archbishop in 1583–5, including Beale's activity and Parliament, Collinson, 243–88; Collinson, *Richard Bancroft*, 39–59. Beale's expectations or, rather, hopes can be seen in Beale's draft 'book', April 1584, BL, Additional MS 48039, fol. 1v.

Barber's: in the margin next to his underlining of the text, Beale scrawled, 'A lye John'.[85] A pointed rebuke from a former pupil, that.

Beale also received other materials from Walsingham relating to proposals for the reform of the Church. These items stretched back a little further but combined well with Beale's concerns in early 1584 when confronting Whitgift. Four items collected in one volume were all, as Beale himself recorded, 'out of a booke of Mr Secretarye Walsingham'. One was 'a Proiect for the increase of the number of Preachers', while the other three were wider ranging and discussed the ordering of ministers and ecclesiastical reform in the context of the initiatives of the House of Commons in 1581.[86] Similarly concerning for Beale were the activities of Edmund Freake, bishop of Norwich from 1575, who endeavoured to increase obedience and uniformity among the Puritan clergy and gentry in East Anglia. Shortly into his tenure, a group of Puritan preachers in Norwich petitioned a sympathizer in high places, quite possibly Walsingham given his position and inclination; interestingly, a copy of their petition worked its way to Beale, who endorsed it accordingly for further reference.[87] Freake's disciplinary articles issued in early 1583 preceded Whitgift's own and accordingly paved the way for increased disciplinary measures among the clergy. In short, Freake had been trying to control the more puritanically inclined gentry of his diocese but met with significant resistance both locally and centrally. Those accused by Freake of opposing the laws publicly established for the government of the Church were in fact justices of the peace who then appealed to Walsingham for support. It might well have been Walsingham who, as with the other materials, supplied Beale with copies of Freake's multiple articles against the JPs as well as their answers.[88]

By the time Whitgift issued his own articles for subscription to enforce greater obedience in October 1583, Aylmer, Freake, and others had been leading the charge against the zealous and enthusiastic who sought further reform of the Church of England and an increasingly preaching ministry. In some respects, there was nothing controversial about a drive for consistency in the Church; after all, part and parcel of the Elizabethan Settlement of Religion was the Act of Uniformity and the Book of Common Prayer. The difference here, though, was in the approach of Whitgift and his allies in the newly reconstructed Court of High Commission, the supreme ecclesiastical court in England. More authoritarian—and more efficient—than traditional diocesan courts, High Commission demanded that the accused swear by oath *ex officio* to answer all questions truthfully, even if

---

[85] Aylmer to Walsingham, 11 March 1583, BL, Egerton MS 1693, fol. 103r (orig.).

[86] BL, Additional MS 48064, fols 188r–91r, 193v–7r, 198v–200v, each with Beale's note regarding these materials' origin.

[87] Petition of John More et al., BL, Additional MS 48101, fols 132r–5v. See also Collinson, 203 *et passim* on Freake.

[88] Freake's articles and the JPs' answers, early 1583, BL, Egerton MS 1693, fols 89r–100r, preceded by Robert Jermyn, JP for Suffolk, to Walsingham, February 1583, fols 87r–8v (orig.).

self-incriminating, rather than face a trial by jury. Of Whitgift's articles approved by Elizabeth, one was particularly troublesome for several hundred ministers in the Church: the Book of Common Prayer contained nothing contrary to the word of God and was the sole book to be used for public prayer and administration of the sacraments.[89] On the face of it, the article seemed inoffensive, but, as will be seen, the devil was in the details. Beale endorsed his copy of Whitgift's articles according to what they seemed like to him—'Articles of the Inquisition'—but he was even more direct in drawing the comparison when he wrote in a summary of the affair for Burghley that the oath and interrogations 'savourethe more of a Spanishe Inquisition then Christian Charitie'. Burghley, as has been pointed out, made the association famous but without credit given to Beale in his letter directly penned to Whitgift, in which he wrote that the articles were 'of great length & curiositie formed in a Romish style to examin all maner of ministers' and compared the articles to the questions used by the inquisitors of Spain and Rome. The association in the minds of Beale and Burghley between the Inquisition(s) and Whitgift's articles clearly 'much troubled' the archbishop, as he later confessed in his correspondence with the lord treasurer.[90]

Opposition to these methods came from ministers and others in Suffolk, Kent, and elsewhere. Through a stroke of good luck or bad timing, depending on the perspective, Beale was sitting in for Walsingham as principal secretary in early 1584 when the petitions to the Privy Council started coming in. Walsingham, as frequently happened, was suffering from an ague (fever) and was not in London; instead, he was in Surrey at Barn Elms.[91] These petitions started a process that led to Beale's encounters with Whitgift at court and Lambeth in February and May. On both occasions Beale was admittedly hot-headed. The meeting at court required of the archbishop by the Privy Council was divisive: Whitgift was annoyed, Beale was insistent, and Aylmer (also present) 'wished that he had as

---

[89] Collinson, 243–8.

[90] Beale's copy of Whitgift's articles, BL, Additional MS 48101, fols 255r–v, with endorsement at 258v. Beale's account of his controversy with Whitgift for Burghley, 1 July 1584, BL, Additional MS 48039, fols 48r–56v, with quotation at 49v. Burghley to Whitgift, 2 July 1584, TNA, SP 12/172/1, fol. 1r; this copy suggests that Burghley wrote to the archbishop the very day after Beale wrote to Burghley, but a different copy of the letter (with similar but not the same spelling), Inner Temple Library, Petyt MS 538/52, fols 14v–15r, is dated 5 July and followed by Whitgift's 'answer to the Lord Treasurer's letter of 5 July 1584' and other correspondence later that month. Collinson, 270, does not cite the Inner Temple manuscript and difference of dating. Whitgift to Burghley, in response to the latter's of 5 July 1584, Inner Temple Library, Petyt MS 538/52, quotation at fol. 15v.

[91] At this time Burghley was also afflicted with a familiar ailment, gout, but he remained at court, while Leicester also appears to have been suffering from an ague. By early March Walsingham and Leicester had recovered. Roger Manners to Rutland, 3 February 1584, Roger Manners to John Manners, 5 March 1584, *Historical Manuscripts Commission [...] Rutland*, pp. 160–2. Beale appears to have travelled between the court and Walsingham during his illness. Walsingham to Stafford, 8 February 1584, TNA, SP 78/11, item 22. On Walsingham's frequent ailments, see Read, *Mr Secretary Walsingham*, 3.445–7.

muche power to beate [Beale] now as ever he had'.[92] After that meeting in February, Beale rapidly produced for Whitgift a 'book' long in coming and the product of Beale's encyclopaedic reference archive and library. It complemented other works of the time on Puritan grievances written by legal minds like John Hammond and annotated in Beale's hand among his papers.[93] It also, however, represented the boldest attack yet on the legality of Whitgift's use of High Commission. Coming from a layman with no formal theological training but a wealth of experience in religious disputes, law, and politics, Beale's 'book' clearly rattled the archbishop.[94] This work for Whitgift was related to another, more finished work that seems to have focused particularly on oaths in ecclesiastical courts and apparently was published overseas about the same time. About this other work little is known. It came to the notice of the famous professor of biblical languages, especially Hebrew, at the University of Leiden, Johannes Drusius (van den Driesche), who had wished that Beale's 'little book' ('*libellus*') had been more than twenty-four chapters.[95] Whitgift remarked later in the year that Beale had distributed copies (presumably in manuscript) of this other work, some of which found their way abroad where it was published in print. That Drusius had acquired or at least knew about this work in Leiden was significant; that Whitgift claimed that copies of it were brought to England in a Scottish ship was all the more so (see Fig. 8).[96]

Although only a draft and not a finished piece, the 'book' for Whitgift demonstrated Beale's knowledge and understanding of scripture, the Church fathers, and more recent efforts to reform the Church during the reign of King Edward VI and in the Elizabethan Settlement. Noting differences in translations (and favourably citing Augustine), Beale thought strict and sole usage of the Bishops' Bible (1568, revised 1572) was unreasonable both because this translation only

[92] Collinson, 255. Beale's account for Burghley, 1 July 1584, BL, Additional MS 48039, fol. 48r. Beale had carried the petitions of those in Suffolk and Kent to Whitgift on 29 January, or, as Whitgift phrased it, 'vpon Sundaie last in the Afternoone' in Whitgift to the Lords of the Privy Council, 4 February 1584, Inner Temple Library, Petyt MS 538/52, fols 8v–10v.

[93] BL, Additional MS 48064, fols 25r–9v; 28r–9v explicitly addressed 'The historie of matters touching the booke of common prayer'.

[94] Although Whitgift sent to Burghley at least one summary of Beale's book, Beale's own draft with annotations is here preferred. Burghley's materials in BL, Lansdowne MS 42, fols 175r–6v, 179r–80v. Beale's draft, BL, Additional MS 48039, fols 1r–39v, with narrative summary of the affair at 40r and later in the same volume.

[95] Drusius to Beale, 20 May 1584, BYU, MS 457, item 22 (orig.). See also Drusius's preface in commendation of Beale, with whom he claimed to have been in company recently, in his work on the Hebrew of the Old Testament: *Animadversorvm Liber II. Ad Rubertvm Belvm Generosvm, et Regii Consilii a Secretis* (Leiden, 1585) (USTC 429015), 3–4. On the different approaches to the Old Testament employed by Franciscus Junius (theological) and Johannes Drusius (grammatical), see Benjamin R. Merkle, *Defending the Trinity in the Reformed Palatinate: The Elohistae* (Oxford, 2015), 149–92.

[96] Whitgift's schedule of Beale's misdemeanours, 1585, printed in Strype, *Whitgift*, 1.401. A tempting possibility is that the Scottish Jesuit, William Crichton, was on the same ship when he was captured in September 1584; Beale's owning of a work in Crichton's possession upon his capture would be a wonderful historical coincidence: BL, Additional MS 48027, fols 252r–7r (including Beale's notes).

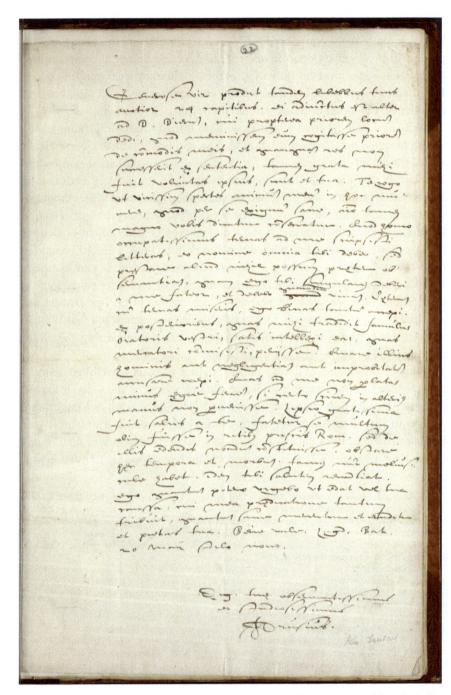

Fig. 8 Johannes Drusius to Beale, 20 May 1584. BYU, MS 457, item 22, fol. 1r (orig.).

came after the three editions of the Book of Common Prayer (and accordingly could not have informed its intentions), and due to the fact that Immanuel Tremellius's 'learned translation [...] was not [yet] published'.[97] It seems probable that Beale used Tremellius's fresh translation into Latin from the Hebrew of the Old Testament and the Syriac of the New, especially considering that all of Beale's citations to scripture were in Latin rather than English.[98] A favourite passage cited by Beale to refute Whitgift's strictures and demands for obedience and orthodoxy as the archbishop understood it was 1 Corinthians 12, in which Paul observed that the Holy Spirit distributes different gifts and abilities to different people, and that different parts of the body are nevertheless unified and working towards a common good. The direct implication was that, although people might have had slightly different ideas regarding the rites and ceremonies of the Church of England, they were all standing together as Protestants in opposition to their common enemy—Roman Catholicism. Beale had used this passage before when he had tried to quell theological discord in Germany and establish an alliance among the Protestant princes in 1577, and he would echo its sentiments again in a letter directly to Whitgift in 1590. Although he admitted to Whitgift that he was 'not by profession a divine', he was 'for the espace almost of these xxxtie yeies [...]' acquaynted with the most famous and learned men abroade and seen and observed the estate of the reformed Churches in ffraunce and Germanye as muche perhappes as anye other of my Callinge'.[99]

The potential for fracture among English Protestants because of Whitgift's demands cut close to the bone for Beale because of his previous efforts among the Protestant princes of Germany to emphasize unity in opposition to Catholicism and downplay differences in comparatively inconsequential matters. Much to his chagrin, the splits among the Germans seemed to grow wider and deeper every day, and he did not want the same thing to happen in England. Accordingly, he went to significant lengths to defend liberty of conscience in things indifferent, *adiaphora*, to which none was bound by anything in the Bible or by laws of the Church or realm. Indeed, he referred to ceremonies as *adiaphora*, the use of which came from faith rather than law, and, because 'the Magistrate cannot alter a thing indifferent', 'Great circumspection [was] to be vsed in indifferent thinges' and 'according to the rule of Charitye'.[100] Specifically, he took issue with Whitgift's

---

[97] Beale's draft, BL, Additional MS 48039, fols 21v–2v, quotation at 22r.

[98] Among books probably owned by Beale, the 'Biblia Latina Trem & Iunil Londini 1585' is found, but he may have also had an earlier impression from 1579–80. BL, Hargrave, MS 107, fol. 10r.

[99] References to 1 Corinthians 12, BL, Additional MS 48039, fols 1v, 17v, quotation at fol. 2r. For the reference in his orations before the princes, copies of which are found in German archives, see, *AGR*, 70–2, 184 n. 57; an English copy, TNA, SP 81/1, item 23. Beale to Whitgift, 22 August 1590, LPL, MS 4267, fols 3r–4v, at 4r (orig.).

[100] Beale's draft, BL, Additional MS 48039, fols 10r–11v, with quotations in the margins; among ceremonies and clerical apparel that seemed Catholic in Beale's eyes, wedding rings also drew Beale's ire because, according to him, 'The Ring cam from Popery' who had 'taken [it] from Pagans' (fols 37v–8r).

demand for clerical subscription to the Book of Common Prayer, as reissued in its third edition at the beginning of Elizabeth's reign, because it contained more changes than were acceptable according to the Act of Uniformity.[101] Citing Martin Bucer's *Censura* of the first prayer book, as well as the *Reformatio Legum Ecclesiasticarum* of 1552, which would have significantly revised canon law in the Church had it been passed by Parliament in 1553, Beale pointed out that the Elizabethan prayer book still needed amendment in some respects, especially bearing in mind that in things indifferent believers were to prioritize their faith over anything pretending to be enforceable law.[102] Beale also justified his position against Whitgift's use of the Court of High Commission in specifically legal terms:

> seinge the name and authoritye of lawe is vsed to enforce the precise observacion of euerye particular thinge conteyned in the last booke: it maye appeare that manye thinges beare the Cloke and color of lawe, which are not lawe, and haue ben and are obtruded as law, wheruppon I thinke manye simple and good men haue bene condemned and punished contrary to lawe.[103]

In content and tone, Beale's 'book' for Whitgift (which he also called a pamphlet) was direct if not aggressive towards the archbishop. According to his own account, Beale delivered his work and was promised an answer, and he hoped that, from now on, Whitgift would proceed more moderately and according to law. He overestimated his position relative to a primate as well as his ability to persuade him. Between March and early May, Beale received no such answer, so he made his way to Lambeth to demand the return of his book so he could finish it. It was, after all, in draft.[104]

The altercation at Lambeth Palace on 5 May 1584 can be seen from at least two angles. In Beale's view, Whitgift answered in a great rage and 'Pontifically'; in Whitgift's, Beale was intemperate and 'fell into verie great passions'.[105] The fallout of their heated discussion in the archbishop's upper chamber was that Whitgift would not return Beale's work, Beale was angry about it, and they both penned vicious accounts of their exchange. The very next day Whitgift sent a letter to

---

[101] Collinson, 255–6.

[102] Beale's draft, BL, Additional MS 48039, fols 23r–8v. Although he also favourably cites Wolfgang Musculus and Ulrich Zwingli, Beale cites Bucer far more frequently, even offering page numbers to the *Censura*. Beale probably owned Bucer's *Scripta Anglicana*, which included the *Censura* and was published at Basel in 1577. BL, Hargrave MS 107, fol. 8r. John Foxe printed the *Reformatio Legum Ecclesiasticarum* in 1571. Beale appears to have borrowed from Foxe a collection of relevant ecclesiastical laws for the reign of Henry VIII, which may have been source material for the book: BL, Additional MS 48040, fols 13r–104v.

[103] Beale's draft, BL, Additional MS 48039, fol. 5r.

[104] Beale's narration of early 1584, BL, Additional MS 48039, fol. 40r.

[105] Beale's narration of early 1584, BL, Additional MS 48039, fol. 40r. Whitgift to Burghley, 6 May 1584, BL, Additional MS 34727, fol. 4r–v (orig.); undated copies, LPL, MS 680, fol. 91r–2r; BL, Lansdowne MS 396/1, fols 30r–2r; and Inner Temple Library, Petyt MS 538/52, fol. 18r–v.

Burghley, complaining of Beale and protesting against his arrogance and pride; never before had the archbishop been so abused as he had been by Beale at Lambeth Palace, or so he claimed. Beale wrote to Whitgift the day after that, probably because he had heard from Burghley. Whitgift wrote again to Burghley on the subsequent day and again complaining of Beale's lack of moderation, or, as one may now recognize, supreme confidence. From Whitgift's relation of his exchange with Beale, the Royalist and anti-Puritan seventeenth-century historian, Peter Heylyn, later understood Beale as impetuous, most eager, rude, and violent.[106] Beale's description of himself and his own thinking may best be described in his letter to the archbishop after the latter refused to return his book. In short, Beale claimed that he had not seen an answer in eight weeks to that which he had written in eight days because there were no justifiable responses Whitgift could muster. Beale thought his own 'knowledge of the estate of the Churche abroade, and the learned men which haue bene of late yeres, [was] not inferior to anye Bishopps or Clergie man in England'; moreover, regarding his study of the civil law, and despite the fact that he was not a practicing lawyer, he would 'be lothe that the greatest doctor that is about Your Lordship [i.e. Whitgift] could so teache me what law is [. . . in] diuinitye I thinke I haue redd as muche as anye Chapleyn Yor Lordship hathe.'[107] Beale's arrogance in his letter of 7 May was noted by Whitgift to Burghley, to whom the archbishop sent a copy of that letter in which, according to Whitgift, Beale's 'stomack, great vanitie, and exceeding malice doth appear'. As for the book, Whitgift described it: 'wherin he so much glorieth, ys without method, and verie frivolus[,] easelie answered both in divinitie[,] law and pollicie'. After more than two weeks without a response from Burghley regarding Beale, the archbishop asked again that Beale be disciplined because Beale's letters to Whitgift 'towch me so neare in creadite, that I can not lapp them vp, the man also ys so Insolent, that he glorieth in them'. Whitgift implored Burghley to correct Beale for the insolence in addressing the archbishop in writing and 'in hys Intemperate speaches which he vsed to me in the counsell chamber at the Cowrte, and in my owne howsse: bearing with hym, doth puff hym upp.'[108] Despite Whitgift's pleading, Burghley seems to have shown little interest in reprimanding Beale.

Had Beale's book been so easily answered, he might have received some response from Whitgift, but none ever came. Just in case the controversy were to return and negatively affect his standing with Burghley and Elizabeth, Beale wrote

---

[106] Whitgift to Burghley, 6 May 1584, BL, Additional MS 34727, fol. 4r–v (orig.). Beale to Whitgift, 7 May 1584, BL, Additional MS 48039, fols 42r–5v (Beale's copy with his marginal annotations); copy sent by Whitgift to Burghley, BL, Lansdowne MS 42, fols 181r–4v. Whitgift to Burghley, 8 May 1584, Longleat, Portland MS I, fol. 108r (orig.); cf. Whitgift's complaint later that month on 26 May at fol. 110r (orig.). Peter Heylyn, *Aërius Redivivus, or, The History of the Presbyterians* 2nd edn (London, 1672), 264.

[107] Beale to Whitgift, 7 May 1584, BL, Additional MS 48039, fol. 44r.

[108] Whitgift to Burghley, 8 and 26 May 1584, Longleat, Portland MS I, fols 108r, 110r (both orig.).

a final summary on 1 July. Along with other vital autobiographical details regarding his early life in Strasbourg and Zurich with Aylmer, Beale's account reiterated his positions on things indifferent, the controversy regarding which 'of late yeres began in Germanye and hathe ben occacion of muche harme, and in the time of Queen Marye[,] who was greater with [Matthias Flacius] Illyricus then the now Bishopp of London [i.e. Aylmer] [?]' Advocating a sense of moderation absent in his confrontation at Lambeth, Beale thought 'there must of necessitie be a toleracion of these thinges as hathe ben hitherto'. As for the multiple versions of the prayer book and the manner in which Whitgift's way of proceeding violated English law, Beale noted, 'I would haue nothing enforced vppon an Englishe subiecte but English lawe. But many of his first articles were directlie against lawe and to abbridge the libertyes graunted vnto Englishe subiectes, Nobles, and others by lawe: and even this subscription and inquisition, which is now vrged[,] is not warraunted by lawe'. Potentially feeling sorry for himself at the end of his account, Beale was simply tired of it all. He recorded for Burghley in dark tones: 'My bodye beinge subiecte to the panges of the Stone and other infirmityes is not able to abyde the toyle of the place[,] and my living is not able to continewe the charge'. He went on to reflect upon the affair and now admitted that his 'nature is perhappes to bruske and playne', or, put another way, he could be a sour, curt, and ungracious complainer. Thinking about his relations with Whitgift, Aylmer, and others, he remembered 'a sayinge of Melanthons, that there is no malice [compared to that] of the Clergie. I haue partelye felt of it heretofore, and am lyke inoughe to be oppressed with it herafter, to my vtter vndoinge'.[109] A moment of clairvoyance, here.

    In the end, Beale came out unscathed. He retained his position as clerk of the Privy Council. He continued to serve Elizabeth in a diplomatic capacity. His relationship with Burghley was not compromised; that with Walsingham was probably strengthened; and, amazingly, Beale learned that Whitgift desired to put the past behind them 'and that he would be gladd of my frendshipp and companye'.[110] Further evidence of his security was a recent grant, to him for life, of the office of the petty customer and supervisor of the petty custom in London and its ports; the annual wage of over £36 will have supplied Beale the financial reassurance to match his growing confidence.[111] Any rapprochement with Whitgift, however, was short-lived. Within a few months, summons for Elizabeth's fifth parliament were sent, and Beale was chosen to represent the borough of Dorchester, Dorset, again almost certainly through the patronage of Francis Russell, earl of Bedford.[112] This parliament had been called because of the international and domestic threats

---

[109] Beale's account of his affair with Whitgift, 1 July 1584, BL, Additional MS 48039, fols 55r, 54r, 55v–6r.
[110] Beale's narration, late 1584, BL, Additional MS 48039, fol. 56v.
[111] Letters patent, 24 January 1584, TNA, C 66/1245, mm. 6–7.
[112] On Bedford and Beale's involvement in the Parliament of 1576, see Chapter 4.

to Elizabeth's safety, most notably in the form of the failed Throckmorton Plot and the implication of Mary Queen of Scots. In some respects, the priorities of this parliament can be seen to fall into two categories: ensuring the queen's safety from Catholic threats (the official goal of the establishment); and advocating reform of the Church and its ministry (the furtive aim of many in the House of Commons).[113] In Beale's mind, though, the two causes were intimately related and vital to the social and religious fabric of the Elizabethan state and society, especially given his several trips to Sheffield alongside his engagements with Whitgift.

Before Parliament opened in November 1584, Beale wrote some advice for Whitgift that he titled 'Meanes how to settle a godlie and charitable quietnes in the churche'.[114] Beale was here attempting to persuade the archbishop to make good on the House of Commons' proposals earlier in 1581 but also to stop the practices that Whitgift himself had put in place since then regarding the articles, the oath *ex officio*, and forced subscription (alongside forcing ministers to perform certain ceremonies or wear specified vestments). Particularly offensive in Beale's eyes was the oath *ex officio*, which he later characterized as a 'diabolicall, paganicall and papisticall proceeding'.[115] The same themes as before, so Whitgift could be forgiven for thinking that Beale was again more than a little presumptuous on this occasion, even froward for a layman before an archbishop. These arguments had been made openly among many persons of note over many years; indeed, as Beale noted a few years later to Lord Chancellor Hatton, 'these things haue not ben don in hugger mugger [secrecy], but all or the most parte of them are knowen to your Lordship'.[116] Beale had addressed his piece to Whitgift, but it was sent via Walsingham, which may suggest that Beale had not warmed to Whitgift no matter how friendly the primate claimed to become. By the time Parliament opened in late November, Beale had not received a reply. His work on various committees aligned with his chief priorities, but his activities regarding procedure in ecclesiastical courts and a conference with representatives from the House of Lords were most significant. Among his papers are found various materials supporting Puritan causes in opposition to Whitgift and the Court of High Commission's proceedings.[117] In all respects, the arguments put forth criticize the bishops' positions and align with Beale's own thinking for reforming the Church from within (rather than wholesale Presbyterianism in opposition to episcopacy).

[113] The classic account of this parliament remains Neale, *Elizabeth I and her Parliaments, 1584–1601*, 13–101, with 58–83 focusing on religious matters. For the Puritan push within and outside the Commons, Collinson, 273–88. For relevant documents, Hartley, *Proceedings*, Vol. 2: *1584–1589*, 20–193. For Beale's committee work, HoP:HoC. D'Ewes, *Compleat Journal*, 332–74, adds nothing of significance regarding Beale's activity.
[114] BL, Additional MS 48039, fols 57r–61r. Discussed in Collinson, 282.
[115] Beale to Hatton, 25 November 1589, BL, Additional MS 48039, fol. 67r.
[116] Beale to Hatton, 25 November 1589, BL, Additional MS 48039, fol. 66v.
[117] BL, Additional MS 48064, fols 37r–43v, 47r.

Beale's most notable effort in this parliament was probably his response to Whitgift's own rejoinder to the petitions of the Commons for reform. As he retold the story to Hatton, he claimed 'all that hearde the aunsweres made' by Whitgift in the Commons 'may well thinck that in all the histories and Records of tymes past, neuer anie prince or subiecte gaue suche an insufficient and opprobrious aunswer'. Beale was one of several MPs who then offered speeches on 25 February 1585 in reaction.[118]

The text of the speech appears to have formed the basis for an extended treatise. Given its tone and addressing to members of the house, it could have been the case that Beale offered a very long and drawn-out speech, but, due to its length (over fifty folios), the treatise was probably intended for manuscript circulation among MPs after 25 February. The only known version exists in draft with Beale's annotations, some of which seem to alter the language used in an oral speech to that in a written treatise.[119] By citing Magna Carta and several other statutes and precedents from the Middle Ages to the reign of Henry VIII, Beale consistently made the case that Parliament, and the House of Commons in particular, was superior to the Church, as was parliamentary law over canon law, save for the fact that Elizabeth was the Supreme Head of the Church on earth. Accordingly, the Church could not imprison or punish men, and it was the Commons' duty to keep the Church in check, especially bearing in mind that the clergy lower than the bishops, such as the ministers currently silenced by Whitgift, were represented in Parliament by the Commons itself. Furthermore, to solidify his position that the Church was to be controlled by Parliament, Beale evaluated the nature and limits of ecclesiastical jurisdiction in the light of the first statutes passed by Elizabeth's first parliament; here the matter of where supremacy lay was clear in Beale's mind. Without going into every minutia, it may suffice to say that Beale was characteristically detailed, forceful, and credible when citing his sources, such as William Lyndwood's *Provinciale* (*Constitutiones Angliae Provinciale*), a collection of ecclesiastical legislation from the province of Canterbury during the thirteenth and fourteenth centuries, a copy of which, printed in 1557, Beale appears to have owned. In short, as Beale put it for his colleagues, 'The Ordinaryes and Bishopps neuer had anye such Spirituall and Ecclesiasticall authoritie, as is

---

[118] Beale to Hatton, 25 November 1589, BL, Additional MS 48039, fol. 67r. Neale, *Elizabeth I and her Parliaments, 1584–1601*, 66–8. See also, Gajda, 'Elizabethan Church', 77–105, with reference to Beale at 94–5.

[119] 'A Treatise made by a Burgess of the lower house in parlement', 1585, BL, Additional MS 48116, fols 154r–211r; 157r, e.g. includes Beale's change of language from 'this place' to 'the lower house'. For brief notice of Beale's speech, which supposedly claimed 'That there was nether law of god nor man, learning, nor witt in the Answer to the petitions. And that the bishops had abused the Queen's lawes and the comission this 26 yeares', TNA, SP 12/175, fol. 97. On what Beale later recorded as his 'first speache in the house' on 3 March 1593, see Chapter 7. See Collinson's comment: 'There is no evidence that this oration of heroically Soviet proportions was in fact delivered and Neale calls it a "treatise"', in 'Puritans, Men of Business and Elizabethan Parliaments', *Parliamentary History*, 7 (1988), 204.

now by them vsurped', but at the same time he wanted to ensure that 'Her Majesty's supreme authority [was] not called in question'.[120] Thus, he was walking a fine line between advocating for further reforms in sympathy with Puritan causes and allegiance to the queen and the Elizabethan Settlement. The key for him was adherence to the law as formulated, enacted, and enforced by Parliament—not the Church. Beale's views on parliamentary sovereignty and supremacy extended back several years and help to explain why he thought that Parliament could comment and advise on matters particularly sensitive to the queen's prerogative and honour—foreign policy and the royal succession.

Despite all the pressure and clamour in the Commons for a more active and engaged ministry, little concrete was accomplished from Beale's perspective; after all, Elizabeth had ordered that religion not be a matter of discussion in the Commons because she, as Supreme Governor, had ultimate say over such matters. Beale, having come out of his altercation at Lambeth relatively unharmed apart from a possible reprimand from Burghley, should probably have been more cautious in the Commons. Burghley had protected him from Whitgift's ire earlier in 1584 when matters were kept comparatively private (though still no 'hugger mugger'); the Commons, as a public forum, was an altogether different arena. However careful he was, if Whitgift's later account is to be believed, Beale might have had his knuckles rapped on at least one occasion: 'In the Lower House of that Parliament he openly spoke of matters concerning ecclesiastical jurisdiction, &c. contrary to her Majesty's express pleasure, afore delivered. For the which he was also at that Parliament time committed.'[121] If Beale had been looking for the limits of his power and influence, and the extent to which Burghley, Walsingham, and others could protect him, he might have found them in early 1585.

Beale's Apogee and Plateau

Between 1578 and 1585 Beale had come to the height of his political power and status on domestic and international fronts. His knowledge and experience in

---

[120] On Lyndwood, *ODNB*. BL, Hargrave MS 107, fol. 16r. Reference to Lyndwood and quotation from 'A Treatise', BL, Additional MS 48116, fols 158v, 159r. Beale also referred to others like Henry of Bracton, whose *De Legibus* appears in Hargrave MS 107 at fol. 44r, and Augustine, but he also referred to his own other works, e.g. at 201v: 'This I haue proued in another booke and cannot be denyed' (on the idea that the ceremonies enforced under Whitgift derived from Judaism, paganism, and popery).

[121] Whitgift's schedule of Beale's misdemeanours, 1585, printed in Strype, *Whitgift*, 1.401. No supporting evidence has yet been located regarding Whitgift's claim, but Beale's overstepping is entirely plausible, especially if his treatise circulated in manuscript among MPs. Despite Neale's claim 'there can be little doubt' that Whitgift's schedule was written in the wake of the Parliament of 1593, Neale's evidence is thin and he does not fully recognize Beale's activity in 1583-4. Neale, *Elizabeth I and her Parliaments, 1584-1601*, 277-8. Beale was more firmly part of a group committed to house arrest in 1593, but the possibility remains that he had also been previously. On those committed, see Richard West to William Pitt, 16 March 1593, BL, Additional MS 22924, fol. 9r.

foreign affairs, from the 1550s forward, continued to pay dividends. Because he was located directly at the centre of the Elizabethan government—as clerk of the Privy Council and as MP in the Commons—he learned how the levers of power operated, and his channels of information continued and diversified. Unsurprisingly, his personal archive and library grew in both depth and breadth, so that he could call on his reference material when serving as acting principal secretary in Walsingham's absence, and he could act like a secretary even when Walsingham was around. Very much like his brother-in-law, Beale had internalized his experience across the seas. His understanding of the Protestant cause on the mainland, including its chances for unity alongside those for fracture, was intimately linked to his perspective regarding Catholics in England who might seek the overthrow of the Elizabethan regime and place Mary Queen of Scots on the throne. With like-minded colleagues and patrons in high places, above all Burghley, it may be unsurprising in retrospect that the resourceful, diligent, and literary Beale climbed the political ladder and had the confidence to match.

He proved enormously useful in his trips to Mary at Sheffield however much he disliked being away from London—either because of his own illness or Edith's pregnancies. He served not only as a courier but also as a negotiator in his own right. His working relationships, even personal friendships, with the earls of Shrewsbury and Rutland were solidified and demonstrate that his orbit of activity and influence in England was not limited to London; one may also recall his prior links with Coventry that would become relevant again in the years ahead. Firm in his resolve when confronting the queen he considered a viper, Beale was similarly resolved when marching into the palace of a primate to tell him that his policies were illegal. To be sure, Beale was confident in his abilities and security. One could say that he was brave in all senses of the word. As a layman and commoner, though, he could realistically go no higher in professional status or development. He discussed matters privately with Elizabeth; he did similarly with Mary as Elizabeth's representative. He enjoyed the support and protection of several peers of the realm. He was respected for his knowledge and ability to impart it. He had few real enemies—he opposed Whitgift's policies more than Whitgift the man, but with Aylmer it was admittedly more personal because of the beatings endured decades before. Nevertheless, Beale had plateaued professionally. In the coming years, he could enjoy the view as long as he did not go too far against Whitgift or cross his sovereign.

A European Elizabethan: The Life of Robert Beale, Esquire. David Scott Gehring, Oxford University Press.
© David Scott Gehring 2024. DOI: 10.1093/9780198902942.003.0006

7

The Highest Highs and Lowest Lows

During the second half of the 1580s and early 1590s, Beale did not slow down. His activity, both personal and professional, kept him busy and moving. As in previous years, he was based principally in the capital, often writing from what he called his 'poore house in London', though later in the 1590s he moved into what the historian John Stow described in 1598 as 'a fayre house lately builded, by M[aster] Beale one of the Clearkes of the Counsell'.[1] The new house was in the same parish as his old one, Allhallows London Wall, so Beale and his growing family may have grown attached to that particular area and community. Indeed, in addition to his and Edith's four children born between 1577 and 1583 (Francis, Ursula, Bridget, and Margaret), their fifth child, Elizabeth, was baptized on 25 October 1584; their sixth, Madeline, on 22 August 1586; their seventh, Katherine, on 27 February 1588; their eighth, Robert, on 9 June 1590; and their nineth, Anne, on 3 February 1592. Then as now, keeping track of Beale's children could be difficult. An increasingly full household helps to explain the newly built house in the mid or late 1590s, but it also justified the string of servants employed, several of whom died in their twenties.[2] Having a household servant will have been important not only because of all the children, but because Beale continued to split his time between the City of London and Barnes, in Surrey, when he, like his brother-in-law Walsingham, needed to get away from the City. His time and intentions in Barnes are signified in his acquiring the formal lease for Milbourne House, along with 116.5 acres, in 1592 (see Fig. 9).[3]

---

[1] Stow, *Svrvay of London*, 110. At pp. 147–8 of Stow's 2nd edn of 1603 (STC 23343), a slight alteration: 'a faire house lately new builded, partly by M. Robert Beale one of the Clerks of the Counsell'.

[2] Jupp and Hovenden, *The Registers*, 10–12, 18, 25; a stillborn child died in January 1589 and was buried at Allhallows London Wall, 110. That child's name is unknown. Baptisms of Elizabeth, Madeline, and Robert were at St Mary's, Barnes, and recorded in Surrey History Centre, P6/1/1, fols 4v–5r. See also the later genealogy, BL, Additional MS 19117, fols 228v–9r. For still another child possibly named Frances, see Chapter 6, n. 4. Beale and Edith's first servant, 'Cuthberd Deytton' it seems, died of jaundice aged 35 in July 1580, but one Ursula Cooth died at 22 'of grieff' in December 1585, William Dalburne at 20 of an unknown cause in February 1591, and Lucretia Duncome at 20 of 'consumption' in 1595. Jupp and Hovenden, *The Registers*, 91, 104, 114, 129.

[3] Lease from the earl of Essex, his wife (Walsingham's daughter, Frances), and Ursula Walsingham, 24 April 1592, recorded among the extracts from the Cartwright muniments at Aynhoe, C(A)2274, Northamptonshire Record Office, in the Richmond Local Studies Library. By this point Beale had acquired what seems to be an additional twelve acres from Walsingham in Barnes according to Walsingham's inquisition post mortem. E. A. Webb, G. W. Miller, and J. Beckwith, *The History of Chislehurst: Its Church, Manors, and Parish* (London, 1899), 361–2. See Chapter 8 and, for an overview of Milbourne House, Caroline Crimp and Mary Grimwade, *Barnes and Mortlake History Society, Milbourne House, Barnes* (Richmond, 1978). I am most grateful to Sue Evans and Anne Monro-Davies (of Milbourne House) for supplying me with a copy of this otherwise rare publication, and for sending me photographs of the surviving Elizabethan features of the house.

Fig. 9 Interior fireplace *c.*1600, at Milbourne House, Barnes, Surrey. Image courtesy of Sue Evans and Anne Monro-Davies.

Reproduced with permission.

Also, as will be seen, he was sent further afield on several occasions. Increasingly during these years, though, Beale's health suffered. Frequently he complained of his pains, some of which were described by others generally as indisposition, but at other times he could be quite explicit regarding his bladder stones and gout. He reported, for example, to Burghley on 16 October 1592 that a bout with the stone 'suppressed [his] water for the espace of ten dayes' earlier that year and had brought him 'even to deathes dore'. That had been bad enough, but a period of five weeks suffering from gout then followed, and after that 'another fit of the Stone for the espace of xxj dayes'. His health was a relatively well-known problem even among friends at a distance like Pietro Bizzarri, who knew of Beale's '*grave et pericolosa indispositione*' in September 1586.[4]

With such pressures on his personal life, Beale needed money. During this period he frequently complained to Burghley regarding his financial situation (and the stone and gout), just as he had previously in the late 1570s and early 1580s. To be sure, he had multiple sources of income from his work as a clerk of the Privy Council since 1572, his grant as the sole importer of steel since 1582, and as supervisor of the petty custom in London since 1584. His financial needs when supporting his family and incurring professional costs soon required further income. His wide range of contacts within England and beyond the seas remained valuable to the Elizabethan regime, and power brokers like Burghley, Walsingham, Leicester, and Hatton recognized Beale's importance in many fields. As a legal scholar with deep historical knowledge, Beale could be called upon for counsel on a wide range of issues—whether international trade, ecclesiastical jurisdiction, or common law. As a specialist in diplomacy with direct experience, he was frequently involved in the formulation and implementation of policy during the late 1580s, especially regarding Germany, France, the Low Countries, and—soon—Denmark; his expertise on the threats posed by Catholic forces in Spain, Ireland, and elsewhere was similarly and frequently sought. As a government bureaucrat and administrator, Beale had competencies admired by all, particularly in the way he handled paperwork. Although none would say that his handwriting was particularly clear (then or now, in any language, some may consider it vile), his skills in diplomatics ensured that he could conduct serious research in the records held in the Tower, compare them with documents held in private archives including his own, and then produce memoranda and summaries on issues of moment.[5] Because during the 1580s he wore so many hats, as it were, it is easy to see why modern scholars have variously seen Beale through legal, religious, international, or archival lenses. Because he was engaging with all these jobs and concerns at the same time, it is best that Beale is understood accordingly. It is best that we understand why he had such sore eyes.[6]

---

[4] Beale to Burghley, 16 October 1592, BL, Lansdowne MS 72/73, fol. 198r (orig.). Bizzarri to Walsingham, writing from the Hague, 7/17 September 1586, TNA, SP 84/10/1, fol. 16r (orig.).

[5] e.g., an extract from charter rolls, 18 Edward I, authenticated for Beale by the keeper of the records at the Tower, Michael Heneage, 1587, BL, Additional MS 48010, fols 718r–20r. On the Tower, see Popper, *Specter of the Archive*, Chapter 1. For comment on Beale's handwriting, Alford, *The Watchers*, 19.

[6] Beale to Davison, 8 July 1585, TNA, SP 12/180, fol. 35r (orig.).

The Busyness of State

Beale had proven his worth in London as a clerk of the Privy Council for well over a decade, but it was clear to all that his principal field of expertise remained in foreign affairs. His official diplomatic missions to the Netherlands in 1576 and Germany in 1577 reaffirmed the value of his personal experience and contacts to the Elizabethan regime; his dealings with Mary Queen of Scots at Sheffield Castle during the early 1580s were a direct consequence of how he understood the threat posed by her in conjunction with Catholic conspirators across Europe. Understandably, many supposed Beale would be chosen for more missions. As has been seen, early in 1585 Jacques de Ségur-Pardaillan, who in 1583–4 had tried to build an alliance with the Protestant princes of Germany in the same manner as had Beale in 1577, wrote to Walsingham in expectation that Beale would soon be Elizabeth's representative again among the princes.[7] Such a prospect was not solely the view of those looking from the outside in, for Burghley himself had supposed a couple of weeks later that Beale would serve Elizabeth by heading into Germany and in particular to see Duke Johann Casimir in the Palatinate. In the end, Beale did not go, but he helped to shape the official instructions for the eventual ambassador, Thomas Bodley, whose embassy that year to Germany and Denmark built upon the efforts of others to secure a Protestant alliance. Beale's notes on the draft instructions highlighted differences of opinion among the German princes, with Adolf, duke of Holstein, previously serving King Philip of Spain, and how best to forge an agreement even if aid were only indirect.[8] Although it remains unclear why Beale, who was without question the most qualified for such a mission, did not serve as Elizabeth's representative in this instance, illness may have been the reason. In fact, the queen intended to send Beale north with articles of league between England and Scotland in May–June, only for 'his indisposicion of health' to prevent him from going.[9]

Due to his family obligations and health considerations, it was understandable that he wanted to stay closer to home in London. It was also financially wiser to do so, especially considering the significant debts Beale, like his colleagues, had previously incurred when serving as Elizabeth's ambassador. It is impossible to know how remunerative his grant for importing steel had been since 1582, but it provided enough for Beale later to complain of his loss of the grant after twelve

---

[7] Ségur to Walsingham, 4/14 March 1585, TNA, SP 78/13, fol. 115r (item 49) (orig.). On Ségur's mission, see Chapter 6 and *AGR*.

[8] Burghley's notes on a consultation, 27 March 1585, CP, 163/76. Beale's notes regarding Bodley's instructions, April 1585, TNA, SP 81/3, fols 174r–5v. On the mission, see *AGR*, 97–102.

[9] Walsingham to Wotton, 11 June 1585, TNA, SP 52/37, item 61 (p. 172, old pagination).

years, stating that it 'was cunningly gotten ouer my heade'.[10] In summer 1585, his grant, however profitable, became a source of contention with those looking to compete with him. A certain Jacob van der Hague, dit. Gotthem, sought a degree of flexibility in the exercise of Beale's license, which, especially given his ill health at the time, Beale was not prepared to relinquish. Despite Van der Hague's efforts over the course of a month, Beale did not yield. After all, the letters patent were clear on his sole ability to import, and Beale justifiably did not want to establish a precedent.[11] As has been and will be seen again, Beale's direct engagement with the Hanseatic merchants of the Steelyard was largely concerned with reciprocal privileges for the Hanse in London and Merchant Adventurers in Hamburg, but the Germans were also aware that, among other English monopolies, Beale's licence for the importation of steel was to their own detriment.[12] Thus, Beale's benefit could also be a liability, especially when he served as the mediator between the Hanse and the English government. He was increasingly aware that his grant could be frowned upon, for about this time he acquired a memorandum by the civil lawyer, William Aubrey, in which multiple authors' opinions were cited on the nature of a monopoly, which, Beale could see in plain writing, was not in the public good but was, rather, for private gain.[13]

His role as supervisor of the petty custom in London will have brought additional income and power, but also demonstrating his wider geographical relevance and interests was Beale's role as secretary to the Council of the North, which he formally took on in October 1586 and which brought a considerable income. The grant was to be for life, but Beale's direct work as secretary at York was cut short because, as he explained, it was not safe for him to be venturing too far north after his role in the execution of Mary Queen of Scots. At first a deputy, Ralph Rokeby (Rookebye) the younger, was installed in 1587, but then two years later in August 1589 Rokeby was made joint secretary and thus able to claim half the fee. The letters patent of 1586 were cancelled with stark crossing out across the roll and with Beale's signature attesting. New letters were accordingly drawn

[10] For the grant in 1582, TNA, C 66/1224, mm. 4–6. For the grant's non-renewal to Beale, and its passing along to Brian Annesley, TNA, C 66/1398, mm. 11–13. Beale to Burghley, 24 April 1595, BL, Lansdowne MS 79, fol. 194r (orig.). On debts and payments for ambassadors, see Bell, 'Elizabethan Diplomatic Compensation, 1–25.

[11] Beale to Davison, 8 and 27 July 1585, TNA, SP 12/180, fols 35r, 97r–v (both orig.). Van der Hague to Davison, 3 letters of 19, 23, and ? July, TNA, SP 84/2, fols 147r, 153r, item 76 (unfoliated) (all orig.).

[12] Richard Saltonstall and Giles Fletcher to Walsingham, 1 August 1587, TNA, SP 82/2, fols 168r–9r (orig.). Cf. Paul Simson (ed.), *Inventar Hansischer Archive des sechzehnten Jahrhunderts, 3. Band: Danziger Inventar 1531–1591* (Munich, 1913), 714, which dates German knowledge of Beale's licence to 1 January 1584 (new style).

[13] Aubrey's memorandum/collections, dated 20 May 1586 by Beale, BL, Additional MS 48126, fols 114r–5v. Beale and Aubrey appear not to have had a close relationship, though the latter did correspond with Thomas Smith in 1574; Beale's copies of their correspondence are in BL, Additional MS 48007, fols 330v–31r. See also, *ODNB*.

for the joint appointment in 1589, which will have dealt a bitter financial blow to Beale, whose later correspondence with Burghley and his son, Robert, frequently includes complaints of losing half the fee (see Fig. 10).[14]

On the side, however, and demonstrating his interest in Coventry and the surrounding area, Beale acquired the manor and lands of Priors Marston and Priors Hardwick, Warwickshire, in April 1586. The property had previously been affiliated with St Mary's Priory, Coventry, but was alienated by, among others, Beale's ward, the younger John Hales. Characteristically, Beale then acquired as much information as he could on his new property, including lists of the inhabitants, rents, acreage, and more. He collected extracts of this material from papers in the Tower or in private hands, as well as from books in Coventry supplied by, among others, 'my brother Charles Hales'.[15] Additionally, in 1590 he took on the office of bailiff and feodary in Warwickshire for lands appertaining to the Duchy of Lancaster. Rather than earn a fee for executing these roles, Beale probably took them on because, first, in all likelihood Walsingham, as chancellor of the Duchy of Lancaster, had put forth Beale's name before he died earlier in 1590, and, second, due to the increased power and influence he could exercise in the area, even he needed to pay for it.[16]

Thus, despite lapses in Beale's health and ability to travel in Elizabeth's service, in 1586 Beale had multiple sources of income, multiple homes, and land in the countryside. He owned a significant library of printed books and archive of manuscripts. He had access, patronage, and power. He was a known expert on legal, historical, and diplomatic issues. In sum, he was a very busy man. Like a few dozen other busy men of the late 1580s and 1590s, he was a member of the Elizabethan College (or Society) of Antiquaries, the ostensible purpose of which

[14] See Chapter 6, n. 71. Letters patent, 20 October 1586, TNA, C 66/1271, m. 25, with Beale's signature in the left margin. Letters patent, 30 August 1589, TNA, C 66/1334, mm. 39–40. Beale to Burghley, 24 April 1595, BL, Lansdowne MS 79/80, fols 192r–4r (orig.), 194r noting the fee as £400 per annum despite rumours that it was £1,000. In other letters Beale notes his fee as considerably less, though he might have been thinking of it quarterly rather than per annum. Beale to Robert Cecil, 24 October 1599, CP, 74/50 (orig.). Copy of the updated letters patent, 30 August 1589, TNA, SP 15/31, fols 53r–9r. Rokeby died early in 1595, leaving Beale as the sole secretary of the North, but it remains unclear whether Beale then was able to collect the full (rather than half) fee. Reid, *King's Council in the North*, 489. Cf. BL, Harley MS 1088, fol. 35r, noting Rokeby's attendance at York starting on 12 July 1587 as deputy secretary and as secretary in his own right from 1589 onwards (36r).

[15] Licence dated 2 April 1586, TNA, C 66/1283, m. 31. See also, Salzman, *History of the County of Warwick*, 140–1. Extracts from cartularies and other monastic records relating to Coventry, St Mary's Abbey and Priory, c.1580–1590, BL, Additional MS 32100, fols 1r–132v, with quotation in Beale's hand at 12r. On the Hales family and Coventry, see Chapter 2. On Beale's use of the cartularies and records, Nicholas Popper, 'From Abbey to Archive: Managing Texts and Records in Early Modern England', *Archival Science*, 10 (2010), 249–66, esp. 256–7.

[16] Bonds of obligation in the area of Kenilworth, Duchy of Lancaster, TNA, DL 41/839 (old reference DL 41/34/2), fol. 269r, noting the £20 due from Beale. For the lack of a fee associated, and for the draft letters patent, 10 July 1590, signed by Thomas Heneage and others, TNA, DL 13/7, box 1, large bound bundle, unfoliated but near bottom, 6 fols. See also, Robert Somerville, *History of the Duchy of Lancaster*, Vol. One: *1265–1603* (London, 1953), esp. 562–3. Walsingham became chancellor after the death of the previous holder in 1587. *ODNB*.

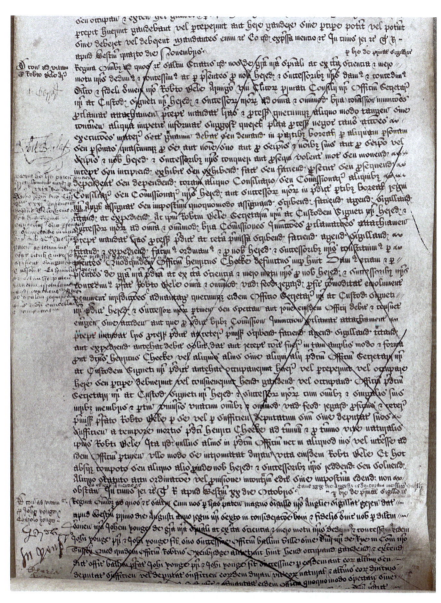

Fig. 10 Letters patent regarding the Council of the North, 20 October 1586. TNA, C 66/1271, m. 25.

was to offer an intellectual forum for historical and antiquarian interests.[17] In reality, this particularly secretive group might have been driven more by concerns for inheritance, law, the ancient constitution, and the royal succession. Either way, his involvement with the College during the early 1590s fit well with his long-standing personal interests and professional development, and among these like-minded men Beale could find, if not entirely scholarly historians, then, in the words of one commentator, 'hard-headed, very ambitious, politically attuned career men'. The vast majority of the College's members were graduates of Oxford or Cambridge, so Beale would have been a very exceptional member; his attendance at meetings seems to have been inconsistent, and he appears not to have contributed much by way of written reports or discussions. Other members of the Society with whom he crossed paths either professionally or personally included William Camden, Michael Heneage, William Lambarde, and John Stow.[18] By way of religion, Beale's Protestantism was unquestioned, even if he erred on the side of Puritans, and his character both at home and abroad was widely acknowledged. In fact, the Spanish ambassador with whom Beale had a history, Bernardino de Mendoza, suggested from Paris that, if English Catholics were successful in rising up and assassinating Queen Elizabeth, then those 'who have great influence with

[17] Beale is listed on two of the earliest extant rolls of members: BL, Stowe MS 1045, fol. 4v (c. February 1591); Norwich Record Office, MS 7198, fol. 65 (c.1590–1 from internal evidence). Cf. Beale's inclusion on another list recorded by an antiquarian of the 17th century, though not of the Elizabethan College, William Burton, recorded on a fly-leaf and reproduced in Notes and Queries, Ser. 1, Vol. 5 (April 17, 1852), 365–6. Lists later compiled by various authors, e.g. Thomas Hearne (ed.), A Collection of Curious Discourses Written by Eminent Antiquaries, Vol. 2 (London, 1773), 423, include Beale but were probably derived from these or other early lists. Two lists for 11 February and 13 May 1591 do not include Beale's name, so his attendance and engagement with the College might have been irregular: BL, Cotton MS Faustina, E. V, fol. 108v. A list of 41 Eliz. (17 November 1598–16 November 1599) does not include Beale: Bodleian, Ashmole MS 763, fol. 197r, with two examples of summons noting the exclusive, even secretive nature of the meetings (195r, 196r). Another list with example of summons, after 1597, does not include Beale's name: BL, Harley MS 5177, fol. 141r; dating suggested by the fact that William Camden is noted as Clarenceux (King of Arms), a role to which he was appointed in October 1597. Joan Evans, A History of the Society of Antiquaries (Oxford, 1956), 12, suggests with reasons unclear a very different date for this list—1591. The College appears not to have met between 1594 and 1597 because of the plague, and Beale's omission from the later lists might be explained by his declining age and infirmities.

[18] Documentation for the Elizabethan College of Antiquaries is more elusive than one may suppose for such a group. For an overview, ODNB. For dedicated studies, Linda Van Norden, 'Sir Henry Spelman on the Chronology of the Elizabethan College of Antiquaries', Huntington Library Quarterly, 13 (1950), 131–60; C. E. Wright, 'The Elizabethan Society of Antiquaries and the Formation of the Cottonian Library', in Francis Wormald and C. E. Wright (eds), The English Library before 1700 (London, 1958), 176–212; Helen Dorothy Jones, 'The Elizabethan Society of Antiquaries Reassessed', MA dissertation, University of British Columbia, 1988, with quotation at 36. The most thorough study to date remains Linda Van Norden, 'The Elizabethan College of Antiquaries', PhD thesis, University of California, Los Angeles, 1946, with discussion of the early primary sources at 24–36, with reference to Beale at 156, 199, 554, 559, 561. Evans, A History, acknowledges indebtedness to Van Norden's work (p. 8 n. 3) and records the numbers of Oxford and Cambridge graduates (21, 16; 2 at both; p. 11). Among Beale's papers are multiple instances of notes and extracts from multiple versions of Lambarde's Archeion, which emphasized common law and prerogative, as well as his Archaionomia, which included a collection of Anglo-Saxon laws, and his work on the Office of Compositions for Alienations. BL, Additional MSS 48023, fols 165r–80r, 48025, fols 103r–7v; 48055; 48063, fols 151r–87r; 48086, fols 19r–20v. Beale also might have owned Lambarde's Perambulation of Kent, 1596 edn; BL, Hargrave MS 107, fol. 28v.

the heretics, as they are terrible heretics themselves', should be either killed or seized. Among those targeted were Burghley and Walsingham, for obvious reasons, as well as Beale, which suggests that Mendoza had not forgotten their exchanges earlier in the 1580s.[19]

Beale's reputation as a strong Protestant opposed to—and targeted by— Catholics in England and elsewhere was well earned. In the parliament of 1586-7, which had been called explicitly because of Mary Queen of Scots' latest attempt against Elizabeth (i.e. the Babington Plot), Beale was predictably active both inside and outside the House of Commons.[20] As he had in 1584-5, Beale sat for Dorchester as a relic of the earl of Bedford's influence in nominating MPs. Although Bedford had died in 1585, the firm and sustained connection between the two men is most visible in the fact that Beale was a witness to (and beneficiary of) Bedford's will dated 7 April 1584 and proved a month before the opening of parliamentary proceedings.[21] Beale's committee work unsurprisingly included that on Mary Queen of Scots and extended to the learned ministry, privilege, and curriers. As was always the case, MPs were formally forbidden by Elizabeth from discussing religion, but that prohibition, as before, did not stop those looking to attack the bishops and advance reform. In many respects, the proceedings of 1586-7 regarding Mary, religious reform, and—importantly—the Netherlands reflected the integrated manner in which Beale understood three of his principal concerns. Rarely isolated, ever inter-dependent, these issues affected the safety of the queen's realm and the security of her subjects' consciences. After concluding its business regarding Mary with an adjournment on 2 December, Parliament resumed on 22 February with discussions regarding Catholic threats within England (it was feared Catholics would have risen to support Mary) and the war in the Netherlands (whence Spanish forces would invade England). In one of Beale's rarely documented oral contributions in the House of Commons, he argued some days later that, according to one diarist, 'all papistes' weapons and furniture for warres might be taken from them'.[22] By this point in late February,

---

[19] Mendoza to Philip, 13 August 1586, Martin A. S. Hume (ed.), *Calendar of State Papers, Spain (Simancas)*, Vol. 3: *1580–1586* (London, 1896), item 469. King Philip wrote on the letter regarding those to be targeted (who also included Henry Carey, Lord Hunsdon, and Francis Knollys): 'It does not matter so much about Cecil, although he is a great heretic, but he is very old, and it was he who advised the understandings with the prince of Parma, and he has done no harm. It would be advisable to do as he says with the others.' On Mendoza and Beale, see Chapter 6.

[20] As before, the classic account remains Neale, *Elizabeth I and her Parliaments, 1584–1601*, 103–91. For relevant documents, Hartley, *Proceedings*, Vol. 2: *1584–1589*, 195–400. For Beale's committee work, HoP:HoC. Simonds D'Ewes, *A Compleat Journal of the Notes, Speeches and Debates, both of the House of Lords and House of Commons Throughout the whole Reign of Queen Elizabeth, Of Glorious Memory* (London, 1693), 391–418, adds nothing of significance regarding Beale's activity other than that Beale was part of a group to investigate matters concerning MPs 'lately committed to the Tower' (p. 415).

[21] Will of Francis Russell, Earl of Bedford, TNA, PROB, 11/69/513, with Beale's inheritance of a 'Cupp gilte worth tenne poundes', fol. 352v/p. 6; at fol. 351r/p. 3, Bedford left for Burghley a particularly fine George and, more interestingly with regard to Beale, 'all my auncient written Englishe bookes of Wycliffes workes, or otherwise within my closett at Bedford howse'; to Bedford's son, John, he left all of his Latin and Italian books whether printed or manuscript (352v/p. 6).

[22] Hartley, *Proceedings*, 2.388; on the date, see also p. 206.

though, Beale had largely shifted focus in what he viewed as the primary danger facing English or, indeed, all European Protestants: King Philip of Spain. Yet that is to look ahead too quickly, to put the cart before the horse; or, rather, to put the tail before the head of the viper.

Beheading a Viper

From London to Fotheringhay is less than 100 miles, but Beale's road to Mary Queen of Scots' execution was more than a decade in the making and reflected the sentiments among many in the regime. As has been seen, since 1571 his thinking regarding Mary and the threat posed by her to Elizabeth's throne incorporated religious and political arguments, legal ideas, and domestic as well as international elements, but about this time he acquired a significant new collection of papers relating to Mary—those of Thomas Norton.[23] Beale and Norton had collaborated and moved in some of the same circles (Parliament, examination of Catholics, law), but it remains unclear how, exactly, Beale acquired this material. During his several trips to see Mary at Sheffield, he needed to swallow his pride in the interest of civil negotiation (no mean feat). The increasing danger brought to English and broader Protestant security with the assassination of William the Silent in 1584, the Parry Plot of 1585, open warfare with Spain in the Netherlands in 1585, and, finally, the Babington Plot of 1586, however, enabled Beale to relish his role in hastening the queen of Scots' end no matter how much she protested (a lot) or whether she signed an oath adhering to the Bond of Association, which stipulated that all signatories pursue and execute any who tried to harm Elizabeth or take her throne (she signed).[24] To recount the whole affair, from Mary's involvement in the Babington Plot to her execution on 8 February 1587, is unnecessary here because it is so well known, but the significance of Beale's role and observations lends further weight to the seriousness of the seismic shifts in winter 1586–7.[25]

---

[23] In addition to the discussions in previous chapters and sources noted, see also BL, Additional MS 48027, a large volume (c.700 fols) of Beale's copies and other papers relating to Mary between 1559 and 1594. Some of Norton's material relating to Mary ended up bound among Beale's existing papers, which makes detecting Norton's from Beale's own a challenge. Relevant volumes include BL, Additional MSS 48023, 48027, 48043, 48048–9. For a schedule listing Norton's papers in Beale's archive, see Taviner, 271–9, with discussion preceding at 265–70.

[24] See Beale's copy of the Bond of Association and Mary's adherence, BL, Additional MS 48027, fols 248r–51v, with Beale's note that 'This haue I Robert Beale seen vnder the hand and seale of ye Scotishe Queene remaining with Mr Secretary Walsingham' (249r).

[25] Julian Goodare's article on Mary in the *ODNB* offers a summary and bibliography, but see also Taviner, 214–43 for a detailed retelling.

A particularly illuminating exchange between Beale and Walsingham in September 1586 helps to set the stage for later events.[26] Walsingham reached out because the proceedings against Mary were gaining steam and he needed information regarding Mary's complaints, Elizabeth's answers, and, more broadly, 'what hath past your owne knowledge'. That half-page request yielded a five-page response from Beale, whose health was at the time not strong. Alongside providing the specific information Walsingham had requested and retelling his five visits to Mary, Beale felt that Mary should be charged in writing—not in speech—on two counts: her dealings with the duke of Norfolk in 1570–2 and the current conspiracy. Citing various legal arguments, he also made the case that Mary was not, in fact a free prince in England (as she claimed) but rather a private subject and, accordingly, subject to the laws of England. The tone of Beale's letter is legalistic, cool, and dispassionate. In his view (as well as Walsingham's), now was not the time for strident vitriol against Catholics or confessional arguments of any sort. No, now was the time for evidence, law, and proper proceedings without any measure of impropriety or irregularity of protocol. In the light of Beale's archive—mental and physical—of Mary's crimes and dissimulation over the years, and soon combined with Norton's own, building the case must have been relatively straightforward.

Beale sat on the parliamentary committee charged to deal with Mary that November, and although the precise nature of his involvement remains obscure, his collection relating the matters and proceedings against Mary at Fotheringhay Castle on 14–15 October 1586, in the Court of Star Chamber on 25 October, and subsequently in Parliament demonstrate the fact that he was very much attuned to the situation (even if looking from afar because still unwell). He was not the author of certain 'notes of ye proceedings of the Parlement' between October and early December, but his copy includes his observation that additional notes concerning this parliament were to be found in a printed volume 'made by Mr R. Cecill, and dedicated to ye Earl of Leycester'.[27] An additional collection of notes detailed the proceedings at Fotheringhay and in Star Chamber, but Beale seems not to have been in either place. Yet again Beale recorded the issue of

---

[26] Walsingham to Beale, 21 September 1586, BL, Additional MS 48027, fol. 374r, with copy of Beale's response at 375r–8r. Beale to Walsingham, 26 September 1586, BL, Cotton MS Caligula, C. IX, fols 445r–7v (orig.); additional copy without addressee, BL, Cotton MS Julius, F. VI, fols 30v–2v. Beale's response discusses many of the themes and papers in BL, Additional MS 48027.

[27] BL, Additional MS 48027, fol. 484r. These 'notes' appear to be transcripts from a parliamentary roll now at Hatfield House. Another transcript is in BL, Cotton MS Titus, F. I. See the discussion in J. E. Neale, 'Proceedings in Parliament Relative to the Sentence on Mary Queen of Scots', *The English Historical Review*, 35:137 (1920), 103–13. The printed work, with dedication dated 25 November 1586, is *The Copie of a Letter to the Right Honourable the Earle of Leycester* (London, 1586) (STC 6052); Beale's clean copy of the translation into French published at London the next year (STC 6053) is BL, Additional MS 48027, fols 511r–28r.

authorship, this time by an appointed notary, 'Mr Ed. Barker Principall Register of ye Delegates', though he was careful also to note that the marginal comments were originally in the hand of Burghley, who was most certainly present at the proceedings and, as Beale would learn, central to the plan to execute Mary.[28] Another collection of documents produced by Star Chamber in October and in Beale's possession were at first of unknown authorship. Beale recorded initially that 'It is thought that Master Sollicitor Generall Drewe this Collection. others think by Mr Somersett the Harold', but nearly a year later he updated his note: 'I haue seen the discours following of the hand of Mr Egerton, her Majesty's Sollicitor Generall so as there is no doubt, but that he was the Author therof'.[29] Still another account of the proceedings at Fotheringhay in mid October includes Beale's observation of Burghley's attitude to Mary. Despite some rumours that Burghley was inclined to favour Mary because of his own grandson's activity in Rome, Beale recorded that, when the rumours came to Burghley and Elizabeth's knowledge, the lord treasurer grew 'more earnest against her'.[30] Again, Burghley's significance and, indeed, centrality were becoming increasingly clear to Beale. The final and possibly most dramatic of all accounts that came into Beale's possession differed from the others because it was a drawing of Mary's trial at Fotheringhay on 14–15 October 1586. Beale most certainly was not the artist (if his handwriting is anything to go by, he cannot be called an 'artist' in any traditional sense), but he did number those in attendance and then list their names on the reverse of the drawing. All of the expected names occur, Beale's own excepted, including Burghley's as 'L Threr' in the second spot behind the Lord Chancellor, Thomas Bromley.[31]

Whatever reason lay behind Beale's lack of active engagement in the proceedings of October seems to have faded by November when he was chosen, along with Thomas Sackville, Baron Buckhurst, to deliver the news to Mary that she had been found guilty of compassing Elizabeth's death and should, accordingly, prepare herself for execution.[32] As noted in their instructions, Elizabeth had been petitioned by Parliament to proceed against Mary because the committee and trial had run their courses. Indeed, on 12 November a formal supplication was

[28] BL, Additional MS 48027, fol. 554r.   [29] BL, Additional MS 48027, fols 558r, 557v.
[30] BL, Additional MS 48027, fol. 574. The passage by Beale is transcribed and discussed in Read, *Lord Burghley*, 350–1, but with a transcription error of 'severe' for 'earnest'.
[31] BL, Additional MS 48027/1, fol. 569r–v, originally part of MS 48027 but now mounted separately. For discussion of the sketch, see Helen Smailes and Duncan Thompson (eds), *The Queen's Image: A Celebration of Mary Queen of Scots* (Edinburgh, 1987), 43–5. Patrick Collinson loosely suggested that this drawing, as well as that of Mary's execution, discussed below, were possibly by Beale himself, but the present author disagrees. While other drawings are among Beale's papers, they only have his annotations in his very characteristic hand. See below, n. 71, and a sketch of an Irish courtroom with Beale's annotations, BL, Additional MS 48015, fol. 260v. No evidence points to Beale's ability as a sketch artist; if anything, the evidence points the other way. Goldring et al., *John Nichols's The Progresses*, Vol. 3: *1579–1595*, 356–8.
[32] Beale and Buckhurst's instructions, mid November 1586, BL, Harley MS 290, fols 196r–7v.

submitted, and as may not be surprising at this point, Beale's copy noted that the amendments ('enterrlinings in the Roman letter') were originally in Burghley's hand.[33] That Burghley sought to move with speed at this time is evident in his letter to the earl of Shrewsbury on 14 November when he reported that Beale and Buckhurst were to repair to Fotheringhay; presumably Beale was feeling a little better by this point. Burghley expected Beale to get more involved, and it seems plausible that Burghley thought Beale would enjoy personally declaring to Mary what, presumably, he had long wanted to declare.[34]

Beale and Buckhurst conveyed the news to Mary in mid or late November 1586 while the committee on Mary in Parliament was still very active.[35] After Parliament adjourned in early December (until its return in February), royal proclamations were made orally and in print; again meeting expectation, Beale recorded his observations from the sidelines even if he was not directly involved. The proclamation was made patent and sealed on 4 December and then announced two days later in London, where Beale seems to have watched the events untold. He recorded how the lord mayor, various earls, the city's aldermen, and many other gentlemen and citizens in rich attire of scarlet gowns, velvet, and gold chains rode on horseback 'in the most solemne maner that could be deuysed' and with the sound of trumpets, making 'open and publyke declaracion and proclamacion of the sentence' against Mary in four locations: at the cross in Cheapside, at Chancery Lane and Fleet Street, at Leadenhall corner, and at St Magnus near London Bridge. When he recorded these notes, Beale knew 'that it is to be seen in print', and when the proclamation was duly printed shortly afterwards, on his own copy he recorded 'how solemly this was proclaimed in the presence of the Lord Maior and diuers of his brethren'.[36] Beale's tendency here and elsewhere in his papers to look forwards and backwards reflects the mentality of an archivist knowing that his papers would be useful either for his own purposes or to later generations.

---

[33] BL, Additional MS 48027, fols 651r–3r, with Beale's note at 653r. The draft with Burghley's changes is discussed and edited in Allison Heisch, 'Lord Burghley, Speaker Puckering, and the Editing of HEH "Ellesmere MS 1191"', *Huntington Library Quarterly*, 51 (1988), 210–26. See also, Hartley, *Proceedings*, 2.244–7.

[34] Burghley to Shrewsbury, 14 November 1586, Longleat, Talbot MS I, fol. 260r (orig.); later copy, BL, Lansdowne MS 982, fol. 74v.

[35] Neale, *Elizabeth I and Her Parliaments, 1584–1601*, 122–33. A retrospective account noting Beale and Buckhurst's going to Mary is in Kent, Beale, Paulet, and Drury to the Privy Council, 8 February 1587, BL, Cotton MS Caligula, C. IX, fols 214r–16r, at fol. 214v.

[36] BL, Additional MS 48027/1, fol. 569*v, originally part of MS 48027 but now mounted separately. BL, Additional MS 48027, fol. 448cr. The solemnity of the occasion remained in Beale's mind for some time. See 'Touching the Commission for the execution of the Scotish Queene', 1587, BL, Additional MS 48027, fols 636r–40v, at 639r; although the title, notes, and comments are in Beale's hand, the possibility remains that Beale was one of several authors. The date of composition is within months of the execution because Christopher Hatton is referred to as 'then' Vice Chamberlain; Hatton becomes Lord Chancellor after Thomas Bromley dies in April 1587.

Mary's sentence had been made official and proclaimed publicly in December, but the real events occurred two months later in February 1587, and if Beale had previously collected as much as he could from the sidelines, in February he was very much at centre stage and collated more than ever. As it turned out, his foresight was valuable because he had good reason to gather what he could. Mary was due to be executed, but that could only happen when the warrant was signed by the queen and then sealed. Multiple copies of the warrant were produced; one survives with Beale's annotations.[37] For Henry Grey, earl of Kent and one of the commissioners at Mary's execution, the warrant is dated 1 February 1587 and written in a customary secretary hand, while Beale has reproduced Elizabeth's signature in the upper left corner. The warrant is formally addressed to Kent, the earls of Shrewsbury, Derby, Cumberland, and Pembroke. Beale's underlining is suggestive because he consistently emphasized 'you', that is, the earls along with, by extension, others of Elizabeth's Council, nobility, and judges. In his underlining Beale seems to have recognized that, although Elizabeth knew that she alone could sign the death warrant, she also sought to put a considerable burden on those around her. Moreover, Beale seems to have seen that they—the earls and others—were identified as complicit or even pushing Elizabeth's hand. When exactly Beale annotated this copy is impossible to know, but it seems probable that he did so only after he carried it along with other materials to Fotheringhay on 4–5 February (see Fig. 11).

Beale's activity during these eventful days can be reconstructed from various sources. Although the timing was potentially awkward and irregular, on 2 February he was admitted to Gray's Inn no doubt owing to his legal expertise but probably also because his membership in an Inn of Court, even if honorary, might provide some degree of future protection if he needed it. Additionally, it did not hurt that Burghley exercised considerable influence over Gray's Inn. As for going north to Fotheringhay, his journeys and physical exertion will have been particularly hard on him because he had only recently recovered from 'a dangerous sicknes which he had longe before'.[38] On Friday, 3 February the Privy Council wrote to the earls of Kent and Shrewsbury to inform them of the

[37] Warrant for the execution of Mary Queen of Scots, 1 February 1587, LPL, MS 4769, no doubt carried with the missive from the Privy Council to Kent dated 3 February. Like the copy at Lambeth, the copy in BL, Harley MS 290, fols 203r–4r, also includes as addressees, following Shrewsbury and Kent, the earls of Derby, Cumberland, and Pembroke, but the latter three were not present at Fotheringhay.

[38] Beale's admission to Gray's Inn on 2 February 1587 recorded without further explanation of the circumstances in The Honourable Society of Gray's Inn Archive, MS ADM 1/1, fol. 103r, and without discussion in Joseph Foster (ed.), The Register of Admissions to Gray's Inn, 1521–1889, together with the Register of Marriages in Gray's Inn Chapel, 1695–1754 (London, 1889), 70. Burghley's connection with Gray's Inn is still visible in the Inn's portrait, Lord Burghley Sitting on an Ass. See also, Stephen Alford, Burghley: William Cecil at the Court of Elizabeth I (New Haven, CT, 2008). The illness noted by Bizzarri seems to have been prolonged. 'Touching the Commission', 1587, BL, Additional MS 48027, fol. 636r.

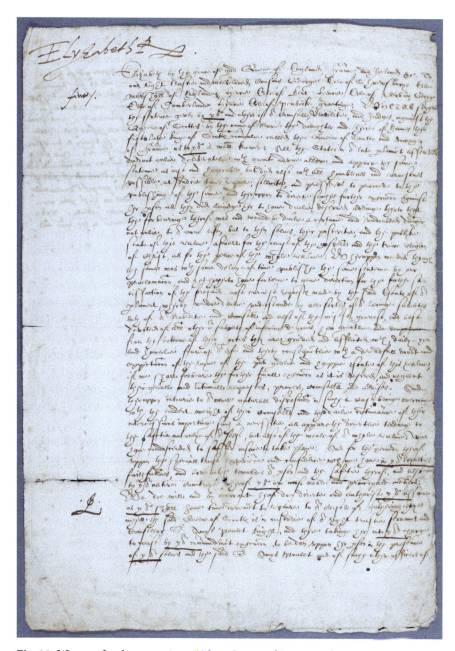

Fig. 11 Warrant for the execution of Mary Queen of Scots, 1 February 1587. LPL, MS 4769, fol. 1r. Image courtesy of Lambeth Palace Library.

Reproduced with permission.

commission to execute Mary, noting Beale as the bearer and as 'a person of greate trust and experyence' (to Kent) and 'honest, wise and trustye' (to Shrewsbury); that to Shrewsbury was, in fact, written by Beale, who would have understood the weight of the moment. By another account, the Privy Council 'had made special Choice of him to carrye it downe [...] for his trustines [in] a matter that required greate speede and secrecye'; by still another, Beale was 'the fittest messenger for that purpose.'[39] The next day he travelled roughly forty miles to Kent's residence at Wrest (Silsoe, in Bedfordshire), where, according to Burghley, the earl 'sent pre-ceptes for the stayinge of such hewes and cryes as had troubled the Countrye'. The next night, Sunday, 5 February 1587, Beale rode another forty miles, arrived at Fotheringhay, and delivered the commission to Mary's keepers, Drew Drury and Amias Paulet. On the 6 February, Beale and Drury rode east six miles to Orton Longueville to meet Shrewsbury. On Tuesday, 7 February, Kent and Shrewsbury individually made their ways to Fotheringhay to speak directly with Mary, Beale and Drury returning with Shrewsbury.[40] So, in a matter of days Beale had ridden many miles at speed while maintaining the utmost secrecy and had gathered the relevant parties to execute the sentence of execution; all the while, he might have still felt tender from his illness of the previous months. Everyone, it seems, was in accord on the plan, and, according to Beale in a comparatively rare use of exclam-ation, 'The lords then promoted among themselues not to reveale the sending down of the commission to her Majesty before the execution were past!'[41] Now was not the time to dither, and yet, amazingly, there was still some deliberation on what, exactly, to do. The plan for execution was clear, but another option had long been in the works.

The proposal to assassinate Mary privately, thereby removing any culpability from Elizabeth and avoiding a public execution, was discussed at Fotheringhay by

---

[39] Privy Council to Kent, 3 February 1587, BL, Cotton MS Caligula, C. IX, fol. 204r. Privy Council to Shrewsbury, 3 February 1587, Longleat, Talbot MS I, fol. 268r (orig.). 'Touching the Commission', 1587, BL, Additional MS 48027, fols 636r, with 'him' in superscript in Beale's hand, with 'me' struck through, 637r. Relation by William Davison, 20 February 1587, BL, Harley MS 290, fol. 223r; Davison's larger discourse of the same date notes Beale 'as the fytteste persone they Could aduise of to whom they myghte comyte that Charge', BL, Harley MS 290, fol. 219v. Discussion of Davison's accounts, with citation to various copies, in Taviner, 215–16.

[40] Multiple copies of the official account exist and suggest something of a circulation: Kent, Beale, Paulet, and Drury to the Privy Council, 8 February 1587, BL, Cotton MS Caligula, C. IX, fols 214r–16r, quotation at 214r; Beale's copy, BL, Additional MS 48027, fols 646v–9r; Newberry Library, Case MS 5089, fols 1r–3v. Burghley's abbreviated summary of the same account, February 1587, CP, 165/20, quotation at fol. 1r. The signed original letter sent has not been located. Beale's own, more private account offering further detail and emphasizing the need for speed and secrecy is 'Touching the Commission', which also notes the 'hues and Cryes' at 638r. The timing of events between 3 and 8 February is corroborated on an endorsement on the address leaf of Privy Council to Shrewsbury, 3 February 1587, Longleat, Talbot MS I, fol. 268r (orig.). Contrast Beale's speed here with his slow pace from London to Dover in 1600, when John Herbert, having left later than Beale, overtook him at Rochester (about halfway). Herbert made the trip of roughly 70 miles in two days. Herbert to Cecil, 15 May 1600, CP, 79/49 (orig.).

[41] 'Touching the Commission', 1587, BL, Additional MS 48027, fol. 637v (marginal comment).

Paulet, Drury, and Beale.[42] Naturally, Beale later wrote a detailed account that included his marginal and summary comments, though he also struck through first-person pronouns like 'me' and 'I', replacing them with 'him' and 'he', probably because he had intended this work for a wider audience. At the very end of the account, which largely deals with the timeline and events before 5 February, he included details about how Paulet and Drury had received a letter seeking to induce them 'to suffer [Mary] to haue ben violentlye murthered by some that should haue bene appointed for that purpose'.[43] That letter was written, as Beale knew, by Walsingham and Davison after Elizabeth had sent John Whitgift, archbishop of Canterbury, to persuade Walsingham to push the matter; the assassination was to be by poison or another method.[44] Although both secretaries Walsingham and Davison 'misliked' the idea that a certain 'Wingfielde (as it was thought)' should do the deed, Beale recorded that 'of all [Elizabeth's] Councellors it is thought, that the Earl of Leycestre did most exhort her un[t]o this course', though Whitgift had also played a role. For their part, Paulet and Drury opposed the idea. When Beale arrived the night of 5 February, 'the matter being in consideration', he appears to have cited the precedents of the kings Edward II and Richard II (both of whom were murdered according to Holinshed, one of Beale's favourite sources for medieval history) and 'it was not thought convenient or safe to proceede covertly, but openly according to the statute of 27 [Eliz., i.e. the Act of Association, 1585]'.[45] Thus, what others like Walsingham and Paulet wanted to avoid potentially because of moral or ethical considerations (it would have been a pardonable offence in legal terms), Beale also opposed on the grounds of historical precedent and what future ills could come of murdering Mary. At the last possible opportunity to rid Elizabeth of the burden (an open and legal process for execution based on her signature), Beale was part of a group opposing their sovereign's wishes. While he sincerely and consistently swore to obey the queen, he was, nevertheless, his own man who understood that history and law, precedent and procedure, were supreme.

---

[42] See the discussions in Neale, *Elizabeth I and Her Parliaments, 1584–1601*, 139–41; Read, *Lord Burghley*, 366–8; Conyers Read, 'The Proposal to Assassinate Mary Queen of Scots at Fotheringay', *The English Historical Review*, 40:158 (1925), 234–5, which includes some of the critical document discussed here: BL, Additional MS 48027, fols 636r–41r. Davison's larger discourse dated 20 February 1587 also notes, if obliquely, Elizabeth's desire that her burden be eased by Mary's assassination. BL, Harley MS 290, fol. 218v.

[43] 'Touching the Commission', 1587, BL, Additional MS 48027, fol. 639v.

[44] Beale's notes, undated, BL, Additional MS 48027, fol. 402v. The letter of 1 February to Paulet, famously including the phrase 'some way to shorten the life of that Queen', with the response of Paulet and Drury, printed in John Morris (ed.), *The Letter-Books of Sir Amias Poulet, Keeper of Mary Queen of Scots* (London, 1874), 359–62.

[45] 'Touching the Commission', 1587, BL, Additional MS 48027, fol. 640r. Raphael Holinshed, *The firste [laste] volume of the chronicles of England, Scotlande, and Ireland* (London, 1577) (STC 13568b), 883, 1129–30; 1587 edn (STC 13569), 341–2, 517. The 1587 edn appears on the list of Beale's books, BL, Hargrave MS 107, fol. 37v, and Beale cites Holinshed elsewhere for his history.

Procedure followed. On the morning of 8 February 1587, with Mary Queen of Scots sitting in front of the block, Beale openly read the commission that he had carried so swiftly and secretly for her execution.[46] He would have been standing on the scaffold so the surrounding audience of knights, gentlemen, and others could hear clearly and respond with 'God save the Queen [Elizabeth]', but in a later drawing of the event Beale is nowhere to be found. The sketch is by the same artist as drew the scene of Mary's trial, with seven parties numbered by Beale and listed on the reverse: the earls of Shrewsbury and Kent, Paulet, Drury, the sheriff of Northamptonshire, the dean of Peterborough, and finally four of Mary's servants. Beale had been in the vanguard of those advocating for the beheading of the woman he thought a 'viper' since the early 1570s, took a leading role in diplomatic discussions with her during the early 1580s, and now took centre stage in reading her commission for execution. Yet, he is not depicted reading or labelled otherwise in this drawing. If Beale had commissioned the artwork, his omission might well have been intentional.[47]

The aftermath of Mary's execution does not need detailed retelling here, but it suffices to say that Elizabeth was furious that her Council had acted so quickly and without her full knowledge as events unfolded. In short, somebody was to blame, and somebody needed to take the fall. That somebody was Walsingham's co-secretary, William Davison, whose downfall and disgrace were carefully watched by Beale for fear of his own similar discredit and dishonour.[48] In truth, Beale was justifiably nervous. Of the nine known accounts of Davison's trial in Star Chamber in March, Beale owned five of them, and, when considered in light of Beale's later comments about his own reputation, it is clear that his concern for Davison was genuine. Even so, his distress regarding his own fate ran much deeper. It could not be known at the time of Davison's downfall that he would be released from imprisonment in the Tower within a year and a half, but Beale's tendency to acquire documentation that might prove valuable later is seen in the fact that he ordered and received a copy of Burghley and Walsingham's letter commanding that Davison be released into private custody. The personal touch and detail here are signified by Beale's notes stating that the original letter was written almost entirely in Walsingham's own hand, save for Burghley's interlinear inclusion that Davison was to be moved from the Tower 'in secret manner';

---

[46] Account of Mary's execution by Robert Wise, 8 February 1587, BL, Lansdowne MS 51, fol. 99v. Beale's own account, written with the others on the same day, does not specify who read the commission. BL, Cotton MS Caligula, C. IX, fol. 215v.

[47] BL, Additional MS 48027/1, fol. 650r, originally part of MS 48027 but now mounted separately. See above, n. 31, for comment on Beale as the possible artist.

[48] On Davison's downfall, a detailed account is Simon Adams' in *ODNB*, but see also the note by R. B. Wernham, 'The Disgrace of William Davison', *The English Historical Review*, 46:184 (1931), 632–6; and the classic narrative by Nicholas Harris Nicolas, *Life of William Davison, Secretary of State and Privy Councillor to Queen Elizabeth* (London, 1823). Beale's papers on Davison's downfall in BL, Additional MS 48027, fols 398r–403r, 666r–90v.

moreover, Beale had an additional copy made, which he personally delivered to Davison 'to be kept by him'.[49] On the reverse of Beale's copy, he included other insights from what he had learned. In the immediate aftermath of Mary's execution, and with Burghley haven taken the lead in the proceedings to ensure her death, the lord treasurer would have been the most likely target for trial, but, according to Beale, 'her Majesty thought that to commit him to the tower wold kill him'. As for Walsingham, he 'was thought to[o] stout and wold vtter all'. Accordingly, 'Mr Dauison most knew the burden'.[50] Among Beale's copies of Davison's trial, he recorded more of his conversations and thoughts regarding Burghley's leading role (partly in saving himself), what the Scottish ambassador knew (and could relay to King James VI), and Davison's eventual release from the Tower and the fine (of 10,000 marks). On Elizabeth's attempt to claim innocence and shift the blame for Mary's execution onto her Privy Council, Beale noted that the Council was not called before Star Chamber, and were the Council to take responsibility for Mary's execution, 'being of so great a moment', it would have been unwisely done ('*Imprudenter*'). Furthermore, he recalled a historical parallel from 1572 that he saw as 'evidence to condemn' Elizabeth's inclination: 'Immediatly appon the Massacre of the Admirall &c the king wold have layed it appon the hands of Guise: and so were his first letters. But they wold not beare yt: and so he was faine to advowe yt himself'.[51]

Given his own role in the drama, in moving so swiftly and secretly, Beale knew that he, along with Paulet, Drury, Kent, and Shrewsbury could also become targets of Elizabeth's ire. Beale's usual insurance policy against later accusations of impropriety was to collect as much documentation as possible, so that is precisely what he did. Along with the others, though, he wrote and signed a letter to Elizabeth that essentially claimed that they were simply obeying orders and could not be held accountable for the contents of a royal commission signed and sealed by the Great Seal of England. They knew that Davison had taken the fall, but they were guarding against their own becoming collateral damage. The letter remains undated, on vellum, and complete with signatures (save Shrewsbury's but also including Thomas Andrews's as sheriff of Northamptonshire). More intriguingly, it seems never to have been sent; rather, three large cuts from scissors have ripped through the letter. Ever the archivist looking to retain documentation, Beale kept the letter for future reference, and it is now appropriately kept in the volume of related papers (see Fig. 12).[52]

It is sometimes difficult to ascertain when, exactly, Beale wrote his notes regarding Davison or expressing concern regarding his own fate, but from other

---

[49] Burghley and Walsingham to Owen Hopton, Lieutenant of the Tower, 23 October 1588, BL, Additional MS 48027, fol. 402r.
[50] Beale's notes, undated, BL, Additional MS 48027, fol. 402v.
[51] Beale's notes, undated, BL, Additional MS 48027, fols 675r, 687r, 690v (quotations).
[52] BL, Additional MS 48027, fols 700v–1r (orig.).

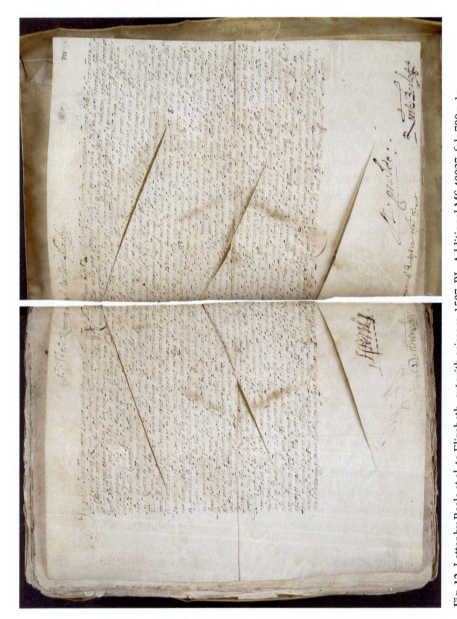

Fig. 12 Letter by Beale et al. to Elizabeth, cut with scissors, 1587. BL, Additional MS 48027, fols 700v–1r. Reproduced with permission from the British Library.

evidence the reputational damage faced by Beale becomes clearer. As expected, the Spanish view of Mary's execution was one-sided, with Mendoza relaying to King Philip in March Beale's role in bringing the warrant; given Mendoza's calling for Beale to be killed or seized less than a year previously, any future conversations or rapprochement between the two were unlikely.[53] Also in March, the Venetian ambassador in Paris relayed to the doge and senate an extract of a letter by the French ambassador in England in which Beale's secret dispatch was noted as well as Beale's informing Mary that Elizabeth had sent to her an English 'Bishop' (actually the dean of Peterborough) to encourage the queen of Scots to a becoming end and consolation.[54] A couple of months later, in May a fuller account of the French ambassadors in England offered still more detail on Beale's discussions with Mary on 5 February upon his arrival at Fotheringhay. According to this report, Beale, addressed as 'Milord Belle' (one of the lords/seigneurs about the queen), 'could well have wished that another than I should have announced to you such ill news', but such courtesy shown to a queen before her death should not lead one to believe that Beale's vitriol for the viper or steadfastness in procedure had been compromised.[55] Beale was painfully aware of how his role could be depicted for the international audience. In one instance, he recorded his notes on an account in French printed in Edinburgh shortly after the execution, even noting the pages on which his name appeared.[56] Germanophone audiences could also learn of Beale's role from printed pamphlets coming out of Munich from a very Catholic perspective and from Cologne in a rare example of a work supposedly translated directly from English into German. Also printed in Cologne was a Latin translation of John Leslie's account of Mary's execution, a fine example of Catholic propaganda that Beale might well have owned. Curiously, just as Beale had been elevated as 'Milord Belle' in the French account, the two German texts referred to Beale as a 'secretary' akin to Davison and Walsingham.[57]

[53] Mendoza to Philip, 7 March 1587, Hume, *(Simancas)*, Vol. 4: *1587–1603* (London, 1899), item 35. On Mendoza, see above.

[54] Extract of a Letter by Monsieur de L'Aubespine, enclosed in Giovanni Dolfin to the Doge and Senate, 13 March 1587, Horatio F. Brown (ed.), *Calendar of State Papers Relating to English Affairs in the Archives of Venice*, Vol. 8: *1581–1591* (London, 1894), items 483–4.

[55] Proceedings of the French Ambassadors, May 1587, BL, Additional MS 30663, fols 436r–69r, at 463v; translated in William K. Boyd (ed.), *Calendar of State Papers, Scotland*, Vol. 9: *1586–88* (London, 1915), item 352.

[56] Adam Blackwood, *Martyre de la Royne d'Escosse* (Edinburgh, 1587; 1588; 1589) (STC 3107–9), Beale's notes on the same, BL, Additional MS 48027, fols 704r–7v, at 704v Beale's (very accurate) noting of his own relevant pages at 329–30, 387, 476. The edition of 1588 is listed as one of Beale's potential books in BL, Hargrave MS 107, fol. 34v.

[57] Anon., *Kurtzer unnd gründtlicher Bericht, wie die Edel und from Königin auß Schotlandt Maria Stuarda* (Munich, 1587) (VD16 M 996), with notice of Beale at sig. Aiv. Anon., *Gründliche vnd Eigentlich Warhaffte Beschreibung von der Königin in Engellandt warumm sie die Königin von Schotlandt hat enthaupten lassen* (Cologne, 1587) (USTC 669525), with notice of Beale at sig. Aiiir. Anon., *Mariae Stuartae Scotorum Reginae* (Cologne, 1587) (possibly VD16 M 991), noted in BL, Hargrave MS 107, fol. 53v. David Chytraeus, based at the University of Rostock, also addressed Beale

As time wore on, Beale showed his sensitivity regarding his reputation, especially across the seas. In a string of letters to Burghley in the early and mid 1590s, when he became increasingly concerned about his finances and then fell from Elizabeth's grace, as will be seen, Beale laid out no small number of details regarding his long and faithful service, which had not always been remunerated financially or recompensed otherwise. In 1592, for example, Beale informed, or perhaps reminded, Burghley that he had supplied Paulet with 'more particular and directe' information regarding Mary and her company than had anyone else, that Buckhurst was witness to 'how plainelie I dealt with [Mary]' when they told her of her impending execution, and that he carried the commission for execution in good faith for Elizabeth's safety. What, Beale asked, had he gained for his service and fidelity? Elizabeth's displeasure, Shrewsbury's suspicion, and 'by sondrie slaunderous libels printed [abroad] in diuers languages' was he defamed as a companion of the hangman.[58] Less than a year later, Beale wrote to Burghley, again noting 'I am so much maligned at home and abroade, for the carrying downe of the Commission for the execution [...] deliuered vnto me by your Lordships, sithe which time I haue neyther had anye Credit or countenaunce'; in the same breath, Beale complained that, 'contrary to promise', he had never been given an official copy of the commission under the Great Seal for his own further reference in self-defence if he were ever called into question.[59] Two years later, in another missive to Burghley, Beale again laid out his history of service and his bad reputation among some who thought he had been 'wonne to a newe Mistresse' (i.e. wooed from Elizabeth by Mary). Far from it, for as he wrote, 'I did nothing but as I was commaunded, and can make good proofe therof for my defence' (from the papers he had collected, no doubt), 'But what gott I by it? As much displeasure at home as anie of the rest, and abroade diffamed with Carryinge downe the hangeman [....] euer sythe I haue lost all my credit and reputation abroade'.[60] Far from his former well-earned status as a legal mind and man of upright character, Beale's reputation after February 1587 was, he feared, tarnished by association with the executioner.

In the end, reputational damage overseas and fear of traveling too far north were significant enough to distress Beale, even if he knew that, both legally and politically, he could not be charged with a crime because all he did in an official capacity was carry the commission for execution as he was commanded to do by the Privy Council. Additionally, although Burghley had advised Beale to go into

as 'secretary' in their early correspondence. See the address leaf, for example, in Chytraeus to Beale, 25 May 1592, AUL, MS 1009/2, item 14 (orig.).

[58] Beale to Burghley, 16 October 1592, BL, Lansdowne MS 72/73, fol. 197v (orig.); at 198r, Beale explains that he is opening up to Burghley 'for that I haue always found your Lordship my especiall good lorde and most relyed vppon your fauor'. By this point Walsingham and Leicester were dead.

[59] Beale to Burghley, 17 March 1593, BL, Lansdowne MS 73/2, fol. 5r (orig.).

[60] Beale to Burghley, 24 April 1595, BL, Lansdowne MS 79, fols 192v, 193v (orig.). The charge regarding a new mistress was also noted in Beale's to Burghley on 16 October 1592.

Star Chamber, presumably during Davison's trial, Beale refused because he did not want to observe the proceedings, potentially be asked a question, and slip in saying something self-incriminating.[61] Back in the 1560s, Beale suffered because of his association with Edward Seymour, earl of Hertford, and his defending the legitimacy of the earl's marriage to Katherine Grey (and, by extension, claim to the succession). Beale remembered all too well how long it took him to earn Elizabeth's trust as a clerk of her Privy Council, and now he feared losing that trust he so cherished. Thus, although in the early 1580s he had become more confident than ever in his position, both politically and religiously, he also knew that his service and rewards were, at bottom, at the queen's pleasure. If Davison's downfall were any barometer of how quickly fortunes could turn, Beale was entirely justified in his fears for his own future and that of his family. In fact, in the aftermath of Davison's downfall Beale contemplated retirement and tried to secure sufficient financial security from Elizabeth to be able to resign quietly and leave his position as a clerk of her Privy Council; the debts and pressure were just too much to bear.[62] Retirement was not to be. He was soon sent abroad in Elizabeth's service. To the Netherlands again, but this time not simply to negotiate for the release of some ships. This time, to sit on a major council.

Another Council (of State)

The queen of Scots was the greatest immediate threat to the stability of the Elizabethan regime, but across the seas the armies of Spain represented the military and existential threat to all Protestant England. The fate of the United Provinces hung very much in the balance during the 1580s. The early 1580s were a difficult time for the nascent Dutch Republic (formally independent since the Act of Abjuration in 1581) because their need for firm leadership and allies went largely unfulfilled. Despite brief episodes of pageantry and military failure associated with the duke of Anjou's assistance, the Dutch rebel provinces in the north were positively independent but also on their heels. When William of Orange was assassinated in 1584, they were left as a ship without a rudder. Also, since 1577, Spanish forces had successfully regained territories in the southern provinces, and by 1585 nearly all of Flanders and Brabant were retaken; by 1589, the Spanish had pushed still farther north with a series of victories under the duke of Parma. The English decision to intervene formally was not taken lightly, but the Dutch rebels led by the provinces of Holland and Zeeland needed help if they were to remain independent, and, after all, it was in England's interest to keep the Spanish from reasserting hegemony over the whole of the Low Countries, the long stretch

[61] Beale's later undated notes, BL, Additional MS 48027, fol. 709v.
[62] Suit of Robert Beale, April? 1587, TNA, SP 12/200, fol. 120r.

of coast opposite English shores very much included. With the Treaty of Nonsuch in 1585 followed by the expeditions of the earl of Leicester to lead military forces, the English became the only thing resembling a firm friend the Dutch had. The period of 1585–87, English leadership under Leicester, was, according to Jonathan Israel, 'in many ways, a formative episode in the history of the Dutch Republic [...and] a time of profound crisis in the Dutch body politic'. As one expects by this point, Beale was painfully aware of how the security of Dutch rebels from Spanish control depended on English assistance—martial, financial, and ideological. Before and after his mission of 1576, he gathered what he could on Dutch affairs relating to trade and treaties with the English, but his and other Protestants' concerns in the mid 1580s looked more towards solidarity in opposition to Catholicism on an international level. His collection of volumes relating to English involvement in the Dutch war is vast and compares favourably to that on Mary.[63] He owned copies of the Treaty of Nonsuch (1585) as well as a memorandum on why Elizabeth should accept the title of 'protector' rather than 'sovereign' of the Netherlands (1585). Also from this period are multiple copies of Leicester's instructions from Elizabeth on his first expedition to the Netherlands; notably, Beale's copy is fuller and more detailed than are other copies. Beale's papers go on to include material on Leicester's expedition and role as governor general, Elizabeth's reproving him for accepting the government of the Netherlands, trade with the Spanish, and so on.[64] As with his papers on Mary, Beale's material on the Netherlands extends back many decades before his own involvement and can bring an overwhelming sense of being lost in a forest. For understanding Beale's position and perspective, a selective use of the evidence can be illuminating.

In summer 1586, for example, when it seems that Burghley had asked Beale for his opinion on Leicester's activity in prohibiting French trade with Spain, Beale assembled his thoughts according to his customary manner.[65] In short, he observed that Leicester had been acting within his authority as an elected governor by the Dutch, not under his commission from Elizabeth, and so these issues were not answerable by the English. Using history as precedent, he pointed to a similar case when the duke of Anjou's actions against Spain stemmed not from his authority as duke of Anjou answerable to the French king but rather from his

---

[63] On the state of the war, see Parker, *Dutch Revolt*, 199–224. Cf. Israel, *Dutch Republic: Its Rise, Greatness, and Fall 1477–1806* (paperback with corrections, Oxford, 1998) 205–30, at 220–1; Simon Adams, 'The Decision to Intervene: England and the United Provinces 1584–1585', in José Martíez Millán (ed.), *Felipe II (1527–1598): Europa y la Monarquía Católica* (Madrid, 1999), 1.19–31. Beale's papers on the war of religion in the Netherlands stretch across several volumes, but important collections include BL, Additional MSS 48014, 48083–4, 48127, 48129; BL, Egerton MS 1694; AUL, MS 1009; BYU, MS 457.

[64] BL, Additional MS 48014, which runs to over 600 fols and includes material gathered before and during Beale's mission from June to October 1587.

[65] 'Beale's Opinion upon the Objections against the Earl of Leicester's Placcard for the Province of Holland', with final paragraphs in Beale's hand, 5 July 1586, TNA, SP 84/9, fols 11r–14v (item 6). Finished version, later misdated to January 1587, BL, Cotton MS Galba, C. XI, fols 103r–6r.

authority as duke of Brabant and answerable to the estates of that region. Nearly a year later in late June 1587, Henry Killigrew, Beale's long-time friend and colleague over many years, was given instructions for his mission to the Netherlands, and while Beale joined him on this occasion, the fact that Beale was not named in the instructions may signify that he had not fully escaped Elizabeth's suspicion after Mary's execution but accompanied Killigrew with the support of Leicester, Walsingham, or Burghley. In any event, Beale kept a journal as a record of his activity between 20 June and 7 October 1587.[66]

The front cover of the journal plainly boasts Beale's position: 'Jornall. When I went with my Lord of Leycester into Holland 1587'. The journal itself is comparatively brief on the daily activities. It notes the comings and goings of various men—English and Dutch—and it briefly mentions the negotiations about men and money. As documentation of Beale's role that summer, the journal is frustratingly thin and mundane when recording movements and dinners. Beale's two nights' dining with the deposed archbishop-elector of Cologne, Gebhard Truchsess, on 24 and 25 July were highlights, as can be seen in Beale's notes kept separately from the journal. Yet, two details relating to family can easily be lost in the banal: first, his writing to his wife Edith and sending of two lanterns and four pairs of bellows; second, his mentioning of a certain 'John' and 'painter' whom he sent to see Bizzarri in Rotterdam.[67] Recording that he wrote to his wife and sent gifts was a nice personal touch. More intriguingly, 'John' was probably Beale's younger brother and the same one who attended previously as a hanger-on of Beale's mission in 1577, while 'painter' had frequently served as a courier across the Channel during the 1580s and might have been one of Walsingham's agents. The journal does not mention John at any other point, but one wonders whether Beale decided to bring his younger brother on this second mission to continue exposing him to the wider world and potentially offer some experience for a future career in government service. When set alongside various other sources, Beale's journal helps to place him at the centre of the action and very much between the Dutch Council of State and the earl of Leicester as governor general.

---

[66] Killigrew's Instructions, 25 June 1587, TNA, SP 84/15, fols 153r–5r. Beale's Journal, 1587, BL, Additional MS 48014, fols 167r–76v. Killigrew's instructions may have been come earlier, or Beale's dates in the journal are a little off; on 25 June Beale and Killigrew had already left London and were at Margate (167v), and on 4 October Beale had made it to London, where he rested for the day (176v).

[67] Beale's Journal, 1587, BL, Additional MS 48014, fols 170v, 175v. Beale had known Painter previously when the latter delivered a book from Henry Brooke in Blois to Beale; the book was *La Sepmaine ou Creation du Monde*, by Guillaume de Saluste du Bartas, first published in Paris in 1578 (e.g. USTC 34602) but reissued many times. Brooke to Beale, 7 April 1581, BL, Cotton MS Otho, E. IV, fol. 20v. See *CSPF* for examples of Painter's activity as a courier; for comment, Read, *Mr Secretary Walsingham*, 2.420. Taviner, 18, mentions the lanterns and bellows as a very rare insight into Beale's personal life; Collinson repeats the incident in a slightly belittling sense: Collinson, 'Servants and Citizens', *Historical Research*, 79:206 (2006), 501. On Beale's younger brother John, see Chapter 2, and on the mission of 1577, Chapter 5. Beale's notes on his dinners with the archbishop-elector follow a copy of Truchsess to Walsingham regarding Leicester, 22 July 1587, BL, Egerton MS 1694, fols 149r–50v. Bizzarri might have been dead by this point, unbeknownst to Beale. *ODNB*.

Killigrew has been more visible to historians than has Beale. Similarly, Leicester's difficulties in the Netherlands in 1586 and 1587 have long been recognized, while Beale's activities have remained in the shadows.[68] From Beale's perspective, the situation in the Netherlands that summer was not good: Leicester's difficulties in fielding and paying sufficient military forces in 1586 weighed heavily and would continue; his personnel choices were controversial among the Dutch; and the Dutch suspected Elizabeth of brokering a peace with Spain that would leave them out to dry. Killigrew and Beale were to serve on the Council of State and negotiate between the Dutch leadership and Leicester and Elizabeth. Their task would not be easy, but Beale was more than capable of representing English interests while also staying in touch with Dutch realities on the ground. His abilities were known to others, so when Thomas Wilkes, who had served for Elizabeth on the Dutch Council until replaced by Beale, informed the Dutch of his replacement in late June, he also offered a glowing endorsement: *'homme de bien, de lettres, de valeur et d'entendement'*. Such praise as a man of competence and understanding (and, as we know, a man of letters) was not without merit, as Leicester soon concurred.[69] By mid July 1587, Beale's eye for detail and his diligent notetaking were evident to Buckhurst when he met with him and Killigrew for a discussion and change of tack because of an evolving situation, and to Walsingham when Beale wrote to the secretary directly from Middelburg regarding the financial difficulties faced by the Dutch, who had simply run out of money and expected Elizabeth to lend significantly more than she already had.[70] Beale and Killigrew continued writing to Walsingham (and Elizabeth directly) about the 'intricate and confused cause', the deteriorating situation more generally, and the little likelihood of defending the town of Sluys (Sluis in Dutch) then under siege. With the loss of Sluys by August 1587 due to the lack of preparation and defence by Dutch forces, Elizabeth was furious because her honour and reputation had been damaged, and she told Beale and Killigrew as much. Despite the lack of organization and money, they hoped on 4 August that God would 'sende vs a good ende, ffor we haue founde a verye confused and waywarde beginninge.' Beale detailed that confused beginning at greater length for Christopher Hatton, now Lord Chancellor, the same day.[71]

---

[68] The classic biography of Killigrew allocates a chapter to its protagonist's role as councillor of state in the Netherlands, but Beale's name is found on just two pages: Miller, *Sir Henry Killigrew*, 199–220, 206–7. On Leicester, Simon Adams's entry in the *ODNB* illustrates the earl's difficulties.

[69] Wilkes to 'M. Deventer', 27 June 1587, TNA, SP 84/15, fol. 166v. On this day Beale dined with various of the Council of State. Beale's Journal, BL, Additional MS 48014, fol. 167v.

[70] Buckhurst to Walsingham, 12 July 1587, TNA, SP 84/16, fols 65r–6v (orig.). Beale to Walsingham, 13 July 1587, TNA, SP 84/16, fols 88r–9v (orig.).

[71] Beale and Killigrew to Walsingham, 13 July, to Elizabeth, 15 July, to Walsingham, 1 August 1587, BL, Cotton MS Galba, D. I, fols 96r–7v, with first quotation at 97r, 100r–2v, 227r–9r (all orig.). Elizabeth to Killigrew and Beale, 1 August 1587, BL, Additional MS 48129, fol. 75r–v (orig.). Beale and Killigrew to Walsingham, 4 August 1587, TNA, SP 84/17, fol. 24r, with second quotation (orig.). Beale's discourse in the form of a letter for Hatton, 4 August 1587, BL, Additional MS 48014, fols

In sitting as the English representatives on the Council of State, Beale and Killigrew were, by all accounts, between a rock and a hard place. They were simultaneously trying to get more commitment and resources from the Dutch to defend their own country, protecting Elizabeth from unexpected financial outlays, and working between Leicester as governor general and the States General of the United Provinces. Although understanding this situation from across the seas might have been difficult in England, Leicester's opinion of Beale's efforts was plain and consistent. To Walsingham in early August he recognized that he was lucky to have Beale with him: 'trulye in my opinnon ther ys not a more suffycient man in England than Mr Beall ys, nor quycker nor of better dispach. He was drownd in England'; moreover, 'I assure ye I euer thought him both an honest & a suffycient man, but never to have that in him that I now have found.'[72] Leicester's candid assessment of Beale's inner character and value for Walsingham was not lost on Beale's brother-in-law, who subsequently wrote to Beale informing him of Leicester's 'favourable report'.[73] As a member of the Privy Council, Burghley was similarly aware. As if he needed further testimony, Leicester wrote about a month later. In a lengthy missive, he observed that regarding the particulars of their daily proceedings Beale and Killigrew would inform separately (they wrote to the Privy Council the same day), but he also included another character assessment of Beale:

Mr Beall [is] an other manner of man than at home he ys accompted of. I do assure ye my Lord I think ther be few so sufficient men as he is[;] he hath tryed him self excellently loued & commended gretly among the best of them for his judgement. and he is both stout & wyse in all matters that [are] brought in questyon almost, he shews him self to be a very sencyble man.[74]

By late September 1587, when it was becoming apparent that Beale would be leaving Killigrew in the Netherlands and heading back to England (much to Beale's own delight after about three months away), Leicester seems to have become a little nervous because he had grown to some degree dependent. Walsingham had written to Leicester, revoking Beale to London, but, in Leicester's view, if Beale were to return while he stayed, 'I shalbe vtterly naked[;] he ys in troth a most suffycient man [...] As for your brother Beall[,] he ys in my books aparte', which is to say a man up to the mighty and grave tasks of international

572r–9v; on Hatton's needing encouragement to keep the faith, see Younger, *Religion and Politics*, 161. For a visual of the siege of Sluys, see the sketch map annotated by Beale in late August, BL, Additional MS 48014, fols 505v–6r.

[72] Leicester to Walsingham, 4 August 1587, TNA, SP 84/17, fols 16v–17r (orig.).
[73] Walsingham to Beale, 7 August 1587, BL, Additional MS 48127, fol. 101r (orig.).
[74] Leicester to Burghley, 11 September 1587, TNA, SP 84/18, fol. 39v (orig.); Killigrew and Beale to the Privy Council follows.

diplomacy for the cause of religion and, moreover, a man of true distinction.[75] Without the greater of his two vital aids, Leicester assumed that he would not have his usual protection in Beale and thus be more vulnerable to slander from (or outmanoeuvring by) the Dutch. As before, he simply referred to Beale for relaying the day-to-day proceedings directly to Elizabeth upon his return to England.[76] Whatever damage had been done by Beale's carrying Mary's death warrant to Fotheringhay, in Leicester's, Walsingham's, Burghley's, and (probably whether she cared to admit it or not) Elizabeth's views, Beale was indispensable in 1587.

Even before his homecoming in early October, he was told to plan a return to the Council of State to serve as a negotiator for peace with Spain. Walsingham and Burghley had known that Elizabeth specifically wanted him in that role, and Walsingham had informed Beale accordingly in early September.[77] Walsingham, for personal reasons, thought it a pity that Beale should go and thought peace with Spain was unrealistic or even advantageous to Spain, while Leicester thought that Beale, as a rather forward advocate for Dutch Protestants against Spain, should most certainly be involved in 'the common service for the church of god'.[78] Characteristically, Burghley was more dispassionate and less certain that Beale would make a good negotiator in this instance. As he put it, 'for diuers respectes I did mislike' the idea, 'for that Mr Beale was not thought a furtherer of the peace but had an opinion that it would neuer be benefitiale, nor yet would be kept', noting also 'Mr Bealls vnwillingness to deale hearin'.[79] So, apart from Walsingham's reasonings or Leicester's desires, Burghley knew that Beale simply did not want to follow his queen's orders and negotiate a peace he thought worthless. His confidence before Archbishop Whitgift in Lambeth Palace in 1584 had grown to such a degree in 1587 that he would expedite the execution of Mary Queen of Scots behind Elizabeth's back and then refuse to serve as her negotiator for a peace he did not believe in. He was a loyal and trusted servant who looked out for what he understood as the best interests of Elizabeth and England, but he was no automaton.[80]

In the end, Beale did not again cross the seas to negotiate a peace in the Netherlands until 1600. Between his return to London in October 1587 and then, he continued collecting as much material as he could on the developments

---

[75] Leicester to Walsingham, 16 September 1587, TNA, SP 84/18, fol. 82r–v (orig.).

[76] Leicester to Elizabeth, 29 September 1587, TNA, SP 84/18 fol. 211 (orig.).

[77] Walsingham to Beale, 2 September 1587, BL, Additional MS 48127, fol. 97r–v (orig.).

[78] Leicester to Walsingham, 16 September 1587, TNA, SP 84/18, fol. 82r (orig.). Cf. Leicester to Beale, 28 October 1587, BL, Additional MS 29549, fols 19r–22v (orig.), in which the earl emphasizes both Beale's intimate knowledge of how to negotiate with the Dutch and his own frustrations: 'I am entred so farr into this comen place [regarding their lack of zeal in religion] as I can hardly get out. Bear with me I pray you' (22r).

[79] Burghley's postscript to a letter dated 11 October, TNA, SP 84/18, fol. 285r.

[80] In the context of the death warrant, Taviner, 243, makes a similar point. Cf. Collinson, 'Puritans, Men of Business', 187–211.

relating to the war. His nervous view of making peace with Spain was shared by many, Walsingham in England as well as the Dutch themselves, including Adrian Saravia, an eager supporter of Leicester and theologian at the University of Leiden who wrote to Beale on exactly this matter.[81] Despite the fact that Beale had not yet been paid the £40 due to him for his services, several months later he put pen to paper for his thoughts on a new treaty to be struck between Elizabeth and the States General. It seems probable that he and Bartholomew Clerk, another assistant in the Netherlands and joint author of this thought piece, were asked to produce it for informing policy, especially given the amount of work they put into the draft version and the existence of multiple finished copies. Also, it would not have been the first time he put his thoughts down regarding a treaty between England and the Netherlands. As Burghley would recall, back in 1584 Beale argued that it was lawful for the princes of the Holy Roman Empire, including those in the Netherlands, to establish their own treaties with foreign powers as doing so was within their privileges and liberties in the Empire.[82] It was possible for Beale to offer such written pieces only because of his experience in the field and personal archive. Not only did he keep copies of what he wrote and originals of what he received, he also acquired and retained many originals of correspondence between others like Leicester and Buckhurst, as well as multiple copies of Leicester's instructions in December 1585. Perhaps unsurprisingly and as noted previously, the copies Beale kept were fuller and of a more particular and private nature than copies found elsewhere.[83] Although he could not have predicted that he would serve as one of Elizabeth's negotiators for peace with Spain within a year of his death in 1601, his proclivity to acquire and retain these and related materials for later use, hoard as it were, was by 1587 his *modus operandi* and, in the view of others, his *raison d'être*.

The Road to Hamburg (almost) and Beyond

Beale's interest and engagement in relations between England and the Hanseatic League had stretched back at least to 1577 and would continue for the rest of his

---

[81] Saravia to Beale and Gilpin, 6 September 1587, enclosing Arnoldus Cornelius to Saravia on the day before, BL, Additional MS 48083, fols 192r–4v (orig.). On Saravia, including his time in England during the previous decades, *ODNB*.

[82] Monies due to various before 12 October 1587, dated 2 March 1588, TNA, SP 84/22, fol. 26r. Notes by Clerk and Beale, 27 April 1589, BL, Cotton MS Galba, D. IV, fols 167r–9v; undated but associated with a letter dated 26 May 1588, BL, Cotton MS Galba, D. III, fols 157r–8v; draft with Beale's amendments, dated 27 April 1589, TNA, SP 103/34, fols 103r–6r. Memorial by Beale, 1584, TNA, SP 83/23, fol. 237r–v.

[83] See above, n. 63. For Beale's versions of Leicester's instructions, BL, Additional MSS 48014, fols 203r–6v; 48084, fols 42r–53v; 48129, fols 80r–v (abstract). Cf. BL, Cotton MS Galba, C. VIII, fols 119v–20r, 215r–v; BL, Harley MS 36, fol. 265r; TNA, SP 84/5, fols 143r–4r (item 80).

life. By the mid 1580s, he had written (at least in part) multiple treatises on the state of play regarding the liberties and trading rights of the Merchant Adventurers in the Hanse towns and the same of the Hanse in England. As ever, his writings were historically grounded and legally informed because he had compiled the relevant documentation to prove his points. His pieces, which exist as drafts in his own archive, were almost certainly sent as finished works for those in the Privy Council who directed policy accordingly. By 1585, the situation had not yet been resolved, and Beale became increasingly involved in direct negotiations with the Hanse.

Two representatives from the Hanse were in London in summer and autumn 1585—Georg Liseman and Dr Joannes Schulte (Johann/John Schultz). They had been sent for exploratory talks but did not have the authorization to conclude a new treaty, yet in reality the English and the Hanseatic towns were looking to see who would blink first. The English wanted their residence restored at Hamburg before privileges would be restored for the Hanse in London's Steelyard, while the Hanse wanted the English to send an embassy to the Low Countries where representatives from all interested parties (including the king of Spain) could attend. In the end, nothing was accomplished other than that mutual mistrust was deepened and prolonged, while Beale was caught in the middle, collecting copies of the Germans' paperwork and correspondence. Given his previous experience and ability to speak in German with the representatives from the Hanseatic League, it is no surprise that he was in the thick of it.[84]

Beale served as something of a messenger and go-between August 1585 and the autumn. From his own and the Hanse representatives' accounts, he participated in the discussions both on behalf of the Privy Council (signing letters as its clerk) and acting of his own accord in writing and verbally (independently of the Privy Council). Because he was writing his own letters apart from those of the Privy Council, a potential difference of opinion or interpretation might arise; in fact, the Hanse pointed it out on multiple occasions that the letters of the 'most learned' ('doctissimus') Beale varied from those of the Council. A particular visit by Beale to the Hanse in the Steelyard on 24 August was a little contentious, with Beale relaying to Walsingham the impasse regarding process between the English and Hanse, and Liseman noting the difficulties between Beale and Adam Wachendorf, secretary of the Steelyard, whom Liseman later noted was entirely familiar with and devoted to Beale. According to Liseman, Beale had mocked the disunity and lack of understanding among the emperor and German princes, and then got into a disagreement with Liseman himself before stopping 'his useless

---

[84] Lloyd, *England and the German Hanse*, 332–4. Beale's copies of relevant papers from Liseman and Schulte's mission, BL, Additional MS 48009, fols 321r–67v; further documents printed in Höhlbaum, *Kölner Inventar*. On Beale's German see Chapter 5.

babble'.[85] Beale's involvement continued despite the low probability of rapprochement between the English and Hanse. Schulte noted his collaboration with Beale and his other activity in his letters that autumn. Just before leaving London to return home, he wrote a letter to Beale bidding him well, requesting assistance for his brother (then in debtors' prison), and sending a smoked salmon. More suggestive of Beale's interests, though, was that Schulte asked Beale to return his letters and other papers that he had lent to Beale for the purposes of copying them.[86]

The culmination of Beale's interests and efforts regarding the Hanse to this point is found in his lengthy treatise of 1586 that extends to over eighty folios. The draft remains among his papers, while a finished version is found elsewhere.[87] Written in Latin to refute the slanders ('*calumnias*') spread in the Holy Roman Empire by the Hanse for their own private interests but contrary to the truth (in Beale's view), the treatise dug deep into the historical record and demonstrated his high-level access to state papers, even dating, for example, letters sent by Elizabeth to the senate of Hamburg. Indeed, Beale refers to Elizabeth's out-letters to the Germans, her in-letters from the German princes and cities, treaties and agreements over the years, and relevant printed works; along the way, one finds occasional trefoils in the margins to draw the reader's attention.[88] The main text of the draft is in a fine secretary hand, but Beale amended the text and added examples and detail in his own hand both in the margins and between the lines. Although it is admittedly plausible that another wrote the text while he simply

---

[85] Commissioners of the Hanse to the Privy Council, 15 and 31 August 1585, TNA, SP 82/2, fols 18r, 33r (orig.). Beale to Walsingham, 29 August 1585, TNA, SP 12/181, fols 230r–1v (orig.). Beale for the Privy Council, 27 August and 11 September 1585, in Höhlbaum, *Kölner Inventar*, 820–1, 831–2. Report by Liseman, September 1585, in Höhlbaum, *Kölner Inventar*, 855–63, noting Beale on 24 August at 862–3. Liseman to Suderman, 12 December 1585, in Höhlbaum, *Kölner Inventar*, noting Wachendorf and Beale at p. 854. Richard Ehrenberg, *Hamburg und England im Zeitalter der Königin Elisabeth* (Jena, 1896), 175. Cf. Beale's letters of 25 August and 11 September (old style) noticed in Simson, *Danziger Inventar*, 750–1.

[86] Schulte to Burghley, 7 September, to Walsingham, 22 October, to Beale, 14 November 1585, TNA, SP 82/2, fols 54r–6v, 68r–9r, 75r–v (all orig.). Beale's copies in BL, Additional MS 48009, fols 321r–67v, are all of one hand and paper stock, and appear to have been copied en masse, which suggests that Beale tried to return the papers to their owner. Whether Schulte ever received his originals remains unknown. Not all was lost for Beale with Liseman, as seen in the latter's letter to Beale of December 1585, printed in Simson, *Danziger Inventar*, 946–53.

[87] 'Vera Declaratio eorum quae inter Serenissima Angliae Reginam [...] et Civitates Hansaticas acta sunt', draft with brief notes following, 1586, BL, Additional MS 48011, fols 82r–164v. Finished version incorporating Beale's amendments but with underlining not found in the draft and probably copied from an intermediary, BL, Harley MS 5112, fols 17r–75v (old foliation 26r–84v), ending at 151r of the draft. Beale's draft is here preferred.

[88] 'Vera Declaratio', 1586, BL, Additional MS 48011, fol. 85r, with marginal annotation dating Elizabeth's letter 8 October 1577; fols 90r and 133r, with reference to the description of Poland by Marcin Kromer (also Martinus Cromerus). Beale's library might have included an impression of Kromer's *Polonia* published in 1588 at Cologne, which, tellingly, was published in Spanish (USTC 339383): BL, Hargrave MS 107, fol. 33r. Various other dates, statutes, and authors are supplied in the margins throughout the treatise. Elizabeth's letter has not been located. Example of trefoil in the finished version, BL, Harley MS 5112, fol. 53r. See the comment on trefoils and Elizabeth's attention in R. B. Wernham, *Before the Armada: The Growth of English Foreign Policy, 1485–1588* (London, 1966), 236.

offered annotations, nobody other than Beale had amassed such a collection of papers relating to the Hanse and had previously demonstrated their engagement in treatises like this one. Much of Beale's research extended back to the fifteenth century to lay the foundations for his discussions of the negotiations and embassies of the 1570s and 1580s, such as the efforts of Englishmen like George Gilpin and William Waad, and the German embassy of Schulte and Liseman in 1585, when Beale was directly involved.[89] After offering a summary of the state of affairs in winter 1585–6, Beale then discussed the establishment and history of the Hanse in London's Steelyard, which at its foundation 'in 1259 or 1260' was called 'Guildhalla Teutonicorum', and offered a discussion of the statutes and international agreements between England and the Empire; clearly he had relatively easy access to the records of the Tower, and, indeed, he appears a year later to have served as one of Burghley's auditors of the Tower's records and staff.[90] Beale's goal in writing this treatise was to counter the rumours and bending of truth in the Empire by setting down a factual narrative based on historical and legal research and with detail, examples, and citation of sources. After all, the draft title page reflected his long-standing flair in manuscript title pages and included his insertion of 'VERA' before 'Declaratio', for he intended this work to be no mere opinion piece. Characteristically, in draft Beale added specificities, struck through generalities, and adjusted grammar and syntax. The audience was unmistakably the princes of the Empire and the emperor himself, whom Beale sought to convince that they should look beyond the complaints of the Hanse who spun the story to their own advantage. Try as he did, the impasse regarding reciprocal trade privileges remained (see Fig. 13).

It remains unknown whether or to what extent the treatise circulated in the Empire, but Beale's expertise demonstrated in the treatise and more broadly had unintended consequences. In time he was to prepare for another embassy. Between 1586 and 1588, he had participated in the execution of Mary Queen of Scots and been overseas with Leicester to help the Dutch defend themselves, but now he was yet again to negotiate commercial grievances. He had also remained directly involved in matters relating to the Hanse, even countersigning and corroborating the queen's promise, signed in her own hand, regarding a favour for Schulte, who, like many overseas, held Beale in higher esteem than most of Beale's own countrymen.[91] More directly still, the Hanse continued to press that,

---

[89] 'Vera Declaratio', 1586, BL, Additional MS 48011, fols 92r, 93r, 96v–113r.

[90] 'Vera Declaratio', 1586, BL, Additional MS 48011, fol. 113v. The charter in question was of 1260. See Lloyd, England and the German Hanse, 19–21. Burghley's instructions for Beale, 1587, BL, Lansdowne MS 103/33, fols 81r–2v (heavily amended draft). On the Tower, see Popper, Specter of the Archive, ch. 1.

[91] Schulte to Burghley and Walsingham, 19 August 1586, TNA, SP 82/2, fol. 140r (orig.); as before, Beale is referred to as 'dominum', rendered by CSPF as 'Sir'. Beale's reputation abroad seemed to cause various people to assume occasionally that his social and political status was greater than, in fact, it was. Cf. Leicester's comments above.

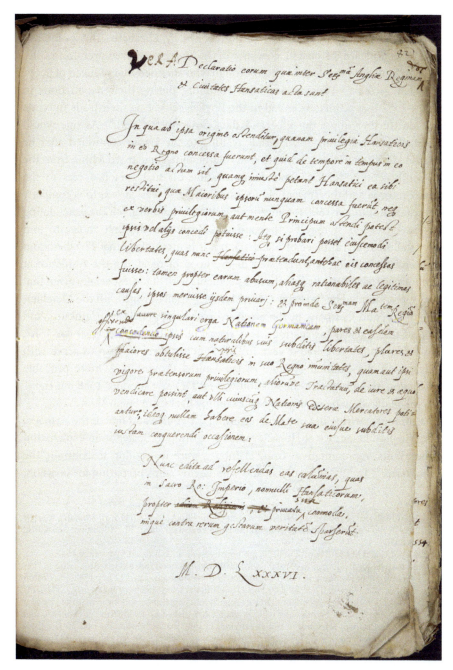

Fig. 13 Beale's treatise on the Hanse, 'Vera declaratio', 1586. BL, Additional MS 48011, fol. 82r.

Reproduced with permission from the British Library.

like other licences granted, Beale's licence for the sole import of steel violated their trading privileges and ought to be revoked by Elizabeth. This point was made when Richard Saltonstall, governor of the Merchant Adventurers, and Giles Fletcher, brother of the dean of Peterborough who attended Mary Queen of Scots' execution, wrote to Walsingham from Hamburg during their negotiations in August 1587 that ultimately ended in the English relocating their trade interests to Stade (further down the Elbe and thus closer to the sea).[92] As one would expect, Beale's collecting of materials relating to the Hanse continued after he completed his treatise in 1586, with one volume in particular stretching from the thirteenth century to 1587 and demonstrating his first-person access to the queen's records and the Tower.[93] It appears that Beale was chosen to accompany Saltonstall in summer 1588 for another mission to Hamburg, but the exact dating remains uncertain. It may be the case that Beale was the first choice to join Saltonstall in 1587 (in place of Fletcher), but it is more likely that Elizabeth and the Merchant Adventurers persisted in the hope of regaining the residence at Hamburg in 1588 even after reaching agreements with Stade, especially given that Beale was appointed by the Privy Council in May 1588 to work with the Merchant Adventurers and Germans in the Steelyard regarding privileges, Hamburg, and Stade. If the undated instructions, two copies of which survive, were for 1587, then Beale would have had a very full year indeed were he also to serve with Killigrew on the Council of State in the United Provinces. A more probable explanation, though, is that the mission was set for early summer 1588 but rightfully called off when news arrived of the coming fleet from Spain.[94]

As rumours swirled in Germany regarding the course and fate of the Armada, with Wilhelm, landgrave of Hesse, eventually writing to Beale for an explanation of the events, representatives from Hamburg were in London to continue the negotiations.[95] In July and August, and with enemy ships preparing for invasion,

---

[92]   Richard Saltonstall and Giles Fletcher to Walsingham, 1 August 1587, TNA, SP 82/2, fols 168r–9r (orig.). See Beale's copies of papers relating to the agreement with Stade, BL, Additional MS 48010, fols 593v–608r.
[93]   BL, Additional MS 48010, with first-person note by Beale at 202r dated 8 May June 1587.
[94]   Instructions for Beale and Saltonstall, with credence, 1587 or 1588, along with a letter of credence from the city of Hamburg to Hatton, Burghley, and Walsingham, dated 12 July 1588, BL, Cotton MS Nero, B. IX, fols 143r–9r; TNA, SP 82/3, fols 21r–33r (letter from Hamburg at 18r, orig.). TNA, PC 2/15, pp. 146–50. From correspondence later in August and September, it is clear that the city also wrote to Elizabeth on 9 or 10 July. The issue of dating was picked up in Ehrenberg, *Hamburg und England*, 181, but without reference to Beale's activities in 1587 that complicate the case for the argument that the instructions come from that year. On Thomas Bodley's planned embassy to Denmark via Hamburg in August 1588, for which admittedly no evidence survives that he went, see *AGR*, p. 125; *ODNB* assumes that he did based on the acts of the Privy Council.
[95]   Wilhelm to Beale, 10 December 1588, AUL, MS 1009/2, item 3 (orig.). Roughly twenty printed pamphlets in German spread the news regarding the Armada, so the landgrave was entirely justified in asking Beale for clarification. For one example, see Anon., *Warhafftige Zeytung vnd Beschreibung von der Gewaltigen Armada* (Cologne, 1588) (USTC 705682). Sebastian van Bergen, representing the city of Hamburg, was in London from late July to late September, having been introduced in the letter to Hatton, Burghley, and Walsingham, 12 July 1588, TNA, SP 82/3, fol. 18r (orig.). On Van Bergen's

the English had other things on their minds than trade grievances with Hamburg, but the city's representative and secretary, Sebastian van Bergen, worked as best as he could with Beale, the Privy Council, and the Merchant Adventurers to secure a deal. Van Bergen reached out directly to Beale seeking his assistance in dealing with the Merchant Adventurers regarding the residence at Stade and the city of Hamburg's desire to have the residence returned to them. After Van Bergen had received an initial response from the Merchant Adventurers that August, Beale and his old friend, John Herbert, who also had experience with the Hanse, were named by Hatton, Burghley, and Walsingham as commissioners and intermediaries 'bycause we haue not leisure our selues to attende the cause'.[96] One of the newer complaints that the English had with Hamburg was the latter's neutrality regarding the war with Spain, a touchy subject that Van Bergen discussed privately with Saltonstall and in writing with Beale. As a Lutheran stronghold, Hamburg could reasonably have been expected to ally with England on the point of religion against Spain, and this issue will not have been lost on Beale, whose activity for international Protestantism had recently kicked into high gear.[97]

The depth of Beale's role that September is seen not only in his copies of relevant papers (propositions and answers, summary accounts) but also in his drafting of Elizabeth's closing statement for Van Bergen on 29 September. The heavily annotated Latin draft in Beale's papers found its final versions sent to Hamburg and translated into English for the state papers.[98] Here he laid out the three principal points of issue: Hamburg's neutrality, the residence at Hamburg, and English ships (men of war) in the Elbe harassing other ships. Beale's amending others' letters was nothing new (plenty of examples are found with his marginal and interlinear annotations), but drafting an entire royal statement was comparatively rare for Beale. Then again, none was better placed to summarize the situation at the end of Van Bergen's embassy that summer; then again, Elizabeth, Hatton, Burghley, and Walsingham had larger concerns than the Hamburgers in September 1588.

mission, Beale's collection of relevant papers in BL, Additional MS 48115, supplies the context and detail behind Elizabeth's response to Van Bergen, late September 1588, TNA, SP 82/3, fols 36r–7r.
[96] Van Bergen to Beale, 18 August 1588, BL, Additional MS 48115, fol. 362r–v (orig.). Letter of commission to Beale and Herbert, 31 August 1588, BL, Additional MS 48115, fol. 183r (orig.); Herbert is named 'A. B.' and Beale 'C. D.' in a minute of Elizabeth to Hamburg, September 1588, BL, Additional MS 48115, fols 60r–5v, which differs from her other response in September, TNA, SP 82/3, fols 36r–7r. Two copies of the replies from the Merchant Adventurers to Van Bergen, dated 23 August 1588, BL, Additional MS 48115, fols 106–9v, 166r–7v.
[97] Van Bergen to Beale, 9 September 1588, BL, Additional MS 48115, fol. 350r–v (orig.). On Hamburg and religion, see Wolfgang Seegrün, 'Schleswig-Holstein', in Anton Schindling and Walter Ziegler (eds), *Die Territorien des Reichs im Zeitalter der Reformation und Konfessionalisierung: Land und Konfession 1500–1650, 2: Der Nordosten* (Münster, 1993), 140–64.
[98] Reply of Elizabeth to Van Bergen, [29] September 1588, BL, Additional MS 48115, fols 359r–61v (Beale's draft omitting day of month); TNA, SP 82/3, fols 36r–7r (English translation omitting day); orig. calendared in Simson, *Danziger Inventar*, 954–5. Proposals from Van Bergen, responses from the Merchant Adventurers, and additional materials of September in BL, Additional MS 48115.

The threats posed by Spain and its Armada that year and subsequently were directly related to English relations with the Hanse because, notwithstanding any claims to neutrality, if Hanseatic merchants delivered to Spain anything that could be considered aid (such as foodstuffs or munitions), then they could be seen as supplying England's enemy during a time of war.

This happened the very next summer and after the Hanse had been warned. In short, Elizabeth's naval forces detained Hanseatic merchants outside Lisbon, thus forbidding them to deliver their goods, which probably included grain of various types, masts and cordage, beans and bacon; powder, ordnance, or other weaponry might also have been aboard the sixty Hanse ships seized.[99] The twin issues were the English retaining of these goods as prizes during wartime and the returning of the vessels themselves. The Privy Council issued a decree listing the reasons why the English proceeded as they did, but soon Beale was charged with writing a full justification for an international audience. At Burghley's request for such a 'declaration', Walsingham told Beale to discuss matters with the civil lawyer John Hammond as well as a certain 'Dr Foorde'. Within a few days Beale drafted what ultimately became the official royal statement, but it was much more than a rehashing of English relations with the Hanse.[100] Alongside the now well-rehearsed English position regarding trading privileges and the Hanseatic League's feigned neutrality, Beale, still smarting from the thought of a Catholic invasion, inveighed strongly against Philip of Spain and the pope. Having been on the inside of the past few years' negotiations, Beale offered commentary and reproduction of key sources during Van Bergen's embassy, and his direct reference to the alderman of the Steelyard, Mauritz Timmerman, is not surprising. Beyond the expected for this piece, Beale wrote that the failing of the Spanish Armada was to the advantage of all Protestant peoples, the Hanse very much included. He noted further that Spanish machinations via Bernardino de Mendoza and others, especially Jesuits, had resulted in various plots to overthrow the English regime. Tying the Hanse directly to Philip, Beale argued that trading with the enemy of Protestantism was making an enemy of oneself, and so the English were entirely justified according to the laws of nations in confiscating the Hanse's cargos as contraband in a time of war. Measures of how successful Beale's

---

[99] Read, *Lord Burghley*, 449–50, offers the context of the previous year's Armada. Order and decree of the Privy Council, TNA, PC 2/16, pp. 192–3. Broader discussion linking to Spanish activity in R. B. Wernham, *After the Armada: Elizabethan England and the Struggle for Western Europe 1588–1595* (Oxford, 1984), 256–8.

[100] Walsingham to Burghley, 15 July 1589, BL, Harley MS 6994, fol. 187r–v (orig.). Robert Beale, *Declaratio Cavsarvm, Qvibvs Serenissimae Maiestatis Angliae Classiarij adducti* (London, 1589) (STC 9197), with English translation for the domestic audience as *A Declaration of the Cavses* (London, 1589) (STC 9196). Latin draft with Beale's heavy annotations, with one finished version that nevertheless varies from the published text, BL, Additional MS 48023, fols 220r–44v; the printed English version is enclosed. The work might also have been included among Beale's books: BL, Hargrave MS 107, fol. 40r.

Latin pamphlet became can be seen in the editions (Latin, German, Dutch) published in Delft, Erfurt, and elsewhere, but they can also be seen in the vigorous and comparatively lengthy confutation Beale's work received on behalf of the Hanseatic city of Lübeck.[101] The author of the Hanse's response, the civilian Kaspar Schuerman, was every bit as detailed, orderly, and biting as Beale would have been if the roles had been reversed. Based in Antwerp as secretary of the Hanse office there, Schuerman had a deep knowledge of the history between the Hanse and England, and his confutation represented enough of a threat for Burghley to ask Beale to prepare an additional refutation. In collaboration with Laurence Tomson, a scholar and administrator of significant experience, Beale was to call on his 'observacions and travayle', never mind his recent experience in writing the *Declaratio*. In the end, a further piece never came to the press, but in his Latin notes Beale dissected Schuerman's work page by page, answering each point as forcefully as possible. After addressing the final issue on Schuerman's page 59 (regarding English Catholics' payment of fines), Beale thought his answers sufficient for a response and was certain that the fair reader would see how false Schuerman's arguments were (see Fig. 14).[102]

Despite the antagonism with Schuerman, Beale established a working if not friendly relationship with another historian and humanist of renown in northern Germany, David Chytraeus, the orthodox Lutheran theologian and professor at the University of Rostock. Chytraeus had an interest in the history of the Hanse and had been a correspondent of Beale's friend, Daniel Rogers, but upon Rogers's death Beale took it upon himself to continue the correspondence in his friend's place. In replying to Chytraeus's final letter to Rogers in which Chytraeus offered a lengthy update on Polish and Swedish affairs, Beale narrated his common history with Rogers, first in Germany under Philip Melanchthon, 'our common teacher of illustrious memory' (*'sub communi praeclarae memoriae praeceptore'*), then in France, and later as clerks of Elizabeth's Privy Council. Offering a tantalizing detail on his early life, Beale observed that he knew the current chancellor of Poland, Jan Zamoyski, formerly to be rector at Padua (*'quem ego olim Rectorem Patauij noui'*), which could only have been between 1563 when Zamoyski was elected rector in law and 1565 when he returned to Poland. This detail offers further evidence that Beale sent his material in favour of the Hertford marriage to Padua in 1563. It seems plausible, given Cecil's information at the time, that the

---

[101] Beale's *Declaratio* in German printed at Erfurt (USTC 615815), German again, n.p. (USTC 2215041), Dutch at Delft (USTC 422717), Latin at Delft (USTC 429242). Kaspar Schuerman's *Confvtatio Cavssarvm* was published at Antwerp in 1590 (USTC 406861). This now very rare work exists in two copies at the Bodleian, in Oxford; the copies at Queen's College, Oxford, Vault: KK.k.56(1), and Balliol College, Oxford, Special Collection: 910 e 6 (2), appear to be of the same impression (not a variant from Lübeck, as suggested by the catalogue). On Schuerman's activity during the late 1580s, see Höhlbaum, *Kölner Inventar*, 280–315.
[102] Burghley to Beale and Tomson, 3 August 1590, BL, Additional MS 48115, fol. 207r (orig.), followed by Beale's notes, fols 208r–16v. On Tomson, *ODNB*.

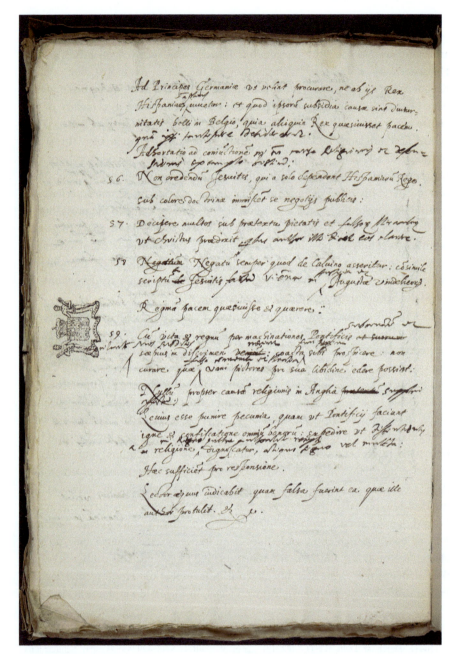

Fig. 14 Beale's notes in refutation of arguments in favour of the Hanse, 1590. BL, Additional MS 48115, fol. 216v.

Reproduced with permission from the British Library.

men of law at Padua replied, possibly also sending to Beale a printed copy of their university's statutes. Also, corroborating his previous knowledge of Chytraeus's interest in the Hanse, Beale mentioned that Rogers had shown him a particular work by Chytraeus on the Hanseatic League, and this work might well have been the 'Hansae Teutonicae Delineatio' discussed previously, on which Beale's notes survive. In any event, Beale asked Chytraeus for more information about the early history of the Hanse, hoping to establish a correspondence just as Chytraeus had previously with Rogers.[103]

Chytraeus responded enthusiastically. Although not all of his letters to Beale survive, those extant show that Chytraeus wrote to Beale relatively frequently with news from Poland and the Baltic more broadly, and Chytraeus is the most likely source for Beale's German copies of Zamoyski's letter to King Sigismund III and broader news from Poland in autumn 1591. He admitted that he could not help Beale very much regarding the early history of the Hanse, but in return he asked Beale for information about their early residence, 'Gildehalla vestra', in London, and widened their correspondence to include Reiner Reineccer, the noted historian not too far from Rostock at the University of Frankfurt an der Oder.[104] Beale and Chytraeus continued to correspond on affairs in the Baltic

---

[103] Chytraeus to Rogers, 24 December 1590, AUL, MS 1009/2, item 13 (orig.). Rogers had died on 11 February 1591 before the letter was delivered in March. *ODNB*. For additional correspondence from Chytraeus to Rogers, see *Davidis Chytraei Theologi ac Historici Eminentissimi, Rostochiana in Academia Professoris quondam primarii Epistolae* (Hanau, 1614) (VD17 1:049418Y). Beale to Chytraeus, April 1591, AUL, MS 1009/1, item 8, quotations from fol. 1r; the draft here does not include a date in April, but a later endorsement offers 16 April; the final letter as sent was dated 10 April and is printed in *Davidis Chytraei [...] Epistolae*, 1210–12. The mention of Padua lends evidence to Cecil's comment in 1564 about Beale's treatise on the Hertford marriage. Cecil's minute on the interrogatories for Hales, 3 May 1564, CP, 154/65. The language Beale uses here does not suggest that he spent any time or learned aspects of civil law at Padua. For the statutes, BL, Hargrave MS 107, fol. 45v. See Chapter 3. On Chytraeus, see *DB*; Karl-Heinz Glaser and Steffen Stuth (eds), *David Chytraeus (1530–1600): Norddeutscher Humanismus in Europa: Beiträge zum Wirken des Kraichgauer Gelehrten* (Ubstadt-Weiher, 2000). On Zamoyski's early travels and Padua, see Michael Tworek, 'Education: The Polish-Lithuanian Commonwealth', in Howard Louthan and Graeme Murdoch (eds), *A Companion to the Reformation in Central Europe* (Leiden, 2015), 359–89, at 365–7; Adam Działyński (ed.), *Collectanea Vitam Resque Gestas Joannis Zamoyscii, Magni Cancellarii et Summi Ducis Reipublicam Polonae* (Posnań, 1861), 9 (on the rectorship); cf. the brief entry in Jerzy Jan Lerski, *Historical Dictionary of Poland, 966–1945* (Westport, CT, 1996), 678. The four letters to Zamoyski in Beale's possession in 1584–5 (in the context of John Herbert's mission to Elbing, Poland, and Prussia) mention nothing of Beale or Padua. BL, Additional MS 48009, fols 437v–8r, 441v–2r, 508r–v, 539r–v. Beale's notes on Chytraeus's history of the Hanse, BL, Additional MS 14029, fols 41v–50r.

[104] Chytraeus to Beale, 15 March 1592/3? (misdated 1597 in the catalogue), BYU, MS 457, item 51 (orig.), with mention of his previous letter of August 1591 at fol. 1r, quotation at 1v. The letter dated the Ides of August 1591 is printed in *Davidis Chytraei [...] Epistolae*, pp. 740–1, which notes Beale's of 10 April. Zamoyski to Sigismund, 26 August 1591, with news from Poland, 14 September 1591, BL, Additional MS 14028, fols 105r–10v, followed by Melanchthon's holograph notes on the succession of kings of Bohemia and Hungary, 113r–v. Cf. German copies of correspondence by Sigismund and his Council, September 1592, BL, Stowe MS 163, fols 34r–42v. In his to Beale of 25 May 1592, AUL, MS 1009/2, item 14 (orig.), Chytraeus mentions another letter of February 1592, to which Reiner Reineccer apparently added his own letter to Beale; no correspondence between Beale and Reineccer has yet been located, but Beale probably owned Reineccer's major work of history, *Historia Julia*, 3 vols (Helmstedt, 1594–7) (VD16 R 886–7); BL, Hargrave MS 107, fol. 20v. On Reineccer, *DB*.

regions and history of the Hanse, sending each other details and examples of the early years. Even more suggestive of Beale's international reputation is that Chytraeus also sent Beale various printed books, including his own *Chronicon Saxoniae* published in 1593. For reasons unclear, the correspondence petered out in the mid 1590s, potentially with Chytraeus writing something he later regretted.[105] In any event, Beale's exchanges with the Lutheran humanist and historian at the University of Rostock demonstrate the breadth of Beale's resources regarding affairs in northern Germany and the Baltic in general, and regarding the Hanse in particular. He pursued multiple avenues of information, both within London and beyond, collected vast quantities of manuscript and printed material, and turned his factual knowledge and broader understanding into useful material for the government. His written accounts on English relations with the Hanse took stock of and illuminated current events by offering a historical and archival perspective unmatched in England (but probably equalled in Schuerman's *Confvtatio*). Beale's service in this regard was practical and utilitarian to serve the immediate purposes of negotiating residences and privileges for the Merchant Adventurers in Hamburg and the Hanse in London, and then later to justify English activity in a time of war. His historical interests here were pragmatic, concrete, and precise in political and economic terms and goals. In other ways, though, his interests and activities could be more ideologically and theoretically motivated (see Figs 15 and 16).

Religion and Parliament

The parliament of 1589 was brief, lasting from 4 February to 29 March.[106] As before, Beale sat for Dorchester, and his work included sitting in February on the committee relating to the subsidy seen as onerous and unwelcome but necessary due to continued threats of Spanish invasion. In fact, an unprecedented double subsidy was granted by Parliament; given Beale's complaints regarding his own finances, a double subsidy would have been particularly taxing his pocketbook. Nevertheless, as he later claimed to Burghley, he was instrumental in getting the subsidy bill passed, for 'I did helpe to ende a greate and longe strife, touching

---

[105] Chytraeus to Beale, 15 July 1593, printed in *Davidis Chytraei [...] Epistolae*, pp. 896–7, noting Beale's own of 12 August 1592. Chytraeus to Beale, 20 August 1593, BL, Egerton MS 1693, fol. 77r–v (orig.). The *Chronicon Saxoniae* (Leipzig, 1593) (USTC 628454), is listed in the booklist, BL, Hargrave MS 107, fol. 25r. Chytraeus to Beale, 26 February 1595/6, AUL, MS 1009/2, item 15 (orig.), noting his inconsiderate letter of the year before.

[106] The classic account remains Neale, *Elizabeth I and Her Parliaments, 1584–1601*, 193–239, but cf. Collinson, 396–400. For documents, Hartley, *Proceedings*, 2.401–97. For Beale's committee work, *HoP:HoC*. D'Ewes, *Compleat Journal*, 428–55, adds the detail (p. 440) that on 27 February Beale joined several others of the Commons in meeting with the Lords regarding a message from Elizabeth, and joined some others on a committee regarding the pier at Hartlepool.

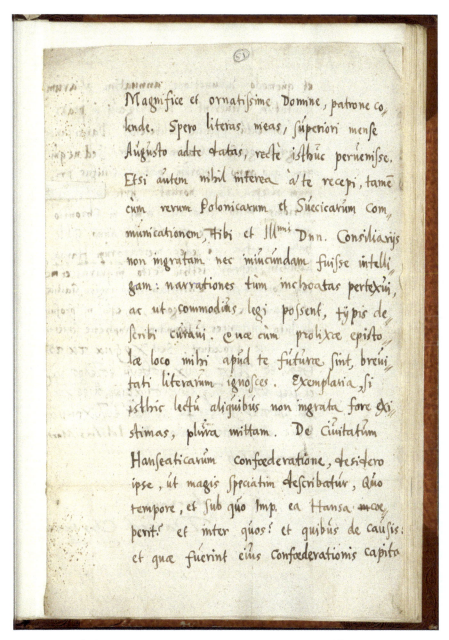

Fig. 15 David Chytraeus to Beale, 15 March 1592/3? BYU, MSS 457, item 51, fol. 1r (orig.).

Reproduced with permission from Tom Perry Special Collections, Harold B. Lee Library, Brigham Young University.

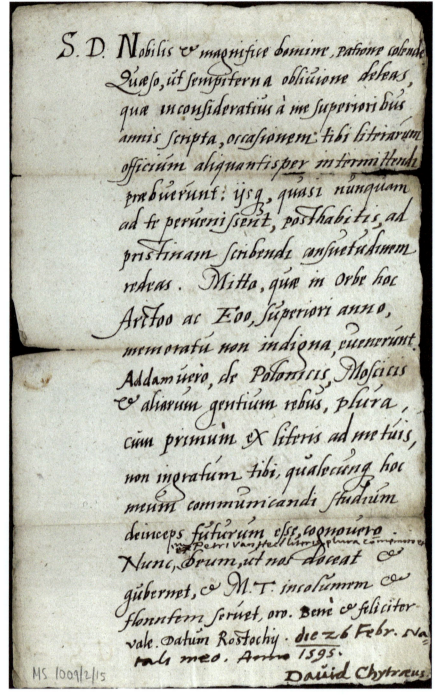

Fig. 16 David Chytraeus to Beale, 26 February 1595/6. AUL, MS 1009/2, item 15, fol. 1r (orig.), in University of Aberdeen Museums and Special Collections, is licenced under CC By 4.0.

the double subsidye'.[107] Later in February he participated in a conference with the House of Lords as part of a delegation from the Commons regarding purveyors to the royal household. John Hare, MP for Horsham, Sussex, had introduced a bill to address corruption in the process, much to the queen's disliking because she saw purveyance to her household as a matter of royal prerogative.[108] Having been named to the conference, Beale was thus involved in a second potentially contentious issue. Equally if not more concerning to Beale, and contentious because of prerogative, were the by now usual complaints in the Commons regarding the state of religion. In late February 'certaine motions for a conference on religion' were penned and circulated among MPs, and from this pressure a bill for religious reform was put forward. Unsurprisingly, Beale owned a copy of these 'certaine motions', which focused on legal questions regarding the oath *ex officio* among other issues, and he found his voice on the floor of the Commons. On the committee to consider pluralities and non-residence of the clergy, Beale knew that discussing religion in the Commons was forbidden and therefore dangerous, but he also, like his colleague, James Morice, MP for Colchester with Walsingham's support, was part of a wider group of Puritans and their sympathizers pushing for further reform by way of enforcement of existing statute law. The evidence for Beale's activity in this regard in March 1589 is admittedly thin, but he gained some notoriety early that month when, as Gilbert, Lord Talbot, reported to Beale's friend, the earl of Shrewsbury, 'There is a byll in the nether house againste the non-residentes of the clergy & agenste pluralities, wherin dyvers pure fellowes are very whott & ernest. Amongeste whom Mr Beale hathe made A very sharpe speche which is nothynge well lyked by the Busshopps.' Among these 'pure fellowes', Beale appears to have, in Collinson's words, 'led the attack'.[109]

Beale's temper got the better of him at Lambeth Palace in 1584, and it appears to have done so again in Parliament in 1589. In the former case, he was arguing against Whitgift's novel use of the *ex officio* oath and a process that resembled, in

---

[107] Beale to Burghley, 17 March 1593, BL, Lansdowne MS 73/2, fol. 4v (orig.), noting also that Beale was assessed at the full fee for his residences both in Surrey and London.

[108] According to Neale, Beale and Morice shared a 'constitutional approach to the campaign against bishops', and it would be difficult to believe that they did not work 'hand in glove' in the parliament of 1593. *Elizabeth I and Her Parliaments, 1584-1601*, 194, 268. Neale projected back into 1589 what he saw more clearly in 1593, for which parliament the documentary record is better. On purveyance in general but also with specific discussion of the situation in 1589, Allegra Woodworth, 'Purveyance for the Royal Household in the Reign of Queen Elizabeth', *Transactions of the American Philosophical Society*, 35 (1945), 1–89.

[109] Beale's incomplete copy of 'Certaine motions' (lacking answers), erroneously dated in the catalogue to 1585, BL, Additional MS 48064, fols 96r–99v; printed from a more complete version dated correctly as 25 February 1589 in Hartley, *Proceedings*, 2.439–69. Collinson has referred to the 'certain motions' as 'a portent of the future growth of legal and constitutional puritanism' (p. 399, with the quotation above). Talbot to Shrewsbury, 3 March 1589, Longleat, Talbot MS II, fol. 89r (orig.). D'Ewes recorded that the second reading of the bill against pluralities and non-residence was on Saturday, 1 March, 'and after sundry Arguments, many with the Bill and some against it', the bill was sent to committee, which included Beale, *Compleat Journal*, 441.

Beale's view, the Spanish Inquisition. In the latter case, he was hot and bothered about a more traditional abuse aimed at by Protestants. As it turned out, he had good and personal reasons. About this time he acquired a copy of a petition of financial grievance regarding William Overton, bishop of Coventry and Lichfield, who appears to have bought his way into the office and subsequently was, regarding diocesan revenues, aggressive and 'possibly downright dishonest' in the view of one biographer.[110] Beale did not apparently know the petitioner, a certain William Plased, but corruption in the diocese where he had previously been schooled and now held good friends and affection will have been a bitter blow. From another quarter, Surrey, Beale learned of a longer petition brought to Thomas Cooper, bishop of Winchester, regarding the failings of clergy in that diocese. The inhabitants of Farnham parish offered various reasons why their vicar needed to be replaced with a sound preacher, not least because of his problems with drinking and his inability to read plainly and distinctly to aid the parishioners' understanding.[111] Beale's copies of these materials included his own notes that nothing in Surrey had been addressed or changed in light of the petition. A third petition or, as Beale labelled it in his own copy, 'supplication' regarding religious causes in March 1589 came from the MP for Great Yarmouth, John Stubbe, whose printed tract of 1579 earned Elizabeth's ire because he dared to advise her against her marriage with the duke of Anjou. No surprise that Beale owned a copy. In any event, Stubbe in 1589 intended to speak for the whole Commons, the third estate. Addressed specifically and, again boldly, to the queen, his grievances extended beyond pluralism and non-residence to include inveighing against an unlearned clergy and, Beale's particular target of the 1580s, the oath *ex officio*. Stubbe appealed to Elizabeth's wisdom and grace to ensure a practising and preaching ministry, and his tone was consistently obedient to the queen in particular, placing blame on those in her Church not holding true to their callings. Very much aligned with Beale's long-held position and other constitutionally minded Puritans, Stubbe also claimed that 'we craue noe innouation, but obseruation of olde lawes, with freedom from Canons & customes abrogated, and that all causes may be determined by the lawes, and liberties of England, & not by mens passionate opiniones'. Furthermore, and as was customary among moderate Puritans at the time, Stubbe abhorred all traitors, schismatics, sectaries, and

---

[110] Petition of William Plased against Overton, February/March 1589, BL, Additional MS 48064, fol. 48r. On Overton, *ODNB*. The only other material relating to Overton in Beale's possession is a letter from the bishop to the Privy Council in which he justified his non-admittance of a certain parson endorsed by the Council, 19 July 1584, BL, Egerton MS 1693, fol. 118r (orig.), which Beale appears to have simply kept as his own.

[111] Petition of inhabitants of Farnham to Sir William More of Loseley, followed by that to the bishop of Winchester, early 1589, BL, Additional MS 48064, fols 72r–4v. Collinson, 400. Although direct evidence connecting Beale to Farnham remains elusive, it may be suggestive that Leicester's intervention was sought from local inhabitants regarding a certain Mr Beale. Papers regarding Leicester, Sir William More, and a petition by John Lanwaye of Farnham, 1580? 1590?, Surrey History Centre, MSS 6729/3/99–100.

separatists.[112] Stubbe, Beale, the petitioners up and down the country, and others in the Commons yearning for action against pluralism and other infelicities would be disappointed by this parliament. The bill did not pass, and nothing substantial was implemented to address their complaints before Parliament was dissolved. At the very least, however, Beale knew that he was by no means alone.

Before and after this parliament a series of tracts by the pseudonymous Martin Marprelate gained national attention for their biting and satirical but deadly serious attacks on the clergy, especially Bishop Cooper of Winchester, Bishop Aylmer of London, and Archbishop Whitgift of Canterbury. These three were, in their own ways, targets of Beale, but Marprelate advocated a thorough reorganization of the Church on a presbyterian model that Beale never endorsed because of his adherence to the Elizabethan Church by statute. Even so, Beale could not avoid some engagement with the arguments and activities of Marprelate. Among Beale's papers is a copy of the examination of John Hodgkin, one of the printers of Marprelate's tracts, in autumn 1589. The copy is not in Beale's hand, nor did he annotate or endorse the paper in any way, no doubt because doing so could potentially implicate himself as a sympathizer or, worse, enabler.[113] Closer to the bone, as it were, was the fact that one of the locations for printing the tracts in March 1589 was the house of John Hales (Beale's former ward since 1573) in Whitefriars, Coventry (Beale's former schoolhouse in the 1550s). By this point Hales had reached majority and was no longer Beale's responsibility, but Beale's interests in and around Coventry could potentially have implicated him as a sympathizer of Marprelate at the heart of the Elizabethan regime, so he wrote to Hatton in support of Hales but distancing himself from Marprelate's means and 'indiscreete words'. Although Beale was certainly in agreement regarding the abuses yet in the Church and the use of the 'diabolicall, paganicall, and papisticall proceadinge ex officio', he also protested 'that truly before the face of Allmightie god, that I neuer was directly or indirectly acquainted to my knowledge withe the person of Martin Marprelate, nor anie of his actions.'[114] Having recently avoided the punishment and embarrassment Davison experienced in 1587, Beale knew to avoid any unnecessary dangers associated with the Marprelate controversy, and he knew that Hatton might have been involved in the government's reaction.[115]

[112] Stubbe's supplication, March 1589, BL, Additional MS 48101, fols 136r–7r, with quotation at 136v; printed in Hartley, *Proceedings*, 2.490–2. Stubbe's *The Discoverie of a Gaping Gvlf* (London, 1579) (STC 23400) is among Beale's annotated papers, BL, Additional MS 48027, fols 152r–95v. On Stubbe, *ODNB*.

[113] Account of Hodgkin's examination, autumn 1589, BL, Additional MS 48064, fol. 146r–v; cf. the notes and extracts not in Beale's hand from Marprelate and related works at fols 253r–6v. For the tracts and discussion, Joseph L. Black (ed.), *The Martin Marprelate Tracts: A Modernized and Annotated Edition* (Cambridge, 2008); by the same author, *ODNB*.

[114] Collinson, 394. Beale to Hatton, 25 November 1589, BL, Additional MS 48039, fols 63r–70r, with quotations at 65v, 66r, 64r. On Hales as Beale's ward, see Chapter 4.

[115] As he later recalled, Beale to Burghley, 17 March 1593, BL, Lansdowne MS 73/2, fol. 7v (orig).

The ensuing crackdown by the establishment led in the next couple of years to the imprisonment of principled and unrelenting ministers opposed to Whitgift's policies. Beale kept an eye on and collected materials, now bound in one volume, regarding deprivations and trials of ministers in various areas of the country— Norfolk, Essex, Surrey, Oxford—but he largely refrained from getting directly involved where possible lest he be accused of presbyterian leanings. Additionally, he acquired materials relating to the stand taken by Francis Knollys, an unrivalled parliamentarian and privy councillor also on the committee against pluralities and non-residence, and who attacked any sentiments from Whitgift or others that suggested episcopacy by divine right.[116] Beale was, to be sure, caught in a balancing act. It might have simply been a matter of time, though, before he was drawn into the conflict because of his past, connections, and legal expertise. At this time he consulted legal texts on ecclesiastical jurisdiction and oaths from the middle ages onwards with a view to establishing what procedures were warranted and within the bounds of English law, and his reputation for legal precision, as well as his resourcefulness, soon led to others asking him for help.[117] His efforts in support of Hales did not save his former ward from a trip to the Fleet prison, but that did not stop others in Coventry asking Beale for help when the vicar of Holy Trinity, Humphrey Fen(n), was in the Clink. Rather than write to Hatton again, on this occasion in 1590 Beale wrote to Whitgift directly seeking bail for the vicar.[118] He started by reminding the archbishop of his history in and affections for Coventry, noting also that 'I have sondrie kinsfolkes, allyes, and frendes in those partes […] a longe time I knowe and am knowen to manie'. After carefully restating his position regarding the issues in controversy because his adversaries said untrue things about him, Beale wrote that 'Although I would gladlie doe my Couentrye frendes anie pleasure that I mighte: yet I doubted, whether I shoulde intermedle in their request or no, least I shoulde doe the partie more harme then good.' In the end, from his house at Barnes Beale informed himself of Fen's case and, 'being fatelie tormented with the goute and stone and farre from bookes and other meanes[,] I drewe these notes enclosed, which I beseeche your Lordship to accept in good parte as I meant them', adding just for good measure as a slight jibe to the archbishop, 'My studie and travell in these Ecclesiasticall causes and Lawes hathe not ben inferior to anye mans.'[119]

---

[116] Papers related to various cases, 1589–91, BL, Additional MS 48064, fols 68r–71r, 90r1v, 118r–31r, 148r–51v, 212r–14r; regarding Knollys, fols 94r–5r, 226r–34r, but see also Collinson, 397.

[117] Materials and notes regarding ecclesiastical jurisdiction and oaths, collected c.1589–90, BL, Additional MS 48064, fols 215r–17v, 238r–52v; cf. BL, Additional MS 48039, fols 89r–202v. Recognition of Beale's position here situated in the wider context of the 1590s in Ethan H. Shagan, 'The English Inquisition: Constitutional Conflict and Ecclesiastical Law in the 1590s', *The Historical Journal*, 7 (2004), 541–65, on Beale at 548.

[118] Beale to Whitgift, 22 August 1590, LPL, MS 4267, fols 3r–4v (orig.); draft with Beale's corrections, BL, Additional MS 48039, fols 74r–5v. On Fen, see Collinson, 412–14, *et passim*.

[119] Beale to Whitgift, 22 August 1590, LPL, MS 4267, fols 1r, 2r (orig.).

What exactly Beale enclosed for Whitgift remains unknown, but his efforts on behalf of Fen and others continued into the next year.

Nine ministers opposing Whitgift's policies were particularly singled out for punishment, with Thomas Cartwright as their leader. Beale had previously known Cartwright, as representative of the Merchant Adventurers in Middelburg, in 1577 when he appointed him to pursue the pirates who attacked him on his crossing the Channel en route to the German princes. Two years previously, in 1575, Cartwright had written a work published in Heidelberg and challenging Whitgift's ideas regarding Church discipline. Thus, his opposition to the archbishop was long in the making, but equally significant is the fact that Beale might have owned a copy of that work. In late 1589, Bishop Aylmer had relayed to Whitgift that Beale attended a meeting with Cartwright and others, and was 'Cosen Germaine [first cousin] to Hailes which is committed'; moreover, Aylmer recorded 'I thinke verily that whatsoever Hayles hath done in this matter [the Marprelate press] it is not without ye knowledge of Beale'.[120] Now in 1591, though, Cartwright needed Beale's help, and among Beale's papers are statements and petitions in support of the ministers, including also a statement by the prisoners themselves against the oath imposed upon them by the Court of High Commission, and Cartwright's replies to a set of interrogatories sent by Whitgift.[121] As with Hales and Fen, so too with the nine ministers, on whose behalf Beale wrote in support.

In his analysis (a tract in the form of a letter) sent to Whitgift, Beale offered what Collinson has referred to as 'a characteristic manifesto'.[122] Beale started boldly: 'In primis it is certaine, that by the lawes of the realme there is as yet no certaine Ecclesiasticall law for the gouernment of the Churche of this realme'. He recognized that, because the overhaul of ecclesiastical law intended in the *Reformatio Legum Ecclesiasticarum* of Edward VI's reign never came into force, government of the Church was imperfect and, in some ways, impinged on Elizabeth's prerogative as well as the customs and laws of the country. Although Beale's putative purpose in writing was to defend the nine, his piece focused primarily on the legal and legislative nature of the Church and realm of England. He, as a principled and proud parliamentarian, reminded Whitgift of the role played by the House of Commons in generating reform and establishing statutes for the Church as it related to the State; indeed, 'It is an error to thinke that the hole authoritie for the establishing of suche ecclesiasticall thinges consisteth in her

[120] Aylmer to Whitgift, 23 November 1589, LPL, MS 3470, fol. 129r (orig.).

[121] BL, Additional MS 48064, fols 102r–3r, 158r 9r, 180₁–1r, 220r–2r. On the nine ministers, Cartwright, and the broader context of their trials, Collinson, 403–31; Collinson, *Richard Bancroft*, 103–28; *ODNB*. On the episode in 1577, see Chapter 5. Cartwright's work, *The second replie of Thomas Cartwright against Maister Doctor Whitgiftes second answer, touching the Churche Discipline* (Heidelberg, 1575) (STC 4714), appears in the booklist, BL, Hargrave MS 107, fol. 9v.

[122] 'Touching the proceedinge against the ministers', draft with Beale's amendments, 1591, BL, Additional MS 48039, fols 77r–88v; copy in Additional MS 48064, fols 134r–43r; discussion in Collinson, 421–2.

Majestie or her Clergie', or 'that parlament men maye not deale in suche causes'. The use of the oath *ex officio*, which he again likened to the Spanish Inquisition and 'popishe tirranie', was, as Beale thoroughly demonstrated by way of various statutes and precedents in English law, clearly prohibited: 'I marvaile that anie man learned in the common lawe should allowe of this kinde of proceadinge'. Among other legal authorities like Henry of Bracton, Anthony Fitzherbert and his *Natura Brevium* were particularly useful for Beale because of his point 'that an Ecclesiasticall person cannot minister an othe but in cases of marages and Testamentes: If he attempt it, there lyeth a prohibicion, then an attachement, a contempt and fine'.[123] For as firm and assertive as he was towards Whitgift, Beale also stated that he would not support any who tried to put in execution their own theories or ecclesiological reforms without due process in Parliament and according to law, never mind schismatics and separatists like the Brownists and Barrowists. Additionally, he was consciously reacting to Whitgift's set of articles for subscription—by lawyers, judges, clergy, and others—stating, in effect, that separatism and ecclesiological revolution were bad, and that obedience and epis-copacy were good (even if just short of divinely ordained). The articles were even-tually abandoned, Beale claimed, because of that latter point and its encroachment on Elizabeth's prerogative, but he nevertheless knew in 1591 when defending the nine that Whitgift and his allies in the Lambeth circle were playing hardball and would not likely be restrained from above.[124]

Whitgift was probably neither surprised nor impressed by Beale's most recent salvo regarding the archbishop's use of High Commission and the oath. It was similarly unlikely that he would relent in his policies now that he had Puritan opposition on the run and in gaol. In the coming years, Beale continued to beat the drum against the oath *ex officio* and broader issues such as pluralism and non-residence, but he was also at work on other legal causes and collaborating with the great legal mind and judge of the High Court of Admiralty, Julius Caesar. From 1589 until shortly before Beale's death in May 1601, the two collaborated on issues of piracy, mercantile complaints, coinage, iron supply, and other issues.[125] Given the stratospheric rise of Caesar through academic and professional

---

[123] 'Touching the proceadinge', 1591, BL, Additional MS 48039, quotations at fols 78r, 80r–v, 82v, 83r. Beale mentions Fitzherbert's work again in his letter to Burghley, 17 March 1593, BL, Lansdowne MS 73/2, fol. 8r (orig.). Beale might have owned multiple editions of Fitzherbert's work, which is noted several times among Beale's likely books, BL, Hargrave MS 107, fols 41r, 44, 45r, 46r, 46v; Bracton's *De Legibus*, edition of 1569, is at 44r.

[124] Beale's copy of the articles with his marginal notes of opposition, March 1591, BL, Additional MS 48064, fol. 88r–v; Burghley's copy with Beale's holograph notes, CP, 167/34–5. Collinson, 408, 499 n. 21 (listing other known copies). The dating of the articles, Hatton's involvement, and inconsisten-cies across the versions are discussed in Younger, *Religion and Politics*, 205. Despite Beale's discourses and letters sent to Hatton, nothing from Hatton to Beale has yet been located, so their relationship remains something of a mystery.

[125] Their working together can be seen in TNA, PC 2/15, p. 449; PC 2/16, pp. 230, 235–6, 562; PC 2/17, pp. 618–19, 981; BL, Lansdowne MSS 155, item 49; 143, item 59; 84, item 2; TNA, HCA 30/840/190, fol. 475r (dated 9 May 1601).

channels, Beale's value and reputation, notwithstanding his entirely informal legal education, can be seen in how his legal knowledge and experience across several decades and a range of issues were used by those in power. Moreover, by this point his collection of manuscripts, both those produced by his own activity and those he acquired or copied from elsewhere, had earned a reputation of its own, especially when combined with his library of printed books, which, as has been seen, he was happy to use and cite in his correspondence with others.[126] A seasoned veteran of court politics and religious disputes both at home and abroad, Beale was enormously valuable, but he was also powerful. Neither peer nor clergy, neither comfortably wealthy nor of landed stock, he was nevertheless confident enough to write to the most powerful men in the realm—Whitgift, Burghley, Hatton—in blunt terms and in all honesty. He had recently weathered various storms, not the least of which was his role in the queen of Scots' execution, and yet he had come out unharmed and still on top. He frequently acknowledged the potential dangers, betraying his insecurity, but he was pushing the limits.

The parliament of 1593 was Beale's last session and the final straw.[127] MPs were summoned for the customary reasons by this point: grave dangers to the realm and financial needs in a time of war. Also as usual, discussion of religious reform was strictly forbidden. Differences from the parliament of 1589, though, were clear. In general, as Beale put it to Burghley, there was 'no suche a readines and desire [among MPs to serve], as was wont to be in former times'.[128] More particularly, Beale sat not for Dorchester, as he had in 1584, 1586, and 1589, but rather for Lostwithiel, Cornwall; after all, Francis Russell, earl of Bedford, Beale's patron regarding his former seat, had now been dead for over seven years. For that matter, Leicester died in 1588, Walsingham in 1590. The passing of the latter was a bitter blow to Beale both professionally and personally because of the family connection through their wives; indeed, Beale was an executor of his brother-in-law's will.[129] Beale's connection to Lostwithiel can be reasonably explained by the influence in that region of the Cecils, Beale's only remaining source of patronage and protection. Also representing a change since 1589, the relative strength of Puritan causes from the 1580s was long gone because, in effect, Whitgift and his

---

[126] See, e.g. Vincent Skinner to Burghley, 14 March 1591, TNA, SP 12/238, fols 107r–8r (orig.).

[127] As before, the classic account is Neale, *Elizabeth I and her Parliaments, 1584–1601*, 241–323. For documents, Hartley, *Proceedings*, Vol. 3: *1593–1601*, 1–176. For Beale's committee work, HoP:HoC. D'Ewes, *Compleat Journal*, 468–521, adds nothing of significance regarding Beale's activity.

[128] Beale to Burghley, 17 March 1593, BL, Lansdowne MS 73/2, fol. 4v (orig.). See Wernham's interpretation that sees not just the decline of a Puritan spirit (Neale's view) but also a general war-weariness and lack of enthusiasm to pay the subsidy. Wernham, *After the Armada*, 438–9.

[129] The other executors, Edward Carey and William Dodington, were also related to Walsingham as 'brethren', the first a half-brother via their mutual father, the second a brother-in-law via Walsingham's sister, Christiana. As tokens of Walsingham's 'good affection towardes them', each was to receive 'one peece of plate of tenne poundes price'. TNA, PROB 11/75/375; printed with connections among the 'brethren' noted in John Gough Nichols and John Bruce (eds), *Wills from Doctors' Commons: A Selection from the Wills of Eminent Persons Proved in the Prerogative Court of Canterbury, 1495–1695* (London, 1863), 69–71. On Dodington as Walsingham's brother-in-law, see Chapter 4, n. 48.

allies had won, and the Puritans were on the run and underground. In sum, the early 1590s marked a real turning point for Beale because he now lacked some of his most vital allies of the previous two decades and was accordingly more vulnerable to attack from Whitgift. Between Parliament's opening on 19 February and early March (it was dissolved on 10 April), Beale sat on committees regarding parliamentary privilege and returns, recusancy, and the subsidy. His involvement in the second was straightforward enough, but the combination of the Commons' ancient liberties and the Crown's financial needs proved for Beale to be difficult territory to navigate.

In the first couple of weeks, two vociferous MPs with abundant principle but lacking sufficient caution got into trouble and demonstrated how times had changed. Peter Wentworth had been foolish enough to wish to discuss the royal succession, while James Morice had again criticized the ecclesiastical commission and Whitgift's proceedings. Along with these two, Beale was, in Neale's view, one of 'three irrepressibles [who] got into immediate trouble and were snuffed out', suggesting to others who wished to push against the establishment that they avoid 'the fate of the intrepid ones'.[130] Given the suppression of Wentworth and Morice, Beale would have been well advised to tread carefully, but a spell of impetuosity and a brief lack of self-awareness took hold. According to the sources recorded at the time, and corroborated by Beale's explanation of events two weeks afterwards, Beale was part of a group in the Commons who questioned whether it were appropriate for the House of Lords to call for a conference with the lower house regarding the subsidy. For Beale, a key difference between this conference and that between the Commons and Lords in 1589 was that previously the call came from the lower, not the upper, house. Also, now the issue was the independence of the Commons and its centuries-old privileges regarding finances. Predictably in retrospect, on Saturday, 3 March, Beale brought forth a legal precedent from the nineth year of the reign of King Henry IV (1407) illustrating, very conveniently, that the Commons should not and could not be pressured to meet with the Lords regarding taxation. One suspects that later that weekend Beale received firm counsel (probably from Burghley) on the need to back down and swallow his pride as soon as possible, for on Monday, 5 March, he took the floor of the Commons and admitted that he had confused the matter. In short, he claimed, he was denying an acquiescent *confirmation* by the Commons of what the Lords wanted (i.e. a greater subsidy, as was the case in 1407), but, in reality, the Lords simply wanted a *conference* between the two houses; as D'Ewes put it nearly a century later, Beale 'acknowledged he had mistaken the question propounded'.[131]

---

[130] Neale, *Elizabeth I and her Parliaments, 1584–1601*, 245, 285. Generally, Neale seems to have assumed more direct connections and collaboration between Beale and Morice, never mind Wentworth, than can be proven; cf. the comment that Beale was Morice's 'brother-in-arms', 277.

[131] Hartley, *Proceedings*, 3.95. D'Ewes, *Compleat Journal*, 485, working from the anonymous journal printed in Hartley, at 487. Neale, *Elizabeth I and her Parliaments, 1584–1601*, 304–5.

Monday, 5 March 1593, is the last date for which evidence survives of Beale's activity in the Commons. Quietly but firmly, he was removed and sent away, his services no longer required. It appears also that he was committed to house arrest, if only for a brief time. As had become his custom, Beale wrote to Burghley on 17 March from his house in London to explain himself and in the hope that he would soon be recalled to Elizabeth's court and Parliament.[132] Explain himself he did, noting his confusion regarding the conference with the Lords and strongly reminding Burghley that he was not opposed to paying a double subsidy (he had in 1589). In his view, it seemed that some confusion and misunderstanding regarding the subsidy, while inconvenient, was not the real reason he was sent packing. Between his dismissal from the Commons and his writing to Burghley, Beale seems to have become more self-aware and realized that his affront to the Lords was only the apparent reason for his being sent away. Rather, Beale's downfall was actually due to his opposition—long-standing, but not voiced in 1593—to Whitgift's proceedings, his relative isolation because his religious and political allies were literally or figuratively underground, and the slanders among his opponents accusing Beale of supporting and fomenting presbyterianism, 'which I take to be the principall cause of my restrainte from the Court and parlament, viz that I should be a plotter of a newe Ecclesiasticall gouernment'.[133] Notwithstanding the fact that he openly criticized the lack of reform in ecclesiastical laws, pluralism, non-residence, and the impinging by the Church on royal prerogative and the common law, Beale held that he never supported separatists or those looking to replace episcopacy, and he had told Whitgift as much on several occasions. Yet, he was exposed to attack because his days at the heart of the Elizabethan regime had always been made possible because of the protection and moral support provided by others now dead, endangered, or disgraced. In 1584 he vehemently confronted Whitgift in the latter's home and came out unscathed. In 1587 he swiftly carried the death warrant for Mary's execution but did not face Elizabeth's fury. In 1589 he, along with other 'pure fellows', spoke sharply in the Commons against the bishops yet nothing happened to him. Now, though, in 1593, his own merits and value to the regime were not enough to keep him on top. Instead, he found their limits. Now he was shunned, humiliated, and uncertain of his future. He had found a new low.

---

[132] If Beale was in fact committed to house arrest as was reported, it was one of the many rumours circulating that was true. On those committed at the same time, see Richard West to William Pitt, 16 March 1593, BL, Additional MS 22924, fol. 9r. See also Chapter 6, n. 121. Beale to Burghley, 17 March 1593, BL, Lansdowne MS 73/2, fols 4r–14v (orig.). Beale curiously claimed that his speech on 3 March was his 'first speache in the house' (4r), but this could only be the case if his previous utterances recorded by others are not considered formal contributions. Also, if this occasion really was his first recorded, formal speech, then his 'A Treatise made by a Burgess of the lower house in parlement' was probably never delivered orally, remaining only in manuscript (potentially for circulation). See Chapter 6.

[133] Beale to Burghley, 17 March 1593, BL, Lansdowne MS 73/2, fol. 5v (orig.).

Sunrise to Sunset

It took Beale several years of service as a clerk of Elizabeth's Privy Council to earn her respect and confidence. It was a lot of hard work, but his sun was very much in the ascendant in the 1570s, with important and like-minded allies in powerful positions. During the 1580s, he kept climbing as high as he reasonably could, given his education, experience, and social status. His expertise was both domestic and foreign, historical and contemporary, political and religious, constitutionally conservative but potentially volatile. He served his sovereign overseas on the Dutch Council of State and north of the Trent in discussions with the queen of Scots. He was the key intermediary for negotiations with the powerful mercantile society of the Baltic, the Hanseatic League. He acquired new properties, grants, and positions, including that as secretary to the Council of the North, even if in absentia. He had served informally as well as formally as principal secretary in Walsingham's absence, and he demonstrated his profound knowledge of the office, its roles, and its dangers in his own treatise for an aspiring secretary in 1592. The treatise represents in microcosm a history of Beale's activity for the previous ten years. Wide ranging but deeply detailed, it reflects his handling of documents, domestic affairs including religion, foreign affairs including intelligence, financial matters, and relations with the queen. With Walsingham dead, Beale felt safe to criticize some of his brother-in-law's habits (e.g. regarding too many private servants), favouring instead the practices of Burghley, who was very much still alive and able to protect Beale. Because of his fall from grace the next year, he would never become principal secretary in his own right despite rumours in 1600 that he might.[134] Financially as well as professionally, it seems that Beale's future looked relatively secure. Before Leicester's death in 1588 and Walsingham's in 1590, Beale had always valued the support and friendship of the earl and his brother-in-law. Walsingham's own position ensured a second powerful buffer (alongside Burghley) between Beale and his opponents (especially Aylmer and Whitgift), but with one of the guard rails removed, he was in danger of overstepping the limits of his station. Without enough powerful allies, including Puritans and their sympathizers in the Commons, the critical mass required for reliable security was gone, and Burghley alone could not protect Beale from the consequences of his own actions. For one so firm in their convictions, so unyielding in their principles, it was only a matter of time before Beale pushed too hard and the sun began to set in 1593.

A European Elizabethan: The Life of Robert Beale, Esquire. David Scott Gehring, Oxford University Press.
© David Scott Gehring 2024. DOI: 10.1093/9780198902942.003.0007

[134] 'A Treatise of the Office of a Councellor and Principall Secretary to her Majestie', BL, Additional MS 48149, fols 3v–9v; transcribed reliably in Read, *Mr Secretary Walsingham*, 1.423–43. See Chapter 6. On the rumours in 1600, see Chapter 8.

8

Abeyance and Drift, or, Forbearance and Shift

Beale's dismissal from the House of Commons in 1593 represents a tempting turning point. Having offended Queen Elizabeth regarding her financial demands at a time of extreme necessity, and having opposed Archbishop Whitgift's procedures for clerical conformity over a much longer duration, Beale was quickly sent away and understandably nervous. Notwithstanding his bright prospects and central roles of the previous decade—when he served as an ersatz principal secretary, sat on the Dutch Council of State, and published in the queen's name at home and abroad—it seemed that, suddenly, the lights went dark. And yet, the signs were already pointing to the fact that the 1590s would be a different decade, and not just for him.[1] The passing of Leicester and Walsingham, as well as the advanced age of Burghley, left those advocating further religious reform vulnerable, punished, or underground—Beale very much included. More personally, Beale was more exposed than he had been since the 1570s, when his role in validating the marriage of the earl of Hertford was still fresh in Elizabeth's memory; his activity in Germany back in 1563 was still, in November 1600 just months before his death, recognized more widely but 'winked at'.[2] His carrying and reading of the commission to execute Mary Queen of Scots imperilled his standing with Elizabeth and was never forgotten, as Beale well knew and recorded in his letters to Burghley. In truth, Elizabeth seems always to have kept Beale at some distance, never including him in the more personal exchanges and rituals of gift-giving at New Year's.[3] Finally, though, it was a matter of simple biology and gradual ageing.

---

[1] For discussion of the scholarship regarding the political implications of shifts in ideologies and practical realities, see Alexandra Gajda, 'Political Culture in the 1590s: The "Second Reign of Elizabeth"', *History Compass*, 8 (2010), 88–100; for the key work, John Guy (ed.), *The Reign of Elizabeth I: Court and Culture in the Last Decade* (Cambridge, 1995).

[2] ? to ?, November 1600, TNA, SP 15/34, fols 77r–8r, quotation at 77v. Beale's interest in the succession continued in the 1590s, but he was very careful not to attract too much attention. See Beale to Robert Sidney, 25 September 1595, Kent History and Library Centre, U1475/C15/2 (orig.), fol. 2r regarding Robert Parsons' polemic; see also below, n. 20.

[3] Beale's complete omission from the lists of those receiving or giving gifts on New Year's Day (or at other times) is slightly surprising. Not even during the early 1580s, when he was closer to Elizabeth than ever before (or after), did Beale's name appear in the rolls. Others of similar station do turn up as receiving gifts, such as Henry Killigrew, who gave a box of gifts to Elizabeth in 1565, and whose daughter in 1585 received from Elizabeth a wedding gift (a gilt cup and cover). Jane A. Lawson (ed.), *The Elizabethan New Year's Gift Exchanges 1559–1603* (Oxford, 2013), 110, 365.

He had complained of sore eyes, bladder stones, and pains from gout and general indisposition at various points in the 1580s, and these afflictions only grew worse in the 1590s.[4] Although he had said that his role in Mary's execution made it unsafe for him to travel too far north, his physical ailments also kept him from travelling to York as secretary of the Council of the North in the 1580s, necessitating a deputy to sit in his stead; there was little likelihood that the situation would change in his final decade. Even attending meetings of the Privy Council became less important for Beale, as the registers indicate his absence after summer 1588, with other clerks stepping in to fill the void. His declining involvement in the regular activities as clerk might have been because he was called to more pressing duties, but his infirmities did not help matters. In sum and as has been pointed out, there is plenty of reason to see Beale after 1593 as more subservient, less influential, and evermore pushed to the sidelines of the Elizabethan regime.[5]

To a remarkable degree, however, Beale remained busy. He was involved in a range of domestic affairs including legal cases, mining, and disputes among London merchants. He remained a key consultant for foreign affairs touching the war in the Netherlands, alliance with France, and trade in the Holy Roman Empire and with Denmark. All the while, he was getting older and more concerned about his financial ability to provide for his wife and children both before and after his departure from this life. The pressure of a large and seemingly ever-expanding household with a servant and new home in London (probably between 1595 and 1598) brought the necessity for Beale to resist any decline in his income, any encroachments on his territory, as it were. Accordingly, he maintained his position both as an expert with profound knowledge and experience and as a diplomatic jack-of-all-trades to ensure that he could provide for his family.[6] Thus, while it may at first seem that Beale was now an outcast of the Elizabethan political machine and sent adrift, his indispensability ensured that he would need to endure the new realities of the 1590s and shift back to working behind the scenes just as he had during the 1560s. He was cast out of the public eye, as it were, for personal reasons, but his utility for government purposes ensured that he would be used (and abused) until the end of his days.

---

[4] See Chapter 7 and, e.g. Beale's letters to Burghley in 1591 and 1592, BL, Lansdowne MSS 68/107, 72/73.

[5] Taviner, 183, with reference to the Privy Council at 153, 304.

[6] On the children, servants, and new home, see Chapter 7. Edith gave birth to Anne in early 1592 and Amy in summer 1593. Jupp and Hovenden, *The Registers*, 25. Surrey History Centre, P6/1/1, fol. 5r records Amy's baptism on 15 July 1593, but 44r records her burial on 6 November 1593. Taviner, 176, makes similar observations regarding Beale as a diplomatic jack-of-all-trades but does not recognize the depth of expertise across the wider range of legal, commercial, political, and maritime issues. Beale's response to a request in 1594 from Burghley regarding, among other topics, papal authority and jurisdiction was characteristically thorough and based on decades of learning and collecting his own archive. See the correspondence and related papers in BL, Additional MS 48101, fols 303r–33r, with possible sources in BL, Additional MS 48037.

Behind the Scenes at Home

By 1593, Beale had amassed a considerable suite of official charges and responsibilities. Long had he served as a clerk of the Privy Council, but more recent roles included those regarding the Council of the North, petty custom in London, importation of steel, commissions of the peace, and administration of interests and lands in Coventry and Warwickshire, whence he also sometimes retreated to get away from London, especially during the plague years of the mid 1590s. As a measure of reciprocity, his history and friendship with Coventry was used by the mayor on at least one occasion in an attempt to lessen the city's financial blow in contributing to Elizabeth's war in Ireland. Additionally, by 1597 at the latest, as a master of the court of Chancery, Beale served as a clerk and legal consultant to the court.[7] Although he had distinguished himself in serving as an MP since 1576, after his dismissal in March 1593 Beale did not sit in the Commons for the parliament of 1597–8. His absence was almost certainly a consequence of his own previous conduct (be it regarding the subsidy or ecclesiastical discipline), but it was also symptomatic of a broader trend during Elizabeth's final decade, when the older generation of Puritans and their sympathizers were either dead or, like Beale, shut out of politics in a formal sense.[8] On a more personal level and reflecting his fall from grace, the twelve-year grant for the importation of steel, and with it the financial benefits, was not renewed in 1594, the grant falling to another for a period of twenty-one years.[9]

His knowledge and experience, however, ensured that Beale would ultimately remain indispensable. As he had demonstrated in 1569 when he descended into a mine in Saxony with Henry Killigrew, Beale's interest in mining and his ability to put that knowledge to use in England continued. As the previous deputy to the governor of the Company of Mines Royal (Walsingham), and as a shareholder of the Company of Mineral and Battery Works, Beale remained attuned to the mining activities in northern England and elsewhere. In 1596, for example, he wrote to Robert Cecil about potential mining activities in Yorkshire, including a draft

---

[7] Beale's references to his properties in Warwickshire are rare, but see, e.g. Beale to Sidney, 25 September 1595, Kent History and Library Centre, U1475/C15/2 (orig.), fol. 1r, where Beale stated that he was about to leave Barnes for Warwickshire 'for some three weekes or a monethe'. John Rogerson (mayor of Coventry) to Beale, 1 September 1598, Coventry History Centre, BA/H/Q/A79/87A. Beale to Robert Cecil, 28 September 1597, CP, 55/79 (orig.). Although he was named as a commissioner of the peace in the northern counties on 26 February 1593 (before his dismissal), he was not on 6 March (thereafter). By July 1594, he had regained sufficient confidence to be named as a commissioner every year until 1599. For convenience, see the series of *Calendar of the Patent Rolls* for 1593–8, various editors, List and Index Society, Vols 309–10, 322, 327–8, 358 (Kew, 2005–18).

[8] Neale, *Elizabeth I and her Parliaments, 1584–1601*, 326, remarks that Beale was 'inexplicably absent from Parliament' in 1597–8 but also that his 'absence cannot have been accidental'. When Elizabeth's final parliament met in late October 1601, Beale had been dead for five months.

[9] License dated 11 August 1593, with effect from expiry of Beale's grant on 21 December 1594, TNA, C 66/1398, mm. 11–13.

minute of a letter for Cecil's consideration in permitting the same to move forward. He also supplied an additional letter, to be signed by Cecil, directed to the officers of the mines at Keswick. This second item was in response to a letter that Beale had received from Leeds, presumably regarding the mining operations at Keswick, where German immigrants had long been involved.[10] Those operations at Keswick (for peat, coal, and various minerals) and the German directors needed attention, especially Beale's: he was named specifically regarding a consultation a few years later on the question of whether the works were to continue or not.[11] Elsewhere, in Monmouthshire, he also had an interest in the mining of iron. Here again, among those of the Privy Council and indeed Julius Caesar, Beale appears to have taken the lead on securing sufficient iron from those mines to keep the workmen employed in the wireworks.[12]

Immigrant communities' involvement in industry and commerce was nothing new in the 1590s, but Beale's long history with the Hanse in London ensured that he would be called upon as needed, and his connections with the Italian and Dutch communities in London could be useful at certain moments.[13] He appears to have been aware of the daily occurrences and key personalities in the Italian Protestant Church, but, more suggestively, he, along with Killigrew and others, were to look into a contentious situation between Dutch artisans and English tradesmen in the City, its suburbs, and Westminster.[14] In short, English tradesmen complained about the number of Dutch tradesmen with whom they needed to compete, while the Dutch complained of the penal statutes imposed upon them. Beale and his colleagues were given no small set of tasks: they were to

---

[10] Beale to Cecil, 25 August 1596, CP, 44/14 (orig.). Cf. Beale to Cecil, 1 July 1596, CP, 40/111 (orig.), noting a recent 'veary sore fitt of the stone'. On Germans at Keswick, see Raingard Esser, 'Germans in early modern Britain', in Panikos Panayi (ed.), *Germans in Britain since 1500* (Hambledon, 1996), 17–27.

[11] Thomas, Lord Burghley, and Henry, Lord Cobham, to Cecil, 1 July 1600, CP, 80/74 (orig.). At this time Beale was in Boulogne to negotiate a peace with Spanish authorities. See below.

[12] Caesar and Beale to Burghley, 19 May 1597, BL, Lansdowne MS 84/2, fol. 4r (orig.). Order of the Privy Council, 25 July 1598, TNA, PC 2/23, 346. Regarding the wireworks and its relation to the companies of Mineral and Battery Works and Mines Royal, see Caesar and Beale to Burghley, 23 May 1597, BL, Lansdowne MS 84/2, fol. 6r (orig.).

[13] Useful overview in Nigel Goose and Liên Luu (eds), *Immigrants in Tudor and Early Stuart England* (Brighton, 2005). Updated discussion for a slightly earlier period, W. Mark Ormrod, 'England's Immigrants, 1330–1550: Aliens in Later Medieval and Early Tudor England', *Journal of British Studies*, 59 (2020), 245–63.

[14] Minute-book of the Consistory of the Italian Protestant Church, 1570–90, BL, Additional MS 48096, fols 17r–123r (orig.); the edition by O. Boersma and A. J. Jelsma omits the fact that Beale owned it: *Unity in Multiformity: The Minutes of the Coetus of London, 1575 and the Consistory Minutes of the Italian Churches of London, 1570–1591*, Huguenot Society of Great Britain and Ireland, Vol. 59 ([London], 1997). Long ago Patrick Collinson observed that '[i]t is just possible that a more formal association existed between the foreign churches in London and the English puritans than has hitherto been suspected', citing this minute-book as evidence for 1570: 'Puritan Classical Movement', 90 n. 1. Collinson followed up the idea in 'Elizabethan Puritans', 528–55; but for an updated and fuller discussion, see Silke Muylaert, *Shaping the Stranger Churches: Migrants in England and the Troubles in the Netherlands, 1547–1585* (Leiden, 2020). Privy Council to Beale et al., 2 June 1592, TNA, PC 2/19, 384.

investigate how many strangers were of every nation in the area, who among them were not permitted in handicrafts and manual labour, where they lived, what occupations they had, how many people lived in their houses, how long they had been in the country, which churches they attended, and whether any English subjects lived in their houses. Furthermore, they were to employ as much secrecy as possible in their investigation lest the English tradesmen be encouraged in their prejudices against the strangers. It seems that Beale then got in touch with the Dutch Church for the specifics, for about two weeks later he received a list from the ministers, who noted the numbers of denizens, non-denizens, English-born, and women who attended the Church and could be comprehended as of that community. Interestingly, though, the ministers also relayed that there were many trades not practiced by the strangers yet still complained about by the English tradesmen as if the Dutch did.[15] A similarly large request was made of Beale and others in 1598, when they were charged with assessing the ability of Italian, French, and Dutch strangers in the City of London to contribute to a loan for English use to put down the Irish rebellion. Those commissioned in this instance, like Beale and his long-time friend and colleague, Killigrew, were connected to the immigrant and mercantile population in one way or another.[16] The situation with the Hanse and their privileges, as will be seen, became even more contentious than it had been previously. Also in 1598 and still writing to Burghley when the Lord Treasurer was in his final decline, Beale informed (presumably on Burghley's request, as usual) on various matters including the debts of the Hanse (and their repayment), travel restrictions on inhabitants of the Steelyard, controversies with English clothiers, and the like for German retailers of Rhenish wine. After the expulsion of the Hanse later that year, controversies remained among the Merchant Adventurers and English clothworkers, and, because of Beale's existing familiarity with the issues, he, Caesar, and others were charged by the Privy Council to investigate further and offer counsel on how best to settle the controversies remaining.[17]

Apart from his ad hoc jobs when called upon, Beale's secretaryship of the Council of the North was a big, financially rewarding position. As he had said previously in his sorrowful letters of complaint to Burghley, in early 1595 Beale recounted how, from the very beginning of his role in 1586, he understood that he was to remain in London to serve there rather than physically at York, where a deputy would serve in his stead. Since that time, his eyes had further decayed and

---

[15] 'The number of the names of the handicraftes menn', date in Beale's hand, 17 June 1592, Folger Shakespeare Library, MS V.b. 142, fol 87r.

[16] Privy Council to Beale, Killigrew, et al., 5 December 1598, TNA, PC 2/24, 169–70, with follow-up at 191.

[17] Beale to Burghley, 24 January 1598, TNA, SP 12/266, fol. 37r–v (orig.). Privy Council to the Lord Mayor of London, Caesar, and Beale, 6 February 1599, TNA, PC 2/24, 303–4; response to the Privy Council, May 1599, TNA, SP 12/270, fols 214v–15r. On Burghley's decline and will, which does not mention Beale (updated, 1 March 1598, TNA, PROB 1/3), see Alford, *Burghley*, 315–31.

the afflictions of stone and gout only increased and had 'sondrye tymes brought me to deathes dore'. Moreover, his financial security was slipping because his license for steel had recently gone to another, who, according to Beale, had so increased the price that he made three times what Beale had. When his deputy at York, Ralph Rokeby, died in early 1595, Beale wondered whether he would then need to travel north or another would be installed as his deputy. Fearing the former, he requested permission that he could quietly but completely retire from formal service and 'withdrawe my self into some corner, where takinge another course, I maye finishe my sorrowfull dayes'.[18] With Rokeby dead, and catching wind of reports that he himself was dead, Beale now heard rumours that a certain Smith, a servant of Robert Devereux, earl of Essex, might be chosen to take his place not only at York but also within the Privy Council, resulting in a potential loss of roughly £33 per annum for the former and £50 for the latter. Rather than speak his mind directly to Elizabeth, an unthinkable prospect, or, in his view, be so presumptuous and offensive in writing directly to her, Beale wrote yet again in distress and at some length to Burghley in April. The idea of addressing his sovereign with so great a concern quite literally struck him dumb, Beale citing Seneca to drive the point home: 'curae leues loquuntur, ingentes stupent'.[19] After reciting, yet again, his decades of service, Beale feared that, if he were to venture north to York on his own without a deputy, he would need to sell his books to cover the costs, and, were 'anye misshape [to] light vppon me there', his wife and children would be left homeless in short order. Given the state of his decaying body, he was bold with Burghley in writing 'I haue neyther harte nor meanes, to make my ordinarye residence there'. As he saw it, either Elizabeth should replace Rokeby so Beale could remain in London, or remove the burden entirely by transferring the offices of secretary to the Council of the North and clerk of the Privy Council to another, while Beale would receive a gift to ensure that his wife and children would be secure, and 'I shall spende the remnant of my dayes as a Countreye Clowne'.[20]

---

[18] Beale to Burghley(?), early 1595, BL, Lansdowne MS 68/111, fol. 248r–v, misdated c.1591 by endorsement, but dating here inferred from corroborating internal evidence and the mentioning of Rokeby's widow in Huntingdon to Lord Keeper Puckering, 31 March 1595, BL, Harley MS 6997, fol. 5r (orig.). For Beale's complaints regarding health, concern for wife and children, and reference to the office at York, see his to Burghley, July/August 1591, BL, Lansdowne MS 68/107, fol. 238r–v.
[19] Beale to Burghley, 24 April 1595, BL, Lansdowne MS 79/80, fol. 192r (orig.). The draft in BL, Additional MS 48116, fols 338r–45v, is suggestive in Beale's interlinear additions emphasizing his merits, e.g. that 'I haue the knowledge of tounges and experience [of service abroad and at home]', fol. 344v. The Smith in question was probably Thomas Smith, Essex's secretary. ODNB.
[20] Beale to Burghley, 24 April 1595, BL, Lansdowne MS 79/80, fol. 194v (orig.). Selling his books would have been a bitter blow, but later in the year Beale clearly wanted to continue building his collection by acquiring Robert Parsons' A Conference abovt the Next Svccession to the Crowne of Ingland (Antwerp, 1595) (STC 19398). Beale to Sidney, 25 September 1595, Kent History and Library Centre, U1475/C15/2, fol. 2r (orig.); cf. Beale's follow-up on 20 December, in which he wrote that he only wanted a copy of Parsons' book for future reference should he need to answer its claims 'when tyme and occacion should requyre', Kent History and Library Centre, U1475/C15/3, fol. 1r (orig.); misdated

Beale was no clown, nor would he be rusticated in the years to come. In the coming months, various candidates were put or came forward to replace Rokeby, one of whom was an old acquaintance from Beale's youth, Thomas Danett, but by mid August John Ferne of Inner Temple was chosen as Beale's deputy. Despite Beale's infirmity and advancing age, his continued if comparatively measured activity can be seen both in the fact that he was still paid the fee of £33.6.8 (to be precise) and in Ferne's and others' subsequent correspondence.[21] In Ferne's letters to Cecil, the loyalty and close collaboration with Beale is clear and consistent, and a frequent concern of Ferne's is that his and Beale's positions be secure and safe from encroachment by others. With the death of Huntingdon as Lord President of the North in December 1595, both Ferne and Beale justifiably feared that a period of uncertainty and shake up of roles would ensue, especially regarding the choice of examiners for the Court and Council of the North (which could bring certain financial remuneration).[22] Beale claimed the selection of such examiners was granted to him as secretary, but that practice was under threat to move to others of the Council, so there was a power struggle and debate about precedence occasioned by Huntingdon's expiry. In defending what he thought was his right, Beale penned a memorandum of things to be considered before the next commission, but it was all for nought.[23] Despite protestations to the contrary, the choice of examinership remained with the president, the Council of the North writing to the Privy Council in brief but clarion terms. At the death of the next lord president (de facto if not formally, Matthew Hutton, archbishop of York) in summer 1599, another threat to Beale's finances came when Edward Hoby, Burghley's nephew, sought to secure Beale's office as secretary and drive Beale in the process to resign the same. Forcefully but graciously did Ferne defend Beale's right to exercise the office however compromised it had become.[24]

to 21 December in Arthur Collins (ed.), *Letters and Memorials of State*, 2 vols (London, 1746), 1.396. A *Conference* is not listed in the booklist, BL, Hargrave MS 107, so it remains an open question whether Beale ever acquired a copy of a text so very dangerous to own.

[21] Danett to Burghley, 1 May 1595, CP, 32/14 (orig.). Among Thomas Norton's papers that worked their way to Beale is an account by Danett on the reasons for the execution for the duke of Norfolk in 1572. BL, Additional MS 48023, fols 160r–2r; additional copy in Additional MS 48027, fols 109r–11v. On Danett, see Chapter 2. ? to Burghley, 6/7? June 1595, TNA, SP 12/252, fol. 103r. Elizabeth to Huntingdon, 13 August 1595, TNA, SP 12/253, fol. 118r. Copy of Elizabeth's warrant for the Council's fees at York, 29 September 1595, CP, 141/102; Ferne does not appear to have been paid in the month after starting the job. His attendance at the Council preceded his appointment as secretary, though he was recognized as secretary from the meeting of 5 July 1596. BL, Harley MS 1088, fol. 39v. According to this list of meetings and attendees, Beale went north to York not a single time during his tenure as secretary of the council despite his suggesting otherwise to Burghley on 24 April 1595; see above, n. 20.

[22] On the issue of examiners and fees, see Reid, *King's Council in the North*, 257–8.

[23] Beale's memorandum relating to officers of the Council of the North, *c.*1596–early 1599, BL, Additional MS 48152, fols 205r–12r, with note regarding the examinership at 207v.

[24] Ferne to Cecil, 25 December 1595, CP, 36/101 (orig.); 25 January 1596, CP, 30/13 (orig.); 11 July 1599, CP, 53/27 (orig.); 1 August 1599, CP, 71/111 (orig.); cf. Ferne to Beale, 3 July 1599, TNA, SP 12/271, fols 123r–4r (orig.). For the argument against Beale's choice of examiners, Richard Cole to Cecil, 24 March 1597, CP, 39/50 (orig.), with enclosure, 39/49; W[illiam?] Slingsby to Cecil, 31 March 1597, TNA, SP 12/262, fol. 153r (orig.); Council of the North to the Privy Council, 20 November 1599,

For his own part, Beale tried to protect his rights as best he could. He had remained in touch and involved with the goings-on at York, defending his position and grant, but he confessed to Cecil in 1599 that his financial reward was so diminished that he wondered whether it was worth the effort. Having by this point lost the argument regarding the examinerships, he claimed that his office at York 'yeildeth not vnto me somoche as may fund my poore house' in London.[25] Indeed, later that year he heard from York that Richard Cole, one of the examiners, had recently died and that the then lord president, Thomas Cecil, Lord Burghley and brother of Robert Cecil, had granted the reversion of the office to one of his own servants. Shut out of the process entirely but also recounting the history of how the choice of examiners had shifted from the office of secretary to that of president, Beale feared that his finances would soon be so reduced that 'all habilitye of liuinge wilbe wholye taken from me'.[26] Adding insult to injury, he also complained that, contrary to his letters patent and the custom that Beale as secretary would officially hold the Signet in the North, Lord President Burghley sought to retain the Signet. Beale could reasonably read this tendency as more than just an oversight of custom or potential slight, for he saw an increasingly slippery slope to his own (and his family's) poverty. In the end and with the first Baron Burghley dead, Beale knew that his only hope for assistance—either in regaining the examinerships or in financial salvation otherwise—lay in Cecil, to whom he wrote again in a tone of servility mixed with shame for his poverty.[27]

During the mid and late 1590s, Beale also took on an increased role as a legal consultant. Long had he offered such advice on parliamentary affairs and religious recusants, for example, frequently peppered with historical context, but in his final decade the net was cast further. He had worked with Caesar at least since 1589, but during these years he also worked with a cast of others, some long familiar like Killigrew and John Herbert, while others were comparatively new colleagues for legal causes like Christopher Perkins (Parkins), Daniel Dun (Donne), William Fleetwood, John Croke, Francis Bacon, Edward Coke, and Christopher Yelverton. All were men of law, civil or ecclesiastical, some of them members of the Inns of Court. Caesar and Coke would go on to have the most significant careers during the subsequent reigns of James and Charles, while

TNA, SP 12/273, fol. 55r (orig.). See also, Hutton and Council of the North to Burghley, 22 December 1595, CP, 36/98 (orig.); Hutton and Council to Burghley, 24 November 1597, CP, 175/132 (orig.); Privy Council to Lord President of the North, 4 November 1598, TNA, SP 12/268, fols 166r–7r; John Benet to Cecil, 3 October 1599, CP, 74/9 (orig.).

[25] Beale to Cecil, 5 May 1599, CP, 70/1, fol. 1r. (orig.). Contrast John Stow's description of Beale's house in 1598 as 'fayre'; see Chapter 7, n. 1.

[26] Beale to Cecil, 24 October 1599, CP, 74/50, fol. 1v (orig.). On Burghley's presidency, as well as that of Huntingdon, see Reid, King's Council in the North, 209–39.

[27] Beale to Cecil, 24 October 1599, CP, 74/50, fol. 2v (orig.). Beale to Cecil, 27 October 1599, CP, 74/55 (orig.).

Beale's bond with Yelverton was solidified by his daughter Margaret's marriage to Henry Yelverton (son of Christopher) sometime in the 1590s.[28]

The breadth of commissions and cases thrust on Beale further demonstrates his continued and indispensable utility. Working with Killigrew, he was charged by the Privy Council in 1594 to investigate matters pertaining to a set of individuals, and while the nature of their infraction(s) remains obscure, perhaps more telling is the fact that Killigrew and Beale had a deputy to assist them, a certain Roger Saunders.[29] With Fleetwood, Beale was to investigate a particularly sensitive issue regarding fraud and estate administration in 1597. To avoid excessive legal fees for the plaintiff, the issue required, according to the Privy Council, 'men of indifferency and good discrecion that may discerne and reporte vnto vs what truthe they finde in this complainte, and be a meanes to procure satisfaccion to the peticioner [...] [f]or which purpose wee haue liked well of you'.[30] Even if Beale was still kept at a distance from Elizabeth and Whitgift, the latter of whom sat on the queen's Privy Council, he was still deemed a legal professional of a dispassionate mind and discrete comportment. Also, just as he had previously been involved in the interrogation of Catholic recusants and Jesuits, especially Campion, Beale was sought in 1594 for the same purpose again for examining, among others, the Jesuit Robert Southwell and the Catholic earl of Arundel, Philip Howard, both of whom had been imprisoned in the Tower.[31] A few years later, Beale was again requested, alongside John Croke, Recorder of London, and Francis Bacon, to examine dangerous criminals from Cumberland then incarcerated for breaking into Carlisle Castle.[32]

Of a similar name and faith to Arundel but of entirely different identity was Thomas Arundell, later Baron Arundell of Wardour (1605), whose early Catholicism put him under suspicion during the 1580s, and whose acceptance of a title (count) from the Holy Roman Emperor in 1595 ensured that he fell foul with Elizabeth. In this instance, Beale was informed that, upon Arundell's release from gaol, the new count would be under house arrest at Beale's own home. As if the financial pressures of his family and servants were not enough, now he was charged with providing for another. As he put it to Cecil from his 'poore house in London', 'my drinke and other prouicions are allmost spent [...] I am lyke to be

---

[28] On all save Fleetwood, see *ODNB*, but use with caution the article on Henry Yelverton, which states that he married Beale's daughter 'Mary'; Beale did not have a daughter so named. The painter, Mary Beale (née Cradock) was born in 1633. For Fleetwood, see *HoP:HoC*, noting the two named William (b. 1551, b. 1566) who both had significant careers in law and politics. Beale's library and archive descended via the Yelverton family. See Chapter 1.

[29] Killigrew and Beale to Saunders, 7 November 1594, CP, 171/22 (orig.).

[30] Privy Council to Beale and Fleetwood, 23 February 1597, TNA, PC 2/22, 135–6, quotation at 136; cf. 145 for the ensuing proceedings.

[31] Richard Young to Lord Keeper Puckering, 14 April 1594, TNA, SP 12/248, fols 159r–61r (orig.).

[32] Privy Council to the Recorder, Bacon, and Beale, 17 July 1597, TNA, PC 2/22, 314.

putt to a further charge, then my poore liuelyhoode will beare.[33] Beale's specific role in treating with Arundell is explained both by the latter's Catholicism and Beale's experience in examination, and in Beale's understanding of the Holy Roman Empire and Arundell's acceptance of a title from Emperor Rudolf II. In short, Beale recorded for Cecil his 'simple opinion, that the Emperor could not Lawfullye grant anie such honor *in Regno non recognoscente superiorem*, without a greate preiudice of her Majestie, and the whole Nobilitye of the realme' of England. Beale based his opinion on his previous knowledge and a fresh reading of Arundell's own account of, and tract defending his, being created Count of the Empire written for Burghley, as well as Rudolf's explanation to Elizabeth that Arundell deserved the title because of his service in war against the Turk.[34] In any event, Arundell lived to serve another English monarch, while Beale proved his worth to the current sovereign in this instance by accommodating uncomfortably and in his home the type of suspect he normally met in the Tower or the Fleet.

Legal matters further afield also called for Beale's attention. In 1598 he was among a party to examine and come to a conclusion regarding a long-running case in Newcastle upon Tyne, and earlier that same year he was commissioned, along with Caesar, for the same in Guernsey; the latter case is suggestive.[35] The jurats of Guernsey had sent to the Privy Council their complaint regarding the governor of the island, and the Council consequently turned to Beale because of his previous experience and knowledge of the island, not through his own travel but rather his research in the early 1580s. Beale had previously collected a considerable amount of material, some stretching back to the reign of Mary, on matters of administration, jurisdiction, and custom in the Channel Islands. Much of it was directly from the Privy Council registers regarding various grievances, but also included was an original letter of John Hammond to Walsingham with the former's opinions on legal matters in Guernsey. No mere collector, Beale also wrote his own set of draft articles on the relationship between Guernsey and Sark, so the Council's calling on him later in the 1590s was not necessarily without precedent.[36] England's relationship with nearby islands and seas was by this point simply part of Beale's overall competency and sphere of responsibility. No surprise, then, that he became increasingly involved in cases of piracy raised by

[33] Beale to Cecil, 9 May 1597, CP, 50/98, quotation at fol. 1v (orig.). Others also knew of Beale's accommodating Arundell; see, e.g. Rowland Whyte to Sidney, 30 April 1597, Kent History and Library Centre, U1475/C12/88 (orig.); statement regarding Beale on fol. 2r. On Whyte, see below.

[34] Beale's copies with memoranda, BL, Additional MS 48126, fols 18r–29v. See also, *ODNB*.

[35] Privy Council to Beale et al. regarding Newcastle, 21 November 1598, TNA, PC 2/24, 147, with follow-up at 180. Privy Council to Caesar and Beale, 23 February 1598, TNA, PC 2/23, 182, with follow-up at 239–40 and TNA, PC 2/25, 401.

[36] Beale's copies of materials relative to the Channel Islands, with special reference to Guernsey, mostly early 1580s, BL, Additional MSS 48001, fols 360r–423v; 48083, fols 201r–3r. Hammond to Walsingham, 28 May 1583, BL, Additional MS 48062, fol. 402r–v (orig.). Beale's 'Touching the Isle Sarck', 1582/3, BL, Additional MS 48062, fols 410r–13v (draft in Beale's hand), 405r–7r (fair copy). On the islands, see David Cressy, *England's Islands in a Sea of Troubles* (Oxford, 2020), esp. 37–57.

Danish and French merchants looking to deliver grain to the Spanish market (thus in conflict with the English understanding that foodstuffs could be considered contraband).

Just as the English could complain of Danish, French, or other countries' pirates, so too could these countries complain of the English. In 1598, the Danes and French having done so, Beale was commissioned along with several others (most significantly Caesar and Herbert, as masters of the requests) to hear and decide cases without appeal brought by foreign subjects accusing the English of piracy or harm otherwise. Although Beale and the others had not met as frequently as they had been instructed at first, their activity picked up in 1599 and continued into 1601.[37] This experience in investigating cases of piracy brought Beale closer to Caesar, other civil lawyers, and the High Court of the Admiralty. Additionally, as can be seen in their correspondence with Cecil, it meant that Beale was a known quantity at the Doctors' Commons, where the society of civilians met and decided cases of comparatively lower significance. Beale had been admitted to Gray's Inn in early 1587, so he had access to the Inns of Court for common lawyers, but he was not formally a member of the deliberately exclusive Doctors' Commons because he never earned the requisite degree in civil law. Even so, his working with Caesar (a member since 1586) will have provided additional access to like-minded and similarly experienced civilians. His work with Caesar might have been some comfort even if only late in life, especially because some who sought his fees were coming from the Inns of Court.[38] Suggesting the degree to which Beale had been absent from meetings of the Privy Council by this point, in these and later official commissions Beale was consistently named not as a clerk of the Council but rather as the secretary of the Council of the North; and yet, in correspondence from the Privy Council to Caesar, Beale, and others, he was named as a clerk of the Council as usual but probably more as a

---

[37] Privy Council to Herbert, Caesar, Beale, Perkins, and Dun, 22 December 1598, TNA, PC 2/24, 201. Commissions regarding piracies against the Danish and French, 3 January 1599, TNA, C 66/1511, mm. 8d–9d; copy of that for the French, TNA, SP 12/270, fols 4r–5r, the calendared version of which cited by Wernham, *Return of the Armadas*, 279, might have led him to ignore similar arguments raised by the Danes. Beale retained copies and drafts of various materials relating to the French complaints in particular: BL, Additional MSS 48100, 48115, fols 304r–48v. Cf. Beale's activity with Caesar regarding the complaints of a Dutchman: Privy Council to Caesar, Beale, et al., 2 April 1598, TNA, PC 2/23, 213. Beale's copy of a commission for Herbert, Caesar, Beale, et al., 12 February 1601, BL, Additional MS 48086, fols 166r–73v.

[38] Caesar, Beale, et al. to Cecil, 14 and 30 August 1599, CP, 72/70, 73/53 (both orig.). Beale's interest in the High Court of the Admiralty is seen in his borrowing from Caesar his copy of the medieval *De Officio Admiralitatis* (temp. Henry VI): BL, Additional MS 48019, fols 180r–6r; cf. Beale's copy of the Black Book of the Admiralty, BL, Additional MS 48028, fols 185r–217r. For an overview of long chronology, see G. D. Squibb, *Doctors' Commons: A History of the College of Advocates and Doctors of Law* (Oxford, 1977), noting Caesar's membership at 163. Joseph Foster (ed.), *The Register of Admissions to Gray's Inn, 1521–1889, together with the Register of Marriages in Gray's Inn Chapel, 1695–1754* (London, 1889), 70. Beale continued to work with Caesar and others at the Doctors' Commons in the run-up to his mission to Boulogne to treat for peace with Spain. See, e.g. Whyte to Sidney, 26 February 1600, Kent History and Library Centre, U1475/C12/217, fol. 1r (orig.).

matter of respect. After all, he had been the senior clerk since Edmund Tremayne's death in 1582. The 1590s were a decade that took Beale away from the floor of the House of Commons and presence of Queen Elizabeth, and while his stature might have declined to the point that he no longer could sit at the table of the Privy Council, the respect he commanded nevertheless ensured that he would have a place at a table in the Doctors' Commons. So, too, did he retain his place as a foreign policy expert.[39]

Informing and Involved Abroad

During the 1560s, 1570s, and 1580s, Beale had been among the most vociferous in advocating for Protestants in theatres of conflict across Europe. He had called for the beheading of Mary Queen of Scots earlier than most, personally sought to unify those opposed to Rome, and collaborated with the Dutch in their resistance against Catholic Spain. By the 1590s, though, the wars of religion in France and the Netherlands were weighing heavily on both the minds and purses of all parties involved, including the English. In his writings and activity during his final decade, Beale, like many, mellowed. He could stand firm on matters of principle and where English rights needed defending, but his stance on the wars softened and, some may say, became more realistic in the face what would otherwise be everlasting war.[40]

In the case of France, his thinking can be seen in a discourse he wrote in 1593 for Robert Sidney, younger brother of Philip and Elizabeth's extraordinary ambassador to France in winter 1593/4, and with whom Beale would later correspond. By this point Henri IV (crowned in February) had abandoned Protestantism in favour of Catholicism in an effort to bring the wars to conclusion, but the state of the ideological and martial conflicts was very much still in flux. In two heavily annotated drafts, Beale's discourse set the question of religious toleration in France in a wider context of how such toleration had worked (or not) in other places, namely the Holy Roman Empire, Poland, and the Netherlands.[41] The discourse employed the Christian fathers and various histories to drive home the point that liberty of conscience should be recognized whenever and wherever possible. Beale's experience with hardline Lutherans in Germany and, more

---

[39] Commissions dated 12 November 1599, 11 December 1600, 2 April 1601, TNA, C 66/1511, mm. 6d–7d; 66/1555, mm. 17d–18d; 66/1554, mm. 10d–11d. Privy Council to Caesar, Beale, et al., 22 August 1600, TNA, PC 2/25, 336.

[40] On war in the 1590s, see Paul E. J. Hammer, *Elizabeth's Wars: War, Government and Society in Tudor England, 1544–1604* (Basingstoke, 2003), 154–235.

[41] 'Touchinge a toleration of two Religions in one Realme', late 1593, BL, Additional MS 48044, fols 253r–74v. Memorandum on religious toleration, October/November 1593, BL, Additional MS 48152, fols 274r–84v. Internal comparisons indicate that the former version incorporated amendments suggested in the latter, with additional changes in Beale's hand.

recently, Whitgift's strict crackdown on—and lack of toleration for—the Puritans was on display. He asked,

> of late yeres in Germanie, what good hathe come to gods Churche by the furious subscriptions, imprisonments, banishments, and other hard vsages of the vbiquitaryes? And this Churche of Englande[,] hathe it receaued anye benefit by the exaction of their newe oathe and subscription, saue that manie good ministers haue ben depriued and putt to silence without cause, and the people left in ignorance, to the intent that they maye haue no knowledge to discerne of the actions of the Clergie, but to be ruled & gouerned in securitie, as they should thincke good?[42]

Beale then anticipated his detractors, that is, those advocating strict conformity either among Protestants or across the Protestant-Catholic divide.

> Some will perhappes saye, that two religions cannot be mainteyned together without continuall civuill contencions and broyles as maye appeare by sondrie examples in the Ecclesiasticall histories and lykewise in our dayes in France and other places. I graunte there wilbe at the first some difficultie in the establishinge of suche a toleracion: but if suche a toleracion be not established, then for one tumult or sedicion, there wilbe twentye, by openinge a gappe to all impietie, iniustice, and licentiousness, as experience hathe taughte vs euerye where. ffor it is true that which Lactantius wrytethe, *Persecutiones* (which must followe, if the toleracion be taken awaye) *introducunt impias religiones, et postremo, ne coli quidem vel a paucis Deum sinunt.*[43]

Thus, Beale held that tolerating differences of conscience, while not ideal because it were better that all agreed on a broad but pure understanding of Christianity, was a practical necessity. His religious idealism aside, the cold realities of political life and ecclesiastical authority had taught him that permitting those of another religious persuasion to worship quietly but without disturbing the peace was the way forward. His reference to Lactantius—for the idea that persecutions lead to impious religions and, in the end, do not even permit God to be honoured by a few—did not mean that English Catholics were off the hook. Indeed, that they had sought so many times to overthrow the government and replace Elizabeth, of course, precluded any toleration towards them.

Beale's knowledge of French history and current affairs extended beyond his own experience in the 1560s or his administrative competencies, for during the

---

[42] 'Touchinge', BL, Additional MS 48044, fol. 265v.
[43] 'Touchinge', BL, Additional MS 48044, fols 265v–6r. The quotation of Lactantius has not been traced but probably derives from his *De Mortibus Persecutorum*.

1590s he had also employed a Frenchman, Pierre Morlet, as tutor in the French language to Francis, Beale's first son (b. 1577) who had followed in his father's footsteps by entering Gray's Inn in 1591. Morlet acknowledged his debt to Beale as patron in a grammar of the language printed in 1596, in which he also named Francis specifically and praised Beale for his travels and linguistic abilities. Offering further detail on Beale's reputation abroad, Morlet noted that Beale was respected in Germany even by those who had never met him personally. One in particular deserved mention: David Chytraeus, who had provided the letter of introduction and commendation for Morlet to Beale. The tuition provided in French appears to have paid off for Francis, who spent time in France a few years earlier in life than had his father but similarly with the support of a Cecil (Robert).[44] These personal connections aside, later in 1596 Beale's expertise in drafting treaties and courting the Germans would again call him into action.

Beale had been adamantly opposed to peace with Spain in the late 1580s lest the Dutch be left without sufficient support. With France now numbering among those opposed to Philip II of Spain and as a potential ally of the Dutch, Beale saw the situation differently. There was still no peace with Spain on the horizon, but an opportunity arose to go on the offensive in a big way and force Spain to accept a treaty favourable to the Dutch. The negotiations that led to the Treaty of Greenwich in May 1596 were at various points 'decidedly stormy' because the requests made by Henri IV for funds and forces met Elizabeth's characteristic hesitation and parsimony.[45] In a work typical of Beale, a lifetime of broadly European intelligence combined with Protestant conviction. Written again for Robert Sidney, who was involved in the negotiations, and with reference to his earlier piece, Beale's 'notes' offered a panoramic view of the offensive and defensive Anglo-French alliance and how it could be expanded to include other parties, just as it later did with the Dutch in the Triple Alliance of October 1596.[46] Beale's position as an observer from the sidelines is evident in the fact that these 'notes' were designed as a proposition to inform the English commissioners. The commissioners were to bear in mind the manifold injuries inflicted upon Europe by Spain, notwithstanding Elizabeth's efforts to achieve piece by way of 'manye messages [...] whereof Mr D. [John] James can geue you out of Mr Secretaryes

[44] Pierre Morlet, *Ianitrix, siue, Institvtio ad Perfectam linguae Gallicae cognitionem acquirendam* (Oxford, 1597) (STC 18114), with letter of dedication dated 'Decimoquinto die Cal. Martij. Anno salutis nostrae 1596' (15 February 1597) at sigs ¶2r–¶4r. The recommendation of Morlet by Chytraeus has not been traced in the known correspondence; see Chapter 7. Foster, *Register of Admissions to Gray's Inn*, 77. On Francis Beale's subsequent career, HoP:HoC. Beale to Cecil, 30 September 1599, CP, 73/111 (orig.).

[45] Wernham, *Return of the Armadas*, 69–81, at 74, offers a narrative and analysis of the public treaty and secret articles but without reference to Beale or Sidney.

[46] 'Notes concerninge a treatie and league offensiue and defensiue betwene her Majestie, the Frenche Kinge &c.' early 1596 (possibly misdated by Beale to September), BL, Additional MS 48044, fols 127r–30v; draft with Beale's amendments, BL, Additional MS 48102, fols 351r–60v.

[Walsingham's] papers, particular notes'. Furthermore, Beale pushed that 'all princes and estates haue an interest in this cause and as the danger is common to them all, so ought the prouicion to be likewise common'.[47] The treaty was to be penned, according to Beale, in an inclusive manner, and 'it were (in mine opinion) good, that her Majestie and the Frenche kinge sent [sic] into Germanye Ambassadors to solicite the princes to ioyne with them'; of special importance were princes in the Palatinate, Württemberg, Hesse, Magdeburg, and Baden, some of whom could at the very least impede Spanish recruitment of mercenaries going into the Netherlands.[48] By citing precedent, Beale cast aside the argument that the princes of Germany could not enleague with foreign powers because of the Imperial constitution, and he pushed further to approach the Danes, Swiss, Venetians, and certain princes in Italy. Ideally, with all agreed, 'a booke might be conceaued in good termes and published concerninge this matter'.[49] In the run-up to the version of the public treaty signed on 14 May, Beale drafted some of the language ultimately approved. Although the number of articles and overall length increased after Beale's draft, the core of Beale's suggestions was incorporated—in some instances verbatim.[50]

In October the alliance widened to incorporate the Dutch formally, but Beale was serious about reaching out to the German princes. On 17 September he wrote to Cecil acknowledging their recent discussions at court regarding Germany, including Cecil's request for a discourse on how the princes could be dealt with and approached regarding the late league. Beale was earnest in deferring to those better acquainted 'with the secret intencions and affayres of her Majestie', but his empty rhetoric that others could improve upon his discourse on the Germans rang hollow. He claimed that, despite his experience in German affairs, he 'had not oportunitye to doe better' and 'my memorie not so good, as to remember all things requisyte'.[51] If indeed he worked from memory for his discourse, one can fairly say that his recollection was still sharp; more likely, he drew on his archive mental as well as physical.

The discourse completed just five days later is extensive and exists in multiple copies, suggesting that it was distributed and taken seriously by Cecil and

---

[47] 'Notes concerning a treatie', BL, Additional MS 48044, fols 128v–29r. On John James and Walsingham's papers, see Hsuan-Ying Tu, 'Dispersal of Francis Walsingham's Papers', 471–92. Contrast the confusion of 'Francis' James in Taviner, 120–1.

[48] 'Notes concerning a treatie', BL, Additional MS 48044, fol. 129v. On the impediment of forces in Germany going to serve Philip in the Netherlands, see AGR and Van Tol, Germany and the French Wars of Religion.

[49] 'Notes concerning a treatie', BL, Additional MS 48044, fol. 130v.

[50] Beale's holograph draft of the Treaty of Greenwich, endorsed 13 May 1596, BL, Additional MS 48126, fols 167r–71v. Comparison with the printed text of the treaty in J. Dumont (ed.), Corps Universel Diplomatique du Droit des Gens, Vol. 5, Part 1 (Amsterdam, 1728), 525–6, demonstrates the level of incorporation.

[51] Beale to Cecil, 17 September 1596, CP, 44/102 (orig.).

others.[52] It incorporated and expanded upon the arguments in Beale's 'notes' for Sidney, even repeating some language in the case of the supposed limitations of the Imperial constitution and expanding the alliance to include the Swiss and Venetians. Surveying several decades of English efforts to get the princes onboard for the Protestant cause, Beale recited some of the familiar points, such as the call for the princes to meet at a central location for consultation (in this case, Bremen), and the need to get the king of Denmark involved (as a duke of Holstein and, thus, prince of the Empire). He also, though, called on his memory and drew attention to certain letters and materials that he himself had seen, such as a letter by Frederik II, King of Denmark, to Elizabeth, 'promisinge her to come and assist her in his owne person, in case she were assayled by the Spaniardes', noting further that '[i]t were conuenient, that Mr D. James should seeke out this letter'. Even more to the point regarding efforts for alliance was Beale's having seen 'the copye of a treatye, betwene kinge Henrie the 7 and king Henrie the 8 and George Duke of Saxonye, greate vncle to the [present] yonge Elector of Saxonye'.[53] Working at least partly from memory, as he claimed, Beale offered some of the same arguments as had been advanced in the 1570s and 1580s, and in so doing he might have looked a little old-fashioned, but such was his experience, such his generation.

As had frequently been the case regarding efforts for Anglo-German alliance building, the timing was off. English relations with the Hanseatic League had been testy for well over a decade, the perennial complaints being the lapsed privileges of the Hanse in the Steelyard, the monopoly held by the Merchant Adventurers regarding the price of cloth, and, more recently, stopping the Hanse's trade with Spain. In July 1595, Emperor Rudolf II wrote to Elizabeth on behalf of the Hanse at Lübeck and requesting that their grievances be addressed, and in response the queen replied in the negative—both in letter form and in print. Beale acquired copies of both letters, Rudolf's in German and Elizabeth's in Latin, endorsing them for later reference as required, and an English translation of Rudolf's soon circulated for those without German.[54] The situation did not

---

[52] Beale's heavily amended draft, September 1596, BL, Additional MS 48044, fols 334r–57r. Final version dated 22 September and ascribed to Beale, damaged by fire and mould, BL, Cotton MS Galba, D. XIII, fols 149r–58r. Final version, 'An aduise in what sorte', dated 22 September, TNA, SP 81/7, fols 230r–7r.

[53] 'An aduise', TNA, SP 81/7, fol. 235r. Frederik's letter has not been traced, but for the king's enthusiasm regarding Elizabeth on at least one rather drunken occasion, see *AGR*, 100. For similar arguments, see Chapter 5. Beale also referred to a Latin collection 'of sondrie vnkindnesses' offered by Philip to Elizabeth 'when Sir Thomas Wilkes and Mr Waad were sent into Spain' (231r–v), though Beale's own collection was written in English and dated 30 May 1591: BL, Harley MS 253, fols 43r–4r, followed by a list of potential objections and responses (to 49r).

[54] Rudolf to Elizabeth, 15 July 1595; Elizabeth to Rudolf, 8 November 1595, BL, Additional MS 48115, fols 23r–5v, 21r–2v. English translation of Rudolf's and printed copy of Elizabeth's, BL, Cotton MS Nero, B. IX, fols 174r–7v; more English versions of Rudolf's, TNA, SP 80/1, fols 173r–8v, followed by drafts of Elizabeth's to 184v. For comment on this episode to January 1598, Lloyd, *England and the German Hanse*, 341.

improve, and by 1597 the city of Gdansk (Danzig) had sent a well-known representative to London, Georg Liseman, along with a newcomer, Pawel Działyński, who also represented Sigismund III, King of Poland. Beale's role in the ensuing drama was not at centre stage, but, armed with decades' worth of papers on the Hanse and, more recently, negotiations with the Poles, he was in a better position than anyone else to inform from behind the scenes.[55] The confrontation between the queen and Działyński on 25 July has been passed down as an example of Elizabethan lore. In short, the ambassador offered a series of complaints from the people of Gdansk and his sovereign, suggesting further that Elizabeth was in violation of the law of nations in banning their trade with Spain. Famously, then and now, Elizabeth lashed back entirely in Latin and, according to Cecil, extempore. Among Beale's copies of these materials, he recorded the ambassador's noble title and possible education at the Catholic citadel of Ingolstadt.[56] The next day, Liseman came to Beale's house 'vnder color of old acquaintance' and to discuss a way forward in light of Działyński's experience. Beale had not witnessed the queen's exchange, but he declared to Cecil (who had) that he hoped a resolution would come soon. Moreover, it appears that, after Liseman's visit, Beale and Perkins went to the ambassador at his lodging to offer counsel because, as Beale put it, 'then wold I haue desired this man to haue sent the message by writing himself, or to haue vsed the meanes of sum other'.[57] In an effort to build bridges, Elizabeth told Cecil to instruct Beale, Caesar, and Perkins—all men of 'knowledges and experiences'—to meet and prepare a summary report for how best to deal with both Liseman and Działyński before their departures from London.[58] By this point, however, the die was cast. On 1 August 1597, Rudolf signed an imperial mandate expelling the Merchant Adventurers from the Hanse towns, including their residence at Stade; they were to be gone in a matter of months (see Fig. 17).

To protect English economic interests, the government sought to limit the damage and offer arguments to the contrary. Beale collected different English translations of the edict, one of which compared some of the original German with the English, and soon he was put to work.[59] A bout with the stone kept him

---

[55] On recent negotiations with the Poles, see BL, Additional MS 48152, fols 133r–7v, with Beale's observations in March 1596.

[56] Beale's copies, BL, Additional MS 48128, fols 50r–6v, with Beale's comment at 51r. Contrast the customary English perspective in Wernham, *Return of the Armadas*, 199–201, and Janet M. Green, 'Queen Elizabeth I's Latin Reply to the Polish Ambassador', *Sixteenth Century Journal*, 31 (2000), 987–1008, with the Polish view in Teresa Bałuk Ulewiczowa, '*Audiatur et Altera Pars*: The Polish Record of the Działyński Embassy of 1597', *British Catholic History*, 33 (2017), 501–33.

[57] Beale to Cecil, 27 July 1597, CP, 53/70, 1r, 1v (orig.). Bałuk-Ulewiczowa, '*Audiatur et Altera Pars*', 529, 531.

[58] Cecil to Beale, Caesar, and Perkins, 18 August 1597, BL, Lansdowne MS 139, fol. 344r (orig.); cf. their response of 24 August, 347r. Caesar's copy, BL, Lansdowne MS 157, fol. 262r.

[59] Imperial edict of 1 August 1597 (new style), BL, Additional MSS 48115, fols 286r–91r; 48126, fols 68r–71v, with marginal comparisons.

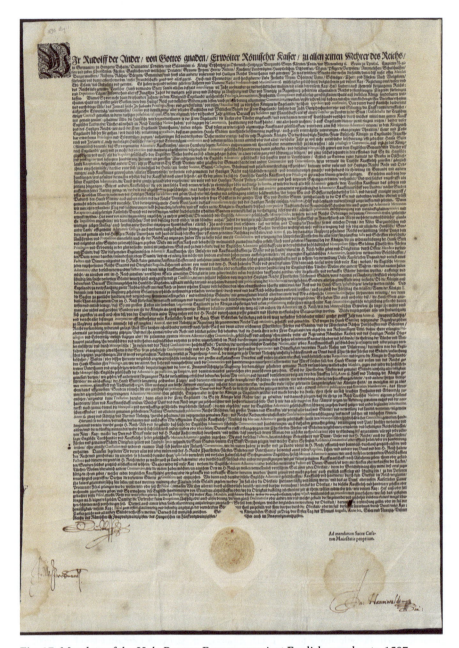

Fig. 17 Mandate of the Holy Roman Emperor against English merchants, 1597.
Geheimes Staatsarchiv Preußischer Kulturbesitz, I. HA GR, Rep. 50, Nr 25 a Fasz. 24.
Reproduced with permission.

on the sideline for a time in September, and a dispute with Perkins regarding precedence occupied his mind later that month. As it turned out, Perkins and Beale had a history. As a doctor in civil law from an unspecified university on the European mainland, Perkins had been offended that Beale's name came before his own in the paperwork regarding Liseman, but Perkins probably also held a grudge against Beale for the latter's role in keeping him as a prisoner under house arrest in late 1589 or early 1590 (because of his Catholic past and as a former Jesuit). In private correspondence, Beale seemed to question Perkins' credentials –'[h]e is (as he saiethe) a doctor of xxv yeres standing: he should doe well to shewe it'— and Beale thought he could better them if he had seen fit—'so might I haue ben xxx yeres agoe, if I had made anie accompt of suche vayne shewes'. Degrees or lack thereof aside, Beale feared 'that suche newe men are preferred before me' and yet insisted 'that in this matter with the Steedes of the Hanse, and in anie other[,] I shall not be founde inferior anye whitt vnto Mr Doctor'.[60] By the end of the year, Beale had reasserted his superiority, even supremacy, on matters relating to the Hanse, and Perkins knew it.

As if he did not already have enough source material for another work on the Hanse, Beale acquired certified transcriptions of the Chancery rolls from Michael Heneage, Joint keeper of the records at the Tower. Annotated by Beale, these records demonstrated the agreements, treaties, and customs of English traders and governments with foreign powers in northern Europe, including the Holy Roman Empire and the Hanse.[61] Having gathered more material and recovered his health and energy, in November Beale proposed how the English could respond to the imperial mandate of 1 August 1597. The principal element in the English response would be an official and published discourse in Latin defending the English position, laying out the reasons why and how the Hanse had deceived Rudolf into issuing the mandate. This book would be printed in 500 or 600 copies and distributed to Liseman, with copies also sent to various princes of the Empire and officials in Poland, including King Sigismund. Elizabeth would complement this book by sending an ambassador and letters to these princes and officials in the hope they would intercede with the emperor and get the mandate either revoked entirely or at least suspended so English merchants in the Empire could continue their trade in security. The book, Beale thought, should be translated into German and secretly printed for those who did not understand Latin, 'especiallie seinge the Emperors Mandate was published in the dutche tongue'. Additionally, because the imperial edict was published at Frankfurt am Main during the last book fair, 'I could wishe, that in the next Marte some Latin and dutche

---

[60] Beale to Cecil 28 September 1597, CP, 55/79, 1r, 1v, 2r (orig.). See also Cecil's comment on 29 August 1597 that only two of the three men (Beale, Perkins, Caesar) signed their letters to Cecil: BL, Lansdowne MS 139, fol. 348r (orig.). On Perkins, *ODNB*.

[61] BL, Additional MS 48086, fols 42r–164r, 175r–230r.

Copyes might be there dispersed secretlye, so as no harme may ensewe vnto the partye, that shall doe it.'[62] The book that Beale had in mind would complement that printed earlier in the year at Amsterdam and on behalf of the States General in reaction to the Polish ambassador. Then again, the book Beale envisioned was considerably longer than the nine pages printed at Amsterdam.[63]

The draft of Beale's book is extensive and the only known copy to survive, though from other sources one can tell that its publication and distribution were widely anticipated. The intention to publish in print is demonstrated by the draft title page, which included the very descriptive title stating that it was a response to Liseman in which the whole controversy between the queen and Hanse was explicated and the lack of resolution explained, with additional confutation of the Hanse's 'false and groundless' suggestions that led the emperor to send forth the mandate against the Merchant Adventurers. A narrative and digest of source material and official embassies in both directions, Beale's response repeated his usual way of proceeding by using and quoting from agreements and treaties both comparatively recent and medieval, and he cited the work of David Chytraeus at several points for good measure.[64] With many, including Elizabeth, wanting Beale's book to be published as the official English response to Liseman (as well as the Polish ambassador, by extension), in early December expectation mounted. The Privy Council instructed Caesar and Herbert to confer with Perkins, Fletcher, Dun, and Beale himself to discuss his discourse. The Council acknowledged 'the paines' taken by Beale, and, '[t]hough the same be written with very good iudgment and knowledge[,] Mr Beale being a man of speciall experience and exercise in those Causes', Elizabeth wanted to be certain that the printed publication be vetted appropriately by several learned minds, not just one. About a week later, Perkins told Burghley what he thought of Beale's work, confirming the

---

[62] 'An aduise what is fitte to be don', November 1597, BL, Additional MS 48011, fol. 256r–v, with quotations on verso, followed by Beale's notes on why this response was directed particularly at Liseman but also with reference to the subjects of the king of Poland. Beale was correct that the imperial mandate was published in German. It had arrived at Frankfurt by 22 September, though it seems that the first printed publication was at Lübeck on 29 September, then at Hamburg on 23 October, and at Stade on 28 October 1597. Ehrenberg, *Hamburg und England*, 195 n. 12, 196; for the longer chronology from 1587 to 1611, see 186–230. Cf. the discussion on the Merchant Adventurers' monopoly in the Empire in Wolf-Rüdiger Baumann, trans. Timothy Slater, *The Merchants Adventurers and the Continental Cloth-Trade (1560s–1620s)* (Berlin, 1990), 191–205; Leng, *Fellowship and Freedom*, 177–201. An excellent example of the now comparatively rare, printed text as a broadsheet (cf. USTC 750534-6), Geheimes Staatsarchiv Preußischer Kulturbesitz, I. HA GR, Rep. 50, Nr 25 a Fasz. 24; translation into French and published as a pamphlet at Brussels in 1597, *Translat du mandement et ordonnance de lempereur, emane en langue hault-allemande contre les Anglois monopoliers dicts marchans aduenturiers, residens à Staden* (USTC 75282).

[63] English translation printed at London in 1597: *The Ansvvere made by the Noble Lords the States, vnto the Ambassadour of Polonia* (STC 18452).

[64] 'Apologetia Responsio ad Georgium Lismannum Dantiscanum / Responsum pro Domino Georgio Lismanno Dantiscano', dated November 1597 at fol. 250r, BL, Additional MS 48011, fols 192r–250v, with references to Chytraeus at 206v, 237v, 238v, 239v, 240v, 241v, 242v, 243v. The work by Chytraeus has not been traced.

'great payns' taken to note 'many things fyt to be had in a rediness for those affares'. Nevertheless, 'the writing as yet is not parfett but in a good forwardness[,] and he is to be incorraged for the finishinge of yt.'[65]

For reasons unclear, Beale's response to Liseman was never printed. It could have been the case that his health prevented his putting the final touches on it, but, then again, he clearly remained active when an embassy was being prepared in December for a mission to Germany. Before Stephen Lesieur and John Wroth left London in early January, Beale acquired copies of Elizabeth's letters to the princes, and upon their return, copies of the princes' replies. Equally if not more significantly, Beale received a written report from Lesieur and an oral one from Wroth.[66] From the former, he learned that the princes of northern Germany would try to persuade Rudolf to revoke the mandate because it was injurious to the Holy Roman Empire, with many princes refusing to print the mandate, but they also admitted that they were subject to his decision in this regard. Lesieur also informed 'that this mandate hath bene procured by the importunate sollicitacion of the ministers of the king of Spayne, and certaine private men of Hamburg and Lubeck' because the Merchant Adventurers had moved their residence to Stade, but the more rogue members of the company did not help relations with the Hanse, either.[67] In sum, from Lesieur Beale had reason for hope that Rudolf had been met with a degree of resistance from the northern princes, whom Elizabeth could try to persuade to further action on her behalf. From Wroth Beale learned that Wroth, who had proceeded without Lesieur to the emperor, had good reason to hope for a revocation of the mandate as long as France did not make peace with Spain, but were that to happen, Rudolf would be emboldened to continue with the mandate in the hope that it would force Elizabeth to come to an agreement with him. In addition to the oral report, Wroth supplied Beale with a copy of Rudolf's written response to Elizabeth.[68] Thus, as ever, Beale was reminded that English relations with the Hanse and the Holy Roman Empire did not exist in a vacuum.

While the ambassadors were in the Empire, Elizabeth expelled the Hanse from the Steelyard and elsewhere in England. From Thomas Wilford, Chamberlain of the City of London, Beale received certified transcriptions of both the order

---

[65] Privy Council to Caesar and Herbert, 4 December 1597, TNA, PC 2/23, 102–3. Perkins to Burghley, 12 December 1597, TNA, SP 12/265, fol. 81r (orig.).

[66] Elizabeth's letters to various, with appropriate clauses, December 1597, BL, Additional MS 48128, fols 110r–17v, with replies at 44r–5v, 119r–24v. Lesieur's report, 1598, BL, Additional MS 48126, fols 50r–5r, with Beale's list of princes who sent replies to Elizabeth, 55v. Beale's note of conversation with Wroth, BL, Additional MS 48011, fol. 250r.

[67] Lesieur's report, 1598, BL, Additional MS 48126, fol. 51v. On the rogues, see Thomas Leng, 'Interlopers and Disorderly Brethren at the Stade Mart: Commercial Regulations and Practices amongst the Merchant Adventurers of England in the Late Elizabethan Period', *The Economic History Review*, 69 (2016), 823–43.

[68] Rudolf to Elizabeth, 24 April 1598, AUL, MS 1009/1, item 2.

written on 13 January for the Hanse to depart by the 28th, the same day that the Merchant Adventurers were to depart from Stade, and the Privy Council's addition that subjects of the king of Poland not allied with the Hanse towns were still permitted to trade according to their existing custom. From William Sebright, Town Clerk of London, Beale received an attested copy of Elizabeth's letter to the Lord Mayor and Sheriffs of London along the same lines regarding the Hanse's expulsion.[69] Even as relations with the Hanse continued to sour and the sands continued to shift, Beale remained informed, and his thinking can be seen in a draft paper he produced at some point in 1598 on the privileges of the Merchant Adventurers both within England and across the seas. He placed the blame for the impasse squarely on the shoulders of the Hanse, but he also considered several hypothetical situations, such as that the Merchant Adventurers might be broken up as a corporation. He also recognized that the Hamburgers had very recently offered some degree of reconciliation, and that the people of Lübeck were also active.[70] Unsurprisingly, when Lesieur was preparing for an embassy to the imperial diet at Speyer in early 1599, Beale had a hand in drafting Elizabeth's general letter of credence to the princes as well as the ambassador's instructions. More significantly, and reminiscent of his experience with the Germans going back to the 1560s, Beale appreciated that some of the princes were more friendly and inclined to assist English efforts than were others, so he drafted Elizabeth's individual letters to those in Hesse, Württemberg, and the electoral Palatinate. Recognizing Beale's role in crafting Elizabeth's position, upon his return Lesieur supplied Beale with copies of the princes' replies for his own reference.[71]

Related to but distinct from English engagements with the Hanse and the Empire were those with Denmark. Although Beale had been played a supporting role regarding Danish affairs since the 1570s, he took the leading role after the death of his friend Daniel Rogers in 1591. What had been an association between England and Denmark that included efforts to collaborate for the Protestant cause in the 1570s and 1580s became, after the death of King Frederik II in 1588, a much more economic and commercial relationship.[72] The string of ambassadors in

[69] Beale's copies, January 1598, BL, Additional MS 48128, fols 28r–9r, 40r–1v.

[70] BL, Additional MS 48126, fols 32r–44v, esp. 36v–7v. Leng has noted Beale's piece as 'impressively well informed on the [Merchant Adventurers'] history', *Fellowship and Freedom*, 191. Beale's copy of ten articles of the Hanse towns agreed at Lübeck, written by Hermanus Molleo, Secretary to Otto, Duke of Brunswick, 28 July 1598, BL, Stowe MS 163, fols 44r–9r.

[71] Beale's heavily amended drafts and copies of Elizabeth's letters, January 1599, with fair copies of replies dated February and March, BL, Additional MS 48128, fols 125r–46v. Comparison with the fair copy of Elizabeth's general letter to those at Speyer, 28 January 1599, demonstrates that Beale's changes were adopted: TNA, SP 81/8, fols 98r–102v. See also Beale's emendations to a draft of the Privy Council's reply to the ambassador from Hamburg, 24 June 1599, BL, Additional MS 48115, fols 111r–17v. Due to a chronological gap between TNA, PC 2/24 and 2/25 (late April 1599 to late January 1600), comparing Beale's amendments with the final response is not currently possible.

[72] Cf. Taviner, 169–70. On the regency government and comparative retreat from foreign causes, see Paul Douglas Lockhart, *Frederik II and the Protestant Cause: Denmark's Role in the Wars of Religion, 1559–1596* (Leiden, 2004), 298–328.

both directions during the late 1590s were, accordingly, sent largely to discuss mercantile issues and resolve complaints. Among Beale's papers relative to the Danish ambassadors' missions to London are accounts of two suggestive episodes. The first, in 1597, came when he bumped into the ambassador, Arild Huitfeldt (anglicized as Arnold Witfeld), on the street in London. Beale had been an acquaintance of Huitfeldt thirty-one years previously, back in 1566 when they were both in France (Huitfeldt pursuing his education in law at the University of Orléans), but now in 1597 he became ashamed when Huitfeldt challenged him regarding a discourtesy and because of 'the small accompte that is made of me' and the fact that other men were now in the ascendant.[73] The next year, Beale learned of the complaint by another Danish ambassador, Niels Krag (anglicized as Nicholas Crag), regarding his lodgings in London that were far inferior to those previously used in Denmark by the English ambassador, Christopher Perkins; Krag's were 'pestred with Cables & ropes' while Perkins was in 'the kings owne Castle'.[74] Also, more broadly, Krag complained that he was dealing with commissioners of lower standing (including Beale) than had Perkins, and Beale thought it important that Cecil and the lords of the Privy Council be aware of the Dane's dissatisfaction. Given Beale's role, he retained copies of Krag's orations and other paperwork that winter and spring of 1598–9, and then drafted the English commissioners' response before Krag's departure.[75]

His drafting of the response was symptomatic of other work preparatory for English ambassadors heading to Denmark at this time. For Edward, Lord Zouche, Beale wrote a memorandum on how to behave and address those in Denmark, this as a supplement to Zouche's official instructions. Beale covered comparatively elementary topics such as how to address King Christian IV and who his primary counsellors were, but he also noted that negotiations would be in Latin, and that Zouche should avoid using scholastic vocabulary and constructions, preferring instead the Danes' custom in speaking Latin. He also, though, offered advice on more specific topics, such as how to convey congratulations to the king and his new queen (and father-in-law) regarding their recent marriage, handle recent mercantile complaints regarding the arrest of goods, address trade into distant regions like Iceland and Muscovy, and navigate the controversy regarding Rudolf's mandate against the Merchant Adventurers. In closing, however, and recognizing

---

[73] Beale to Cecil, 28 September 1597, CP, 55/79 (orig.); at 1v Beale notes this exchange. He did not name the ambassador but refers to him only as the chancellor of Denmark, who was indeed Arild Huitfeldt, and who was in London in September 1597 for an embassy from Denmark. Beale acquired and retained copies of relevant papers from Huitfeldt's mission: BL, Additional MS 48152, fols 125r–31v. On Huitfeldt, see the entry in the *Dansk Biografisk Leksikon*, online at https://biografisklek-sikon.lex.dk.

[74] Beale to Cecil, 20 December 1598, TNA, SP 12/269, fol. 37r (orig.).

[75] Krag's oration, December 1598, BL, Additional MS 48128, fols 105r–9v. Krag's propositions and orations, commissioners' response and Beale's memorandum, April 1599, BL, Additional MS 48152, fols 14r–17r, 23r–24r, 28r–40r, 63r–84v, 89r–94r, 99v–105v.

his own diminished status in the machinery of governance and the formulation of foreign policy, Beale reminded Zouche that he offered only 'my simple opinion' and that he did not know the exact specifics behind the mission; as he admitted, Beale had 'onelye aymed at thinges' he suspected lay ahead of the ambassador.[76] In truth, his own derogation might have been overstated, for Beale also ended up drafting at least one of Elizabeth's later responses in these ongoing negotiations, carry on as they did later in 1598 and into 1599 in the embassy of Lesieur. Indeed, because of his satisfactory drafting in Elizabeth's name, Cecil informed Beale that 'Her Majesty requires you, that wrote the last letter, to consider for some draught of another' on behalf of certain English merchants seeking redress from the Danish king. As had been the case regarding Germany for decades, now in the 1590s Beale was the primary English expert on Denmark both historically and currently. To ensure that he remained abreast of the situation, especially because it potentially involved not only the Hanse but also Spanish pretentions in the Netherlands and elsewhere, he retained his drafts and acquired copies of all relevant paperwork—including the royal correspondence.[77]

Never far off in the background of Beale's mind was the war with Spain and fate of the Dutch Protestants. He had functioned as an official ambassador to the Low Countries in 1576, just four years after formally entering Elizabeth's service, and again as Leicester's assistant and English representative on the Dutch Council of State in 1587. In the mid and later 1590s, the war continued to drag on, and many looked for a way towards peace that would provide political freedoms and liberty of conscience for the Dutch. In 1595, Beale, along with Killigrew and Arthur Atye (Leicester's former secretary), both of whom had been with Beale in the Netherlands in 1587, were ordered by Burghley to conduct research and deliver a report on the outstanding debts owed by the Dutch to Elizabeth. This was no small task. In short, they were to consult the relevant agreements and disbursements either from their own collections (Beale's and Atye's, principally) and those of others if they could get access. Between June and September, they acquired additional papers from Walsingham's collections, then in the possession of John James, and those of Thomas Digges, conferring also with William Davison. Digges had been muster master in the Netherlands between 1585 and 1588, and he was involved in the initial discussions in 1595; after his death, his papers relevant to the project were acquired from his widow and, perhaps unsurprisingly, incorporated into Beale's own. Together with Killigrew and Atye, Beale came to realize that the Dutch 'haue ben to[o] cunninge for vs, according to the olde

---

[76] Beale's memorandum for Zouche, May 1598, BL, Additional MS 48152, fols 6r–13r, quotation at 12v.

[77] Cecil to Beale, September 1599, BL, Additional MS 48152, fol. 107r (orig.). Working drafts and copies, with related papers, BL, Additional MS 48152, fols 18r–26*v, 45r–60r, 85r–8r, 107r–20v. Propositions, replies, and royal correspondence, BL, Additional MSS 48126, fols 130r–1v, 135r–41r; 48128, fols 42r–3v. Additional, later copies c. 1600, BL, Additional MSS 48001, fols 149r–78r; 48094.

imperfection, which Philip de Comines reportethe to be in our nation, to be ouertaken by others with whome we are to treate'. Although he acknowledged the help of Killigrew and Atye, Beale informed Cecil that 'I drewe two books' on the topic, 'wherof the papers and proofes remayne in my hands, and can hardly be sorted out by an other, that is not so wel acquainted with them as I am'.[78]

Between Beale's drafts/copies and the finished discourses sent to Burghley (and the Privy Council) in July and September, the former are more useful.[79] The shorter report of July worked from a more limited set of sources (the accounts of Richard Huddleston and Thomas Shirley, Treasurers-at-War between 1585 and 1589), while the larger report incorporated the supplementary material. Both reports endeavoured to sum up how much was owed to Elizabeth in ordinary charges agreed at Nonsuch as well as extraordinary charges sent in addition. At the close of the first, the authors informed the Privy Council that they could produce the sources upon which they had drawn for this 'Collection made as the shortnes of time wold permit vs'.[80] They could do so easily because, in Beale's copy, he included citations to specific volumes and article numbers in his own and Atye's collections. To a significant degree had Beale, by this point, organized at least some of his papers into bound volumes with shelf marks of a letter followed by a number. Most telling, perhaps, is his annotation on the back of the first declaration's title page, where he recorded 'The Coppyes of my Treatyes are in my great booke. N. 1. & 2. & 6.'[81] Beale's copy of the second, larger declaration also included these marginal citations to volumes in his and Atye's personal collections, but, having included the closing note in the prior declaration, Beale had already informed the Privy Council that his archive could easily provide the evidence to back up their positions when demanding repayment of the loans or, if necessary, a new treaty. Given the disagreements between the English and

---

[78] Digges' memorial of a conference, 17, 18, 21 June 1595, TNA, SP 84/50, fols 205r–8v (cf. fol. 219r–v). Digges' papers, 1585–95, BL, Additional MSS 48084, fols 232r–311v; 48083. Beale to Davison, 11 August 1596, TNA, SP 12/253, fol. 109r (orig.). Beale to Sidney, 2 September 1595, Kent History and Library Centre, U1475/C15/1, quotation regarding Commines at fol. 1v (orig.); an edition Commines' memoires (1559) was probably among Beale's books, BL, Hargrave MS 107, fol. 20v (cf. 25r); cf. the follow-up in Beale to Sidney, 25 September 1595, Kent History and Library Centre, U1475/C15/2 (orig.). Beale to Cecil, 16 September 1595, CP, 44/99, quotation regarding 'books' at fol. 1r–v (orig.). Killigrew, Beale, and Atye to Burghley, 18 September 1595, TNA, SP 12/253, fol. 160r (orig.); Beale's copy, BL, Additional MS 48116, fol. 150r. On Atye's papers, see Simon Adams, 'The Papers of Robert Dudley, Earl of Leicester, II: The Atye-Cotton Collection', *Archives*, 20 (1993), 131–44.

[79] First declaration, 3 July 1595, with associated memorandum, second declaration, 18 September 1595, BL, Additional MS 48084, fols 333r–73r; additional drafts of the first, BL, Additional MS 48116, fols 110v–44v. Declarations as sent, with occasional marginal notes by Burghley but with significant damage by fire, BL, Cotton MS Galba, D, XI, fols 106r–19v, 138r–64r.

[80] First declaration, 3 July 1595, BL, Additional MS 48084, fol. 344v.

[81] First declaration, 3 July 1595, BL, Additional MS 48084, fol. 333v. On the lettering of Beale's volumes during his lifetime, see the discussion in Taviner, 36–8, especially with reference to Basing's introduction to the Yelverton catalogue. In the 1570s Beale certainly collated his material into coherent bundles based on subject matter, but his more formal process of having these items bound might have started as early as 1587. Popper, 'From Abbey to Archive', 257. Two drafts of the first declaration, with rough notes, BL, Additional MS 48116, fols 110v–44v.

Dutch governments regarding debts, repayment periods, and other issues, a renewal and update of the Treaty of Nonsuch was in order. Perhaps unsurprisingly, Beale, with this reference archive at the ready, was involved in the drafting (if not deliberation) of the new treaty as finalized in August 1598. Taviner has offered an appropriate illustration of Beale's role: a diplomatic clerk working largely behind the scenes in support of the official English negotiators but nevertheless with a central and crucial responsibility in advising and framing the content in Latin and French. Without clerks like Beale, the treaty simply could not possibly have been completed. This image, of the indispensable clerk on the shoulder of the councillor in 1598, would be a welcome complement to the painting at the National Portrait Gallery in commemoration of the peace treaty between England and Spain at the Somerset House Conference in 1604.[82]

A draftsman and clerk advising and preparing in London in 1598, Beale got an opportunity to be one of the principal negotiators to end the war with Spain at Boulogne in 1600. He had long considered how peace might be best achieved, even as recently as May 1598 when he offered his thoughts to Burghley. Characteristically and echoing his previous work, Beale addressed the situation from the English, French, and Dutch perspectives, and made the call to include (in opposition to Spain) the kings of Poland, Scotland, and Denmark; the Protestant princes, cities, and cantons of the Holy Roman Empire; as well as powers in Venice and Florence.[83] Beale was happy to advise on such matters from a distance, but his aversion to long-distance travel (or, at this point, any travel at all) was well known and voiced frequently in the 1590s. In 1596, for example, he complained to Cecil of his health and poverty, firmly trying to avoid any further service abroad whether across the seas in the Netherlands or north of the border in Scotland.[84] Even when, in April 1600, he received Elizabeth's orders via Cecil, Thomas Sackville (Lord Treasurer), and Charles Howard (Lord Admiral) to prepare himself for the imminent mission, he protested on account of his poverty: 'I am indebted, without apparell, without credite, or meanes to repay', begging them in his holograph to move the queen to bestow an advance on Beale or to excuse him altogether from service abroad.[85] Despite his efforts, Elizabeth remained unmoved, probably because by this point Beale was in too deep. In February, he was part of a team charged with considering previous treaties between England and Spain (and Burgundy) and conferring with English merchants trading in those areas. The fruits of Beale's labour can be seen in his archive, which includes

[82] Papers of Thomas Lake in Beale's possession, August–October 1598, BL, Additional MS 48129, fols 3r–47r. See also Beale's copy of Buckhurst's draft preamble to the treaty, 8 August 1598, BL, Additional MS 48078, fols 11r–20v. Taviner, 172–4, offered an evocative analysis and depiction later celebrated by Collinson, 'Servants and Citizens', 501.
[83] Beale's notes regarding a peace with Spain, May 1598, BL, Lansdowne MS 103/88, fols 252r–7r, with reference to additional allies at fol. 256r; this piece follows Burghley's own thoughts on the matter.
[84] Beale to Cecil, 16 September 1595, CP, 44/99 (orig.).
[85] Beale to Cecil, Sackville, and Howard, 18 April 1600, CP, 180/85 (orig.).

an entire volume of such treaties compiled at this time, and a batch of papers regarding merchants' grievances regarding Spain. Within a week of being assigned the tasks, Beale produced and sent to Cecil a 'proiecte of a Treatye' based on his research in the Spanish and Burgundian treaties, though he also offered his usual but rhetorical modesty, 'wherin I haue roued as a blinde man, rather wishing well, then knowing how to direct it aright'. True to form, Beale's 'proiecte' included the Protestant kings, princes, and other powers included in his previous notes of May 1598.[86]

In the months preceding the conference at Boulogne, Beale had been at the centre of activity, so his going was probably unavoidable notwithstanding his complaints. Rumours swirled in the days before his departure from London. Some understood 'how he was made [to] belyue he shld be advaunced to the same place of Honor', that is be made a privy councillor and 'Secretary of state' alongside Robert Cecil, and such an offer from Elizabeth, even if only speculative, could only have been to persuade Beale to go to Boulogne in exchange for such a financially remunerative position. Whatever reason he had was quickly dashed when his friend, John Herbert, was promoted in Beale's stead, no doubt to bolster Herbert's honour and credentials as one also sent to Boulogne ('to grace the intended service'). Not all was lost, however, because the queen made a private promise to Beale (though others knew of it, too) that his family's security would be ensured by the promotion of his son, Francis, to serve as fellow secretary of the Council of the North and earn the associated fee by patent.[87] Rumours and promises aside, with instructions dated 12 May 1600, Beale was commissioned along with Herbert, Henry Neville, and Thomas Edmondes.[88] Herbert, Edmondes, and Beale left London at different times (Neville was already in France as resident ambassador in Paris), but Beale's inability to keep pace in travel soon became

[86] Privy Council to Herbert, Caesar, Beale, Edmonds, and Lake, 24 February 1600, TNA, PC 2/25, 62. BL, Additional MSS 48000, 48126, fols 73r–7*v; cf. material relating to the Treaty of Vervins, 1598, BL, Additional MS 48152, fols 145v–60v. Beale to Cecil, 1 March 1600, CP, 68/63, with quotation (orig.); cf. Beale to Cecil, 26 March 1600, CP, 77/98 (orig.), sending 'the thing which your honour desisrers [sic]'. Beale's draft of the 'proiecte', BL, Additional MS 48035, fols 95r–8v.

[87] Whyte to Sidney, 10 May 1600, Kent History and Library Centre, U1475/C12/240, quotations at fol. 1r (orig.); printed partially but omitting the passage regarding Beale's expected promotion in Collins, *Letters and Memorials of State*, 2.192–3; passage summarized in *Historical Manuscripts Commisson Report on the Manuscripts of Lord De L'Isle & Dudley Preserved at Penshurst Place: Vol. 2*, ed. C. L. Kingsford (London, 1934), 459. Elizabeth's 'priuely promise' noted in Whyte to Sidney, 12 May 1600, Kent History and Library Centre, U1475/C12/241 (orig.), with 'a priuely' struck through by a later hand (in preparation of the Collins volume) and 'her Royal' inserted above 'promis'; the *HMC* volume, 461, is more faithful to the original than is Collins, 194. On Elizabeth's promise, see below. Sidney later wrote to Beale directly from Ostend on 18 June 1600 regarding Beale's negotiations in Boulogne, noting Herbert's role as Secretary but mentioning nothing of the promise: BL, Additional MS 48035, fol. 93r (orig.).

[88] Among the multiple extant copies of these instructions, Beale's annotated copy is BL, Additional MS 48035, fols 34r–41, but see also BL, Cotton MS Vespasian, C. VIII, fols 379r–83v, followed by Cecil's dated letter to the commissioners at 384r (also included with Beale's copy). See the discussion in Wernham, *Return of the Armadas*, 319–34, with reference to Beale at 330, 413.

apparent to his old friend Herbert, who reported to Cecil from Dover that he needed to look after Beale because he was 'somewhat heavy, and vnwildy [paunch-bellied] to travell'.[89] The ensuing two and a half months accomplished little by way of negotiations towards peace, liberty, amity, and trade agreements because of the initial stumbling block—establishing precedence. In sum, Elizabeth wanted to maintain the degree of superiority over Spain, while the latter would have it the other way around, so between late May and late July the commissioners on both sides discussed little more than seals, powers to negotiate, and who should precede whom.[90] Among the four English representatives, Beale and Edmondes were most active in trying to advance the process, and one could justifiably suppose that Beale, having resisted this mission as much as he could but ultimately succumbing to serve his sovereign, simply wanted to get something out of it rather than return to London having been unproductive. Measures of success aside, Beale did not return entirely empty-handed, for he retained copies and some originals of the correspondence and commissions of both sides, and it is clear from his collection that Elizabeth's official letters patent for the commissioners were drafted by Beale himself. Additionally, he might also have helped to inform Robert Cotton's discussion of the issue of precedency between England and Spain.[91] His centrality in the planning and negotiations was also plain to at least one of the Spanish negotiators, Jean Richardot, President of the Council of the Southern Provinces of the Netherlands. After all parties had departed from Boulogne and royal tempers cooled, Beale and Edmondes continued to engage with Richardot in correspondence. From October 1600 to his death in May 1601, Beale disagreed with Richardot on some points but did not entirely lose hope that progress could be made in achieving the peace for which he had worked so tirelessly. In the end, Edmondes continued to write to Richardot after Beale's death, noting on 20 June 'that it hath pleased God, to call Mr Beale to his mercy'.[92]

---

[89]   Herbert to Cecil, 15 May 1600, CP, 79/49 (orig.).
[90]   The difficulties and strains in the negotiations are laid bare in the correspondence between the commissioners and London: TNA, SP 78/44, fols 119r–258v (orig. and copies). Succinct discussion in Wernham, *Return of the Armadas*, 324–5. Beale returned home in London on 6 August. Neville to Cecil, 6 August 1600, CP, 81/19 (orig.).
[91]   BL, Additional MS 48035, fols 2r–100v, with draft commission at 2r–5r. Cf. a stray item, a copy of Philip II's will with a note by Beale on 10 June, in BL, Additional MS 48126, fols 259r–60v. Among the copies of Cotton's discussion dated about 1600, a volume associated with Beale contains a part of the work: BL, Additional MS 48088, fols 2r–5r.
[92]   Richardot to Beale and Edmondes, 5/15 October 1600, TNA, SP 77/6, fol. 213r–v (orig.). Richardot to Beale and Edmondes, 8/18 November 1600, BL, Cotton MS Vespasian, C. VIII, fols 375r–6v (orig.), acknowledging theirs of 25 October and recapitulating the summer's negotiations; Beale's copy, AUL, MS 1009/1, item 21. Beale and Edmondes to Richardot, 12 December 1600, BL, Cotton MS Vespasian, C. VIII, fol. 377r–v; Beale's copy, BL, Additional MS 48152, fol. 173r–v. Richardot to Beale and Edmondes, 1/11 January 1601, TNA, SP 77/6, fols 242r–3v (orig.). Beale and Edmondes to Richardot, 3 May 1601, TNA, SP 77/6, fols 264r–5r. Richardot to Beale and Edmondes, 31 May/10 June 1601, TNA, SP 77/6, fol. 275r–v. Edmondes' copies and originals in BL, Stowe MS 167, fols 148r–9r, 247r–66v, with quotation from a minute of Edmondes to Richardot, 20 June 1601, fol. 255r.

Beale could no longer work towards peace, but a few years later Richardot would be depicted at the table in the painting of the Somerset House Conference in 1604. Would that Beale lived longer, he, rather than Henry Howard, earl of Northampton, might well have sat opposite Richardot.

The End of a Life's Work

Towards the end of the 1590s, Beale could sense that the end was coming. He survived the years of plague in the middle of the decade, but he was nervous about his health among other things. Having fallen from Elizabeth's grace but still invaluable as a specialist in legal and diplomatic matters, he could in some ways rest on the fact that his collections of state and personal papers, as well as his library, were valuable. As had often been the case when he opened his heart and spoke his mind, he adamantly maintained in a series of letters to Burghley and Cecil that he collected this material not for his own gain but in service to the queen. Putting aside for the moment the fact that his gain and serving his sovereign were not mutually exclusive categories, it seems that Beale was sincere. In 1595, in two particularly downtrodden letters, Beale wrote that 'I haue spent the better parte of my yeres and substaunce in gettinge of bookes and papers, to be able to serue her Majestie, not lookinge to myne own proffit. I haue not ben ambitious, but kept my self within the boundes of lawes and my duetye', noting also that, due to his charges, he needed to start selling his books.[93] The next year in a letter to Cecil regarding his work with Killigrew and Atye, he claimed that his collections—'papers and proofes'—were very much his own and in the service of the queen. A few years later to Cecil among others, Beale appeared to have second thoughts on his previous financial decisions. While others had sought personal advancement, he had never done so; rather, 'I haue giuen my self more to study to learne how to serue her Majesty, then sought myne own commodity', and, as a result, he found himself begging for further patronage and financial compensation for services rendered in the past.[94] In an understandable but potentially bittersweet turn of events, after Beale's death his archive and life's work had a reputation of their own. When Lesieur was considering matters relating to a treaty with Denmark in 1602, he noted that the secretary to the company of Merchant Adventurers, a certain Mr Robinson, possessed 'certain books of collections made by Mr Beale' about the Hanseatic League and their activities in England.

---

[93] Beale to Burghley(?), early 1595, BL, Lansdowne MS 68/111, quotation at fol. 248r; on date, see above, n. 18. Beale to Burghley, 24 April 1595, BL, Lansdowne MS 79/80, fol. 194v (orig.); see above, n. 20. Beale's language is admittedly vague on whether he did, in fact, start selling his books or would soon need to.

[94] Beale to Cecil, 16 September 1596, CP, 44/99 (orig.). Beale to Cecil, Sackville, and Howard, 18 April 1600, CP, 180/85 (orig.).

It remains unclear whether Beale delivered these materials to Robinson while he lived or whether Robinson acquired them after Beale had passed, but either way Beale's material on the Hanse continued to serve Elizabeth's purposes. When in 1610 Thomas Milles, the nephew of Robert Glover, Somerset Herald, published his uncle's book on nobility, he did so having received help from his 'learned friends'. Sandwiched in this list between Robert Cotton and William Camden was 'Worthy Robert Beale that graue cleark of the Counsel'; Milles's putting Beale on the same level as Cotton and Camden is worth consideration.[95]

His concern for his family was justifiably serious. The 1590s were a difficult decade for many, with poor harvests, continued warfare, bouts of plague, and inflation biting into family budgets.[96] As he stated several times, Beale feared for his wife and family were he to die suddenly. Because of his debts and what must have been considerable regular expenses for running a household of a wife, many children, and a servant, he appears not to have amassed any savings to leave his family. Granted, he had multiple positions earlier in the decade, but by the latter years, when his children's needs were becoming more financially onerous, his income had been reduced in both nominal and real terms despite his being granted another wardship in 1597 (almost certainly via the Cecils). Indeed, his salary as clerk of the Privy Council in the 1590s nominally remained the same £50 as it had been in 1572, but that sum was worth dramatically less by way of spending power (by some measures it declined by about 40 per cent). Additionally, although he held lands in Warwickshire, a house and land at Barnes, and a house in London, any realized financial gains from the first and second remain obscure, while he frequently described the second and third as 'poor'. However self-deprecating he might have been about his houses, Beale clearly had a difficult and costly relationship with a former servant and neighbour in London who attempted building projects visually offensive (a privy under Beale's window) and struck down Beale's shed with access inside the house, thus leaving the Beales vulnerable to thieves when Edith was yet again about to give birth to a child in May 1599 at about 46 years of age (see Fig. 18).[97]

---

[95] Thomas Milles, *The Catalogve of Honor or Tresvry of Trve Nobility Pecvliar and Proper to the Isle of Great Britaine* (London, 1610) (STC 17926), sig. [A4r].
[96] Jim Sharpe, 'Social Strain and Social Dislocation, 1585–1603', in John Guy (ed.), *The Reign of Elizabeth I: Court and Culture in the Last Decade* (Cambridge, 1995), 192–211. For a more specific discussion of Beale's locale, see M. J. Power, 'A "Crisis" Reconsidered: Social and Demographic Dislocation in London in the 1590s', *The London Journal*, 12 (1986), 134–45.
[97] Grant to Beale of wardship of George Purefye, with yearly value of £24.6.8, 25 October 1597, TNA, C 66/1466, m. 32. Beale to Cecil, 16 September 1596, from 'my porre house at Barnes', CP, 44/99 (orig.). For an example of the same £50 in four instalments over the year, see TNA, E 403/2282, unfoliated (for 1597–8). Comparison of purchasing power via https://www.nationalarchives.gov.uk/currency-converter/. The lease for the house at Barnes, Milbourne House, included 116.5 acres and cost Beale a yearly rent of £10.13.4; his landlords were the earl of Essex and Ursula Walsingham. Extracts from the Cartwright muniments at Aynhoe, C(A)2274, Northamptonshire Record Office, in the Richmond Local Studies Library. Beale to Cecil, 24, 27 October 1599, both from 'my poore house in London', CP, 74/50, 74/55 (both orig.). In contrast, Beale wrote to Cecil 'from my house in London'

Fig. 18 Edith Beale's funerary monument, 1628. St Michael and All Angels, Eastington, Gloucestershire.

Photograph taken by the Author and reproduced with permission.

Beale had consistently tried during these years to avoid diplomatic service overseas or north to Scotland because he knew from experience how financially debilitating the experience could be. His complaints of poverty went back to spring 1578, when, in the wake of his missions of the two previous years, he wrote to Burghley accordingly. In 1599, before Elizabeth ordered him to Boulogne but at the same time as the potential new addition to the household, Beale had an increased sense of desperation in his calls for help, noting on several occasions that he was 'at last cast'. He was probably uncertain whether he would continue to be paid regularly as clerk of the Privy Council because his quarterly payment of £12 and 10 shillings for Christmas 1598 was missed and only made up for at the next quarterly payment period (Annunciation, 25 March 1599).[98] No surprise, then, that Herbert caught up to Beale on the way to Dover. He was downtrodden and tired. He was slowing down.

With his immediate family's needs weighing heavily on his mind, Beale also looked out for others. When he was of greater means in the mid 1580s, Beale played the role of a patron for a surgeon, John Banester, who praised Beale as 'well knowen to be skilfull in the varietie of tongues, and endewed with all other good learning: so haue you sounded the depth of this art'. Beale also might have been on good terms with Stephen Bredwell, a physician who identified some of the plants at Beale's home in Barnes for John Gerard, who subsequently included this observation in his printed work on plants in 1597. The suggestion that he was interested in medicine is later corroborated by his generosity in 1599, when he was of considerably less means but nevertheless donated a very substantial £40 to the upkeep of a local hospital for children, Christ's, Bridewell, where in exchange for his donation a physician of his choice would be appointed to look after the children and staff.[99] Perhaps thinking back to his lean years during the 1560s,

(not poor this time) on 20 December 1598, TNA, SP 12/269, fol. 37r–v (orig.). Again, contrast Stow's comments about Beale's house. From the account of relations between Beale and his neighbour, Robert Browne, it also appears that Walsingham's erstwhile servant, Painter, lived next to Beale. Account of injuries, 3 May 1599, TNA, SP 12/270, fol. 183r–v. The child does not appear to have been baptized and might have been stillborn. Accounting for known baptisms at All Hallows London Wall and St Mary's, Barnes, and references to other births in 1580 and 1589, the child in 1599 was Edith's thirteenth since 1577. If Edith died at the age of 75 in 1628, thus born in 1553, as plausibly suggested by her funerary monument, then she was roughly 46 years old during this, her final pregnancy. The monument was recorded in Ralph Bigland, *Historical Monumental and Genealogical Collections, Relative to the County of Gloucester* (London, 1791), 1.540, and still exists at St Michael and All Angels Church, Eastington, Gloucestershire; the monument names the two sons and nine daughters. Edith probably resided at Eastington in the autumn of her life because her daughter, Katherine, had married Nathan Stephens of that village. One calls to mind Languet's comment to Philip Sidney that Beale did not think anyone was able to lead a happy life in celibacy. Languet to Sidney, 8 January 1578, in Roger Kuin, *Correspondence*, 2.804–8. See Chapter 5, n. 41.

[98]   Beale to Cecil, 5 May and 24 October 1599, CP, 70/1, 74/50 (both orig.). Exchequer Issue Book for 1598–9, TNA, E 403/2283, unfoliated.

[99]   Johann Wecker, trans. John Banester, *A Compendiovs Chrvrgerie* (London, 1585) (STC 25185), sig. *3r–v. John Gerard, *The Herball or Generall Historie of Plantes* (London, 1597) (STC 11750), 504. 'Robert Beale's Gift', 20 February 1599, LMA, CLC/210/G/BBK/001/MS12930.

when he sought the patronage of Hales and Cecil, in 1595 he wrote to the earl of Essex in favour of a young inventor seeking support. This man deserved the earl's patronage because of the benefit that could redound to the state, for, indeed, '[m]anye times poore men maye haue giftes to doe good, if they shalbe supported by men of credit and authoritie.'[100] Beale and Essex together then helped Ursula Walsingham, widow of Francis, sister-in-law of Beale, and mother-in-law of Essex, regarding the acquisition of land near Westminster that could provide financial assistance to Ursula in her time of significant need. Beale and Essex went one step further for her, with Beale drafting a memorial for Francis Vere, commander of military forces in the Netherlands, to deal with the States General on Essex's behalf regarding a debt owed by them to Ursula. Tracing a complicated ownership of loans and debts, Beale identified Francis's personal share in the debt in 1578 and made the case that the Dutch now needed to repay that debt to his widow.[101] It seems unlikely that Ursula ever saw anything from the Dutch.

Beale was certainly a family man who tried to help others, but this sense of altruism could get in the way of his providing for that very family. As he proudly professed at various points, he never took a degree of any sort. He matriculated at the University of Wittenberg but did not stay around long enough to complete a course, probably frequented the halls of the University of Heidelberg but did not even matriculate. Having this exposure, having learned the methods and intellectual traditions, Beale became more of an auto-didact and eventually claimed superiority in knowledge of civil law and divinity relative to Whitgift's entourage despite his not having the titles or post-nominals to show for it. If he had taken a degree or multiple, he probably could have advanced higher up the ranks of the

---

[100] Beale to Essex, 8 December 1595, LPL, MS 652, fol. 314r (orig.). Beale knew of Essex's political clout and was leasing property from him, but his writing to the earl on behalf of another does not suggest that the two were close. As will be recalled, one of Essex's servants had earlier that year been put forward for taking Beale's roles as both clerk of the Privy Council and secretary of the Council of the North. A few months previously, Beale had learned of Essex's implication (dedication) in a book printed at Antwerp on the royal succession in favour of King Philip of Spain. That book was *A Conference abovt the Next Svccession to the Crowne of Ingland* written by Robert Parsons (Antwerp, 1595) (STC 19398). Beale to Sidney, 25 September 1595, Kent History and Library Centre, U1475/C15/2, fol. 2r (orig.). For a lively discussion and notice of Beale's interest, see John Guy, *Elizabeth: The Forgotten Years* (New York, 2016), 237–53, on Beale at 251. After Essex's downfall in 1598, Beale acquired copies of relevant correspondence but, having seen the downfall of Davison and experienced his own, Beale kept his distance from Essex. BL, Additional MS 48126, fols 97r–100v. For a broader discussion of Essex and dedications, see Alzada Tipton, '"All mens eyes are fixed vpon you": Dedications of Printed Works to the Earl of Essex and the Creation of Essex's Public Persona', *The Sixteenth Century Journal*, 52 (2021), 111–32. On Essex more broadly, see Paul E. J. Hammer, *The Polarisation of Elizabethan Politics: The Political Career of Robert Devereux, 2nd Earl of Essex, 1585–1597* (Cambridge, 1999); Alexandra Gajda, *The Earl of Essex and Late Elizabethan Political Culture* (Oxford, 2012).

[101] License to alienate lands, 2 April 1597, TNA, C 66/1470, m. 30. Beale's memorial for Vere, 1598, BL, Additional MS 48116, fols 86r–90r. In May 1590 Beale tallied the accounts of Walsingham's debts and credits at his decease, no doubt to assist Ursula, though Caesar later questioned Beale's accuracy. Read, *Mr Secretary Walsingham*, 3.444. Beale's relationship with Essex and Ursula was complicated because of their family ties and financial relationship in Milbourne House. See above, n. 97.

government (like Walsingham) or in the London law scene (like Caesar). Just as he could boast of his own knowledge and experience, though, he could complain that others with less expertise but more degrees were preferred over him (like Perkins). Indeed, complaining was, by his own admission, one of his less desirable attributes: 'my nature is perhappes to bruske and playne'.[102] His grievances regarding his health were by all measures genuine and recognized by others as such. His suffering from gout and bladder stones went back to the early 1580s, and these ailments only seemed to increase in severity and frequency throughout the 1590s. So, too, were his eyes continuing to deteriorate. His use of a secretary for his letters to others, signing his name only, as opposed to writing the letters entire, as in a holograph, increased in the 1590s. Missives wholly in his own hand were, by and large, reserved only for those most intimate—Burghley and Cecil—but they also indicate declining eyesight and deteriorating manual dexterity relative to a few years earlier. If he wrote to Cecil by way of a secretary, it was with good reason, as when he complained of a 'deflux' (i.e. rheumatism) in one of his arms, 'an ache [...] which grieueth me not a lytle', or 'a fall vppon my backe' that rendered him unable to move with ease just a month before he was sent to Boulogne.[103]

No wonder that Beale thought that he was in danger of expiry throughout the decade. When informing Burghley in 1592 of a serious bout with gout and the stone while at death's door, he also complained of other unspecified 'dangerous accidentes' that came with the bladder stones. His fear of accidents and mishaps continued and might have been instances of foresight or fatalism; it might also simply be that he was accident-prone and others knew it, with overstated rumours of his own death swirling prematurely in 1595.[104] His journey to and from Boulogne seems to have gone without issue, even if more slowly than normal, but Beale's financial necessity drove him to extreme measures upon his return. He was of course accustomed to writing to Burghley and then Cecil when asking for financial assistance or release from financial burdens, with a view to their approaching Elizabeth on his behalf. He thought—he knew—it presumptuous to approach the queen directly. And yet, at last cast, he did. On 4 May 1601, he wrote to his sovereign, sending a copy to Cecil for reference.[105] Beale was bold to remind Elizabeth that, 'at my goinge ouer to Boulogne [...] it pleased you [...] to promise vnto me somwhat at my comminge home, for the better maintenance of my poore estate'. Again, that promise was not entirely private, for others at court had heard of it, such as Rowland Whyte, who reported to his employer, Robert

---

[102] Beale's account of his affair with Whitgift, 1 July 1584, BL, Additional MS 48039, fol. 55v.

[103] e.g., Beale to Cecil, 5 May 1599, CP, 70/1 (holograph, orig.). Cf. Beale's acknowledgement that Cecil had received that of 5 May and sought to help, 9 May 1599, CP, 70/14 (holograph, orig.). Beale to Cecil, 20 December 1598, TNA, SP 12/269 fol. 37r–v (autograph, orig.). Beale to Cecil, 1 March 1600, CP, 68/63 (autograph, orig.).

[104] Beale to Burghley, 16 October 1592, BL, Lansdowne MS 72/73, fol. 198r (orig.). Beale to Burghley, 24 April 1595, BL, Lansdowne MS 79/80, fols 194v, 192r (orig.).

[105] Beale to Elizabeth, 4 May 1601, CP, 182/15.

Sidney, that Elizabeth 'gaue a priuely promis that at [Beale's] return, his Sonne shuld be ioined in patent with hym in his office at Yorke, which is worth 300 l. a yeare, and more'.[106] Beale further noted that his solicitations of his friends to advocate for his cause 'auayled litle for my reliefe', so he tried to meet personally with Elizabeth. One hurdle or another prevented his access, 'and so hitherto I haue wanted that fauor, which I expected at your Majesties handes. And therefore haue ben forced at this present, to vse this last meanes of writing, most humblie to beseeche your Majestie, to extende your fauorable liberalitie vnto me'. Beale claimed that he was 'no importunate [annoyingly persistent] suter' (the Cecils probably thought otherwise) and emphasized his fidelity and long duration of service, 'allmost these 28 yeres', writing also,

> If my vnfortunate case hath bene, to haue spent so longe a time of my seruice vnfruitefullie: my humble desire is, that it would please your Majestie to vouch-safe me what aunswer your Majestie shall thinke good: to the intent I maye, before a greater burthen of debt, age, and pouertie fall vppon me, prouide to liue with lesse charge, wherin I maye not discredit or disappoint your Majesties seruice with my pouertie.

How Elizabeth reacted to Beale's letter is unknown, but clear enough is that she broke her promise and Beale was heartbroken. Three weeks later, he was dead (see Fig. 19).

The precise cause of his death is obscured by a surprising dearth of documen-tation, but a later petition from Edith and her son Francis to the queen records that Beale died 'by an infortunate accident in your Highnes seruices'.[107] Thus, Beale's fear of an accident taking his life proved eerily far-sighted. What mishap befell Beale has not come to light; the parish register for St Mary's, Barnes, records simply that he died at 8 p.m. on Monday, 25 May 1601.[108] Because it is unlikely that he would have been on Elizabeth's service in Barnes, after the accident he probably made a conscious decision to retire to his suburban home in Barnes either for recuperation or because he knew his end was coming. Getting away from his neighbour in London during a period of distress for the whole family would also have been a plus. Two days later, on 27 May, he was recorded in another parish register as buried at his more usual church of All Hallows London

---

[106] Whyte to Sidney, 12 May 1600, Kent History and Library Centre, U1475/C12/241, fol. 1v (orig.); see n. 87. Whyte's understanding of Beale's income seems wildly inaccurate. On Whyte, see Michael G. Brennan, '"Your Lordship's to Do You All Humble Service": Rowland Whyte's Correspondence with Robert Sidney, Viscount Lisle and First Earl of Leicester', *Sidney Journal*, 21 (2003), 1–38.
[107] Petition of Edith and Francis Beale, July 1601, CP, Petitions 1429.
[108] Surrey History Centre, P6/1/1, fol. 44v, including also that he was buried 'at london'.

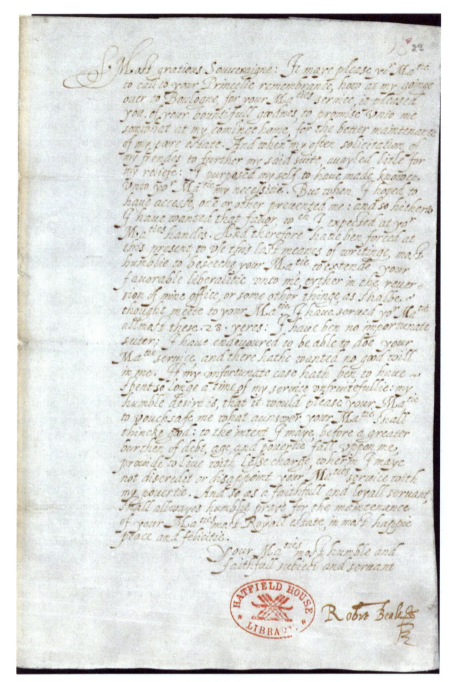

Fig. 19 Beale to Queen Elizabeth, 4 May 1601. CP, 182/15.

Wall, where he had been a parishioner since 1583 at the latest.[109] Forasmuch as Beale had long suffered from various illnesses and foresaw his own death at so many points in the previous decade, because he was so painstakingly detailed in providing and retaining documentation of all sorts, and since he had been involved in the last wills and testaments of others (Bedford and Walsingham at least), it seems highly unlikely that Beale died intestate—and yet, no will is recorded in the usual place in the probate series. In fact, however, a gap exists for the month of May 1601 between two volumes that previously were two halves of one volume, so it remains possible that Beale did record a last will and testament but that it was lost when the volume was split in two. Moreover, the covenant Beale made with the hospital in exchange for his donation stipulated that the agreement would extend to his heirs, executors, and administrators, the latter two of which suggest that Beale already had a will in place in February 1599.[110] Although he claimed to have considerable debts and insufficient funds to meet them, Beale also retained properties in multiple locations and an valuable library of printed books and archive of manuscripts. That his library and archive passed not to his firstborn son, Francis, who in 1602 inherited but then sold the Warwickshire properties (Priors Marston for £1,700 probably in support of his mother and siblings), but to Margaret, the third-born daughter who married Henry Yelverton, cannot have been by accident.[111]

The issue of Beale's last will and testament or lack thereof may forever remain a mystery, but his family's needs in his absence were abundantly clear. In Edith's petition to the queen she recalled that Elizabeth had promised to help her and the children, now 'orphanes', so Edith requested a grant of a fee farm valued at roughly £30 per annum in recognition of her husband's long services. About this time or

---

[109] Jupp and Hovenden, *The Registers*, 136, verified in LMA, P69/ALH5/A/001/MS05083 and P69/ALH5/A/002/MS05084. Churchwardens' Accounts for All Hallows, London Wall, LMA, P69/ALH6/MS05090, fol. 63v includes Beale among those contributing to the upkeep of the church; various payments occur through to 1601 (fol. 154r).

[110] TNA, PROB 11/97–98 are the two halves of the previous 'Woodhall' volume of the Prerogative Court of Canterbury, but among the wills for May in 11/97 Beale's is not found, while in 11/98 a considerable gap remains between the will of Robert Pulham, 4 April 1601, and that of Samuel Hales, 3 June 1601. TNA, PROB 10/202 does not include an original will proved in May or June 1601. 'Robert Beale's Gift', 20 February 1599, LMA, CLC/210/G/BBK/001/MS12930. Taviner, 25, suggests that Beale died intestate and hypothesizes that he died 'quietly in his bed'.

[111] Tracing the exact ownership history of Priors Marston and Priors Hardwick is difficult, but they seem to have followed the same trajectory. The Spencers purchased the manor of Priors Marston from Francis Beale in 1602 but later acquired the manor of Priors Hardwick in 1633 from a certain Arthur Samwell (or Samuel) of Upton; it might be that Francis sold the latter to that intermediary at the same time he sold the former to the Spencers. Mary E. Finch, *The Wealth of Five Northamptonshire Families 1540–1640* (Oxford, 1956), 176. Inquisition post mortem, April 1602, TNA, C 142/269/34. Francis retained Milbourne House, Barnes, acquiring a new lease in 1602. Extracts from the Cartwright muniments at Aynhoe, C(A)2274, Northamptonshire Record Office, in the Richmond Local Studies Library. On Francis Beale, see also *HoP:HoC*. On Beale and the Yelverton collection, see the discussion by Michael Borrie in the introduction to the catalogue, ix–xviii but NB the error that Beale died on 27 May and suggestion that he died intestate. Cf. the error that Beale 'left no son to succeed him' in B. Schofield, 'The Yelverton Manuscripts', *The British Museum Quarterly*, 19 (1954), 3–9, at 8.

shortly afterwards, she wrote to Cecil from Barnes seeking his favour and furtherance of her petition, informing him also of Elizabeth's 'late promise, to extende
her princelie bountie towards me, in this shipwracke of my fortunes'.[112] Elizabeth
did not care for the idea of the fee farm, so Edith wrote again from Barnes to Cecil
with another idea—that Elizabeth bestow upon the Beales, Edith and her six children, £2,000 in lump sum from the fines collected from the recent offenders
against the queen (supporters of the Essex rebellion).[113] With a lump sum not
forthcoming from the queen, Edith tried again several months later in January
1602 by way of two intermediaries—one of Elizabeth's ladies in the Privy Chamber
(Lady Scudamore) and Cecil. Writing again to Cecil, this time from her 'poore
house in London', 'in expectacion of her Majestes promised grace & goodnes
towards me', she asked for 'some competent annuitye'.[114] The annuity did not
come, either. The next and final time she wrote to Cecil (December 1602), she was
responding to a letter from him and others of the Company of Mines Royal seeking the repayment of £100 owed to them by her husband. With now only a fleet-
ing hope for financial assistance from Elizabeth, Edith, writing from an
unspecified location in London, asked for whatever mercy the company could
manage, especially since her husband had helped to right the company's finances
some years previously. Any bounty from Elizabeth in the queen's final months
was unlikely, as was Edith's ability to repay such a substantial debt without significant assistance. It might have been that she even needed to give up the house in
London, 'poor' or otherwise; her residence for tax purposes in 1602 was noted as
in Barnes. At the very least, her son, Francis's sale of the Warwickshire properties
would have helped to settle debts and provide a little breathing room (see Fig. 20).[115]

[112] Petition of Edith and Francis Beale, July 1601, CP, Petitions 1429. Edith Beale to Cecil, 11 July
1601, CP, 86/156 (orig.). Edith signed this and subsequent letters to Cecil, and her signature is suggestive regarding her level of literacy. For discussion of signatures and literacy, see the discussion (and
bibliography) in Eleanor Hubbard, 'Reading, Writing, and Initialing: Female Literacy in Early Modern
London', *Journal of British Studies*, 54 (2015), 553–77.
[113] Edith Beale to Cecil, 29 July 1601, CP, 87/29 (orig.). Which children Edith was counting in her
'six' is potentially awkward. Edith's first, Francis, was 23 years old by this point, so hardly a child, while
her two most recent were Amy, born in July 1593 and died a few months later, and an unnamed child
in May 1599 who died before baptism could be recorded. Surrey History Centre, P6/1/1, fols 5r, 44r.
The surviving offspring in 1601 certainly included Francis (b. 1577), Margaret (1583), Elizabeth
(1584), Katherine (1588), and Anne (1592), though Ursula (1579), Madeline (1586), and Robert
(1590) all might be included.
[114] Edith Beale to Cecil, 11 January 1602, CP, 84/57 (orig.). Scholarly notice of Edith's activity to
provide for her children in Susan Doran, *Elizabeth I and Her Circle* (Oxford, 2015), 203; James
Daybell, 'Gender, Politics and Diplomacy: Women, News and Intelligence Networks in Elizabethan
England', in Robyn Adams and Rosanna Cox (eds), *Diplomacy and Early Modern Culture* (Basingstoke,
2011), 110. More generally, see James Daybell, *Women Letter-Writers in Tudor England* (Oxford,
2006); James Daybell, *The Material Letter in Early Modern England: Manuscript Letters and the Culture
and Practices of Letter-Writing, 1512–1635* (Basingstoke, 2012); James Daybell and Andrew Gordon
(eds), *Women and Epistolary Agency in Early Modern Culture, 1450–1690* (London, 2016).
[115] Edith Beale to Cecil, 13 December 1602, CP, 96/108 (orig.). Certificate of residence for Edith
Beale, October 1602, TNA, E 115/29/88. Previously, Robert had been noted as resident at the court for
tax purposes in 1590, 1597, and 1601: TNA, E 115/38/10, E 115/42/17, E 115/27/106. On Francis's
sale, see above, n. 110.

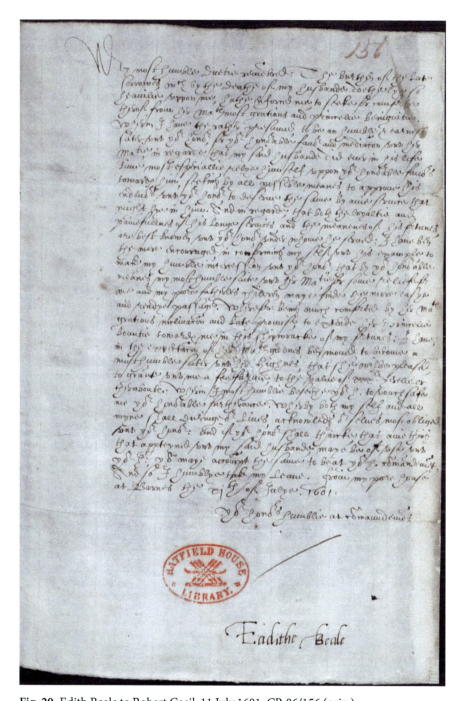

Fig. 20 Edith Beale to Robert Cecil, 11 July 1601. CP, 86/156 (orig.).

Robert Beale had much to show for a particularly rich life. Having come from a modest but comfortable family in London, he travelled for his education first to Coventry and then to Strasbourg, Zurich, Wittenberg, and elsewhere. With the help of his step-uncle and ersatz father, John Hales, he was introduced to those in the Elizabethan government and society who could provide patronage if they found him useful. Useful Beale became. As a specialist on the political and religious affairs of the Holy Roman Empire, and with a special emphasis on civil law, he demonstrated a profound, embedded knowledge and linguistic ability uncommon among Elizabethans. In France, Beale increasingly understood the integrated nature of the wars of religion, with events and personalities intimately connected across national borders for, indeed, religious ideologies and political motivations often disregard such boundaries. Back in England and involved in the proceedings of the queen's Privy Council, Parliament, and policy formation, he put his skills and collections of print and manuscript to use. Drafting others' letters, recording memoranda, and penning treatises both short and long, he produced a volume of written work across a vast range of subjects—so vast, in truth, that Burghley recognized that Beale alone could do it. He was recognized as an expert in civil law, even admitted into an Inn of Court, like so many other MPs and Elizabethans of the professional classes. It is tempting to refer to Beale as an Elizabethan success story of social advancement, a 'man of business' on whom upper statesmen could rely to do the dirty work of research, intelligence gathering, and writing, but Beale was no automaton. He decided not to pursue university degrees, and so could not reap their consequent rewards. He chose not to seek gain at the expense of others, often thinking of others before himself. Unlike Henry Killigrew or Francis Walsingham, he was never knighted and thus addressed as 'Sir', despite the assumptions of those abroad who knew him. Unlike Christopher Perkins or Julius Caesar, he never earned a doctorate in law and was accordingly referred to as 'Dr', notwithstanding his experience in both civil and common law.

He preferred, rather, Mr Robert Beale, Esquire.

A European Elizabethan: The Life of Robert Beale, Esquire. David Scott Gehring, Oxford University Press.
© David Scott Gehring 2024. DOI: 10.1093/9780198902942.003.0008

9

England in Europe

Robert Beale was far from ordinary. From a modest but comfortable family background, he benefited at an early age from his connections to John Hales and Richard Morison. His formal education began in earnest at Hales's school in Coventry but shifted into international and more informal directions in Strasbourg, Zurich, Wittenberg, and elsewhere. He learned at the feet of some of Protestant Europe's greatest minds, especially Johann Sturm and Peter Martyr Vermigli, and he soon learned the value of historical and legal knowledge for present and future purposes in the form of his personal library and archive. Even in the 1560s, when he had little financial means and even less professional security, he was building his private collection because he knew that he could be useful to potential patrons by way of his knowledge, travel, and experience. Useful he became, first regarding the royal succession and second broader intelligence. Matters of the succession, it turned out, would be close to Beale's life for decades to come, and he learned early the consequences of earning the queen's distrust. The proverbs he recorded in English, Latin, and Greek on the cover page for his notes taken in 1563 regarding the *Reichskammergericht* in Speyer would hold meaning for the rest of Beale's life: he would live and learn in hope and fear, and make God the beginning and end of all things. As a clerk of Elizabeth's Privy Council and her formal ambassador in the 1570s, he stepped up from the third tier of government life as a servant and intelligencer to be recognized in the second tier of administration and royal representation. Additional minor offices came in the following decade, with Beale even serving as temporary principal secretary in Francis Walsingham's stead while he was away or unwell. Beale's confidence in his abilities and role grew proportionately, especially while he had the patronage and protection of William Cecil, Lord Burghley; Robert Dudley, earl of Leicester; and his brother-in-law, Walsingham. That self-assurance could be seen in his religious convictions and confrontations with John Whitgift, archbishop of Canterbury, even within Lambeth Palace, and in his committee work in the House of Commons over various parliaments. Beale's Protestantism was both grounded in English law and firmly international in reach. His observations regarding the English Church in the 1580s echoed his previous ones regarding Lutherans in Germany during the 1560s, and he thought that those opposed to Rome had more in common than in difference. If one were pressed to find his favourite chapter in the New Testament, a logical choice would be 1 Corinthians 12, where Paul wrote that the Holy Spirit gives different gifts and abilities to different people, and that different parts of the body are nevertheless unified and working towards a common good. So too, thought Beale, should differences among Protestants be understood as insignificant when these groups could work together; the alternative, suspected Beale, was that hardline religious authorities (in England, Germany, or elsewhere) would work against themselves and ultimately bring the downfall of all Protestants. For as vitriolic as he could be against Catholic threats to the regime, he preferred to proceed against Catholics in a legal, formal manner above board and avoiding the use of torture behind closed doors. If Whitgift is to be believed, and in this instance he should be, Beale's moral aversion to torture as cruel and barbarous combined with his view that the its use was against the law and liberties of English subjects. For as outspoken and abrasive as he could be, for as much of a complainer as he was, the level of Beale's power and protection was evident in the fact that he came out of the 1580s unscathed. Bearing in mind the consequences of his role in defending the Hertford-Grey marriage and claim to the succession in the 1560s, he usually recognized his own precarity and thoroughly documented his activities to guard against any future accusations of impropriety, as in the case of Mary Queen of Scots' execution. His final decade, though, was a different matter because Leicester and Walsingham were dead, Burghley was increasingly infirm, and a new generation was displacing the old. His fall from grace for opposing Whitgift's religious proceedings demonstrated the limits of Beale's immunity in 1593, but recognition of his expertise continued such that many looked to him for matters of law and foreign affairs, rumours even floating that he, at nearly sixty years of age, was considered for the role of principal secretary in his own right alongside Robert Cecil. The secretaryship went to another, and Elizabeth's promise to ensure the financial security of Beale's family went unfulfilled. He never made it to the first tier of Elizabethan political society either because of his controversial roles and positions regarding the royal succession and religious policy, or due to the innate social conservatism of the age. Probably a bit of both, but his significance need not lie in the limits of his career advancement or whether William Camden thought Beale vehement and bitter while Thomas Milles considered him worthy and grave. Rather, it is found in his life lived and his archive of history, religion, and politics assembled for private purposes long before the English state started doing the same in as systematic a manner. Other early Elizabethans like Matthew Parker, archbishop of Canterbury, and Burghley sought and collected similarly for different purposes related to the state, but Beale's archive was, in its genesis and substance, *sui generis*.

The proliferation of personal archives like Beale's caused more and more papers to get shared and copied. That copies of private correspondence and diplomatic instructions, for example, occur across various personal and state collections of the period has long been recognized by modern scholars, but we are also increasingly aware that these early modern archives were far from static entities in fixed locations. Rather, the circulation, lending, borrowing, to-ing and fro-ing of such papers within and across archives can serve as indications of Elizabethans' and the broader European thirst for inside information and state secrets. Within Beale's own archive he kept as many of his own original documents as he could, but he was also rapacious in getting additional material from others. Despite his mourning over the dispersal of Walsingham's papers after the principal secretary's death, Beale had previously used his brother-in-law's materials and almost certainly acquired more of them without any intention of returning them to Walsingham's widow, Ursula. Ascertaining exactly which materials Beale acquired from others' collections in every case would help to establish clear and direct lines of patronage and other relationships at precise moments. Yet, by stepping back more broadly, one can at the very least recognize that an early modern archive, like the notion of home for many exiles and immigrants, was more fluid than fixed and relied more upon communities and colleagues than bricks and mortar. Just as important as archival fluidity is the recognition that Beale's archive was broadly symptomatic of other private archives in England and in contrast to a more state-centred approach elsewhere in Europe, especially Spain, France, and Italy.[1] Because the official state papers in the Tower were in such disarray for nearly all of the sixteenth century, and because of the blurring of boundaries between matters public and private, men like Burghley, Walsingham, and Leicester retained as much of their paperwork as they could, creating their own archives for further reference in matters of state; Beale's archive was very much his own but it could also serve the state and had historical value in the same way that, later, Robert Cotton's did. That Beale also kept an archive and library is thus not surprising, but it is worth remembering that his archival practice stemmed not from lessons learned in England during the 1570s but rather from those learned in Strasbourg and elsewhere in the Holy Roman Empire during the 1550s and 1560s.

Part of the challenge in retracing Beale's steps has been to keep track of his ever-expanding list of friends and contacts across various countries. Sometimes letters between him and his correspondents survive, while at other times one can only infer contact from references and asides in other material. He corresponded surprisingly little with some of his longest-standing friends at relatively close proximity (e.g. Henry Killigrew), while others at a greater distance received more attention (e.g. Hubert Languet). The lack of surviving documentation illuminating Beale's friendships with Killigrew, Daniel Rogers, John Herbert, John Dee, and others comparatively nearby may simply be because they did not write to each other as much as they saw each other in person either at work or over meals. One can only wonder, for example, how Beale and Rogers felt when working

---

[1] For relevant discussions, see Liesbeth Corens, Kate Peters, and Alexandra Walsham (eds), *Archives and Information in the Early Modern World* (Oxford, 2018).

together in Germany in 1577, or what Beale, Edith, and Dee spoke about over dinner in 1593. What did they eat and drink (in Germany or at Dee's)? How frequently did Beale raise a glass of wine or flagon of beer? What foods did he enjoy? We simply cannot tell. The sources available offer only a partial list of Beale's associates, but his correspondence with Christoph Ehem in the 1560s, René Hennequin in the 1570s, Wilhelm, landgrave of Hesse, in the 1580s, and David Chytraeus in the 1590s can be seen as representative of the esteem in which Beale was held across the seas, as can be Beale's relationship with André Wechel, the great publisher in Frankfurt am Main. An Englishman with international experience and contacts, and with broadly European but still firmly Protestant intellectual tendencies, he resembled predecessors like Thomas Cromwell and Thomas Cranmer and contemporaries like Philip Sidney and Walsingham but was on a lower social stratum. Comparison could be made to successors like Samuel Hartlib and the Scotsman John Durie. As in the case of his archive, Beale can be understood as both a product of a previous age and a harbinger of things to come. Thus, he was not ordinary, but he was in some ways representative of a certain strand of sixteenth-century life—ambitious and international but vulnerable and insecure.

Recognizing that the voluminous sources regarding Beale's professional life can only tell part of the story, one must also accept that they tell us much less regarding his personal life. And yet, he appears to have had a loving relationship with his wife, Edith, a marriage that produced at least thirteen children (not all of whom survived), and a close connection with his sister- and brother-in-law, Ursula and Francis Walsingham. He owned (or at least rented) multiple homes and properties but had increasing financial difficulties and debts. He suffered from multiple debilitating ailments, not the least of which included bladder stones. Having benefited from the patronage offered by others, he extended the same and supported a local hospital. He received gifts great and small, but little record remains of any gifts from Beale to others. Despite his matriculation at the University of Wittenberg, he never earned a formal university degree and seemed to wear that lack as a badge of honour; indeed, he scorned such ambition for personal gain. He could write with warmth, sympathy, and understanding among friends on one hand, but then bring a dispassionate coolness and precision in legal analyses on the other. With Burghley he could be sarcastic, noting on two occasions that if it could proven he had behaved covetously or sought a new ecclesiastical government, he desired no further favour than to be hanged at the court gates.[2] In general, he seems to have been as dependable a friend with a hand to lend as he was an obstreperous adversary with a fiery temper. Intellectually, he understood complex situations and the need for diplomatic nuance, yet sometimes

---

[2] Beale to Burghley, 15 April 1578, BL, Lansdowne MS 27/32, fol. 62r (orig.). Beale to Burghley, 7 March 1593, BL, Lansdowne MS 73/2, fol. 6r (orig.).

saw the world in very black and white terms regarding Catholic threats and Protestant survival in England, France, the Netherlands, and elsewhere. Very much an Englishman in the Commons and when defending parliamentary rights and legal precedents, Beale was also a European by way of his reading habits, travels, languages, connections, and worldview. He was, in short, a complex man. He was, in truth, a European Elizabethan.

This book began with an appreciation that the causes and developments of the European mainland mattered in the English theatre. Earlier in the sixteenth century, the ways in which the mainland influenced or otherwise affected the island could be seen in, for example, King Henry VIII's receiving of agents from the Schmalkaldic League, Archbishop Cranmer's courting of international Protestants, and Queen Mary's welcoming of Philip of Spain and his entourage. At the beginning of Elizabeth's reign, hundreds of English Protestants who had found refuge in German and Swiss lands during Mary's reign returned to English shores and brought back ideas from Strasbourg, Zurich, Geneva, and elsewhere. The shaping and character of the Elizabethan Church of England has been hotly debated ever since. As the wars of religion unfolded in France and the Netherlands, religious refugees found safe harbour in London and elsewhere in England, while English engagement and defence of their brethren opposed to Rome became a political issue. Beale's engagement with internationals in the capital and involvement in the informing and implementation of English foreign policy in this regard can be seen in his writings and activity in those countries. In Beale one can see not only how the mainland mattered to the island, but also how the island mattered to the mainland.

Issues such as the royal succession, character of the English Church, status of Mary Queen of Scots, and monopoly of the Mercant Adventurers were not uniquely English. These concerns involved various parties either directly or indirectly, especially by way of the broader international Protestant community and potential aid to and military engagement with the wars in France and the Netherlands. With keen interest did Huguenots, the Dutch, and German Protestants look to Beale and upon England more generally. The contexts into which Beale sits are many and overlapping. From religious exile and identities to the push for further reform of the Church, Beale was deeply embedded. From concerns for the royal succession and the stability of the realm to foreign policy and defence of the Protestant cause, Beale was intimately involved. From questions of common and civil law and parliamentary rights to issues of counsel at court and in the Privy Council, Beale was better schooled than most. These matters were not always easily distinguishable, for indeed they were often intermingled and interdependent. Like Walsingham, Burghley, and others, Beale understood Mary Queen of Scots to be a nexus for all that threatened Protestant England from within and from across the seas. Part of an orchestrated attempt by Catholic powers to reassert their political power across Europe, Mary was the head and a viper in her own right, in Beale's view, and his role in the drama of her life at Sheffield and death at Fotheringhay helped to focus his attention because he understood her in both domestic and international contexts. If Beale was right in doing so, and if we are right in understanding Beale in the same way, then Beale and Mary may have more in common for our understandings today than either would have ever dared to admit. Stepping back from Beale and Mary, one can now more easily see how the direction and character of the English Church mattered to Protestants elsewhere in Europe, how the English royal succession related to the European wars of religion, how Beale's reading of a royal commission for execution reverberated across much of the Catholic world. As much as Europe was in England, England was in Europe.

By 1601, England's position in Europe had become stronger and more self-confident relative to its neighbours. As the traditional rival, France had been wracked by decades of internal violence, religious conflict, and social strife, rendering it incapable of projecting and wielding the same levels of power it had earlier in the century. Spain, the assumed invincible hegemon of Europe with unimaginable wealth and colonies around the world, had been beaten back from English shores and tasted defeat at English hands. The Holy Roman Empire, after the splitting of the Habsburg patrimony (Spain and its possessions to Philip, the Empire to Ferdinand) and the territorial religious division between Catholics and Lutherans of the 1550s, was not commanding the same level of international respect that it had under Emperor Charles V. Internal rifts across and within religious denominations meant that any English efforts to collaborate with Protestants in Germany, or with France, necessitated informed and current intelligence from reliable and trusted contacts; here Beale found his entrée. In the Netherlands, the nascent United Provinces of the Dutch Republic were caught in the middle of all these shifting sands. For reasons religious, political, and cultural, the Dutch rebelled against their Spanish lords and sought refuge and support from allies in Germany, France, and, ultimately, England. Throughout these lands and in various others, many Protestants across the spectrum of religious opinion and practice looked to England as their leader and potential saviour. Elizabethans with experience and contacts abroad—such as Killigrew, Rogers, Sidney, and, naturally, Beale—were painfully aware of the role that England could (in their view, should) play in the struggle for the Protestant cause. In the mid 1580s, men like Walsingham, Leicester, and Sidney advocated strongly for English intervention on behalf of the Dutch against Spain, their fears of Spanish political domination of Europe combining with a dread that they would all become subject to Roman Catholicism once again. Beale was thinking along these lines in the early 1570s and saw religious causes on the mainland as integrated with those in England, and with the Spaniard, the pope, and Mary Queen of Scots allied against Elizabeth and all she stood for as Defender of the Faith in Protestant England. For Beale and various others, Europe was in England, and England was in Europe.

Not everyone saw it that way; nor is it the case today. Some, such as those who never left English shores, Queen Elizabeth very much included, preferred a more cautious approach that left England more removed from the rest of Europe than those like Beale would have wished. Some, such as those who knew the dangers of travel first-hand, Elizabeth's tutor Roger Ascham comes to mind, warned against international travel lest, for example, the Englishman Italianate become the devil incarnate.[3] The English did not hold a monopoly on conflicting ideas regarding engagement with other European powers of the sixteenth century; nor is it the case today. From Spain to Sweden, from Scotland to Sicily, a variety of opinion could be found in each land and people, so in this respect England was intimately a part of a heterogeneous Europe that shared a common cultural foundation but differed according to political and religious traditions. In Robert Beale we can see the push and pull of religious and national identities, the reflections on indebtedness and instincts for self-reliance, and the nuanced deliberations alongside knee-jerk reactions that seem familiar four centuries after Beale's own.

A European Elizabethan: The Life of Robert Beale, Esquire. David Scott Gehring, Oxford University Press.
© David Scott Gehring 2024. DOI: 10.1093/9780198902942.003.0009

---

[3] Roger Ascham, *The Scholemaster* (London, 1570) (STC 832), fol. 26r. Cf. the later view in Joseph Hall, *Quo vadis? A Ivst Censvre of Travell as it is commonly vndertaken by the Gentlemen of our Nation* (London, 1617) (STC 12705), 38, 93–4.

Bibliography

Primary Sources

Manuscripts
United Kingdom
Aberdeen University Library
MSS 1009/1-2

Belvoir Castle
MSS V-VII

Bodleian Library, University of Oxford
Ashmole MSS 763, 826, 1729

British Library
Additional MSS 5935, 14028-9, 15943, 19117, 22924, 29549, 30663, 32091, 32100, 34727, 48000 1, 48007, 48009-11, 48014-15, 48017-20, 48023-8, 48030, 48032-3, 48035-7, 48039-40, 48042-4, 48047-9, 48055, 48062-4, 48066, 48078, 48080, 48083-6, 48088, 48094, 48096, 48098, 48100-2, 48110, 48114-8, 48126-9, 48149-50, 48152, 48195
Cotton Charter XV, 42
Cotton MSS Caligula, C. III, IX; E. VI; Faustina, E. V; Galba, C. V, VIII, XI; D. I, III-IV, XI, XIII; Julius, F. VI; Nero, B. IX; Otho, E. IV; Titus, F. I, III; Vespasian, C. VIII; F. III, VI
Egerton MSS 1693-4, 2790
Hargrave MS 107
Harley MSS 36, 253, 290, 1052, 1088, 1110, 1561, 1582, 5112, 5177, 6035, 6990, 6993-4, 6997
Lansdowne MSS 12, 18, 27, 39, 42, 51, 68, 72-3, 79, 84, 100, 103, 139, 155, 157, 396, 982
Royal MS 13, B. I
Sloane MS 2442
Stowe MSS 163, 167, 1045

Cambridge University Library
MSS Add. 4467-8
MS Dd.iii.85
MS Ii.v.3

Coventry History Centre
BA/H/Q/A79/87A
PA244/37/7
PA1798/2

Hampshire Record Office
21M65 A1/26

Hatfield House
CP, 2, 30, 32, 36, 39, 40, 44, 50, 53, 55, 68, 70-4, 77, 79, 80-1, 84, 86-7, 96, 141, 151-2, 154, 156, 159, 162-3, 165, 167, 171, 175, 180, 182, 185, 246
CP, Petitions 1429

Honourable Society of Gray's Inn Archive
MS ADM 1/1

Inner Temple Library
Petyt MSS 538/50, 538/52

Kent History and Library Centre
U1475/C12/88, 217, 240-1
U1475/C15/1-3

Lambeth Palace Library
MSS 647, 652, 680, 3197-8, 3206, 3470, 4267, 4769

London Metropolitan Archives
CLC/210/G/BBK/001/MS12930
CLC/313/P/036/MS25202
P69/ALH5/A/001/MS05083
P69/ALH5/A/002/MS05084
P69/ALH6/MS05090

Longleat House
Dudley MS II
Portland MS I
Talbot MS I
Talbot MS II

Magdalen College, University of Cambridge
MSS PL 2502-3

Norwich Record Office
MS 7198

Richmond Local Studies Library
Extracts from the Cartwright muniments at Aynhoe, C(A)2274, Northamptonshire Record Office

Somerset Record Office
D/D/Ca 48
D/D/B Register 15

Staffordshire Record Office
B/A/1/15
LD30/2/7/96
LD30/12/10

Surrey History Centre
P6/1/1
MSS 6729/3/99-100

The National Archives
C 66/1090, 1105, 1224, 1245, 1271, 1283, 1334, 1398, 1466, 1470, 1511, 1554-5
C 142/269/34
DL 13/7, box 1
DL 41/839 (old reference DL 41/34/2)
E 115/27, 29, 38, 42
E 331/CoventryandLich/2
E 403/2261-85
HCA 30/840/190
PC 2/10-11, 13, 15-7, 19, 22-5
PRO 30/5/5
PROB 11/75/375
PROB 11/97-98
PROB 1/3; 10/202; 11/32, 11/55; 11/69
SP 12/77, 141, 144, 150, 154, 175, 180-1, 200, 238, 248, 252-3, 262, 265-6, 268-73
SP 15/27, 31, 34
SP 46/16
SP 52/37
SP 53/11-13, 21
SP 68/5
SP 70/4, 25, 34, 49, 86 7, 89, 94, 96, 116-17, 119-24, 134, 146
SP 75/1
SP 77/6
SP 78/8-11, 13-14, 44
SP 80/1
SP 81/1-3, 7-8
SP 82/2-3
SP 83/2, 4, 5, 20 23
SP 84/2, 5, 9-10, 15-18, 22-3, 50
SP 94/1
SP 99/1
SP 103/34
SP 104/163

Germany
Geheimes Staatsarchiv Preußischer Kulturbesitz
Rep. 13, Nr 15cd, Fasc. 8

Hauptstaatsarchiv Dresden
GR, Loc. 7278/1

Hauptstaatsarchiv Hannover
Cal. Br. 21, Nr 362

Hauptstaatsarchiv Munich
Kasten schwarz 16682
Kurbayern Äußeres Archiv MS 4515

Hauptstaatsarchiv Stuttgart
Bestand A 63, Bü. 54
Bestand A 114, Bü. 8

Hauptstaatsarchiv Weimar
Ernestinisches Gesamtarchiv, Reg. D. 94

Staatsarchiv Marburg
Bestand 4, Abteilung I, Nr 82

United States of America
Brigham Young University
MS 457

Folger Shakespeare Library
MS V.b. 142

Huntington Library
HM 31188

Newberry Library
Case MS 5089

Denmark
Rigsarkivet, Copenhagen
TKUA, SD, England, AI, 1
TKUA, SD, England, AII, 9

France
Bibliothèque Nationale de France
Latin MS 8583

Ireland
Trinity College Dublin
MS 706

Spain
Bibliotheca Nacional de España
MSS 3821

Original Printed Works

Anon., *Gründliche vnd Eigentlich Warhaffte Beschreibung von der Königin in Engellandt warumm sie die Königin von Schottlandt hat enthaupten lassen* (Cologne, 1587) (USTC 669525).

Anon., *Kurtzer unnd gründtlicher Bericht, wie die Edel und from Königin auß Schotlandt Maria Stuarda* (Munich, 1587) (VD16 M 996).

Anon., *Mariae Stuartae Scotorum Reginae* (Cologne, 1587) (possibly VD16 M 991).

Anon., *The Ansvvere made by the Noble Lords the States, vnto the Ambassadour of Polonia* (STC 18452).

Anon., *Warhafftige Zeytung vnd Beschreibung von der Gewaltigen Armada* (Cologne, 1588) (USTC 705682).

Aratus, *Arati Solensis Phænomena, et Prognostica, Interpretius, M. Tullio Cicerone* (Paris, 1559) (USTC 750689).

Ascham, Roger, *The Scholemaster* (London, 1570) (STC 832).

Bartas, Guillaume de Saluste du, *La Sepmaine ou Creation du Monde* (Paris, 1578) (USTC 34602).

Bauduin, François, *Ad Edicta Veterum Principum Rom. de Christianis* (Basle, 1557) (VD16 B 762).

Bauduin, François, *Oratio in Fvnere Illvstriss. Principis Othonis Henrici Electoris Palatini etc. Habita XII Cal. Mar. MDLIX* (Heidelberg, 1559) (VD16 B 775).

Beale, Robert, *A Declaration of the Cavses [. . .]* (London, 1589) (STC 9196).

Beale, Robert, *Declaratio Cavsarvm, Qvibvs Serenissimae Maiestatis Angliae Classiarij adducti* (London, 1589) (STC 9197); German translations at Erfurt and n.p. (USTC 615815, 2215041); Dutch and Latin at Delft (USTC 422717, 429242).

Blackwood, Adam, *Martyre de la Royne d'Escosse* (Edinburgh, 1587; 1588; 1589) (STC 3107–9).

Buchanan, George, *De Maria Scotorum Regina totaque eius contra Regem coniuratione, foedo cum Bothuelio adulterio, nefaria in maritum crudelitate & rabie, horrendo insuper & deterrimo eiusdem parricidio: plena & tragica plane historia* (London, 1571) (STC 3978); English translation of (1571) (STC 3981.

Camden, William, *Annales Rervm Anglicarvm, et Hibernicarvm, Regnante Elizabetha* (London, 1615) (STC 4496); edns in English (1625; 1635) (STC 4497, 4501).

Camden, William, *Britannia, or, A Chorographical Description of the Flourishing Kingdoms of England, Scotland, and Ireland [. . .] Enlarged by the Latest Discoveries*, trans. Richard Gough (London, 1789).

Cartwright, Thomas, *The second replie of Thomas Cartwright against Maister Doctor Whitgiftes second answer, touching the Churche Discipline* (Heidelberg, 1575) (STC 4714).

Cecil, Robert, *The Copie of a Letter to the Right Honourable the Earle of Leycester* (London, 1586) (STC 6052).

Chytraeus, David, *Chronicon Saxoniae* (Leipzig, 1593) (USTC 628454).

Chytraeus, David, *Davidis Chytraei Theologi ac Historici Eminentissimi, Rostochiana in Academia Professoris quondam primarii Epistolae* (Hanau, 1614) (VD17 1:049418Y).

Cuningham, William, *The Cosmographical Glasse* (London, 1559) (STC 6119).

D'Ewes, Simonds, *A Compleat Journal of the Notes, Speeches and Debates, both of the House of Lords and House of Commons Throughout the whole Reign of Queen Elizabeth, Of Glorious Memory* (London, 1693).

Drusius, Johannes, *Animadversorvm Liber II. Ad Robertvm Belvm Generosvm, et Regii Consilii a Secretis* (Leiden, 1585) (USTC 429015).

Fuller, Thomas, *The Church-History of Britain* (London, 1655).

Gerard, John, *The Herball or Generall Historie of Plantes* (London, 1597) (STC 11750).

Hall, Joseph, *Quo vadis? A Ivst Censvre of Travell as it is commonly vndertaken by the Gentlemen of our Nation* (London, 1617) (STC 12705).

Heylyn, Peter, *Aërius Redivivus, or, The History of the Presbyterians [. . .] The Second Edition* (London, 1672).

Holinshed, Raphael, *The firste [laste] volume of the chronicles of England, Scotlande, and Ireland* (London, 1577) (STC 13568b), 1587 edn (STC 13569).

Jewel, John, *Apologia Ecclesiae Anglicanae* (London, 1562) (STC 14581).

Kromer, Marcin, *Polonia* (Cologne, 1588) (USTC 339383).

Leslie, John, *A defence of the honour of the Right High, Right Mighty, and Noble Princesse, Marie Queene of Scotlande* (1569) (STC 15505), renamed slightly in 1571 (STC 15506).

Leslie, John, *A Table Gathered ovvt of a Boke Named A Treatise of Treasons against Q. Elizabeth and the Croune of England* (Antwerp, 1572) (STC 23617.5).

Leslie, John, *A Treatise of Treasons against Q. Elizabeth, and the Croune of England* (Leuven, 1572) (STC 7601).

Milles, Thomas, *The Catalogve of Honor, or, Tresvry of Trve Nobility Pecvliar and Proper to the Isle of Great Britaine* (London, 1610) (STC 17926).

Morlet, Pierre, *Ianitrix, siue, Institvtio ad Perfectam linguae Gallicae cognitionem acquirendam* (Oxford, 1597) (STC 18114).

Parsons, Robert, *A Conference abovt the Next Svccession to the Crowne of Ingland* (Antwerp, 1595) (STC 19398).

Reineccer, Reiner, *Historia Julia*, 3 vols (Helmstedt, 1594–7) (VD16 R 886–7).

Rudolf II, *Translat du mandement et ordonnance de lempereur, emane en langue hault-allemande contre les Anglois monopoliers dicts marchans aduenturiers, residens à Staden* (Brussels, 1597) (USTC 75282); German original in multiple impressions (USTC 750534–6).

Schuerman, Kaspar, *Confvtatio Cavssarvm* (Antwerp, 1590) (USTC 406861).

Sleidan, Johann, *A Famovse Cronicle of oure Time, called Sleidanes Commentaries*, trans. John Daus (London, 1560 (STC 19848).

Stow, John, *A Svrvay of London* (London, 1598, 1603) (STC 23341, 23343).

Stubbe, John, *The Discoverie of a Gaping Gvlf* (London, 1579) (STC 23400).

Tillet, Jean du, *Commentariorum [...] de rebus Gallicis libri duo* (Frankfurt am Main, 1579) (VD16 D 3066).

Vermigli, Peter Martyr, *In Librum Judicum [...] Commentarij Doctissimi* (Zurich, 1561) (VD16 B 3038).

Verweij, Johannes, *Nova Via Docendi Græca* (Amsterdam, 1691).

Wechel, André, *Rerum Hispanicarvm Scriptores Aliqvot, quorum nomina versa pagina indicabit. Ex Bibliotheca clariβimi viri Dn. Roberti Beli Angli* (Frankfurt am Main, 1579) (VD16 R 1163–4).

Wecker, Johann, trans. John Banester, *A Compendiovs Chrvrgerie* (London, 1585) (STC 25185).

Zanchi, Girolamo, *Opera Omnia Theologica: Opervm Theologicorvm D Hieronymi Zanchii, Tomus Septimus, Epistolarvm Libri Dvo* (Geneva, 1619) (possibly USTC 6700274).

Printed Editions

Andrich, Giovanni Luigi, and Biagio Brugi, *De Natione Anglica et Scota Iuristarum Universitatis Patavinae ab a. MCCXXII p. ch. n. usque ad a. MDCCXXXVIII* (Padua, 1892).

Anon. (ed.), *Epistolae Tigurinae* (Cambridge, 1848).

Anon. (ed.), *Journal of the House of Commons, Vol. 1: 1547–1629* (London, 1802).

Black, Joseph L. (ed.), *The Martin Marprelate Tracts: A Modernized and Annotated Edition* (Cambridge, 2008).

Boersma, O., and A. J. Jelsma (eds), *Unity in Multiformity: The Minutes of the Coetus of London, 1575 and the Consistory Minutes of the Italian Churches of London, 1570–1591*, Huguenot Society of Great Britain and Ireland, 59 ([London], 1997).

Boyd, William K. (ed.), *Calendar of State Papers, Scotland, Vol. 9: 1586–88* (London, 1915).

Brown, Horatio F. (ed.), *Calendar of State Papers Relating to English Affairs in the Archives of Venice, Vol. 8: 1581–1591* (London, 1894).

Collins, Arthur (ed.), *Letters and Memorials of State*, 2 vols (London, 1746).

Controversia et Confessio, https://www.controversia-et-confessio.de.

Cooper, Charles Henry, and Thompson Cooper (eds), *Athenae Cantabrigienses*, Vol. 2 (Cambridge, 1861).

Cooper, Thomas, *An Admonition of the People of England. 1589*, ed. Edward Arber (Birmingham, 1882).

Croft, Pauline (ed.), *The Spanish Company* (London, 1973).

Digges, Dudley (ed.), *The Compleat Ambassador, or, Two Treaties of the Intended Marriage of Qu: Elizabeth [...] Comprised in Letters of Negotiation of Sir Francis Walsingham, her Resident in France* (London, 1655).

Dumont, J. (ed.), *Corps Universel Diplomatique du Droit des Gens*, Vol. 5, Part 1 (Amsterdam, 1728).

Förstemann, Karl Eduard, et al. (eds), *Album Academiae Vitebergensis: Ältere Reihe in 3 Bänden 1502–1602* (Leipzig and Halle, 1894; repr. Aalen, 1976).

Foster, Joseph (ed.), *Alumni Oxonienses: The Members of the University of Oxford, 1500–1714* (Oxford, 1891).

Foster, Joseph (ed.), *The Register of Admissions to Gray's Inn, 1521–1889, together with the Register of Marriages in Gray's Inn Chapel, 1695–1754* (London, 1889).

Gehring, David Scott (ed.), *Diplomatic Intelligence on the Holy Roman Empire and Denmark during the Reigns of Elizabeth I and James VI: Three Treatises*, Royal Historical Society, Camden Fifth Series, 49 (Cambridge, 2016).

Gerlo, Aloïs, and Rudolf De Smet (eds), *Marnixi Epistulae: De briefwisseling van Marnix van Sint Aldegonde: een kritische uitgave. Pars I (1558–1576)* (Brussels, 1990).

Goldring, Elizabeth, Faith Eales, Elizabeth Clarke, and Jayne Elisabeth Archer (eds), *John Nichols's The Progresses and Public Processions of Queen Elizabeth I: A New Edition of the Early Modern Sources, Vol. 2: 1572–1578* (Oxford, 2014).

Hales, John, *A Declaration of the Succession of the Crowne Imperiall of Ingland*, 1563, in Francis Hargrave (pseud. George Harbin), *The Hereditary Right of the Crown of England Asserted* (London, 1713).

Halliwell, James Orchard (ed.), *The Private Diary of Dr John Dee* (London, 1842).

Hartley, T. E. (ed.), *Proceedings in the Parliaments of Elizabeth I*, 3 vols (Leicester, 1981, 1995).

Hearne, Thomas (ed.), *A Collection of Curious Discourses Written by Eminent Antiquaries*, Vol. 2 (London, 1773).

Höhlbaum, Konstantin (ed.), *Kölner Inventar, 2. Band: 1572–1591* (Leipzig, 1903).

Holleran, James V. (ed.), *A Jesuit Challenge: Edmund Campion's Debates at the Tower of London in 1581* (New York, 1999).

Horn, Joyce M. (ed.), *Fasti Ecclesiae Anglicanae 1541–1857, Vol. 2: Chichester Diocese* (London, 1971).

Horn, Joyce M. (ed.), *Fasti Ecclesiae Anglicanae 1541–1857, Vol. 10: Coventry and Lichfield Diocese* (London, 2003).

Horn, Joyce M. and Derrick Sherwin Bailey (eds), *Fasti Ecclesiae Anglicanae 1541–1857, Vol. 5: Bath and Wells Diocese* (London, 1979).

Hughes, Charles (ed.), 'Nicholas Faunt's Discourse Touching the Office of the Principal Secretary of Estate, &c. 1592', *English Historical Review*, 20 (1905), 499–508.

Jupp, Edward Basil, and R. Hovenden (eds), *The Registers of Christenings Marriages and Burials in the Parish of Allhallows London Wall within the City of London from the Year of Our Lord 1559 to 1675* (London, 1878).

Kervyn de Lettenhove, J. M. B. C. (ed.), *Relations Politiques des Pays-Bas et de L'Angleterre, sous le règne de Philippe II*, 11 vols (Brussels, 1882–1900).

Kausler, Eduard von, and Theodor Schott (eds), *Briefwechsel zwischen Christoph, Herzog von Württemberg, und Petrus Paulus Vergerius* (Tübingen, 1875).

Kluckhohn, August (ed.), *Briefe Friedrich des Frommen Kurfürsten von der Pfalz mit verwandten Schriftstücken*, 2 vols (Brunswick, 1868–72).

Kolb, Robert, and James A. Nestingen (eds), *Sources and Contexts of the Book of Concord* (Minneapolis, MN, 2001).

Kolb, Robert, and Timothy J. Wengert (eds), *The Book of Concord: The Confessions of the Evangelical Lutheran Church* (Minneapolis, MN, 2000).

Kuin, Roger (ed.), *The Correspondence of Sir Philip Sidney*, 2 vols (Oxford, 2012).

Labanoff, Alexandre (ed.), *Lettres, instructions et mémoires de Marie Stuart, Reine d'Écosse*, 7 vols (Paris; London, 1844–52).

Lawson, Jane A. (ed.), *The Elizabethan New Year's Gift Exchanges 1559–1603* (Oxford, 2013).

Lodge, Edmund (ed.), *Illustrations of British History* (Howard Papers), 3 vols, 2nd edn (London, 1838).

Martin, Charles Trice (ed.), *The Camden Miscellany, Volume the Sixth [...] Journal of Sir Francis Walsingham from December 1570 to April 1583. From the Original Manuscript in the Possession of Lieut.-Colonel Carew* (London, 1870/1).

Morris, John (ed.), *The Letter-Books of Sir Amias Poulet, Keeper of Mary Queen of Scots* (London, 1874).

Nichols, John Gough, and John Bruce (eds), *Wills from Doctors' Commons: A Selection from the Wills of Eminent Persons Proved in the Prerogative Court of Canterbury, 1495–1695* (London, 1863).

Powell, Edgar (ed.), *The Travels and Life of Sir Thomas Hoby, Kt. of Bisham Abbey, written by Himself* (London, 1902).

Robinson, Hastings (ed.), *Original Letters Relative to the English Reformation*, 2 vols (Cambridge, 1846–7).

Robinson, Hastings (ed.), *The Zurich Letters [...] the Reign of Queen Elizabeth*, 3 vols (Cambridge, 1842, 1845, 1846).

Simson, Paul (ed.), *Inventar Hansischer Archive des sechzehnten Jahrhunderts*, 3. Band: *Danziger Inventar 1531–1591* (Munich, 1913).

Snow, Vernon F. (ed.), *Parliament in Elizabethan England: John Hooker's 'Order and Usage'* (New Haven, CT, 1977).

Tanner, Thomas, *Bibliotheca Britannico-Hibernica, sive, De Scriptoribus, qui in Anglia, Scotia, et Hibernia [...] Commentarius* (London, 1748).

Toepke, Gustav (ed.), *Die Matrikel der Universität Heidelberg von 1386 bis 1662*, Vol. 2 (Heidelberg, 1886).

Vos, Alvin (ed.), *Letters of Roger Ascham*, trans. Maurice Hatch and Alvin Vos, (New York, 1989).

Wright, Thomas (ed.), *Queen Elizabeth and Her Times*, Vol. 1 (London, 1838).

Calendars and Catalogues

Acts of the Privy Council of England, ed. John Roche Dasent, 32 vols (London, 1890–1907).

The British Library Catalogue of Additions to the Manuscripts: The Yelverton Manuscripts [...] Additional Manuscripts 48000–48196, 2 vols (London, 1994).

Calendar of the Cecil Papers in Hatfield House, various editors, Vols 1–14 (London, 1883–1923).

Calendar of State Papers Domestic: Elizabeth, various editors, 8 vols (London, 1856–72).

Calendar of State Papers Foreign: Elizabeth, various editors, 23 vols (London, 1863–1950).

Calendar of State Papers Relating to English Affairs in the Archives of Venice, various editors, Vols 7–9 (London, 1890–7).

Calendar of State Papers, Scotland, various editors, 11 vols (London, 1898–1936).

Calendar of State Papers, Spain (Simancas), ed. Martin A. S. Hume, 4 vols (London, 1892–9).

Calendar of the Patent Rolls, various editors, List and Index Society, Vols 309–10, 322, 327–8, 358 (Kew, 2005–18).

The Forty-fifth Annual Report of the Deputy Keeper of Public Records, (London, 1885).

Historical Manuscripts Commission Report on the Manuscripts of Lord De L'Isle & Dudley Preserved at Penshurst Place Volume Two, ed. C. L. Kingsford (London, 1934).

Historical Manuscripts Commission Twelfth Report, Appendix, Part IV: The Manuscripts of His Grace the Duke of Rutland, G. C. B., Preserved at Belvoir Castle, Vol. I, ed. H.C. Maxwell Lyte (London, 1888).

Pollard, A. W., and G. R. Redgrave, *A Short-title Catalogue of Books Printed in England, Scotland, & Ireland and of English Books Printed Abroad 1475–1640*, 2nd edn rev. W. A. Jackson, F. S. Ferguson, and K. F. Pantzer (London, 1976–1991), online at http://estc.bl.uk.

Proceedings of the Privy Council of Queen Elizabeth I, 1582–1583, ed. David Crankshaw, 3 vols (Woodbridge, forthcoming).

Universal Short Title Catalogue, online at http://ustc.ac.uk/index.php.

Verzeichnis der im deutschen Sprachbereich erschienenen Drucke des 16. Jahrhunderts, online at www.gateway-bayern.de.

Secondary Sources, Published

Adams, Simon, 'Favourites and Factions at the Elizabethan Court', repr. in Simon Adams, *Leicester and the Court: Essays on Elizabethan Politics* (Manchester, 2002), 46–67.

Adams, Simon, 'The Decision to Intervene: England and the United Provinces 1584–1585', in José Martíez Millán (ed.), *Felipe II (1527–1598): Europa y la Monarquía Católica* (Madrid, 1999), I.19–31

Adams, Simon, 'The Lauderdale Papers, 1561-1570: The Maitland of Lethington State Papers and the Leicester Correspondence', *Scottish Historical Review*, 67 (1988), 28–55.

Adams, Simon, 'The Papers of Robert Dudley, Earl of Leicester, I: The Browne-Evelyn Collection', *Archives*, XX (1992), 63–85.

Adams, Simon, 'The Papers of Robert Dudley, Earl of Leicester, II: The Atye-Cotton Collection', *Archives*, XX (1993), 131–44.

Adams, Simon, 'The Papers of Robert Dudley, Earl of Leicester, III: The Countess of Leicester's Collection', *Archives*, XXII (1996), 1–26.

Adams, Simon, 'Tudor England's Relations with France', *State Papers Online 1509–1714*, Cengage Learning EMEA Ltd., 2009; https://www.gale.com/intl/essays/simon-adams-tudor-englands-relations-france.

Adams, Simon, 'Two "Missing" Lauderdale Letters: Queen Mary to Robert Dudley, Earl of Leicester, 5 June 1567, and Thomas Randolph and Francis Russell, Earl of Bedford to Leicester, 23 November 1564', *Scottish Historical Review*, 70 (1991), 55–7.

Adams, Simon (ed.), *Household Accounts and Disbursement Books of Robert Dudley, Earl of Leicester*, Royal Historical Society, Camden Fifth Series, 6 (Cambridge, 1995).

Alford, Stephen, *Burghley: William Cecil at the Court of Elizabeth I* (New Haven, CT, 2008).

Alford, Stephen, *The Early Elizabethan Polity: William Cecil and the British Succession Crisis, 1558–1569* (Cambridge, 1998).

Alford, Stephen, *The Watchers: A Secret History of the Reign of Elizabeth I* (London, 2012).

Allen, Gemma, 'The Rise of the Ambassadress: English Ambassadorial Wives and Early Modern Diplomatic Culture', *Historical Journal*, 62 (2019), 617–38.

Anderson, Marvin W. 'Vermigli, Peter Martyr', in Hans J. Hillerbrand (ed.), *The Oxford Encyclopedia of the Reformation* (Oxford, 1996); online edn.

Andreani, Angela, *The Elizabethan Secretariat and the Signet Office: The Production of State Papers, 1590–1596* (London, 2017).

Astbury, Leah, 'When a Woman Hates her Husband: Love, Sex and Fruitful Marriages in Early Modern England', *Gender & History*, 32 (2020), 523–41.

Astbury, Leah, 'Being Well, Looking Ill: Childbirth and the Return to Health in Seventeenth-century England', *Social History of Medicine*, 30 (2017), 500–19.

Atkinson, E. G., 'The Cardinal of Châtillon in England, 1568-71', *Proceedings of the Huguenot Society of London*, 3, for 1888–92 (London, 1892), 172–285.

Bałuk-Ulewiczowa, Teresa, '*Audiatur et Altera Pars*: The Polish Record of the Działyński Embassy of 1597', *British Catholic History*, 33 (2017), 501–33.

Basing, Patricia, 'Robert Beale and the Queen of Scots', *British Library Journal*, 20 (1994), 65–82.

Baumann, Wolf-Rüdiger, trans. Timothy Slater, *The Merchants Adventurers and the Continental Cloth-Trade (1560s–1620s)* (Berlin, 1990).

Bowden, Caroline, and James E. Kelly (eds), *The English Convents in Exile, 1600–1800: Communities, Culture and Identity* (Farnham, 2013).

Bechtold, Jonas, 'Divergierende Formalitätszuschreibungen und die Skalierbarkeit (in) formeller Akteure der Diplomatie: Christopher Mundt als englischer Gesandter am Reichstag 1566', *Frühneuzeit-Info*, 33 (2022), 17–31.

Beckett, Margaret J., 'Counsellor, Conspirator, Polemicist, Historian: John Lesley, Bishop of Ross 1527-96', *Scottish Church History*, 39 (2009), 1–22.

Bell, Gary M., *A Handlist of British Diplomatic Representatives 1509–1688* (London, 1990).

Bell, Gary, 'Elizabethan Diplomatic Compensation: Its Nature and Variety', *Journal of British Studies*, 20 (1981), 1–25.

Benedict, Philip, 'The Saint Bartholomew's Massacres in the Provinces', *Historical Journal*, 21 (1978), 205–25.

Bigland, Ralph, *Historical Monumental and Genealogical Collections, Relative to the County of Gloucester*, Vol. 1 (London, 1791).

Blok P. J., and P. C. Molhuysen (eds), *Nieuw Nederlandsch Biografisch Woordenboek, part 4* (Leiden, 1918).

Bossy, John, *Under the Molehill: An Elizabethan Spy Story* (New Haven, CT, 2001).

Brennan, Michael G., '"Your Lordship's to Do You All Humble Service": Rowland Whyte's Correspondence with Robert Sidney, Viscount Lisle and First Earl of Leicester', *Sidney Journal*, 21 (2003), 1–38.

Budke, Tobias, *Die geschenkte Reformation: Bücher als Geschenke im England des 16. Jahrhunderts* (Frankfurt am Main, 2015).

Burton, A. A. C., et al., *King Henry VIII School, 1545–1945* (Coventry, 1945).

Burton, William, *Notes and Queries*, Ser. I, Vol. V (April 17, 1852), 365–6.

Chalmers, Alexander, *The General Biographical Dictionary: A New Edition* (London, 1812), Vol. 4.

Collinson, Patrick, *Archbishop Grindal, 1519–1583: The Struggle for a Reformed Church* (London, 1979).

Collinson, Patrick, 'England and International Calvinism, 1558–1640', in Menna Prestwich (ed.), *International Calvinism 1541–1715* (Oxford, 1985), 197–223.

Collinson, Patrick, 'Puritans, Men of Business and Elizabethan Parliaments', *Parliamentary History*, 7 (1988), 187–211.

Collinson, Patrick, *Richard Bancroft and Elizabethan Anti-Puritanism* (Cambridge, 2013).

Collinson, Patrick, 'Servants and Citizens: Robert Beale and other Elizabethans', *Historical Research*, 79:206 (2006), 488–511.

Collinson, Patrick, *The Elizabethan Puritan Movement* (London, 1967).

Collinson, Patrick, 'The Elizabethan Puritans and the Foreign Reformed Churches in London', *Proceedings of the Huguenot Society of London*, 20 (1964), 528–55.

Collinson, Patrick, 'The Monarchical Republic of Queen Elizabeth I', *Bulletin of the John Rylands University Library of Manchester*, 69 (1987), 394–424.

Cooper, John, *The Queen's Agent: Francis Walsingham at the Court of Elizabeth I* (London, 2011).

Corens, Liesbeth, *Confessional Mobility and English Catholics in Counter-Reformation Europe* (Oxford, 2019).

Corens, Liesbeth, Kate Peters, and Alexandra Walsham (eds), *Archives and Information in the Early Modern World* (Oxford, 2018).

Coster, Will, *Baptism and Spiritual Kinship in Early Modern England* (Aldershot, 2002).

Craigwood, Joanna, and Tracey A. Sowerby (eds), *Cultures of Diplomacy and Literary Writing in the Early Modern World* (Oxford, 2019).

Craigwood, Joanna, and Tracey A. Sowerby (eds), 'English Diplomatic Relations and Literary Cultures in the Sixteenth and Seventeenth Centuries', special issue of *Huntington Library Quarterly*, 82 (2019).

Crankshaw, David J., 'The Tudor Privy Council, *c.*1540–1603', *State Papers Online 1509–1714*, Cengage Learning EMEA Ltd., 2009, accessible at https://www.gale.com/intl/essays/david-j-crankshaw-tudor-privy-council-c-1540-1603.

Cressy, David, *England's Islands in a Sea of Troubles* (Oxford, 2020).

Crimp, Caroline, and Mary Grimwade, *Barnes and Mortlake History Society, Milbourne House, Barnes* (Richmond, 1978).

Daussy, Hugues, 'London, Nerve Centre of the Huguenot Diplomatic Network in the Later Sixteenth Century', in Vivienne Larminie (ed.), *Huguenot Networks, 1560–1780: The Interactions and Impact of a Protestant Minority in Europe* (New York, 2018), 29–40.

Davies, Norman, *God's Playground: A History of Poland, Vol. 1: The Origins to 1795*, rev. edn (Oxford, 2005).

Daybell, James, 'Gender, Politics and Diplomacy: Women, News and Intelligence Networks in Elizabethan England', in Robyn Adams and Rosanna Cox (eds), *Diplomacy and Early Modern Culture* (Basingstoke, 2011), 101–19.

Daybell, James, *The Material Letter in Early Modern England: Manuscript Letters and the Culture and Practices of Letter-Writing, 1512–1635* (Basingstoke, 2012).

Daybell, James, *Women Letter-Writers in Tudor England* (Oxford, 2006).

Daybell, James, and Andrew Gordon (eds), *Women and Epistolary Agency in Early Modern Culture, 1450–1690* (London, 2016).

Dewar, Mary, *Sir Thomas Smith: A Tudor Intellectual in Office* (London, 1964).

Diefendorf, Barbara B., *Beneath the Cross: Catholics and Huguenots in Sixteenth-Century Paris* (Oxford, 1991).

Dingel, Irene, '*Caritas christiana* und Bekenntnistreue: Johannes Sturms Einsatz für die Einheit des Protestantismus in den Auseinandersetzungen um die lutherische Konkordienformel', in Matthieu Arnold (ed.), *Johannes Sturm (1507–1589): Rhetor, Pädagoge und Diplomat* (Tübingen, 2009), 375–90.

Dingel, Irene, 'The Culture of Conflict in the Controversies Leading to the Formula of Concord (1548–1580)', in Robert Kolb (ed.), *Lutheran Ecclesiastical Culture, 1550–1675* (Leiden, 2008), 15–64.

Domínguez, Freddy Cristóbal *Radicals in Exile: English Catholic Books during the Reign of Philip II* (University Park, PA, 2021).

Donald, M. B., *Elizabethan Monopolies. The History of the Company of Mineral and Battery Works from 1565 to 1604* (Edinburgh, 1961).

Doran, Susan, *Elizabeth I and Her Circle* (Oxford, 2015).

Doran, Susan, *Monarchy and Matrimony: The Courtships of Elizabeth I* (London, 1995).

Doran, Susan, 'Religion and Politics at the Court of Elizabeth I: The Habsburg Marriage Negotiations of 1559–1567', *The English Historical Review*, 104:413 (1989), 908–26.

Doran, Susan (ed.), *Elizabeth and Mary: Royal Cousins, Rival Queens* (London, 2021).

Doran, Susan, and Paulina Kewes (eds), *Doubtful and Dangerous: The Question of Succession in Late Elizabethan England* (Manchester, 2014).

Dorsten, J. A. van, *Poets, Patrons, and Professors: Sir Philip Sidney, Daniel Rogers, and the Leiden Humanists* (Leiden, 1962).

Działynski, Adam (ed.), *Collectanea Vitam Resque Gestas Joannis Zamoyscii, Magni Cancellarii et Summi Ducis Reipublicam Polonae* (Posnań, 1861).

Ehrenberg, Richard, *Hamburg und England im Zeitalter der Königin Elisabeth* (Jena, 1896).

Erbe, Michael, *François Bauduin (1520–1573): Biographie eines Humanisten* (Gütersloh, 1978).

Esser, Raingard, 'Germans in early modern Britain', in Panikos Panayi (ed.), *Germans in Britain since 1500* (Hambledon, 1996), 17–27.

Evans, Joan, *A History of the Society of Antiquaries* (Oxford, 1956).

Finch, Mary E., *The Wealth of Five Northamptonshire Families 1540–1640* (Oxford, 1956).

Flood, John L., and David J. Shaw, *Johannes Sinapius (1505–1560): Hellenist and Physician in Germany and Italy* (Geneva, 1997).

Franklin, Julian H., *Jean Bodin and the Sixteenth-Century Revolution in the Methodology of Law and History* (New York, 1963).

Frigo, Daniela (ed.), *Politics and Diplomacy in Early Modern Italy: The Structure of Diplomatic Practice, 1450–1800*, trans. Adrian Belton (Cambridge, 2000).

Gajda, Alexandra, 'Political Culture in the 1590s: The "Second Reign of Elizabeth"', *History Compass*, 8 (2010), 88–100.

Gajda, Alexandra, *The Earl of Essex and Late Elizabethan Political Culture* (Oxford, 2012).

Gajda, Alexandra, 'The Elizabethan Church and the Antiquity of Parliament', in Paul Cavill and Alexandra Gajda (eds), *Writing the History of Parliament in Tudor and Early Stuart England* (Manchester, 2018), 77–105.

Gallagher, John, *Learning Languages in Early Modern England* (Oxford, 2019).

Garrett, Christina Hallowell, *The Marian Exiles: A Study in the Origins of Elizabethan Puritanism* (Cambridge, 1938).

Gehring, David Scott, *Anglo-German Relations and the Protestant Cause: Elizabethan Foreign Policy and Pan-Protestantism* (London, 2013).

Gehring, David Scott 'From the Strange Death to the Odd Afterlife of Lutheran England', *The Historical Journal*, 57 (2014), 825–44.

Gehring, David Scott, 'Intelligence Gathering, *Relazioni*, and the *Ars Apodemica*', *Diplomacy & Statecraft*, 33 (2022), 211–32.

The Gentlemen's Magazine (May 1825).

Gibbons, Katy, *English Catholic Exiles in Late Sixteenth-Century Paris* (Woodbridge, 2011).

Glaser, Karl-Heinz and Steffen Stuth (eds), *David Chytraeus (1530–1600): Norddeutscher Humanismus in Europa: Beiträge zum Wirken des Kraichgauer Gelehrten* (Ubstadt-Weiher, 2000).

Goetze, Dorothée, and Lena Oetzel (eds), *Early Modern European Diplomacy: A Handbook* (Berlin, 2024).

Goldring, Elizabeth, Faith Eales, Elizabeth Clarke, Jayne Elisabeth Archer (eds), *John Nichols's The Progresses and Public Processions of Queen Elizabeth I: A New Edition of the Early Modern Sources. Volume III 1579–1595* (Oxford, 2014).

Goose, Nigel, and Liên Luu (eds), *Immigrants in Tudor and Early Stuart England* (Brighton, 2005).

Green, Janet M., 'Queen Elizabeth I's Latin Reply to the Polish Ambassador', *Sixteenth Century Journal*, 31 (2000), 987–1008.

Gründler, Otto, 'Zanchi, Girolamo', in Hans J. Hillerbrand (ed.), *The Oxford Encyclopedia of the Reformation* (Oxford, 1996); online edn.

Gunnoe, Jr., Charles D., *Thomas Erastus and the Palatinate: A Renaissance Physician in the Second Reformation* (Leiden, 2011).

Guy, John, *Elizabeth: The Forgotten Years* (New York, NY, 2016).

Guy, John (ed.), *The Reign of Elizabeth I: Court and Culture in the Last Decade* (Cambridge, 1995).

Ha, Polly, 'Reorienting English Protestantism', *Journal of Medieval and Early Modern Studies*, 53 (2023), 1–23.

Ha, Polly, and Patrick Collinson (eds), *The Reception of Continental Reformation in Britain* (Oxford, 2010).

Hammer, Paul E. J., *Elizabeth's Wars: War, Government and Society in Tudor England, 1544–1604* (Basingstoke, 2003).

Hammer, Paul E. J., *The Polarisation of Elizabethan Politics: The Political Career of Robert Devereux, 2nd Earl of Essex, 1585–1597* (Cambridge, 1999).

Harding, Vanessa, 'Families in Later Medieval London: Sex, Marriage and Mortality', in Elizabeth A. New and Christian Steer (eds), *Medieval Londoners: Essays to Mark the Eightieth Birthday of Caroline M. Barron* (London, 2019), 11–36.

Harkins, Robert, 'Calvinism, Anti-Calvinism, and the Admonition Controversy in Elizabethan England', in Bruce Gordon and Carl R. Trueman (eds), *The Oxford Handbook of Calvin and Calvinism* (Oxford, 2021), 141–54.

Heal, Felicity, *The Power of Gifts: Gift Exchange in Early Modern England* (Oxford, 2014).

Heffernan, David, *Debating Tudor Policy in Sixteenth-Century Ireland: 'Reform' Treatises and Political Discourse* (Manchester, 2018).

Heffernan, David, 'Six Tracts on "Coign and Livery", c.1568–78', *Analecta Hibernica*, 45 (2014), 1, 3–33.

Heffernan, David (ed.), *'Reform' Treatises on Tudor Ireland, 1537–1599* (Dublin, 2016).

Heisch, Allison, 'Lord Burghley, Speaker Puckering, and the Editing of HEH "Ellesmere MS 1191"', *Huntington Library Quarterly*, 51 (1988), 210–26.

Hennings, Jan, 'The Failed Gift: Ceremony and Gift-giving in Anglo-Russian Relations, 1660–1664', in Tracey A. Sowerby and Jan Hennings (eds), *Practices of Diplomacy in the Early Modern World c.1410–1800* (London, 2017), 237–53.

Heuser, Peter Arnold, 'Zur Bedeutung der Vor- und Nachkarrieren von Reichskammergerichts-Juristen des 16. Jahrhunderts für das Studium ihrer Rechtsauffassungen: Eine Fallstudie', in Albrecht Cordes (ed.), *Juristische Argumentation: Argumente der Juristen* (Cologne, 2006), 153–218.

Hildebrandt, Esther, 'Christopher Mont: Anglo-German Diplomat', *Sixteenth Century Journal*, 15 (1984), 281–92.

Hobbs, R. Gerald, 'Strasbourg: Vermigli and the Senior School', in Torrance Kirby, Frank A. James II, and Emidio Campi (eds), *A Companion to Peter Martyr Vermigli* (Leiden, 2009), 35–69.

Holt, Mack P., *The French Wars of Religion, 1562–1629*, 2nd edn (Cambridge, 2005).

Hubbard, Eleanor, 'Reading, Writing, and Initialing: Female Literacy in Early Modern London', *Journal of British Studies*, 54 (2015), 553–77.

Hunt, Alice, and Anna Whitelock (eds), *Tudor Queenship: The Reigns of Mary and Elizabeth* (Basingstoke, 2010).

Hunt, Arnold, 'The Early Modern Secretary and the Early Modern Archive', in Liesbeth Corens, Kate Peters, and Alexandra Walsham (eds), *Archives and Information in the Early Modern World* (Oxford, 2018), 105–30.

Ilić, Luka, *Theologian of Sin and Grace: The Process of Radicalization in the Theology of Matthias Flacius Illyricus* (Göttingen, 2014).

Iordanou, Ioanna, *Venice's Secret Service: Organizing Intelligence in the Renaissance* (Oxford, 2019).

Israel, Jonathan, *The Dutch Republic: Its Rise, Greatness, and Fall 1477–1806* (paperback with corrections, Oxford, 1998).

Jones, Norman, *Governing by Virtue: Lord Burghley and the Management of Elizabethan England* (Oxford, 2015).

Jones, Norman, *The English Reformation: Religion and Cultural Adaption* (Oxford, 2002).

Kaplan, Josef (ed.), *Early Modern Ethnic and Religious Communities in Exile* (Newcastle, 2017).

Keblusek, Marika, and Badeloch Vera Noldus (eds), *Double Agents: Cultural and Political Brokerage in Early Modern Europe* (Leiden, 2011).

Kelley, Donald R., *Foundations of Modern Historical Scholarship: Language, Law, and History in the French Renaissance* (New York, 1970).

Kelley, Donald R., 'Historia Integra: François Baudouin and his Conception of History', *Journal of the History of Ideas*, 25 (1964), 35–57.

Kelly, James E. *English Convents in Catholic Europe, c.1600–1800* (Cambridge, 2020).

Kilburn-Toppin, Jasmine, 'Gifting Cultures and Artisanal Guilds in Sixteenth- and Early Seventeenth-Century London', *Historical Journal*, 60 (2017), 865–87.

Kingdon, Robert M., *Myths about the St. Bartholomew's Day Massacres 1572–1576* (Cambridge, MA, 1988).

Kittleson, James M., 'Marbach vs. Zanchi: The Resolution of Controversy in Late Reformation Strasbourg', *Sixteenth Century Journal*, 8 (1977), 31–44.

Kouri, E. I., *England and the Attempts to Form a Protestant Alliance in the Late 1560s: A Case Study in European Diplomacy* (Helsinki, 1981).

Lake, Peter, *Anglicans and Puritans? Presbyterianism and English Conformist Thought from Whitgift to Hooker* (London, 1988).

Lake, Peter, 'The "Political Thought" of the "Monarchical Republic of Elizabeth I", Discovered and Anatomized', *Journal of British Studies*, 54 (2015), 257–87.

Lake, Peter, and Michael Questier (eds), *Conformity and Orthodoxy in the English Church, c.1560–1660* (Woodbridge, 2000).

Lasry, George, Norbert Biermann, and Satoshi Tomokiyo, 'Deciphering Mary Stuart's Lost Letters from 1578–1584', *Cryptologia*, 47:2 (February, 2023). https://doi.org/10.1080/01611194.2022.2160677

Lazzarini, Isabella, *Communication and Conflict: Italian Diplomacy in the Early Renaissance, 1350–1520* (Oxford, 2015).

Leader, John Daniel, *Mary Queen of Scots in Captivity: A Narrative of Events* (Sheffield, 1880).

Leimon, Mitchell, and Geoffrey Parker, 'Treason and Plot in Elizabethan Diplomacy: The "Fame of Sir Edward Stafford" Reconsidered', *English Historical Review*, 111:444 (1996), 1134–58.

Leng, Thomas, *Fellowship and Freedom: The Merchant Adventurers and the Restructuring of English Commerce, 1582–1700* (Oxford, 2020).

Leng, Thomas, 'Interlopers and Disorderly Brethren at the Stade Mart: Commercial Regulations and Practices amongst the Merchant Adventurers of England in the Late Elizabethan Period', *The Economic History Review*, 69 (2016), 823–43.

Lerski, Jerzy Jan, *Historical Dictionary of Poland, 966–1945* (Westport, CT, 1996).

Levine, Mortimer, *The Early Elizabethan Succession Question 1558–1568* (Stanford, 1966).

Lloyd, T. H., 'A Reconsideration of Two Anglo-Hanseatic Treaties of the Fifteenth Century', *English Historical Review*, 102:45 (1987), 916–33.

Lloyd, T. H., *England and the German Hanse, 1157–1611: A Study of their Trade and Commercial Diplomacy* (Cambridge, 1991).

Lockhart, Paul Douglas, *Frederik II and the Protestant Cause: Denmark's Role in the Wars of Religion, 1559–1596* (Leiden, 2004).

Lyon, Gregory B., 'Baudouin, Flacius, and the Plan for the Magdeburg Centuries', *Journal of the History of Ideas*, 64 (2003), 253–72.

MacCaffrey, Wallace, T., *Queen Elizabeth and the Making of Policy, 1572–1588* (Princeton, NJ, 1981).

McCoog, Thomas M. (ed.), *The Reckoned Expense: Edmund Campion and the Early English Jesuits: Essays in Celebration of the First Centenary of Campion Hall, Oxford (1896–1996)* (Woodbridge, 1996).

MacCulloch, Diarmaid, 'Changing Historical Perspectives on the English Reformation: The Last Fifty Years', *Studies in Church History*, 49 (2013), 282–302.

MacCulloch, Diarmaid, 'Putting the English Reformation on the Map (The Prothero Lecture)', *Transactions of the Royal Historical Society*, 15 (Cambridge, 2005), 75–95.

MacCulloch, Diarmaid, 'Sixteenth-century English Protestantism and the Continent', in Wendebourg, Dorothea (ed.), *Sister Reformations: The Reformation in Germany and in England: Symposium on the Occasion of the 450th Anniversary of the Elizabethan Settlement, September 23rd–26th, 2009 = Schwesterreformationen: Die Reformation in Deutschland und in England: Symposion aus Anlass des 450. Jahrestages des Elizabethan Settlement, 23.–26. September 2009* (Tübingen, 2010), 1–14.

MacCulloch, Diarmaid, 'The Church of England and International Protestantism, 1530–1570', in Anthony Milton (ed.), *The Oxford History of Anglicanism, Vol. 1: Reformation and Identity, c.1520–1662* (Oxford, 2017), 316–32.

MacCulloch, Diarmaid, 'The Latitude of the Church of England', in Kenneth Fincham and Peter Lake (eds), *Religious Politics in Post-Reformation England* (Woodbridge, 2006), 41–59.

MacCulloch, Diarmaid, *Thomas Cranmer: A Life* (New Haven, CT, 1996).

MacCulloch, Diarmaid, *Thomas Cromwell: A Life* (London, 2018).

McDiarmid, John F. (ed.), *The Monarchical Republic of Early Modern England: Essays in Response to Patrick Collinson* (Aldershot, 2007).

McFarlane, I. D., *Buchanan* (Oxford, 1981).

McGovern, Jonathan, 'The Development of the Privy Council Oath in Tudor England', *Historical Research*, 93:260 (2020), 273–85.

McGovern, Jonathan, 'Was Elizabethan England Really a Monarchical Republic?', *Historical Research*, 92:257 (2019), 515–28.

McLaren, Anne, 'Reading Sir Thomas Smith's *De Republica Anglorum* as Protestant Polemic', *The Historical Journal*, 42 (1999), 911–39.

Marshall, Peter, *Heretics and Believers: A History of the English Reformation* (New Haven, CT, 2017).

Marshall, Peter, 'Tudor Brexit: Catholics and Europe in the British and Irish Reformations', *Studies: An Irish Quarterly Review*, 106:424 (2017–18), 417–24.

Matheson-Pollock, Helen, Joanne Paul, and Catherine Fletcher (eds), *Queenship and Counsel in Early Modern Europe* (Basingstoke, 2018).

Mears, Natalie, 'Counsel, Public Debate, and Queenship: John Stubbs's "The Discoverie of a Gaping Gulf", 1579', *The Historical Journal*, 44 (2001), 629–50.

Mears, Natalie, 'Courts, Courtiers, and Culture in Tudor England', *The Historical Journal*, 46 (2003), 703–22.

Mears, Natalie, *Queenship and Political Discourse in the Elizabethan Realms* (Cambridge, 2005).

Merkle, Benjamin R., *Defending the Trinity in the Reformed Palatinate: The Elohistae* (Oxford, 2015).

Miller, Amos C., *Sir Henry Killigrew; Elizabethan Soldier and Diplomat* (Amsterdam, 1963).

Millstone, Noah, *Manuscript Circulation and the Invention of Politics in Early Stuart England* (Cambridge, 2016).

Mortensen, Lars Boje, 'François Bauduin's *De Institutione Historiæ* (1561): A Primary Text Behind Anders Sørensen Vedel's *De Scribenda Historia Danica* (1578)', *Symbolae Osloenses*, 73 (1998), 188–200.

Muller, Aislinn, *The Excommunication of Elizabeth I: Faith, Politics, and Resistance in Post-Reformation England, 1570–1603* (Leiden, 2020).

Muylaert, Silke, *Shaping the Stranger Churches: Migrants in England and the Troubles in the Netherlands, 1547–1585* (Leiden, 2020).

Neale, J. E., *Elizabeth I and her Parliaments, 1559–1581* (London, 1953).

Neale, J. E., *Elizabeth I and her Parliaments, 1584–1601* (London, 1957).

Neale, J. E., 'Proceedings in Parliament Relative to the Sentence on Mary Queen of Scots', *The English Historical Review*, 35:137 (1920), 103–13.

Neale, J. E., *The Elizabethan House of Commons*, rev. edn (Harmondsworth, 1963).

Nicolas, Nicholas Harris, *Life of William Davison, Secretary of State and Privy Councillor to Queen Elizabeth* (London, 1823).

Nicollier-de Weck, Béatrice, *Hubert Languet (1518–1581): Un Réseau Politique International de Melanchthon à Guillaume d'Orange* (Geneva, 1995).

Nugent, Donald, *Ecumenism in the Age of the Reformation: The Colloquy of Poissy* (Cambridge, MA, 1974).

Ó hAnnracháin, Tadhg, *Confessionalism and Mobility in Early Modern Ireland* (Oxford, 2021).

Ormrod, W. Mark, 'England's Immigrants, 1330–1550: Aliens in Later Medieval and Early Tudor England', *Journal of British Studies*, 59 (2020), 245–63.

Osborn, James B., *Young Philip Sidney, 1572–1577* (New Haven, CT, 1972).

Page, Augustine, *A Supplement to the Suffolk Traveller: Or Topographical and Genealogical Collections, Concerning that County* (Ipswich and London, 1844).

Parker, Geoffrey, *Imprudent King: A New Life of Philip II* (New Haven, CT, 2014).

Parker, Geoffrey, *The Dutch Revolt: Revised Edition* (London, 1988).

Parker, Geoffrey, 'The Place of Tudor England in the Messianic Vision of Philip II of Spain', *Transactions of the Royal Historical Society*, 12 (Cambridge, 2002), 167–221.

Parry, Glyn, 'Foreign Policy and the Parliament of 1576', *Parliamentary History*, 34 (2015), 62–89.

Parry, Glyn, *The Arch-Conjuror of England* (New Haven, CT, 2011).

Patterson, W. B., 'The Anglican Reaction', in L. W. Spitz and W. Lohff (eds), *Discord, Dialogue, and Concord: Studies in the Lutheran Reformation's Formula of Concord* (Philadelphia, PA, 1977), 150–65.

Paul, Joanne, *Counsel and Command in Early Modern English Thought* (Cambridge, 2020).

Pettegree, Andrew, *Foreign Protestant Communities in Sixteenth-Century London* (Oxford, 1986).

Pitkin, Barbara, 'Calvin's Mosaic Harmony: Biblical Exegesis and Early Modern Legal History', *The Sixteenth Century Journal*, 41 (2010), 441–66.

Platt, F. Jeffrey, 'The Elizabethan Clerk of the Privy Council', *Journal of the Rocky Mountain Medieval and Renaissance Association*, 3 (1982), 123–42.

Platt, F. Jeffrey, 'The Elizabethan "Foreign Office"', *The Historian*, 56 (1994), 725–40.

Popper, Nicholas, 'An Information State for Elizabethan England', *The Journal of Modern History*, 90 (2018), 503–35.

Popper, Nicholas, 'An Ocean of Lies: The Problem of Historical Evidence in the Sixteenth Century', *Huntington Library Quarterly*, 74 (2011), 375–400.

Popper, Nicholas, 'From Abbey to Archive: Managing Texts and Records in Early Modern England', *Archival Science*, 10 (2010), 249–66.

Popper, Nicholas, *The Specter of the Archive: Political Practice and the Information State in Early Modern Britain* (Chicago, IL, 2024).

Powell, Jason, 'Building Paper Embassies: A Prehistory of *The Compleat Ambassador*', *The Journal of Medieval and Early Modern Studies*, 50 (2020), 541–64.

Power, M. J., 'A "Crisis" Reconsidered: Social and Demographic Dislocation in London in the 1590s', *The London Journal*, 12 (1986), 134–45.

Pulman, Michael Barraclough, *The Elizabethan Privy Council in the Fifteen-seventies* (Berkeley, CA, 1979).

Questier, Michael, 'Going Nowhere Fast? The Historiography of Catholicism in Post-Reformation Britain', *Huntington Library Quarterly*, 84 (2021), 405–31.

Read, Conyers, *Lord Burghley and Queen Elizabeth* (London, 1960).

Read, Conyers, *Mr Secretary Walsingham and the Policy of Queen Elizabeth*, 2 vols (Oxford, 1925).

Read, Conyers, 'The Proposal to Assassinate Mary Queen of Scots at Fotheringay', *The English Historical Review*, 40:158 (1925), 234–5.

Reid, R. R., *The King's Council in the North* (London, 1921).

Rose, Jacqueline, 'Kingship and Counsel in Early Modern England', *The Historical Journal*, 54 (2011), 47–71.

Rose, Jacqueline (ed.), *The Politics of Counsel in England and Scotland, 1286–1707* (Oxford, 2016).

Rott, Jean, and Robert Faerber, 'Un anglais à Strasbourg au milieu du XVIᵉ Siècle: John Hales, Roger Ascham, et Jean Sturm', *Études Anglaises*, 21 (1968), 381–94.

Russell, Alexander, 'The Colloquy of Poissy, François Baudouin and English Protestant Identity, 1561–1563', *Journal of Ecclesiastical History*, 65 (2014), 551–79.

Ryrie, Alec, 'Tudor Brexit: From *Ecclesia Anglicana* to Anglicanism', *Studies: An Irish Quarterly Review*, 106:424 (2017–18), 425–30.

Salzman, L. F. (ed.), *A History of the County of Warwick*, Vol. 5: *Kington Hundred* (London, 1949).

Samson, Alexander, *Mary and Philip: The Marriage of Tudor England and Habsburg Spain* (Manchester, 2020).

Schindling, Anton, and Walter Ziegler (eds), *Die Territorien des Reichs im Zeitalter der Reformation und Konfessionalisierung: Land und Konfession 1500–1650*, 7 vols (Münster, 1989–97).

Schofield, B., 'The Yelverton Manuscripts', *The British Museum Quarterly*, 19 (1954), 3–9.

Seger, Donna A., *The Practical Renaissance: Information Culture and the Quest for Knowledge in Early Modern England, 1500–1640* (London, 2022).

Shagan, Ethan H., 'The English Inquisition: Constitutional Conflict and Ecclesiastical Law in the 1590s', *The Historical Journal*, 7 (2004), 541–65.

Sharpe, Jim, 'Social Strain and Social Dislocation, 1585–1603', in John Guy (ed.), *The Reign of Elizabeth I: Court and Culture in the Last Decade* (Cambridge, 1995), 192–211.

Shaw, Dannielle, and Matthew Woodcock (eds), 'New Explorations in Early Modern Espionage', a special issue of *History*, 108:381 (2023).

Sherman, William H., 'Decoding Early Modern Cryptography', *Huntington Library Quarterly*, 82 (2019), 31–19.

The Sixteenth Century Journal, 'The Formula of Concord: Quadricentennial Essays', 8:4 (1977).

Smailes, Helen, and Duncan Thompson (eds), *The Queen's Image: A Celebration of Mary Queen of Scots* (Edinburgh, 1987).

Smith, Frederick E., *Transnational Catholicism in Tudor England: Mobility, Exile, and Counter-Reformation, 1530–1580* (Oxford, 2022).

Soetaert, Alexander, 'Catholic Refuge and the Printing Press: Catholic Exiles from England, France, and the Low Countries in the Ecclesiastical Province of Cambrai', *British Catholic History*, 34 (2019), 532–61.

Soetaert, Alexander, and Violet Soen, 'A Catholic International or Transregional Catholicism? The Printing Press, English Catholics, and their Hosts in the Early Modern Ecclesiastical Province of Cambrai', *The Catholic Historical Review*, 106 (2020), 551–75.

Somerville, Robert, *History of the Duchy of Lancaster*, Vol. 1: *1265–1603* (London, 1953).

Sowerby, Tracey A., '"A Memorial and a Pledge of Faith": Portraiture and Early Modern Diplomatic Culture', *English Historical Review*, 129:537 (2014), 296–331.

Sowerby, Tracey A., 'Early Modern Diplomatic History', *History Compass*, 14 (2016), 441–56.

Sowerby, Tracey A., 'Francis Thynne's *Perfect Ambassadour* and the Construction of Diplomatic Thought in Elizabethan England', *Huntington Library Quarterly*, 82 (2020), 539–57.

Sowerby, Tracey A., *Renaissance and Reform in Tudor England: The Careers of Sir Richard Morison c.1513–1556* (Oxford, 2010).

Sowerby, Tracey A., and Jan Hennings (eds), *Practices of Diplomacy in the Early Modern World c.1410–1800* (London, 2017).

Spitz, Lewis W. and Barbara Sher Tinsley, *Johann Sturm on Education: The Reformation and Humanist Learning* (St. Louis, MO, 1995).

Squibb, G. D., *Doctors' Commons: A History of the College of Advocates and Doctors of Law* (Oxford, 1977).

Stephen, Leslie (ed.), *Dictionary of National Biography* (London, 1885), Vol. 4.

Stephens, W. B. (ed.), *A History of the County of Warwick, Vol. 8: the City of Coventry and Borough of Warwick* (London, 1969).

Stewart, Alan, 'Familiar Letters and State Papers: The Afterlives of Early Modern Correspondence', in James Daybell and Andrew Gordon (eds), *Cultures of Correspondence in Early Modern Britain* (Philadelphia, PA, 2016), 237–52.

Stillman, Robert E., *Philip Sidney and the Poetics of Renaissance Cosmopolitanism* (Aldershot, 2008).

Strype, John, *Annals of the Reformation and Establishment of Religion [...] a New Edition*, 4 vols (Oxford, 1824).

Strype, John, *The Life and Acts of John Whitgift*, 3 vols (Oxford, 1822).

Strype, John, *The Life of the Learned Sir Thomas Smith [...] a New Edition* (Oxford, 1820).

Taylor, Kathryn, 'Matters Worthy of Men of State: Ethnography and Diplomatic Reporting in Sixteenth-Century Venice', *The Sixteenth Century Journal*, 51 (2020), 715–36.

Tinsley, Barbara Sher, 'Sturm, Johann', in Hans J. Hillerbrand (ed.), *The Oxford Encyclopedia of the Reformation* (Oxford, 1996); online edn.

Tipton, Alzada, '"All mens eyes are fixed vpon you": Dedications of Printed Works to the Earl of Essex and the Creation of Essex's Public Persona', *The Sixteenth Century Journal*, 52 (2021), 111–32.

Tol, Jonas van, *Germany and the French Wars of Religion* (Leiden, 2018).

Tol, Jonas van, 'Religion or Rebellion? Justifying the French Wars of Religion and Dutch Revolt to German Protestants', *The Sixteenth Century Journal*, 51 (2020), 445–64.

Torre, Victoria, de la, '"We Few of an Infinite Multitude": John Hales, Parliament, and the Gendered Politics of the Early Elizabethan Succession', *Albion*, 33 (2001), 557–82.

Tremml-Werner, Birgit, and Dorothée Goetze (eds), 'A Multitude of Actors in Early Modern Diplomacy', a special issue of *Journal of Early Modern History*, 23 (2019).

Tremml-Werner, Birgit, Lisa Hellman, and Guido van Meersbergen (eds), 'Gift and Tribute in Early Modern Diplomacy: Afro-Eurasian Perspectives', a special issue of *Diplomatica*, 2 (2020).

Trim, David J. B., 'English Military Émigrés and the Protestant Cause in Europe, 1603–c.1640', in David Worthington (ed.), *British and Irish Emigrants and Exiles in Europe, 1603–1688* (Leiden, 2010), 237–58.

Trim, David J. B., 'Immigrants, the Indigenous Community and International Calvinism', in Nigel Goose and Liên Luu (eds), *Immigrants in Tudor and Early Stuart England* (Brighton, 2005), 211–27.

Trim, David J. B., 'Protestant Refugees in Elizabethan England and Confessional Conflict in France and the Netherlands, 1562–c.1610', in Randolph Vigne and Charles Littleton (eds), *From Strangers to Citizens: The Integration of Immigrant Communities in Britain, Ireland, and Colonial America, 1550–1750* (Brighton, 2001), 68–79.

Tu, Hsuan-Ying, 'The Dispersal of Francis Walsingham's Papers', *The Sixteenth Century Journal*, 50 (2019), 471–92.

Turchetti, Mario, *Concordia o Tolleranza? François Bauduin (1520–1573) e i 'Moyenneurs'* (Milan, 1984).

Tworek, Michael, 'Education: The Polish-Lithuanian Commonwealth', in Howard Louthan and Graeme Murdoch (eds), *A Companion to the Reformation in Central Europe* (Leiden, 2015), 359–89.

Van Norden, Linda, 'Sir Henry Spelman on the Chronology of the Elizabethan College of Antiquaries', *Huntington Library Quarterly*, 13 (1950), 131–60.

Vigne, Randolph, and Charles Littleton (eds), *From Strangers to Citizens: The Integration of Immigrant Communities in Britain, Ireland, and Colonial America, 1550–1750* (Brighton, 2001).

Vivo, Filippo de, 'How to Read Italian *Relazioni*', *Renaissance and Reformation*, 34 (2011), 25–59.

Walsham, Alexandra, *Generations: Age, Ancestry, and Memory in the English Reformations* (Oxford, 2023).

Warneke, Sarah, *Images of the Educational Traveller in Early Modern England* (Leiden, 1994).

Warnicke, Retha M., *Mary Queen of Scots* (London, 2006).

Webb, E. A., and G. W. Miller, and J. Beckwith, *The History of Chislehurst: Its Church, Manors, and Parish* (London, 1899).

Weis, Monique, 'Philip of Marnix and "International Protestantism": The Fears and Hopes of a Dutch Refugee in the 1570s', *Reformation & Renaissance Review*, 11 (2009), 203–20.

Wendebourg, Dorothea, and Alec Ryrie (eds), *Sister Reformations II: Reformation and Ethics in Germany and in England / Schwesterreformationen II: Reformation und Ethik in Deutschland und in England* (Tübingen, 2014).

Wendebourg, Dorothea, Euan Cameron, and Martin Ohst (eds), *Sister Reformations III: From Reformation Movements to Reformation Churches in the Holy Roman Empire and on the British Isles / Schwesterreformationen III: Von der reformatorischen Bewegung zur Kirche im Heiligen Römischen Reich und auf den britischen Inseln* (Tübingen, 2019).

Wernham, R. B., *After the Armada: Elizabethan England and the Struggle for Western Europe 1588–1595* (Oxford, 1984).

Wernham, R. B., *Before the Armada: The Growth of English Foreign Policy, 1485–1588* (London, 1966).

Wernham, R. B., *Return of the Armadas: The Last Years of the Elizabethan War against Spain, 1595–1603* (Oxford, 1994).

Wernham, R. B., 'The Disgrace of William Davison', *The English Historical Review*, 46:184 (1931), 632–6.

Whaley, Joachim, *Germany and the Holy Roman Empire, Vol. 1: Maximilian I to the Peace of Westphalia 1493–1648* (Oxford, 2012).

White, Jason, *Militant Protestantism and British Identity, 1603–1642* (London, 2012).

Williamson, Elizabeth, 'Diplomatic Letters as Political Literature: Copying Sir Henry Unton's Letters', *Huntington Library Quarterly*, 82 (2019), 559–78.

Williamson, Elizabeth, *Elizabethan Diplomacy and Epistolary Culture* (London, 2021).

Wolfe, Heather, and Peter Stallybrass, 'The Material Culture of Record-Keeping in Early Modern England', in Liesbeth Corens, Kate Peters, and Alexandra Walsham (eds), *Archives and Information in the Early Modern World* (Oxford, 2018), 179–208.

Wooding, Lucy, *Tudor England* (New Haven, CT, 2022).

Woodworth, Allegra, 'Purveyance for the Royal Household in the Reign of Queen Elizabeth', *Transactions of the American Philosophical Society*, 35 (1945), 1–89.

Woolfson, Jonathan, 'Padua and English Students Revisited', *Renaissance Studies*, 27 (2013), 572–87.

Woolfson, Jonathan, *Padua and the Tudors: English Students in Italy, 1485–1603* (Cambridge, 1998).

Wright, C. E., 'The Elizabethan Society of Antiquaries and the Formation of the Cottonian Library', in Francis Wormald and C.E. Wright (eds), *The English Library before 1700* (London, 1958), 176–212.

Younger, Neil, *Religion and Politics in Elizabethan England: The Life of Sir Christopher Hatton* (Manchester, 2022).

Zim, Rivkah, 'Religion and the Politic Counsellor: Thomas Sackville, 1536–1608', *English Historical Review*, 122:498 (2007), 892–917.

Zins, Henryk, trans. H. C. Stevens, *England and the Baltic in the Elizabethan Era* (Manchester, 1972).

Secondary Sources, Unpublished

Bell, Gary McClellan, 'The Men and their Rewards in Elizabethan Diplomatic Service, 1558–1585', PhD thesis, University of California, Los Angeles, 1974.

Brewerton, Patricia Ann, 'Paper Trails: Re-Reading Robert Beale as Clerk to the Elizabethan Privy Council', PhD thesis, Birkbeck College, University of London, 1998.

Collinson, Patrick, 'The Puritan Classical Movement in the Reign of Elizabeth I', PhD thesis, University of London, 1957.

Diemer, Kurt, 'Die Heiratsverhandlungen zwischen Königin Elisabeth I. von England und Erzherzog Karl von Innerösterreich 1558–1570', PhD thesis, University of Tübingen, 1969.

Jones, Helen Dorothy, 'The Elizabethan Society of Antiquaries Reassessed', MA dissertation, University of British Columbia, 1988.

Taviner, Mark, 'Robert Beale and the Elizabethan Polity', PhD thesis, University of St Andrews, 2000.

Trim, David J. B., 'Fighting "Jacob's Wars": The Employment of English and Welsh Mercenaries in the European Wars of Religion: France and the Netherlands, 1562–1610', PhD thesis, King's College, University of London, 2002.

Tu, Hsuan-Ying, 'The Pursuit of God's Glory: Francis Walsingham's Espionage in Elizabethan Politics, 1568–1588', PhD thesis, University of York, 2012.

Van Norden, Linda, 'The Elizabethan College of Antiquaries', PhD thesis, University of California, Los Angeles, 1946.

Vaughan, Jacqueline D., 'Secretaries, Statesmen and Spies: The Clerks of the Tudor Privy Council, c.1540–c.1603', PhD thesis, University of St Andrews, 2007.

Websites

Clergy of the Church of England Database, online at https://theclergydatabase.org.uk

Dansk Biografisk Leksikon, online at https://biografiskleksikon.lex.dk

Deutsche Biographie, online at www.deutsche-biographie.de

History of Parliament: House of Commons, online at www.historyofparliamentonline.org

Oxford Dictionary of National Biography, online at www.oxforddnb.com

Index

Since the index has been created to work across multiple formats, indexed terms for which a page range is given (e.g., 52–53, 66–70, etc.) may occasionally appear only on some, but not all, of the pages within the range.